This book provides an exciting reinterpretation of the sayings and actions of Jesus. Setting him firmly in the context of first-century Judaism, it asks how important the city of Jerusalem and the theological traditions centred on it were to Jesus. At this time, Zion had become 'the symbol of the life, beliefs and hopes of all Jews'. Those Jews who expected the coming of a messianic Davidic king assumed that it would be from Zion that he would reign. Dr Tan examines how Jesus viewed the significance of Jerusalem in relation to his own vocation, and asks why he went there in what proved to be the last weeks of his life. Skilfully integrating what Jesus is recorded to have said with what he is recorded to have done, the author argues that, as a prophet, Jesus was attracted inevitably to the city of Zion. His message concerned the establishment of God's sovereignty on earth, and this in itself impelled him to go to the city to bring it under the divine rule. Jesus' actions in Jerusalem can also be interpreted as part of a common theme of the restoration of God's people for the fulfilment of their promised destiny.

An understanding of the importance to Jesus of the Zion traditions, therefore, not only helps us to understand the unifying aim behind his ministry, but can also provide us with the key to the riddle of who Jesus thought he was.

SOCIETY FOR NEW TESTAMENT STUDIES

MONOGRAPH SERIES

General Editor: Margaret E. Thrall

91

THE ZION TRADITIONS AND THE AIMS OF JESUS

The Zion traditions and the aims of Jesus

KIM HUAT TAN

Trinity Theological College, Singapore

CAMBRIDGE
UNIVERSITY PRESS

Published by the Press Syndicate of the University of Cambridge
The Pitt Building, Trumpington Street, Cambridge CB2 1RP
40 West 20th Street, New York, NY 10011–4211, USA
10 Stamford Road, Oakleigh, Melbourne 3166, Australia

First published 1997

Printed in Great Britain at the University Press, Cambridge

A catalogue record for this book is available from the British Library

Library of Congress cataloguing in publication data

Tan, Kim Huat.
The Zion traditions and the aims of Jesus / Kim Huat Tan.
   p.   cm. – (Monograph series / Society for New Testament Studies : 91)
Originally presented as the author's thesis (Ph. D. – University of
London, 1993).
Includes bibliographical references and index.
ISBN 0 521 58006 4 (hardcover)
1. Jesus Christ – Biography.   2. Jerusalem – Social life and customs.
3. Bible – History of Biblical events.   I. Title.
II. Series: Monograph series (Society for New Testament Studies) : 91.
BT301.2.T36   1996
232.9'5–dc20   96–13034   CIP

ISBN 0 521 58006 4 hardback

CONTENTS

CONCLUSIONS

ACKNOWLEDGMENTS

This book is a revised version of a Ph.D. thesis submitted to the University of London in January 1993. In the two years between the completion of the thesis and this revision, the output of scholarly works on Jesus research does not seem to have abated. I have tried to take into account all the relevant literature published during this period, but the sheer immensity of the material precludes any possibility of complete coverage.

One incurs many debts in writing a book and most of these are not easily repaid. I am extremely grateful to my supervisor, Professor G. N. Stanton, for his unstinting advice and perceptive criticisms given during my studies at King's College, London. His friendliness and his prompt response to my written work have eased my difficult journey through the 'dense jungle' of scholarly studies. The examiners of the thesis, Professor J. L. Houlden and Dr W. R. Telford, offered many constructive criticisms for which I am most grateful. My heartfelt thanks go to Dr M. E. Thrall, the editor, for accepting this book into the SNTS monograph series. Her incisive comments saved me from committing many an embarrassing error and helped me to clarify my argument. Needless to say, I alone take full responsibility for mistakes which still remain.

The completion of the thesis has been made possible through the funding I received from many sources. The committee of vice-chancellors and principals of the universities and colleges in the United Kingdom provided an overseas research studentship. The Tyndale House Council helped with a grant and the provision of a desk in its renowned library, where most of my research was carried out. The time spent in Tyndale House, Cambridge, and the friendships forged there are some of the things which will be indelibly marked in my memory.

A word of thanks is also due to the members and pastoral team of the Chinese Church in London. Their Christian fellowship helped to keep one research student sane and I hope, saintly too. The pastoral team has graciously allowed me time to finish my revision of the thesis for publication. I want especially to thank the Revd Walter Lau for his constant queries about the progress of my revision. These have enabled me to overcome a natural tendency to procrastinate. Mention must also be made of Betty Chow's kindness in allowing me to use her computer.

Profound thanks are due to the Emmanuel Baptist Fellowship in Singapore for their generous support and prayers. I trust that their decision to send me abroad for further theological studies has not been in vain.

Finally, my family back in Singapore deserves special mention. Words alone cannot fully express my gratitude and thanks to them. My brother, Kim Eng, has been extremely encouraging in many ways. Without his sacrificial support, my trip to Britain would not have been possible. My sister, Siew Lian, bore the brunt of the household responsibilities during my absence from home. To them and to the rest of the family, I trust that this book will not be disappointing.

ABBREVIATIONS

The following abbreviations are used for journals or reference works.

ABD   *Anchor Bible Dictionary*, ed. D. N. Freedman (New York: Doubleday, 1992)

ANRW   *Aufstieg und Niedergang der römischen Welt*, eds. H. Temporini and W. Haase (Berlin and New York: de Gruyter, 1972–)

BAGD   W. Bauer, *A Greek English Lexicon of the New Testament and other Early Christian Literature*, translated and adapted by W. F. Arndt, and F. W. Gingrich, 2nd edition revised and augmented by F. W. Gingrich and F. W. Danker (Chicago: University of Chicago Press, 1979)

BDF   F. Blass and A. Debrunner, *A Greek Grammar of the New Testament and Other Early Christian Literature*, translated and revised by R. W. Funk (Cambridge: Cambridge University Press, 1961)

Bib   *Biblica*

BJRL   *Bulletin of the John Rylands Library*

BTB   *Biblical Theology Bulletin*

BZ   *Biblische Zeitschrift*

CBQ   *Catholic Biblical Quarterly*

EQ   *Evangelical Quarterly*

ExpT   *Expository Times*

HeyJ   *Heythrop Journal*

HTR   *Harvard Theological Review*

HUCA   *Hebrew Union College Annual*

ICC   International Critical Commentary

IEJ   *Israel Exploration Journal*

Int   *Interpretation*

JBL	*Journal of Biblical Literature*
JQR	*Jewish Quarterly Review*
JRelEth	*Journal of Religion and Ethics*
JSJ	*Journal for the Study of Judaism*
JSNT	*Journal for the Study of the New Testament*
JTS	*Journal of Theological Studies*
NA[26]	Nestle–Aland, *Novum Testamentum Graece*, 26th edition, eds. K. Aland, M. Black, C. M. Martini, B. M. Metzger and A. Wikgren; based on an original work by Eberhard Nestle and Erwin Nestle (Stuttgart: Deutsche Bibelgesellschaft, 1979)
NovT	*Novum Testamentum*
NTS	*New Testament Studies*
OTP	*Old Testament Pseudepigrapha*, ed. J. H. Charlesworth, 2 vols. (New York: Doubleday, 1983 and 1985)
RevQum	*Revue de Qumran*
RHPR	*Revue d'historie et de philosophie religieuses*
SB	H. L. Strack and P. Billerbeck, *Kommentar zum Neuen Testament aus Talmud und Midrasch*, 6 vols. (Munich: Oskar Beck, 1922–56)
SJT	*Scottish Journal of Theology*
TDNT	*Theological Dictionary of the New Testament*, eds. G. Kittel and G. Friedrich, 10 vols., translated by G. W. Bromiley (Grand Rapids: Eerdmans, 1964–76)
TDOT	*Theological Dictionary of the Old Testament*, eds. G. J. Botterweck and H. Ringgren, many vols., translated by J. T. Willis, G. W. Bromiley and D. E. Green (Grand Rapids: Eerdmans, 1974–)
TynB	*Tyndale Bulletin*
TZ	*Theologische Zeitschrift*
VE	*Vox Evangelica*
ZAW	*Zeitschrift für die alttestamentliche Wissenschaft*
ZNW	*Zeitschrift für die neutestamentliche Wissenschaft*
ZTK	*Zeitschrift für Theologie und Kirche*

(*Note:* The Hebrew transliteration adopted in this book follows the system of the ICC series.)

PART I

The background

1

INTRODUCTION

Research on the historical Jesus is once again prominent in biblical scholarship. The recent output of major works[1] on this subject testifies to a new phase in an old study and terms like 'The Renaissance in Jesus Research'[2] or 'The Third Quest'[3] have been introduced to describe this phenomenon. Thus, the impasse in historical Jesus research, to which Drury refers,[4] is now regarded as *passé*. This is to be welcomed in that Jesus as a historical figure is a proper object of historical research.[5] The impact on the world of a movement which names him as founder makes such research urgent and relevant.[6]

---

[1] G. Vermes, *Jesus the Jew*; B. F. Meyer, *The Aims of Jesus*; J. Riches, *Jesus and the Transformation of Judaism*; A. E. Harvey, *Jesus and the Constraints of History*; E. Bammel and C. F. D. Moule (eds.), *Jesus and the Politics of His Day*; M. J. Borg, *Conflict, Holiness and Politics in the Teachings of Jesus*; G. W. Buchanan, *Jesus: The King and His Kingdom*; E. P. Sanders, *Jesus and Judaism*; and recently his *The Historical Figure of Jesus*; D. E. Oakman, *Jesus and the Economic Questions of His Day*; R. A. Horsley, *Jesus and the Spiral of Violence*; G. Theissen, *The Shadow of the Galilean*; I. M. Zeitlin, *Jesus and the Judaism of His Time*; J. Gnilka, *Jesus von Nazaret*; B. Witherington III, *The Christology of Jesus*; J. D. Crossan, *The Historical Jesus: The Life of a Mediterranean Jewish Peasant*; M. de Jonge, *Jesus, the Servant-Messiah*; J. P. Meier, *A Marginal Jew: Rethinking the Historical Jesus*; M. N. Bockmuehl, *This Jesus: Martyr, Lord, Messiah*; B. D. Chilton and C. A. Evans (eds.), *Studying the Historical Jesus: Evaluations of the State of Current Research*.

[2] This term is used by M. J. Borg, 'Portraits of Jesus in Contemporary North American Scholarship', *HTR* 84:1 (1991), 1–22.

[3] This phrase was coined by Wright in S. Neill and N. T. Wright, *The Interpretation of the New Testament 1861–1986*, p. 379.

[4] J. Drury, *The Parables in the Gospels*, p. 3.

[5] Cf. the comments of J. I. H. MacDonald, 'New Quest – Dead End? So What about the Historical Jesus?', in E. A. Livingstone (ed.), *Studia Biblica 1978 II. Papers on the Gospels*, p. 168.

[6] Significantly, an elaborate seminar called 'The Jesus Seminar' was started in the USA in 1985 (headed by R. W. Funk) in order to enhance co-operative research and to disseminate the results obtained by the Seminar to a wider public. See R. W. Funk, 'A Forum for Informed Discussion', *Forum* 1 (1985), 2–3.

Two main features stand out in this new phase of Jesus research. The first concerns the Jewishness of Jesus.[7] Recent books on the historical Jesus take seriously this characteristic of Jesus and attempt to understand him (his intentions and message) within the limits of first-century Judaism.[8] The second concerns the intentions of Jesus.[9] The focus on these by recent works[10] represents a shift from the preoccupation with the *kerygma* of Jesus (or the post-Easter community) characteristic of the infant period of the New Quest whose inauguration is usually attributed to Käsemann's lecture, 'Das Problem des historischen Jesu'.[11] It also represents a shift from scepticism to optimism regarding the possibility of recovering what Jesus intended in his ministry. That this is a step in the right direction is well argued by Meyer: 'History is reconstruction through hypothesis and verification. Its topic is aims and consequences, for history involves first of all, the grasp of aims in relation to the dynamics of time...'[12] These two features are to be welcomed.[13]

---

[7] See the observations of D. J. Harrington, 'The Jewishness of Jesus: Facing Some Problems', *CBQ* 49 (1987), 3. Harrington tries to account for the interest in this particular aspect on pp. 1–2. This aspect has become even more prominent since the completion of our original research. Controversies over the possible connection between Jesus of Nazareth and the Qumran community were stirred up over the erstwhile unpublished fragments of the Qumran scrolls. Popular books were written to capitalise on this and they exaggerated the significance of these unpublished fragments. Through these books, public awareness of the identity and aims of Jesus of Nazareth has become greatly aroused. This subject need not detain us here. A good assessment of the impact of these fragments on Jesus research can be found in C. A. Evans, 'The Recently Published Dead Sea Scrolls and the Historical Jesus', in Chilton and Evans (eds.), *Studying*, pp. 547–65. There appears to be a counterpoint to the general trend of understanding Jesus according to his Jewish environment, and this approach emphasises the Graeco-Roman background instead and regards Jesus as a cynic teacher. It is predominantly a North American phenomenon represented mainly by the Claremont Graduate School, California and the Jesus Seminar in the USA. A British representative of this viewpoint is F. G. Downing, *Christ and the Cynics: Jesus and Other Radical Preachers in First-Century Tradition*.

[8] Most of the works cited in the first note take seriously this aspect.

[9] Cf. Neill and Wright, *Interpretation*, pp. 398–9.

[10] See especially Meyer, *Aims*. But cf. also Sanders, *Jesus*; Borg, *Conflict*; Oakman, *Jesus*; Horsley, *Spiral*, where what Jesus was attempting to achieve in the context of his Jewish background receives the main focus.

[11] *ZTK* 51 (1954), 125–53 (ET: 'The Problem of the Historical Jesus', in E. Käsemann, *Essays on New Testament Themes*, pp. 15–47).

[12] *Aims*, p. 19.

[13] It should also be mentioned that the political and social contexts of Jesus' ministry are important features in many works cited in the first note. However, these two contexts can be subsumed under the two features we have highlighted.

The present book follows in the same vein and focuses on these two features. We hope to make a contribution to a better understanding of the aims of the historical Jesus by bringing to light certain important questions which have been left unanswered so far.

1 The questions posed

The first question

To ascertain the overall aims of Jesus by taking into account the whole sweep of his life and ministry would be a task too wide-ranging for the compass of this book. The focus has to be narrowed and the attendant problem is how to avoid any misrepresentations caused by the necessity of a narrower focus. Working on the assumption that it is reasonable to suppose that Jesus' aims during his last days in Jerusalem were in continuity with his aims in his ministry prior to that fateful journey (if not its crowning explanation),[14] we propose to study the former set of aims.

Schweitzer wrote that 'one might use . . . as a principle of division . . . to clarify the lives of Jesus, whether they make him go to Jerusalem to work or to die'.[15] Hence, according to Schweitzer, how a scholar is to portray Jesus depends very much on his or her understanding of why Jesus made that final trip to Jerusalem. The first question posed in our study, then, is 'What intentions did Jesus have when he made that final trip to Jerusalem?' It may be that he had no intentions whatsoever and that he was simply overtaken by events. But whether or not this is the case has to be investigated. If he had intentions, the results of such an enquiry would be significant for Jesus research. In this connection, the significant *actions* of Jesus during this period would be of importance in the ascertaining of these intentions.[16] A detailed study which searches for an explanatory hypothesis of Jesus' intentions in Jerusalem[17] by

---

[14] In a semi-popular work, G. N. Stanton observes that the key to the story of Jesus' ministry and intentions is the ending in his *The Gospels and Jesus*, p. 274.

[15] A. Schweitzer, *The Quest of the Historical Jesus*, p. 389 n. 1.

[16] This should not be taken to mean that the sayings are of no importance. See discussion in next section.

[17] Hereafter, the phrase 'Jesus' intentions in Jerusalem' (and other similar phrases) will be a shorthand way of referring to his intentions during his last days in Jerusalem. It does not presuppose that Jesus made only one trip to Jerusalem

taking into account the significant actions performed in that city has yet to be carried out. Nor has there been a quest for a unifying hypothesis to explain these actions. This study will attempt to address these matters.

The second question

The mention of the word 'Jerusalem' recalls the rich stream of traditions which developed in the first and second temple periods (perhaps even before that), often called, in OT scholarship, 'the Zion traditions'.[18] These traditions have ingrained in the minds of the Jews of Jesus' day the concept that Jerusalem is the city which God has promised to dwell in and save. Hence, in the political and religious ferment of first-century Palestine, Jerusalem (regarded as both a political and religious centre of Israel) inevitably became involved and implicated.[19] What then is the relationship between Jesus' conception of his own ministry and these important traditions (the importance of which we hope to demonstrate in chapter 2)? Did the latter influence the former? This important question has yet to be explored even with the resurgence of interest in the Jewishness of Jesus. Hence the second question posed is 'Did Jesus appropriate the Zion traditions for his ministry?'

The two questions posed are related, for it is legitimate to ask whether or not the intentions of Jesus (and his significant actions) in Jerusalem were informed by the Zion traditions. The conjoining of these two questions implies our prior commitment to test their relatedness. And this relatedness forms the hypothesis which we hope to verify in the course of our study.

---

during his public ministry, nor does it suppose that the pericopae of the passion narrative in the Synoptic gospels are chronologically arranged or accurate.

[18] We shall give a proper definition of what we understand by the term 'Zion traditions' in chapter 2. But for an example of how certain OT scholars define the Zion traditions see J. J. M. Roberts, 'Zion in the Theology of the Davidic–Solomonic Empire', in T. Ishida (ed.), *Studies in the Period of David and Solomon and Other Essays*, p. 94. For a recent and succinct exposition of these traditions see J. D. Levenson, 'Zion Traditions', *ABD* VI, pp. 1098–102.

[19] J. Jeremias mentions that Jerusalem was bound to be the objective of every messianic movement in his *Jerusalem in the Time of Jesus*, p. 73. See also G. Theissen, *Social Reality and the Early Christians: Theology, Ethics and the World of the New Testament*, pp. 96–7 for a similar viewpoint.

2 Method

Overview of approach taken

Our study will use a broadly based approach. We shall first show the importance of the Zion traditions to the Jews of the first century in the remainder of Part I of the book. The next two major parts (II and III) will be devoted to a study of Jesus' sayings which may shed light on his intentions in Jerusalem and his attitude towards the Zion traditions, and his actions in Jerusalem respectively.

One should not reconstruct the intentions of Jesus purely out of the sayings tradition. It has been pointed out by Sanders that the methodological uncertainty over ascertaining the authenticity of the sayings of Jesus makes them too shaky a foundation on which to build.[20] Hence, there is a need to broaden our study by an investigation into the actions of Jesus. But it has also been observed that investigating the meaning of actions without recourse to sayings may lead to fanciful speculations as actions by themselves are often not transparent.[21] However, it is admitted that, in principle, the authenticity of an action may be easier to ascertain[22] than is that of a saying. None the less, both actions and sayings are to be given due weight in order that our reconstruction of the aims of Jesus be founded relatively securely.

One insight derived from form criticism is that the pericopae of the gospels may not have been arranged in chronological order and that even their narrative and chronological frameworks may have been the creation of the evangelists.[23] In order to circumvent this problem, we propose to investigate the sayings relevant to our study without any attempt to situate them chronologically or geographically. Given the constraint on space, we shall focus on

---

[20] Sanders, *Jesus*, p. 4.
[21] As has been observed by J. Riches in his critique of Sanders' *Jesus* in 'Works and Words of Jesus the Jew', *HeyJ* 27 (1986), 53.
[22] To Sanders, the actions are 'facts'! See his *Jesus*, p. 5.
[23] So K. L. Schmidt, *Der Rahmen der Geschichte Jesu*, p. v. For good critiques of the weaknesses of form criticism, see the essays by G. N. Stanton, 'Form Criticism Revisited', in M. D. Hooker and C. J. A. Hickling (eds.), *What About the New Testament? Essays in Honour of C. F. Evans*, pp. 13–27; P. Stuhlmacher, 'Zum Thema: Das Evangelium und die Evangelien', pp. 2–12; and E. E. Ellis, 'Gospels Criticism: A Perspective on the State of the Art'. These last two essays are found in P. Stuhlmacher (ed.), *Das Evangelium und die Evangelien*.

only a few key sayings and not attempt to analyse every saying which might be relevant. We hope to draw these sayings from diverse streams of tradition (Mark, Q, L and M). As for the actions, they could be much more easily situated chronologically and geographically by virtue of their very nature.

The approach adopted for Part III of our study is relatively straightforward. We shall try to show that the actions selected for investigation (the 'triumphal' entry, the incident in the temple and the last supper) did occur during the final days of Jesus in Jerusalem[24] and were performed in chronological proximity to one another. Whenever a saying is purportedly attached to a certain action (according to the data offered by the evangelists' accounts), we shall ascertain whether the two were originally joined.

Two other methodological points ought to be noted here. First, we shall refrain from using as evidence any saying or pericope from the gospel of John that does not have a parallel in the Synoptic gospels. This, however, is not meant to prejudge the question of the historicity of John's peculiar material. Rather, this is done because of space limitation and the prevalent scholarly doubt over this question.[25] Nevertheless, any Johannine parallel to a saying or pericope found in the Synoptic gospels will be considered.

Second, this study presupposes the viability of the two-document hypothesis as an explanation of Synoptic relationships. We are aware of the resurgence of scholarly support for the Griesbach hypothesis but, in our opinion, such a hypothesis creates more problems than it solves. We are also aware that the two-document hypothesis has its own problems but we concur with scholars who view this hypothesis as the simplest and least problematic explanation of Synoptic relationships.[26]

---

[24] It is of course obvious that if the actions selected were authentic, they must have occurred in Jerusalem.

[25] Classically set forth by D. F. Strauss, *The Life of Jesus Critically Examined*, p. 649 and *passim*. See also the commentaries by R. Bultmann, *The Gospel of John*; B. Lindars, *The Gospel of John*; and C. K. Barrett, *The Gospel According to St John*, especially pp. 141–2. But cf. recently the cautiously positive assessment of D. Moody Smith in his 'Historical Issues and the Problem of John and the Synoptics', in M. de Boer (ed.), *From Jesus to John: Essays on Jesus and New Testament Christology in Honour of Marinus de Jonge*, pp. 252–67.

[26] For a good defence of this hypothesis, see G. M. Styler, 'The Priority of Mark', in C. F. D. Moule, *The Birth of the New Testament*, pp. 285–316; C. M. Tuckett, *The Revival of the Griesbach Hypothesis*; R. H. Stein, *The Synoptic Problem: An Introduction*. See also the collection of essays in C. M. Tuckett (ed.), *Synoptic Studies. The Ampleworth Conferences of 1982 and 1983*.

Criteria of authenticity

Intrinsic to research on the historical Jesus is the important matter of establishing criteria for ascertaining whether or not a certain saying or action is authentic. Recently, great interest has been generated on this particular matter as can be seen from the numerous articles which have been published.[27] Hence, a brief word about our stance towards these criteria is necessary before the study proper begins.

In the past, great importance has been assigned to the criterion of double dissimilarity as the key tool to be used.[28] With this criterion, critical scholars isolate a pool of authentic traditions of Jesus on which to work and use them as a basis for ascertaining other traditions which may be authentic (the criterion of coherence).[29] Any tradition which does not pass the test of this criterion is judged inauthentic. The results obtained by the use of this criterion are often considered more assured than those obtained from other criteria formulated (e.g., the criterion of multiple attestation).[30]

It is becoming increasingly recognised that the negative use of this criterion (i.e., any material which does not pass the test of this criterion is judged inauthentic) is untenable. The primary weaknesses of this criterion which have been pointed out by scholars are

---

[27] R. Riesner, *Jesus als Lehrer*, pp. 86–96; R. H. Stein, 'The Criteria for Authenticity', in *Gospel Perspectives I*, pp. 225–63; S. C. Goetz and C. L. Blomberg, 'The Burden of Proof', *JSNT* 11 (1981), 39–63; M. E. Boring, 'Criteria of Authenticity: The Lucan Beatitudes as a Test Case', *Forum* 1,4 (1985), 3–38; D. Polkow, 'Method and Criteria for Historical Jesus Research', in D. J. Lull (ed.), *SBL 1987 Seminar Papers*, pp. 336–56; and Meier, *Marginal Jew*, pp. 167–84.

[28] So Käsemann, 'Problem', p. 37; J. M. Robinson, *A New Quest of the Historical Jesus*, pp. 116–19; R. H. Fuller, *The Foundations of New Testament Christology*, p. 18; N. Perrin, *Rediscovering the Teaching of Jesus*, p. 89 and his *What is Redaction Criticism?*, p. 71; D. L. Mealand, 'The Dissimilarity Test', *SJT* 31 (1978), 41–50. It was probably Bultmann who pioneered this criterion, see his *The History of the Synoptic Tradition*, p. 205.

[29] So Perrin, *Redaction Criticism*, p. 71. Polkow observes that 'it [the criterion of double dissimilarity] is the real basis for the entire "new quest" of the historical Jesus' in his 'Method and Criteria', p. 347.

[30] Cf. the statement of Käsemann: 'In only *one* case do we have more or less safe ground under our feet [in the search for authentic Jesus traditions]; when there are no grounds either for deriving a tradition from Judaism or for ascribing it to primitive Christianity' in 'Problem', p. 37. Emphasis mine. Such an outlook is also echoed in Perrin, *Rediscovering*, pp. 39–43 and R. H. Fuller, 'The Criterion of Dissimilarity: The Wrong Tool?', in R. F. Berkey and S. A. Edwards, *Christological Perspectives*, p. 48.

the following. (1) By its very nature, it goes in search of a peculiar Jesus and not a characteristic one.[31] What may be characteristic of Jesus is not necessarily unique. And by focusing only on the unique aspects, a skewed picture of Jesus is obtained. (2) It presupposes that Jesus must be divorced from his Jewish environment.[32] (3) It assumes that Jesus made no influence on the post-Easter community whatsoever.[33] The assumptions of (2) and (3), if correct, make Jesus a man without parallel in history since he neither depended on his predecessors nor influenced his followers at any point.[34] (4) For this criterion to be viable, complete knowledge on our part of first-century Judaism and the theology of the early church is required.[35] But such knowledge is not available to us.

As a result of these criticisms, we propose that this criterion should not be the key tool and that it should be used positively and not negatively.[36] In other words, any material from the Jesus tradition which does not meet the requirements of this criterion should not be judged categorically as inauthentic. Instead, other criteria (and considerations) should be brought into service to ascertain the possibility of its authenticity. And if any material passes the test of this criterion, it will be judged authentic (the positive use).

Hence, we are not committed to any particular criterion but shall use all of them as appropriate and recognise, at the same time, their limitations. The particular material under consideration will prompt the tool. In our arguments for the authenticity of the sayings and actions we shall choose later, the procedure will be as follows: we shall attempt to show how past arguments against their authenticity are mistaken[37] and provide arguments to show why we

---

31 So M. D. Hooker, 'On Using the Wrong Tool', *Theology* 75 (1972), 574.
32 This assumption is rejected in principle by most works cited in note 1.
33 Meyer observes that 'if authentic materials contrary to church tendencies were conserved, authentic materials in accord with church tendencies were *a fortiori* conserved' in *Aims*, p. 83. This observation sounds the death-knell for this assumption.
34 So Goetz and Blomberg, 'Burden of Proof', 43.
35 So Hooker, 'Tool', 575.
36 Even as a positive tool it has an inherent weakness. This is implied in criticism (4). In other words, the results obtained through the positive use of this criterion are always in danger of being overturned by future research into first-century Judaism as it may demonstrate that what was once understood as unique of Jesus is attested elsewhere.
37 S. Westerholm has made the interesting proposal that criteria for inauthenticity should also be formulated. His attempts at such a formulation can be found in his *Jesus and Scribal Authority*, pp. 8–10.

consider the contrary to be correct.[38] As the question of authenticity is a very important issue in historical Jesus research, much attention will be devoted to it in our study.

Obviously, the prior task of isolating the most primitive materials through source, form and redactional criticism will also be performed.

3   Review of research

In the history of scholarship on the historical Jesus, different answers have been given to the first question posed[39] but often only in a brief manner. A connection between the three significant actions of Jesus in Jerusalem (the 'triumphal' entry; the incident in the temple; and the last supper) has only rarely been sought. The second question posed[40] is largely ignored. It is the concern of this section, then, to give a brief survey of such scholarship. Basically, there are three lines of interpretation of the intentions of Jesus in Jerusalem: (1) Jesus intended to stage a coup in Jerusalem (the *putsch* theory); (2) Jesus intended to bring about his death; (3) Jesus intended to challenge the city with his message (Jesus might have *expected* death but he did not *intend* to die).

The Reimarus–Brandon line: the *putsch* theory

Why Jesus went to Jerusalem was a question of paramount importance to H. Reimarus, who is often regarded as the initiator of the 'Old Quest'.[41] According to him it was Jesus' intention to establish in the immediate future an earthly kingdom with himself as king. Hence, Jesus went to Jerusalem in order to stage a coup. He made a grand entry into Jerusalem near Passover, amid the acclamation of the crowds. The entry was deliberately timed to get maximum exposure, as Passover was a pilgrimage festival. Jesus

---

[38]   Scholars have often debated the issue of where the burden of proof ought to lie. Should it be on the person who claims authenticity or the one claiming inauthenticity? Or perhaps it should be on anyone who wants to make his case (whether for authenticity or inauthenticity). On this important issue, see Goetz and Blomberg, 'Burden of Proof', 39–63. For our study we align ourselves with the third view although we judge that the second view has most merits.

[39]   That is, 'What intentions did Jesus have when he made that final trip to Jerusalem?'

[40]   That is, 'Did Jesus appropriate the Zion traditions for his ministry?'

[41]   See C. H. Talbert (ed.), *Reimarus: Fragments.*

intended to incite the people of Israel gathered in Jerusalem to proclaim him as king.[42] After the entry, he went straight into the temple, began a disturbance and committed acts of violence, like one who suddenly considered himself possessed of worldly power for the purpose of expressing his messiahship.[43] Unfortunately, Jesus' incitement of the crowds to rebellion was not successful and he died as a disillusioned man on the cross with the cry, 'My God, my God, why hast thou forsaken me?'[44] Thus, in Reimarus' view, it was clearly the intention of Jesus not to die but to build up a worldly kingdom and deliver the Israelites from bondage. Unfortunately, Reimarus did not seek to understand the last supper in connection with these events.[45]

Reimarus' errors in his reconstruction are well known[46] and will not be rehearsed here. However, it is seldom recognised that there are intrinsic strengths in Reimarus' account of the intentions of the historical Jesus. For instance, Reimarus was sensitive to three important matters. First, he took seriously into account the political aspect of the Jewish hope for the kingdom of God and the political circumstances in which the Jewish contemporaries of Jesus found themselves. Secondly, Reimarus' interpretation involves a broad sweep of the key events in Jesus' life and thus lends a certain amount of coherence and conviction to it. And lastly, Reimarus recognised that, to a first-century Jew, Jerusalem was both politically and theologically important (Jerusalem being the place where the kingdom of God will be revealed).[47]

The strengths of the *putsch* theory of Jesus' intention ensure that it will not simply fade into oblivion. And this is exactly what we witness in the twentieth century. This theory, which has been espoused in fits and starts,[48] found new expression in 1967 in S. G. F. Brandon's work.[49]

Reimarus' account could easily be dismissed as being based on a

---

[42] *Fragments*, p. 146.   [43] Ibid.
[44] *Fragments*, p. 150.   [45] *Fragments*, pp. 118–22.
[46] See the criticisms found in M. Hengel, *Was Jesus a Revolutionist?*; and E. Bammel, 'The Revolution Theory from Reimarus to Brandon', in Bammel and Moule (eds.), *Politics*, pp. 11–68.
[47] Reimarus, *Fragments*, p. 124, cf. p. 138.
[48] See the magisterial survey of Bammel in 'Revolution Theory', pp. 11–68. It is interesting to note that during this period, the historical Jesus was interpreted according to the social and political issues which confronted the various interpreters.
[49] *Jesus and the Zealots*.

very uncritical reading of the gospels. The same cannot be said for Brandon's work. Like Reimarus, Brandon recognised the political dimension of the hope for the kingdom of God.[50] Although Jesus was not a zealot, he had emphases in his ministry which were similar to those of the zealots. The difference between Jesus and the zealots was that Jesus did not challenge the Romans directly, but directed his challenge at the Jewish authorities.[51] The entry into Jerusalem was intended to be such a challenge, and was also meant to signify his messianic role.[52] The action in the temple constituted an attack on the Jewish sacerdotal system, which was regarded by Jesus as corrupt and in need of purification.[53] The resurrection of Reimarus' hypothesis in Brandon's work (albeit in an altered form) came about precisely because of the strengths noted above. Of course, Brandon avers that these political aspects of Jesus' ministry were masked by the first gospel to be written, Mark, in order to 'depoliticise' Jesus after 70 CE.[54]

Although Brandon's theory has been severely criticised,[55] the *putsch* theory lives on. G. W. Buchanan's book, *Jesus: The King and His Kingdom* (1984) adopts a similar line of interpretation but bases its results on his research on chreia.[56] He comes to the conclusion that Jesus was committed to the principle of Jewish conquest theology (which he believes to be central to the covenant faith of the Jews).

Jesus intended to die in Jerusalem

Another line of approach is to interpret Jesus' intention in Jerusalem as the intention to die in order to bring about certain results.

(i) A. Schweitzer

Schweitzer's book, *Von Reimarus zu Wrede*,[57] is acclaimed as having brought the 'Old Quest' to a close by arguing that the historical Jesus is irrelevant to the modern world.

Schweitzer's Jesus was thoroughly eschatological. He was a man

---

[50] Brandon, *Jesus*, p. 337.   [51] *Jesus*, p. 356.
[52] *Jesus*, p. 350.   [53] *Jesus*, pp. 332, 335.   [54] *Jesus*, pp. 322–4.
[55] See especially Hengel, *Revolutionist*, and Bammel, 'Revolution Theory'.
[56] Buchanan, *Jesus*, pp. 43–128.
[57] Hereafter, the citations will be taken from the English translation, *The Quest of the Historical Jesus*.

who believed that he was now the secret messiah who would be enthroned later following a period of πειρασμός.[58] But as that period did not materialise, the kingdom of God could not dawn. At Caesarea Philippi, he came to the decision that it would be through his own suffering and death that the kingdom of God would come.[59] With this notion in mind, Jesus went into Jerusalem and did provocative acts (e.g., the 'triumphal' entry and the action in the temple) so that he might be killed. Hence, Jesus went to Jerusalem in order to die. For Jesus, the necessity of his death was grounded in dogma, not external historical circumstances.[60] It is important to note that Schweitzer's notion of the death of Jesus included a strain of atonement theology. Jesus was 'to give his life for them, the many ... and to make in his own blood the atonement which they [the disciples] would have had to render in the tribulation. The kingdom could not come until the debt which weighed heavily upon the world was discharged.'[61] But even so, the kingdom did not come. His words describing this failure are poignant: '[Jesus] lays hold of the wheel of the world to set it moving on that last revolution which is to bring all ordinary history to a close. It refuses to turn, and he throws himself upon it. Then it does turn; and crushes him. Instead of bringing in the eschatological conditions, he destroyed them!'[62]

What is of interest in Schweitzer's reconstruction of the historical Jesus is that he set out to find an inner connection between the intentions of Jesus and his death.[63] Jesus' journey to Jerusalem was treated as climactic and no statement about his intentions could be more succinct than Schweitzer's: Jesus went to Jerusalem to die in order to bring in the kingdom. Therefore, a certain coherence between Jesus' earlier ministry, his aims and his activities in Jerusalem is obtained. In some studies on the historical Jesus, this important connection is not even sought.

The weaknesses of Schweitzer's reconstruction are well known and we shall not repeat them here,[64] but we would like to offer some observations which are seldom noticed. With all his vaunted claims of interpreting Jesus in a thoroughly eschatological manner, Schweitzer has failed to exploit or take notice of the fact that Jerusalem was the place where Jewish eschatological hopes were

---

[58] *Quest*, p. 362.   [59] *Quest*, p. 386.   [60] *Quest*, p. 389.
[61] *Quest*, pp. 387, 389.   [62] *Quest*, pp. 368–9.
[63] As is also observed by Sanders, *Jesus*, p. 23.
[64] See Sanders, *Jesus*, p. 23 for a good summary.

centred. Furthermore, if Jesus intended to die, why did he provoke the Jewish authorities? Why not provoke Herod or the Romans? This question may not be as pedantic as it seems. It will be seen later that Dodd and Borg took cognisance of this and drew some important conclusions from it.

(ii) The modern period

Schweitzer insists that Jesus went to Jerusalem to die. How did scholars who came after him regard this claim? Most modern scholars today believe that Jesus at least expected to die although he did not intend to die. However, two scholars have recently followed a line of explanation similar to Schweitzer's. J. C. O'Neill believes that Jesus went to Jerusalem with the expressed purpose of sacrificing himself for mankind as God's Son.[65] N. T. Wright argues that Jesus' overall intention in his ministry concerned the 'reconstitution' of Israel and that he believed he *was* Israel.[66] Hence, Jesus' main intention in Jerusalem was to die the death of Israel by taking on the wrath of Rome, the historical embodiment of the wrath of God, so that Israel would not 'die'.[67]

Mention should also be made of P. Stuhlmacher's recent article.[68] While it was not his intention to discuss primarily Jesus' aims, some statements he made in the course of his argument merit our attention. Stuhlmacher believes that as the messianic Son of Man, Jesus held in the face of death his belief in the validity of the Zion traditions.[69] Jesus saw himself, then, as being sent by Yahweh to gather the 'Zwölfstämmevolk' and he wanted to sanctify the sanctuary on Zion for the type of worship which he was pioneering and leading.[70] The action in the temple came about because of its failure to be the true place of worship.[71] That action signified judgment and called into question the temple as the place of offering.[72] However, Jesus would himself step in to be the sin

---

[65] J. C. O'Neill, *Messiah. Six Lectures on the Ministry of Jesus*, p. 58. O'Neill regards the title 'God's Son' as messianic (p. 56).

[66] N. T. Wright, 'Jesus, Israel and the Cross', in K. Richards (ed.), *SBL 1985 Seminar Papers*, pp. 93, 83.

[67] 'Jesus', pp. 90, 93.

[68] P. Stuhlmacher, 'Die Stellung Jesu und des Paulus zu Jerusalem', *ZTK* 86 (1989), 140–56.

[69] 'Stellung', 146.   [70] 'Stellung', 144–5.   [71] 'Stellung', 144; cf. 143.

[72] 'Stellung', 143.

offering to replace all sin offerings.[73] Thus, in Stuhlmacher's view, Jesus' death was part and parcel of his intentions in Jerusalem. Stuhlmacher's essay attempts to fit Jesus' intentions in Jerusalem with his attitude towards the Zion traditions. The result Stuhlmacher arrives at is that Jesus did not reject the Zion traditions *per se*. In fact, Zion remained for him the central place of salvation in spite of judgment on the temple and Jerusalem.[74]

A scholarly discussion on Jesus' attitude towards Jerusalem and how that fits in with his intentions to go there is long overdue. Stuhlmacher's short article has pointed to the direction we should take, but it cannot be a substitute for intensive scholarly work in this area.

It should be noted that the scholars who adopt this line of explanation find it difficult to fit Jesus' significant actions in Jerusalem with his expressed intention to die. Most regard these actions as being performed to provoke the powers that be to execute him (so Schweitzer and Wright). But this appears to be a highly implausible hypothesis. An important question is thus raised: if Jesus intended to die, why those actions?

Jesus intended to challenge Jerusalem with his message

Scholars in this category believe that death came to Jesus as result and not intention. Jesus, therefore, went to Jerusalem to confront the capital with his message.

(i) G. Bornkamm

What is of paramount importance to Bornkamm in his book *Jesus of Nazareth* is not so much who Jesus thought he was or what his intentions were, but his message.[75] That stands supreme.[76]

According to Bornkamm, the central thrust of Jesus' message was to make the reality of God present.[77] The decisive turning-point in his ministry came when he made the resolution to go to

---

[73] 'Stellung', 144.   [74] 'Stellung', 146.

[75] This was also observed by W. B. Tatum, *In Quest of Jesus*, p. 75. Years ago, S. Neill made a similar point: 'though the book presents itself as a piece of historical research, it is not the work of the historian', in *The Interpretation of the New Testament 1861–1961*, p. 279. Cf. Sanders, *Jesus*, p. 30.

[76] This may be a result of the influence of Bultmann, Bornkamm's teacher.

[77] G. Bornkamm, *Jesus of Nazareth*, p. 62.

Jerusalem with his disciples to confront the people there with his message, because, in Jesus' view, Jerusalem was connected with the destiny of the Jewish nation.[78] How does Bornkamm explain the actions of Jesus in Jerusalem? First of all, Bornkamm rejects the passion predictions and hence concludes that Jesus did not seek his own death in Jerusalem.[79] Secondly, he has doubts about the 'triumphal' entry episode.[80] Thirdly, he regards the action in the temple as being carried out to cleanse the sanctuary for the approaching kingdom of God.[81] Further than that Bornkamm did not go. In his view, the message of Jesus was all-important.

(ii) C. H. Dodd

Dodd's little book *The Founder of Christianity* is replete with pertinent observations and contains a brilliant hypothesis which is seldom noticed. Sanders, who is not sympathetic towards Dodd's non-eschatological framework, admits that he none the less offered a thorough and complete hypothesis.[82]

Dodd is confident of his ability to psychologise Jesus and to recover the chronology of his ministry.[83] Regarding the Markan outline in general as authentic, Dodd takes as his starting-point the notion that historic Israel was in a state of crisis. It was doomed and it had to die in order to rise again.[84]

Hence, Jesus' aim during his ministry was 'to constitute a community worthy of the name of a people of God, a divine commonwealth through individual response to God coming in his kingdom'.[85] And as Jerusalem is the heart and central shrine of historic Israel, it is inevitable that Jesus should go and challenge the city for a decisive response to the presence of God.[86] As renunciation of self is the principle which validates total commitment to God and his kingdom, the whole conception of a new people of God is based on the principle of 'dying to live'.[87] In Jesus' death, the ideal of sacrifice was translated into brute fact. Dodd explains the cause of Jesus' death thus: 'pointers afforded by the outward course of events coincided with the inner promptings of his

---

[78] *Jesus*, pp. 154–5.   [79] *Jesus*, p. 154.   [80] *Jesus*, p. 158.
[81] *Jesus*, p. 159.   [82] Sanders, *Jesus*, p. 44.
[83] As also observed by Tatum, *Quest*, p. 86.
[84] C. H. Dodd, *The Founder of Christianity*, p. 89.
[85] *Founder*, p. 90.   [86] *Founder*, p. 139.   [87] *Founder*, p. 95.

vocation: he must go to Jerusalem – and die there'.[88] In short, intention, premonition and result coalesced. How does Dodd then interpret the 'triumphal' entry and the temple episode in the light of his central thesis? They were both symbolic acts. The entry challenged the people to rethink their ideas and hopes for the nation (Jesus had in mind Zech. 9.9).[89] The action in the temple was not meant to be political as it was the worship of God and not the independence of the Jewish state that Jesus was concerned with.[90] In that act, Jesus was making the charge that the priesthood was exploiting the sanctity of the temple by making it a stronghold of a powerful and exclusive faction.[91] The parable of the wicked husbandmen, which Dodd believes to be authentic in both form and setting, signified that the existing Jewish religious establishment was to be replaced by a different leadership.[92]

Clearly, it can be seen that Dodd's reconstruction is coherent and wide-ranging with many fresh and interesting ideas. His strength lies in his ability to see the picture as a whole. It is only the compass of the book which prevents him from grounding his ideas more firmly.

(iii) B. F. Meyer

To date, Meyer's *The Aims of Jesus* is the most comprehensive treatment of the intentions of Jesus. Meyer believes that Jesus was concerned with a particular hope of Israel, namely 'restoration'. His reconstruction is similar to Dodd's. The major difference between them, however, is that, for Meyer, Jesus' mission was eschatological through and through.[93] He posits that Israel was in a state of crisis and judgment was about to fall which would also inaugurate God's eschatological reign.[94] Hence, it was Jesus' intention to seek *publicly* the national, eschatological restoration of Israel, while in *private* teaching his disciples, as they faced the coming ordeal, about his understanding of himself as the messianic builder of the house of God and about the resolution of all these at the day when he, the Son of Man, was to be enthroned.[95]

In Meyer's understanding of Jesus' overall aims, what was Jesus' intention in going to Jerusalem? Meyer believes that Jerusalem was

---

[88] *Founder*, p. 151.   [89] *Founder*, p. 143.   [90] *Founder*, p. 145.
[91] *Founder*, p. 146. It is noteworthy that Dodd anticipated many of Borg's ideas.
[92] *Founder*, p. 150.   [93] Meyer, *Aims*, p. 211.
[94] Ibid.   [95] *Aims*, pp. 221–2.

intended by Jesus to be the place for the climax of his ministry.[96] As a result, there was a 'strain on the secret' of Jesus' messiahship, during which time Jesus pressed Israel for a decision in the hope of winning it over to the reign of God.[97] Therefore, the 'triumphal' entry and the action in the temple (which Meyer seems to regard as one event[98]), while being symbolic, were also at the same time indicative of Jesus' messiahship and the messianic restoration of Israel.[99] The action in the temple is interpreted by him to have a very wide significance: as demonstration, prophetic critique, fulfilment, imminent judgment and restoration.[100] All these unite to point to the restoration of the temple on a restored Zion.[101] In Meyer's account, the symbolism of Zion or Jerusalem is readily acknowledged and utilised although he does not explore it fully. To his credit, he is aware of the centrality of the Zion symbol in Jesus' ministry.

What about Jesus' death? Meyer concludes that it was not Jesus' *intention* to be repudiated and killed. However, as he did *expect* repudiation and death, his intention was actually to charge them with meaning.[102] Jesus interpreted his foreseen death as expiatory for the world[103] and he tried to combine the promise of God's reign with the prospect of his own violent death.[104]

(iv) M. J. Borg

For Dodd and Meyer politics is on the periphery. In Borg's book,[105] it occupies centre stage. However, Borg's Jesus did not intend to stage a coup.

Borg starts from the premise that conflict in the context of the hope of Israel is the key to understanding the intention of the historical Jesus.[106] He posits that in the first century there operated within Jewish society a powerful cultural dynamic, the quest for holiness, which pushed Judaism increasingly towards a collision with Rome.[107] Jesus appeared in history as a holy man who rejected that quest, offered an alternative paradigm (mercy as *imitatio Dei*)

[96] *Aims*, p. 169.   [97] *Aims*, p. 199.
[98] *Aims*, p. 168.   [99] *Aims*, p. 199.
[100] *Aims*, pp. 197–8. It is surprising that Wright could write that Meyer consistently plays down the element of judgment! See Neill and Wright, *Interpretation*, p. 383.
[101] Meyer, *Aims*, p. 198. Cf. p. 183.
[102] *Aims*, p. 218.   [103] *Aims*, pp. 217–18.   [104] *Aims*, p. 216.
[105] *Conflict, Holiness and Politics in the Teachings of Jesus.*
[106] *Conflict*, p. 24.   [107] *Conflict*, p. 70.

and redefined the concept of holiness. That is, holiness, and not uncleanness, was contagious.[108]

In light of this overall thrust of Jesus' ministry, what was his intention in going to Jerusalem? Jesus' entry into Jerusalem and his action in the temple were symbolic acts which amounted to a protest against the quest for holiness undertaken by many of his contemporaries.[109] Borg gives much weight, as does Dodd, to Zechariah 9.9 (where the motifs of universalism and anti-resistance can be found) in determining the meaning of Jesus' entry.[110] The action in the temple was meant to be an indictment against it for it had become a centre of nationalistic resistance.[111] But Borg does not answer the question why Jesus went to Jerusalem as clearly as he does in his later book, *Jesus: A New Vision*. In that book, Borg states that Jesus' concern was the renewal of Israel: he created within Israel a sectarian revitalisation or renewal movement, the purpose of which was the transformation of the Jewish social world.[112] Jesus went to Jerusalem, believing it to be the climax of his prophetic mission, and made a final appeal to his people to change their ways before it was too late.[113] The actions in Jerusalem are to be seen in this light. Such a reading of the gospel data bespeaks an attempt on the part of Borg to 'de-eschatologise' Jesus in order to 'politicise' him.[114]

Why then did Jesus die? According to Borg, Jesus was not simply a victim of circumstances but one who provocatively challenged the ethos of his day. He was killed because he sought the transformation of his own culture: 'For that goal he gave his life, even though his death was not his primary intention.'[115] Hence Jesus did not intend to die but was killed because he was perceived to be a threat. All that can be said about Jesus' death is that he died for a cause.

(v) E. P. Sanders

According to Sanders, Jesus saw himself as God's last messenger before the establishment of the eschatological kingdom of God.[116]

---

[108] *Conflict*, pp. 123, 133.   [109] *Conflict*, p. 176.

[110] Cf. Dodd, *Founder*, p. 143.   [111] Borg, *Conflict*, pp. 174–7.

[112] M. J. Borg, *Jesus: A New Vision*, p. 124.   [113] *Vision*, p. 172.

[114] See especially chapter 8 of his *Conflict*, 'Jesus and the Future', pp. 201–27; cf. his article 'An Orthodoxy Reconsidered: The End-of-the-World Jesus', in L. D. Hurst and N. T. Wright (eds.), *The Glory of Christ in the New Testament: Studies in Christology in Memory of George Bradford Caird*, pp. 207–17.

[115] *Vision*, p. 183.   [116] Sanders, *Jesus*, p. 319.

Jesus, working in the framework of restoration eschatology,[117] believed that God, not himself, would bring in the kingdom miraculously.[118] Sanders further suggests that Jesus may not have had a well-thought-out plan or programme.[119] In the light of this framework, why did Jesus go to Jerusalem? Jesus went there to offer symbolic gestures to indicate what was to come, and his own role in that future.[120] Sanders believes Jesus was aware of the fact that the religious leaders might not be convinced by his claims and thus had a premonition that he might be rejected and be put to death. However, he did look to God to redeem the situation and to vindicate him.[121] Sanders does not spell out how this was to be achieved. But it is to be noted that Sanders holds that it was not Jesus' intention to die although he did not seek to escape from it.[122]

Methodologically speaking, Sanders relies heavily on the acts of Jesus and not the sayings, for he believes that the latter are more liable to be distorted during oral transmission.[123] And it is Jesus' action in the temple which forms the starting-point in Sanders' book. That action pointed to the fact that God's eschatological restoration was about to begin in that it signified the destruction of the old temple and its replacement with the new.[124] Hence, Jesus did not criticise or pass judgment on the temple. The 'triumphal' entry is almost stripped of its significance, as Sanders believes that the event as narrated in the gospels has been grossly exaggerated.[125] But he does allow for the possibility that the event was intended by Jesus to symbolise the coming kingdom and his own role in it.[126]

The works surveyed in this subsection, although adopting different paradigms (eschatological, political or otherwise) to interpret Jesus' ministry, all agree (with the possible exception of Dodd) in stating that Jesus did not intend to die. Death might have been expected, but Jesus' intentions were something other than that. The question this line of explanation faces is, 'If Jesus expected to die, how did he relate that expectation to his intentions in going to Jerusalem? Did he simply set the expectation of death aside in the considerations of those intentions?'

---

[117] *Jesus*, p. 329.   [118] *Jesus*, p. 235.   [119] *Jesus*, pp. 226, 235.
[120] *Jesus*, p. 235.   [121] *Jesus*, p. 332.   [122] *Jesus*, p. 332.
[123] *Jesus*, p. 5; cf. pp. 13–18.   [124] *Jesus*, pp. 69, 71.   [125] *Jesus*, p. 306.
[126] *Jesus*, p. 308.

We shall now offer some remarks to conclude our survey:

(i)   As can be seen from the above survey, a scholarly con-
       sensus on Jesus' intentions in Jerusalem has yet to be
       reached. Some old hypotheses still have currency in the
       modern period. However, it is significant to note that
       several recent works agree in attempting to understand
       Jesus' intentions *vis-à-vis* the hopes of Israel (whether
       political or eschatological ones).

(ii)   In some works surveyed, it can be seen that there is
       difficulty relating the death of Jesus to his actions in
       Jerusalem. To a certain extent, then, Schweitzer's dictum
       still applies: 'one might use ... as a principle of division ...
       to clarify the lives of Jesus, whether they make him go to
       Jerusalem to work or to die'.[127]

(iii) No full-scale attempt has been devoted to the two ques-
       tions posed earlier. Stuhlmacher's essay is the only one
       which tries to link these two questions together. His treat-
       ment encourages us to explore these issues thoroughly.

---

[127] Schweitzer, *Quest*, p. 389 n.1.

2

ZION IN THE FIRST AND SECOND TEMPLE PERIODS

1   Introduction

It is no exaggeration to say that Zion is of immense importance in the OT and in Jewish religious and eschatological thought.[1] A study of the use of the term Zion or Jerusalem during the first and second temple periods will reveal that it is constantly referred to and has attracted to itself many strands of Jewish national and eschatological hopes. The purpose of this chapter is not just to survey the use of these terms during the said periods.[2] Rather, it will also attempt to highlight important motifs connected with them, and assess how they have influenced Jewish thought. To use Steck's terminology, we are interested in tracing those 'notional elements' which have been connected to Zion and Jerusalem during this period, and in understanding how these 'notional elements' are related to each other and point to more extensive 'intellectual spheres'.[3] In addition to that, we hope to demonstrate that, against great odds, Zion/Jerusalem retains its centrality through the vicissitudes of Jewish history. However, the question of the origin of the Zion traditions[4] and the social setting which gave rise to them will

---

[1]   D. E. Gowan writes that in OT eschatology Jerusalem appeared with a prominence unparalleled by any other theme. Indeed, he ventures to suggest that Jerusalem could serve as its centre in his *Eschatology in the Old Testament*, p. 3.

[2]   For useful surveys on this topic see G. Fohrer and E. Lohse, 'Σιών κτλ' in *TDNT* VII, pp. 292–338; T. L. Donaldson, *Jesus on the Mountain*, pp. 35–69; J. A. Beagley, *The 'Sitz im Leben' of the Apocalypse with Particular Reference to the Role of the Church's Enemies*, pp. 113–78 (his survey covers the prophetic corpus and the NT).

[3]   O. H. Steck, 'Theological Streams of Tradition' in D. A. Knight (ed.), *Tradition and Theology in the Old Testament*, pp. 183–214, especially p. 193.

[4]   We owe the specific identification of the 'Zion traditions' among the many traditions emanating from the OT to E. Rohland, 'Die Bedeutung der Erwähl-ungstradition Israels für die Eschatologie der alttestamentlichen Propheten' (D.Theol. dissertation, University of Heidelberg, 1956). Since then, discussion has moved on apace. On this see B. C. Ollenburger, *Zion, the City of the Great*

not be discussed. Much work has been done on this topic, although a consensus has yet to be reached.[5]

A statement of what we mean by 'Zion traditions' is in order. By Zion traditions we mean the use of Zion or Jerusalem as a focus and symbol of Jewish national and eschatological thought.[6] By the first century, this usage has developed elaborately and become a heritage of the Jews. The plural of the term is used to indicate that there was no set understanding regarding Zion or Jerusalem.

An inherent danger in the procedure adopted is that it may be insensitive to the course of development of the Zion traditions and link writings which may not be related in time or geographically, thus giving a false impression of homogeneity. But such weaknesses can be mitigated if the purpose of this chapter is simply to show that particular strands of thought about Zion can be found enshrined in the canonical texts of Israel (i.e., the OT) and that their influence can also be found in Jewish life of the second temple period.

A clarification regarding the relationship of the terms 'Jerusalem' and 'Zion' is in order here. 'Jerusalem' and 'Zion'[7] are used synonymically in the OT (see especially Zech. 8.2–3; Micah

---

King, pp. 15–19 and R. E. Clements, *Isaiah and the Deliverance of Jerusalem*, pp. 73–4.

5 On the question of the origins of the Zion traditions, three positions are held by scholars.
   1. The Jebusite theory. This view holds that the Zion traditions were a complete takeover of the Jebusite traditions about Jerusalem. See Rohland, 'Die Bedeutung'; G. von Rad, *Old Testament Theology* II, pp. 155–8, 293–4; R. E. Clements, *God and Temple*, pp. 41–8; J. H. Hayes, 'The Tradition of Zion's Inviolability', *JBL* 82 (1963), 419–26.
   2. The Davidic court's creation theory. As the name indicates, this view holds that the Zion traditions originated as a creation of the Davidic court. See N. W. Porteous, 'Jerusalem-Zion: The Growth of a Symbol' in his *Living the Mystery*, pp. 93–111; J. J. M. Roberts, 'The Davidic Origin of the Zion Traditions', *JBL* 92 (1973), 329–44.
   3. The Canaanite theory. This view holds that the Zion traditions came about through a transfer of older Israelite theology, already richly infused with Canaanite motifs, to a new geographical context, Jerusalem. See M. Noth, 'Jerusalem and the Israelite Tradition' in his *The Laws in the Pentateuch and Other Essays*, pp. 132–44; E. Otto, 'Silo und Jerusalem', *TZ* 32 (1967), 65–77; J. A. Soggin, 'Der offiziell geförderte Synkretismus in Israel während des 10. Jährhunderts', *ZAW* 78 (1966), 179–204; D. L. Eisler, 'The Origin and History of Zion as a Theological Symbol in Ancient Israel' (Th.D. dissertation, Princeton Theological Seminary, 1978).

6 Cf. J. D. Levenson's explanation in his 'Zion Traditions', *ABD* VI, p. 1098.

7 On the question of their etymology, see Fohrer and Lohse, 'Σιών', pp. 293–9.

3.12–4.2 among others). Fohrer has attempted to understand more precisely how the terms are used in the OT. He claims that Zion is a term normally used when eschatology is on the writer's horizon, although it is also used to describe present realities connected with the city of Jerusalem. However, Jerusalem is used 'fairly evenly for all aspects'.[8] There are therefore no grounds for denying the synonymity of the two terms, although it could arguably be said that Zion is more evocative of eschatology.

2   Zion in the OT

It has often been observed that Jerusalem is a relative latecomer as an Israelite sanctuary.[9] It is also not the most suitable place for a political capital in terms of physical geography, as it is not centrally positioned nor on important traffic routes.[10] Alt observes that other sanctuaries (e.g., Gibeah and Shechem) would have been better choices if physical geography was the main consideration.[11] Nevertheless, Jerusalem did become the religious and political capital of Israel during the monarchy, and, even after its destruction, its centrality was not overtaken by another city or shrine. The unsuitability of Jerusalem as a capital only serves to accentuate the religious and theological dimension of its importance.[12]

Although one may not be certain about the origins of the Zion traditions, it is incontrovertible that the introduction of the ark into the Jebusite city (i.e., Jerusalem) and its being chosen as the capital city by David gave the impetus, if not the origin, for its importance in Jewish eschatological and theological thought.[13] The mystique of the city was further enhanced by the ceremonies and festivals celebrated by the nation in the temple on Mt Zion. The enthronement[14] and royal psalms,[15] possibly composed for these occasions,

[8] Fohrer and Lohse, 'Σιών', pp. 301–2.
[9] Gowan, *Eschatology*, p. 6.
[10] Beagley, *Apocalypse*, p. 113.
[11] A. Alt, 'Jerusalems Aufstieg' in *Kleine Schriften zur Geschichte des Volkes Israels*, pp. 245–6.
[12] It has been observed that many a renowned city of the ancient orient lies today in ruins like a burnt-out crater, its former splendour reduced to a heap of stones or crumbling bricks. This is not so in the case of Jerusalem. In spite of many a disaster and many a consequent metamorphosis, it remains a living city, a holy city to three great religions. See Porteous, 'Jerusalem-Zion', p. 94.
[13] See Gowan, *Eschatology*, p. 6.
[14] Pss. 47; 93; 96–9. See P. C. Craigie, *Psalms 1–50*, p. 347.
[15] Pss. 2; 18; 20; 21; 45; 72; 89; 101; 110; 132; 144.1–11. See J. Day, *Psalms*, pp.

allow one a window into the understanding of the Israelites concerning the importance of Zion. Much study has been done on this subject and what we shall attempt in this section instead is a general overview of the use of Zion in the OT. We shall also posit an organising concept behind the various motifs connected with it.

Analysis of motifs connected with Zion

Fohrer's delineation of the meanings of Zion and the motifs connected with and generated by it will be our starting-point in the discussion which follows. He lists eight aspects:[16] (i) royal residence and capital; (ii) court-sacral aspect; (iii) symbol of the people or community; (iv) seat and city of God, cultic centre and temple city; (v) city of sin and judgment; (vi) city of the eschatological age of salvation;[17] (vii) mythical aspect; and (viii) city of the theocracy. Fohrer's full treatment has one important drawback: he does not analyse how these motifs became attached to the symbol Zion, what their relationship to each other is, and what their organising centre might be. The discussion which follows will, I hope, remedy this.

Schreiner argues that the most fundamental feature of OT Zion theology is the concept of election: Mt Zion has been chosen by Yahweh as the place of his abode.[18] This forms the central feature of the royal cult in Jerusalem before the destruction of the first temple in 586 BCE. As Clements observes, 'the entire ideology of the Jerusalem temple centred in the belief that, as his chosen dwelling-place, Yahweh's presence was to be found in it, and that from there he revealed his will and poured out his blessing upon his people'.[19] Among the variety of ways in which Yahweh is pictured as present on Mt Zion, the most prominent one is his kingship – Yahweh is king in Zion.[20] These two important aspects of Zion theology, that is, Yahweh dwells in Jerusalem and Yahweh is king

---

88–90 and also H. J. Kraus, *Theology of the Psalms*, pp. 107–23 for further discussion.

[16] Fohrer and Lohse, 'Σιών', pp. 307–18.

[17] Under this heading, Fohrer also discusses the motif of the pilgrimage of the nations to Jerusalem.

[18] J. Schreiner, *Sion-Jerusalem: Jahwes Königssitz. Theologie der heiligen Stadt im Alten Testament*, pp. 19–71, especially pp. 67–8.

[19] Clements, *Temple*, p. 76.

[20] As has been demonstrated conclusively by Ollenburger, *Zion*, pp. 23–52.

in Jerusalem, hold together the nexus of motifs and concepts connected with Zion.

It is this fused concept which lends legitimacy to Jerusalem as the political capital of Israel. Indeed, it may not be inaccurate to say that at least some groups in Israel believed the election of Jerusalem to be prior to the election of David.[21] This would suggest that David was elected so that Yahweh could exercise his kingship through a vicegerent in Jerusalem. As is pointed out by Schreiner, no earthly king is ever spoken of as 'King of Zion'.[22] Hence, the priority of Zion over David is clear, even though the two are in some sense connected. In this light, the election of David is inseparable from the election of Zion as the place in and through which Yahweh would exercise his kingship through a vicegerent.

It is precisely because Zion is the dwelling-place and throne of Yahweh that many motifs connected with it cohere. In the first place, Zion is conceived as inviolable precisely because it is Yahweh's dwelling-place. Taunts are made against the aggressors for their futile attempts to assault Zion (Pss. 2; 46; 48; 76). But this should not blind one to the fact that Zion is inviolable only as long as Yahweh dwells in it and not because of some intrinsically sacred character on its part.[23] Although some circles in Israel did possibly conceive of Zion's independent inviolability (see Jer. 7.4), the prophetic perspective is decisively against it (Jer. 7; 24; 26; 29; Ezek. 5; 10.18–19; 11.22–3).

It should be noted that the prophets were not slow to indict Jerusalem for its sins. Yet, for all these indictments, the hope for a better, restored and glorified Jerusalem was not discarded[24] but forcefully expressed. An example from the prophetic corpus serves to demonstrate this. Ezekiel 16 can be described as a prophetic attack on Jerusalem.[25] Jerusalem is depicted as an ungrateful and unfaithful wife who prostituted herself (vv. 15–20). Judgment is passed on her (vv. 35–41). Yet Ezekiel 16 ends with a promise of forgiveness (v. 63) and an establishment of an everlasting covenant (v. 60). This nexus of judgment and restoration can also be found

---

[21] See Ps. 132.11–13 where it is suggested that Yahweh covenanted with David because (כִּי, *ki*, v. 13) he has chosen Zion. Cf. Ollenburger, *Zion*, pp. 61, 86 and H. Seebass, 'בחר', *bachar'*, *TDOT* II, p. 81.

[22] *Sion-Jerusalem*, pp. 129–30.

[23] See Ollenburger, *Zion*, p. 74.

[24] So Beagley, *Apocalypse*, pp. 149–50.

[25] Cf. W. H. Brownlee, *Ezekiel 1–19*, pp. 239–41.

in Isaiah and Jeremiah.[26] Such a nexus points to the fact that while the prophets might be harsh with Jerusalem's sins, they could not abandon the notion that Jerusalem was loved by Yahweh despite its sins.

Following from what is said above, Zion is also conceived of as a refuge (Pss. 20.2–3; 46.6). Hence, political alliances without due recognition of Yahweh's protection over its people were criticised in Isaiah as they were tantamount to rejecting Yahweh's refuge for another (Isa. 7.1–17; 30.1–5; 31.1–3). In addition, this motif implies that the distressed of Israel can find refuge in it (Ps. 9.12–13).[27] Zion therefore can be a symbol of security and also of judgment for those who looked for other sources of security.

One other corollary of the idea that Yahweh is king in Zion is that, through a chosen king, his rule over all the nations is exercised in Zion (Ps. 2). This aspect is later given an eschatological colouring in the prophecies of the restoration of Jerusalem in which mention is made of the pilgrimage of the nations to the city to worship Yahweh (Isa. 2.2–4; 66.18–23; Jer. 3.17; Zech. 2.11; 8.20–3).

Finally, the motif of election is also related to the concept of the possession of the land. Clements observes that in the recitation of *Heilsgeschichte* in Psalm 78 and Exodus 15.1–18, 'both follow a similar pattern in which the climax is found in the establishing of Mount Zion as Yahweh's abode, and Israel's possession of the land of Canaan. In both of these psalms the land of Canaan is closely identified with Yahweh's holy mountain.'[28]

But the most significant use of Zion in the OT is its function and role in eschatology. The destruction of Jerusalem and its temple in 586 BCE can be said to be a watershed in the history of Israel.[29] The cherished hopes connected with Jerusalem appeared to be dashed. However, an unexpected phenomenon occurred. With its destruction, the city did not diminish in importance. In fact, its significance increased after that very event![30] As Porteous has observed, 'the names Zion and Jerusalem ... shine through the darkness of those years and lend themselves as the vehicles of meanings which were not disconnected with earlier, pre-Israelite

[26] Among the many references, the following are representative: Isa. 1.21–31; 3.1–4.6; 3.14–18; Jer. 7.4–11; 29.10–14.

[27] Ollenburger, *Zion*, p. 108 and cf. Kraus, *Theology*, pp. 152–3.

[28] Clements, *Temple*, p. 51. Cf. Fohrer and Lohse, 'Σιών', pp. 308–9.

[29] W. D. Davies, *The Gospel and the Land*, pp. 133–4.

[30] Davies, *Land*, p. 134. Cf. Clements, *Deliverance*, pp. 107–8.

beliefs but became enriched, transformed and deepened by the experiences through which Israel passed'.[31]

Post-exilic prophets prophesied the restoration of Jerusalem to a splendour grander than before. It therefore became a vehicle for eschatological hopes. Many traditional elements of Zion theology reappeared in different guises in the Zion eschatology of the prophets[32] and the concept of an eschatological Zion is found widely distributed over the entire prophetic corpus (both pre- and post-exilic prophets).[33] It is therefore clear that, with the destruction of Jerusalem, the Zion traditions were not discarded but experienced development. Indeed, instead of a repudiation of the Zion traditions, exilic Judaism had eschatologised them, and had found a way to take account of judgment and to express its hope for a divinely accomplished future in which these traditions would be fulfilled.[34]

The restoration of Israel to its land, of Israel's relationship with Yahweh, and of Zion's former glories were the one preoccupation of many OT prophets. They looked towards the time when the people would be brought back to Zion amidst great rejoicing. This could only come about when Yahweh had forgiven the sins of the people and restored Zion. A restored people without a restored Jerusalem was inconceivable. Pastoral imagery was used to describe the action of Yahweh in the regathering of his people (Isa. 40.11; Jer. 23.3; 31.10; Ezek. 34.10–16). He would be a shepherd to his people and punish those negligent shepherds whose actions brought about the exile of the people (Jer. 23.2; 25.34–6; Ezek. 34.7–10; Zech. 10.3). From this controlling idea of restoration, two important strands of thought connected with the eschatological Zion proceeded. The first was that the nations which had been a source

---

[31] Porteous, 'Jerusalem-Zion', p. 94. Cf. also Gowan, *Eschatology*, p. 9.

[32] Donaldson, *Jesus*, p. 48.

[33] This occurs twenty times in Isa. 1–39 (1.24–6; 2.2–4; 4.2–6; 11.6–9; 18.7; 24.21–3; 25.6–8; 26.1; 27.13; 28.16; 29.8; 30.19–26, 29; 31.4–5; 32.14–20; 33.4–9, 17–24; 34.8; 35.10; 37.30–2); twenty-three times in Isa. 40–66 (40.2; 40.9; 41.27; 44.24–8; 45.13; 46.13; 48.2; 49.14–26; 51.1–3; 51.9–11; 51.12–16; 52.1–10; 54.1–17; 56.3–8; 57.11–13; 59.20; 60.10–14; 61.1–11; 62.1–12; 65.17–25; 66.1, 6; 66.10–14; 66.18–21); thirteen times in Jer. (3.14; 3.15–18; 27.22; 29.10–14; 30.18–22; 31.6, 10–14, 23, 38–40; 32.36–41, 44; 33.4–9, 10–11, 12–13, 14–16; 50.4–5); ten times in Ezek. (16.59–63; 17.22–4; 20.40–4; 34.20–30; 37.24–8; 40.2; 43.12; 45.6–8; 47.1–12; 48.35); eight times in Zech. (1.14–17; 2.1–12; 3.2; 8.1–23; 9.9–10; 12.1–9; 13.1; 14.1–21); Dan. 9.24–6; Obad. 15–21; Mic. 4; Zeph. 3.14–20; Hag. 2.9; Mal. 3.4.

[34] Gowan, *Eschatology*, pp. 8–9.

of constant distress to the Israelites would now come to Jerusalem to bring tribute to Yahweh and worship there (either voluntarily or in subjugation) and Yahweh would be king over all the earth (the motif of the pilgrimage of Gentiles to Zion, see Isa. 2.2–4; 66.18–23). Indeed, world peace was not outside its purview (Isa. 2.2–4). The second was that the restoration of Zion would result in the transformation of nature (Isa. 11.6–9; 65.17–19). As Donaldson has observed, the eschatological restoration of Zion is like a magnet which has attracted other eschatological themes to itself, resulting in a traditional and yet fluid pattern, and this forms one of the most prominent and persistent strands of OT eschatological expectation.[35] It is precisely this particular strand (i.e., the eschatological restoration of Zion) which was being handed down from generation to generation as a tradition which was later reflected on and enlarged upon during the second temple period and had control over much of Jewish eschatological thought.[36] And it is possible to argue that it is precisely this tradition which shaped much of the thinking and praxis of many Jewish contemporaries of Jesus. We hope to demonstrate this later.

Summary

The important organising concept of the Zion traditions is that Yahweh has chosen to dwell in Jerusalem and exercise his kingship in and through the city. From this important bipolar concept many strands of these traditions (as evident in the OT) receive their impetus and origin: the inviolability of Zion; Zion as a place of refuge, security and salvation; Zion as a place of blessing; Zion as the place of the pilgrimage of the nations; Zion as the place of the universal dominion of Yahweh. With the destruction of Jerusalem, these ideas were not discarded but were given an eschatological dress. The one preoccupation of the post-exilic prophets was the

---

[35] Donaldson, *Jesus*, p. 50.

[36] Note that L. Gaston has asserted that Deutero-Isaiah has no place for a Hebrew messiah or a new temple, and hence, in the post-exilic writings, the Zion traditions and not that of the messiah or the temple are developed in his *No Stone on Another*, pp. 105–6. But see the disagreement of A. Chester, 'The Sibyl and the Temple' in W. Horbury (ed.), *Templum Amicitiae*, pp. 43–4. The issue of whether there was a dichotomising of the two entities (city and temple) is too large for us to take up here. However, there might be tentative steps taken in this direction; see our discussion in section 3 of this chapter.

regathering of the exiles. This future restoration is expected to take place in a glorified Zion.

3   Zion in inter-testamental literature

The eschatological restoration of Zion and related ideas, enshrined in the OT Psalter and prophetic corpus, were constant themes in numerous Jewish writings of the second temple period which emanated from different circles. Indeed, at least one scholar has concluded that eschatological hopes for a glorified Jerusalem were central to Judaism of this period although this subject has rarely been studied.[37] The centrality of Jerusalem for Judaism during this period serves to show the *tenacity* of the Zion traditions. In addition, the traditions emanating from this period also exhibit development and intensification.

Once it became possible, the Israelites returned from exile to rebuild their own homes. Yet there was a sense that the glorious promises given in Deutero-Isaiah (e.g., Isa. 49.14–23) were not fulfilled. The return had materialised, but was that the true return Yahweh had promised? The temple was rebuilt but its splendour paled in comparison with that of the former. Could this be the temple described in Ezekiel 40–8? Such questions loomed large in the thoughts of the returned Israelites and such thoughts were also found expressed in the apocrypha and pseudepigrapha. Almost invariably, yearnings for the eschatological city, temple and restoration were prominent. Indeed, during this period fraught with tumult when 'external forces on several occasions threatened the annihilation of Judaism and internal tensions seemed ready to bring about its disintegration, it was the Zion ideal which along with the Torah, provided the ideology that enabled Judaism to survive'.[38] While it is to be expected that new circumstances[39] would give rise to creative reinterpretation of the traditions (and

---

[37]   Gowan, *Eschatology*, p. 16. Gowan cites A. Causse, 'Le mythe de la nouvelle Jerusalem du Deutero-Esaire à la IIIᵉ Sibylle', *RHPR* 18 (1938), 397.

[38]   Donaldson, *Jesus*, p. 51.

[39]   Davies points out that, in the post-exilic period, the life of Jewry was mainly centred in Jerusalem and in the area surrounding it, so that it was probably inevitable that the city should gather to itself the hopes of Israel. Geographical actualities demanded this. But Davies also concedes that it was not only, and not chiefly, the physical modality of Jerusalem that accounted for its increasingly representative character. It was rather rooted in the history and religion of Israel (in *Land*, p. 131).

this is best seen in the apocalyptic literature of that period), by and large the same themes found in the OT were being used in the writings of this period.

The apocrypha

In the Zion poem of Baruch[40] (4.5–5.9), Jerusalem's election is affirmed: 'take courage, Jerusalem: he who gave you that name will console you' (4.30). This strand of thought is not confined to Baruch but can also be found in Tobit 1.4; Sirach 24.11; 3 Maccabees 2.9–10. Tied closely to this idea is the insistence that the temple is God's dwelling-place (Tob. 1.4) and Jerusalem the place of God's rest and sanctuary (Sir. 35.15–16).

The regathering of exiles back to Zion is also ardently yearned for in the apocrypha. This, in turn, is closely tied up with the yearning for Zion's restoration (cf. Tob. 13.5, 6; cf. 13.12; Bar. 4.36–7; 5.5–6). Hence, in 2 Maccabees 2.17 (cf. 1.27), there is an entreaty for exiles to be gathered (Jerusalem is not mentioned but the temple is) and, in Sirach 36.12–14,[41] there is a very moving entreaty for Zion to be restored:

> Have mercy, Lord, on the people who have invoked your
>   name,
> On Israel whom you have treated as a first-born.
> Show compassion on your holy city,
> On Jerusalem, the place of your rest.
> Fill Zion with songs of your praise
> And your sanctuary with your glory.

However, in Tobit,[42] the regathering of the exiles to Zion and the rebuilding of Jerusalem are confidently asserted (Tob. 13.5, 16–18) without any note of entreaty. This is significant as it shows Tobit's confidence in the promises of Yahweh concerning Zion. It is also interesting to note that in 1 Maccabees 5.53–4 the author describes

---

[40] Written no later than 116 BCE. See G. W. E. Nickelsburg, *Jewish Literature Between the Bible and the Mishnah*, p. 113.

[41] Written between 198 and 175 BCE. See Nickelsburg, *Literature*, p. 64.

[42] Nickelsburg points out that, in contrast to the book of Job, the fate of the nation in Tobit is of great concern and not just the innocent sufferer. Tobit's own suffering therefore is secondary and the problem of the exile and dispersion and the hope for a regathering of the people are foremost in his mind (*Literature*, p. 33; Nickelsburg gives the date of Tobit as pre-168 BCE, p. 35).

Judas' action in encouraging the stragglers in terms reminiscent of the regathering of exiles as prophesied in second Isaiah. As Goldstein has observed, 'our author's echoes here of prophecies of Isaiah are so audacious that he must be hinting that he saw this fulfilment in Judas' victories'.[43] Clearly, one can conclude from this short discussion that the expectation of the regathering of exiles and the restoration of Zion was one chief preoccupation of the Jews living in that period. Interestingly, the expectation for regathering and restoration would presumably (excepting perhaps 1 Maccabees 5.53–4) imply that they have yet to be fulfilled even though there was already a large community of returned Jews living in Palestine.[44] Political realities of that period might have caused such an ongoing expectation. But such a phenomenon also indicates that hopes for their fulfilment have been pushed into the eschatological future (in the case of Tobit and Baruch).

Other motifs connected with Zion in the OT are also found in the apocrypha: the pilgrimage of the nations to Jerusalem (Tob. 13.13–14.); Jerusalem as the mother of Israelites (2 Macc. 7); Yahweh as king on Mt Zion (Jub. 1.28; cf. Isa. 24.33). That there is continuity of thought with regard to Zion between the OT and the apocrypha is a fact which cannot be denied.

In addition to this continuity, one may perhaps discern an interesting development. In Baruch 4, Jerusalem is personified (probably after the manner of Lamentations) not as lamenting its fate (as in Lamentations) but as lamenting for its children (Bar. 4.8) and praying for them (Bar. 4.20). Nowhere in the OT is Jerusalem depicted as lamenting for its children. There might be therefore an implicit distancing of Jerusalem from the sins which had led to its downfall. This is in contrast to the prophetic and Deuteronomistic denunciation of Jerusalem found in the OT. More significantly, the book of Lamentations is implicitly turned on its head in that it is not Jerusalem which is being lamented for but Jerusalem lamenting for her children. Blame is levelled at the Israelites, not the city. This may reflect a tendency to glorify Jerusalem during the second temple period.

---

[43] J. Goldstein, *1 Maccabees*, p. 304.
[44] This is confirmed by the extent of the Jewish boundaries during the Maccabean period. On this, see E. Schürer, *The History of the Jewish People in the Age of Jesus Christ* I, pp. 140–3.

The apocalyptic literature

The nature of the apocalyptic writings would inevitably lead to a more pronounced eschatological treatment of the traditions inherited from the OT. Hence, Zion is greatly eschatologised in these writings and is often treated in conjunction with other eschatological motifs: the messiah and the new age. It is in these writings that one finds a very pronounced development of the Zion traditions.

It is to be noted that, in the apocalyptic literature, traditions are retained as well as developed. There is nothing novel in such a procedure as this phenomenon was already present in the prophetic corpus (e.g., Isa. 60–2). Hence, Jerusalem is affirmed to be elect (T. Levi 10.5) and, in the new Jerusalem, the Lord's presence is said to be there in particular (T. Dan 5.12, 13; cf. Ezek. 48.35).[45] This is worthy of note as Jerusalem can function as the city of God only if God dwells in it. This has been seen already in our discussion of the Zion songs.

In Psalms of Solomon 17,[46] the messianic-Davidic king is connected with Zion. Clearly, the roots of this conception can be traced back to the royal psalms. It is therefore affirmed once again that Yahweh exercises his rule through a vicegerent, in this instance, the messianic-Davidic king (17.21, 32, 34). Allotted to him is the task of regathering the people (17.26) and purging Jerusalem of Gentiles (17.22). In 17.30, the messianic-Davidic king performs a role similar to that of Josiah (cf. 2 Chron. 34.3) by purging Jerusalem (here, probably of the Gentiles) and making it holy 'as it was from the beginning'. The connection of the messiah with Zion in Psalms of Solomon 17 cannot be overemphasised as it serves as an important background for the understanding of the first-century CE messianic movements (including the Jesus movement) and why they had Jerusalem as their target.[47]

---

[45] H. C. Kee dates the composition of the testaments of the twelve patriarchs to the second century BCE in 'Testaments of the Twelve Patriarchs', *OTP* I, pp. 777–8. M. de Jonge claims that they should be read as Christian writings in *The Testaments of the Twelve Patriarchs: A Study of their Text, Composition and Origin*. His case has not convinced many scholars and he has modified his view. See his 'The Testaments of the Twelve Patriarchs' in *Jewish Eschatology, Early Christian Christology and the Testaments of the Twelve Patriarchs*, p. 234.

[46] Composed probably around 70 to 45 BCE. See R. B. Wright, 'The Psalms of Solomon', *OTP* I, p. 641.

[47] Cf. J. Jeremias, *Jerusalem in the Time of Jesus*, p. 73.

The motif of the regathering of exiles and the attendant impact on the Gentiles are also treated (1 En. 90.30–3; Pss. Sol. 17.34; Sib. Or. 3.772–5). The connection between the two must be highlighted even though the exact relationship between them may be ambiguous. That the Gentiles would make a pilgrimage, bringing the exiled Jews as tribute to Jerusalem, is clear enough (Sib. Or. 3.772–5; Pss. Sol. 17.31).[48] But what is not clear is the status of the Gentiles. Are they the subdued or the converted? The former conception appears to be supported by 1 Enoch 90.33, but, three verses earlier, the Gentiles are said to have been converted. In Psalms of Solomon 17.34, the Gentiles are said to have been shown compassion by the messiah. But there are many references to the destruction of the Gentiles (1 En. 91.9; T. Mos. 10.7; Jub. 23.30; Pss. Sol. 17.25–7; Sib. Or. 3.517–18, 669–72, 761). Such an ambiguous state of affairs may not seem significant if one also bears in mind the fact that in the OT the same ambiguity is found (cf. Isa. 49.23; 66.18–23; 2.2–4 and also Zech. 14.12–19).[49] Perhaps, circumstantial factors have a large influence on the Jewish conception of the status of the Gentiles in the new age.

We now come to 1 Enoch 90.28–38,[50] where the new Jerusalem is described. Some scholars have seen in this description the genesis of the idea of a heavenly Jerusalem. Thus Davies: 'the belief in a heavenly Jerusalem ... probably first occurs in 1 Enoch 90.28–38'.[51] Scholars of this persuasion normally cite as support the fact that God is said to be the builder of the 'house' (i.e., Jerusalem) in v. 29. But this is insufficient evidence. In agreement with Rowland,[52] it must be said that, first of all, conceptions of the heavenly Jerusalem which occur in post-70 CE Jewish literature (e.g., 4 Ezra; 2 Bar.) are of a different nature as they make explicit the idea that it is a celestial city which takes the place of an earthly one (4 Ezra 10). Secondly, it seems better to view the description of

---

[48] Interestingly, in Pss. Sol. 17.31, the Gentiles make a pilgrimage to Jerusalem in order to see (i) the messiah and (ii) the glory of God manifested there in addition to bringing the exiled Jews as tribute.

[49] For more references in the apocalyptic works which pertain to this phenomenon, see E. J. Schnabel, 'Jesus and the Beginnings of the Mission to the Gentiles' in J. B. Green and M. Turner (eds.), *Jesus of Nazareth: Lord and Christ*, p. 41.

[50] 1 En. 90 occurs in a section often termed as the 'Animal Apocalypse' and it is probably written around 164 to 160 BCE. See Nickelsburg, *Literature*, p. 93. See also E. Isaac, '1 (Ethiopic Apocalypse of) Enoch', *OTP* I, p. 7.

[51] Davies, *Land*, p. 143.

[52] C. C. Rowland, 'The Second Temple: Focus of Ideological Struggle?' in W. Horbury (ed.), *Templum Amicitiae*, p. 186.

the new Jerusalem in 1 Enoch 90 as a miraculous rebuilding of the *earthly* Jerusalem (possibly through human agents) on the old site rather than as a descent of a heavenly city. None the less, it appears that the 'house' in 1 Enoch 90.28–38 can easily be misinterpreted as a celestial 'house' and one can perhaps detect here the tentative steps taken in that direction which would later be developed into a full-scale concept of a heavenly Jerusalem by other writers.

The above passage also raises another interesting problem. It appears that the eschatological renewal of Israel is conceived in terms of a new Jerusalem but without a new temple (!) as there is no explicit mention of one in that passage. Presumably, the 'tower' is seen as the symbol for the temple (1 En. 89.50, 73) and in the description of the eschatological Zion, no mention is made of the 'tower'. As Rowland observes, in this passage we may well be faced with a restored city without a temple.[53] While one may assume that whenever Jerusalem is mentioned the temple is also in view, the lack of mention of one and the constant reference to the other may prove to be significant. Perhaps one can see here the incipient stages of the displacement of one in favour of the other in eschatological thought.

To conclude our survey of the apocalyptic literature, mention must again be made of the fact that traditional elements connected with Zion are faithfully adhered to although the eschatological thrust is pronounced. Although this does not constitute a new development, as already in the prophets such a tendency was present, it does, however, show once again the impact that the Zion traditions had on Jewish eschatological and theological reflections, and also their tenacity. Eschatological hopes are focused on Zion and the lack of mention of a new temple in 1 Enoch 90.28–38 may be significant.

The Qumran scrolls

The Qumran community's history, which explains their antagonism towards the Jerusalem cult, temple, priesthood and rulers,[54] can also easily mislead one into thinking that the temple and the status

---

[53] Rowland, 'The Second Temple', p. 186.

[54] For a brief account of this, see M. A. Knibb, *The Qumran Community*, pp. 3–6; G. Vermes, *The Dead Sea Scrolls in English*, pp. 19–35. For a detailed treatment of the history of the community see P. R. Callaway, *The History of the Qumran Community*.

of Jerusalem as the city chosen by God and imbued with eschatological hopes are all rejected by them. A survey of the extant scrolls which are published[55] reveals, instead, that Zion/Jerusalem is not rejected. In fact the impact of the Zion traditions on the Qumran community was so great that the eulogising of Zion reached a pinnacle with them. Moreover, the temple (albeit a restored one) is not obsolete in Qumranic thought.

(i) Qumran and Zion

As the city and the temple are usually inseparable in Jewish thought,[56] separate treatment of Qumran *vis-à-vis* Zion without due regard to Qumran *vis-à-vis* the temple may lead to a misrepresentation. But as there may be some implicit separation between these two entities in some quarters, and as the Qumran polemic against the temple is of a more intense nature, there is justification for a separate treatment.

Some passages may indicate an antagonism towards the city of Jerusalem. In 4QpNah 3–4 2.1, the 'city of blood' most probably refers to Jerusalem.[57] The city of Ephraim becomes identified with the city of the present priesthood (i.e., Jerusalem) because the Hasmonean king who usurped the high priesthood and ousted the Zadokite high priest originated from Modin in Ephraim.[58] The city of Jerusalem is likened to a city of blood because of the defilement by illegitimate sacrifices. Hence the community distanced themselves from the priesthood in Jerusalem. Another text which offers a similar accusation is 1QpHab 12.7–8.

In addition to the tendency just noted above, we find in 1QH 6.22–34 an interesting phenomenon where the community are likened to a city. There are good grounds for viewing 6.25–8 as containing Zion language:[59]

---

[55] Since this study was completed, more scroll fragments were published. It has not been possible to incorporate all of these data into the present study. But as far as our knowledge goes, nothing significant in this section needs modification. For a recent assessment of these fragments for Jesus research, see C. A. Evans, 'The Recently Published Dead Sea Scrolls and the Historical Jesus' in B. D. Chilton and C. A. Evans (eds.), *Studying the Historical Jesus: Evaluations of the State of Current Research*, pp. 547–65.

[56] Davies, *Land*, pp. 150–2.

[57] Knibb, *Qumran*, p. 215.

[58] For a demonstration of this, see J. A. Draper, 'Korah and the Second Temple' in W. Horbury (ed.), *Templum Amicitiae*, pp. 154–5.

[59] See S. Holm-Nielsen, *Hodayot: Psalms from Qumran*, p. 119, n. 151.

I am (25) as one who entereth into a fortified city and seeketh refuge in a high wall for salvation; and [I lean upon] Thy truth, O my God.

For Thou (26) layest foundations upon the rock, and crossbeams to thy right measure, and a plumb-line ... to ... chosen stone for a (27) strong [building], and all they that enter therein falter not, for [the man of violence] entereth not [therein]; its [gates] are armoured gates, which do not allow (28) entry, and mighty gate bolts, which do not break.[60]

The author finds refuge within his community, the true city of God. This city is fortified and is depicted as impregnable to the invasion of the enemy.[61] The use of such imagery would therefore imply that the traditions and symbolism of the city of God are still being used by way of transference even though the community have distanced themselves from the establishment in Jerusalem.

Not only was the Zion symbol not rejected, it is arguable that Zion remained the focus of the eschatological hopes of the community. Even though, in CD 20.22b–3, the sanctuary is pronounced as unclean, Jerusalem is still called in the same passage, following tradition, the 'holy city'. In 1QM 1.3, the camp of the Israelites in preparation for the final war is in the wilderness of Jerusalem (בְּמִדְבַּר יְרוּשָׁלַיִם, *bĕmidbār yĕrušālayim*). This phrase does not occur in the OT nor in the rabbinic literature[62] but it indicates where the decisive battle is to be fought – in the vicinity of Jerusalem. It is possible that the ambiguous ending of 1QM 1.3 refers to going up to Jerusalem,[63] since in 3.11 the community return from battle to Jerusalem. In other words, the battle is conducted from Jerusalem.[64] All this would imply that Jerusalem is still the place where the community would be during the last battle and that they would have an important role to play in it.[65] This can be compared with 4QpPs^a 3.8–13 where the expectation that the

---

60   Translation taken from Holm-Nielsen, *Hodayot*, p. 102.
61   So also Nickelsburg, *Literature*, p. 139.
62   See Y. Yadin (ed.), *The Scroll of the War of the Sons of Light Against the Sons of Darkness*, p. 257.
63   So the translation of Vermes, *Scrolls*, p. 105 but cf. Yadin, *War*, p. 258.
64   Cf. 1QM 2.3 where the chiefs and fathers of tribes stand perpetually in the gates of the sanctuary.
65   And, in 4QMMT, Jerusalem is identified with the holy camp of the wilderness (כי ירושלים היאה מהנה הקדש) and is set apart from all the other cities of Israel (כי ירושלים היא ראש מהחנות ישראל). See J. Strugnell and E. Qimron,

Qumran community would one day 'possess the mountain of the height of Israel' is expressed. Undoubtedly, Mt Zion is being referred to.[66]

Moreover, the songs of thanksgiving for the successful conduct of the war in 1QM 12.12–15 explicitly exhort Jerusalem and Zion to rejoice. In this passage, the motifs of the subjugation of the nations, the pilgrimage of the nations, and the kingship of God (motifs connected with Zion) can be found.

The texts discussed above would therefore support the contention that the current temple and city were rejected by the community only because of defilement caused by the illegitimate sacrifices and priesthood, and not on account of anything intrinsic to the institutions themselves. Hence, hopes for a better and purified temple and city were cherished. Even the traumatic experience of being forced to leave Jerusalem and the temple could not shake the community from the belief that the city was the focus of their eschatological hopes. Such a state of affairs speaks eloquently for the great impact the Zion traditions had on the Qumran community.

Not only were traditional motifs connected with Zion retained in the Qumran community, there were also developments. The first has been highlighted earlier; that is, the community were being depicted as a city. This implies that the community was functioning as the true city of God outside corrupt Jerusalem (1QH 6.25–8). This may represent a reversal of the OT conception of the relationship between people and city. In the OT, the city represented the people,[67] but, in the aforesaid passage, the community of people represented the city!

In 5Q15 we find yet another interesting development. This document (extant in fragmentary form) describes the new Jerusalem. It has often been observed that much of its language derives from Ezekiel 40–8.[68] What is of interest here is that in Ezekiel 40–8 only the temple is measured, but in 5Q15 the whole city, including houses, streets, rooms, stairs and windows, is measured! The idea

---

'An Unpublished Halakhic Letter from Qumran', in *Biblical Archaeology Today*, pp. 400–7.

[66] So also Donaldson, *Jesus*, p. 65.

[67] See discussion in Fohrer and Lohse, 'Σιών', pp. 308–9 and the relevant texts they cite.

[68] See Vermes, *Scrolls*, p. 271.

of measuring probably signified protection[69] and hence, the protection of God over the temple as in Ezekiel is extended to the entire city and all the buildings in it. Even Revelation 21.15–21 (which includes the measuring of the walls and gates) could not match it in detail.

But the most interesting development in the conception of Zion as the focus of eschatological hopes is found in 11QPs[a] 22, better known as 'the Apostrophe to Zion'. This eulogy to Zion marks the pinnacle in the idealisation of Zion, for, in this writing, terms usually applied to Yahweh himself are applied to the city.[70] L'Heureux has put scholarship in his debt by his thorough analysis of this apostrophe.[71] This writing evidently borrowed much of its language and imagery from the Zion songs in Isaiah 54; 60–2; 66.[72] But it also went a step further. Two examples will suffice. First, line 1a mentions that Zion will be 'remembered'[73] by the author 'in blessing'. The verb used for 'remembered' is אַזְכִּירֵךְ (*'ezkarĕkå*), the *Hiph'il* of זָכַר (*zåkar*). As noted by L'Heureux, this is a technical cultic expression meaning 'to name the name'.[74] Noteworthy here is that the 'name' envisaged is Zion and not Yahweh.

Secondly, the words in line 1b, 'with all my might I love you', should be compared with Deuteronomy 6.5, 'and you shall love the Lord your God with all your heart, and with all your soul, and with all your might'. A similar phenomenon is found. One is therefore led to conclude with L'Heureux:

> In its manner of adapting and modifying old material, the Apostrophe is not lacking in creative originality. It marks a stage in the process of the idealization of Zion. At first, Zion was praised because of the Lord who dwelt there. But Zion herself becomes more and more an object of praise

[69] Cf. J. Sweet, *Revelation*, p. 183. See also the interesting discussion in F. G. Martinez, 'The "New Jerusalem" and the Future Temple of the Manuscripts from Qumran' in *Qumran and Apocalyptic: Studies on the Aramaic Texts from Qumran*, pp. 180–213.

[70] Davies, *Land*, p. 141.

[71] C. E. L'Heureux, 'The Biblical Sources of the Apostrophe to Zion', *CBQ* 29 (1967), 60–74.

[72] See J. A. Sanders, *The Psalm Scrolls of Qumran Cave 11 (11QPs[a])*, p. 85.

[73] Following Vermes' translation in his *Scrolls*, p. 212.

[74] L'Heureux, 'Apostrophe', 61.

until concepts previously applied to the Lord are applied to Zion.[75]

It is noteworthy that a community which have been distanced from the Jerusalem cult and leadership could produce what can be said to be the pinnacle of the idealisation of Zion. This alone speaks volumes of the importance of Zion in the community's understanding of eschatology. Hence, in spite of their traumatic experiences, the Qumran sectaries did not reject the use of Zion as the appropriate place and symbol of God's eschatological salvation.

(ii) Qumran and temple

This matter will be treated briefly.[76] While it is true that the community regarded the temple as being defiled because of illegitimate sacrifices and priesthood, the temple *per se* as the place of God's presence and the divine–human encounter was not rejected. This explains the presence of a document like the Temple Scroll (11QT), in which it is unambiguously stated that the second temple is to be the place of God's glory until another temple, created by God's hand, replaces it (11QT 29.8–10).[77] Evidence from the War Scroll (1QM) suggests that the sanctuary would play a vital role in the final eschatological war between the sons of light and the sons of darkness (1QM 2.3). It is only through a serious reckoning with these texts that we can appreciate why the community understood themselves as the 'interim' temple (1QS 8.8–9; 9.4–5)[78] and as making atonement for the iniquities of the land. It was precisely because the present temple was defiled that the community conceived themselves as serving a vicarious function for the land of Israel (1QS 8.1–10). Nickelsburg shrewdly observes that, in the light of the statements in the scrolls about the defilement of the temple, this cultic language suggests that the community and their pious conduct are understood to be a substitute for the Jerusalem cult.[79] It can therefore be seen that the Qumran community did not

---

[75] L'Heureux, 'Apostrophe', 73–4.
[76] For extensive discussions see B. Gärtner, *The Temple and the Community in Qumran and in the New Testament*; and G. Klinzig, *Die Umdeutung des Kultus in der Qumrangemeinde und im Neuen Testament*.
[77] Y. Yadin, *The Temple Scroll: The Hidden Law of the Dead Sea Sect*, pp. 112–15.
[78] Cf. G. Vermes, *The Dead Sea Scrolls: Qumran in Perspective*, p. 181.
[79] Nickelsburg, *Literature*, p. 133.

repudiate the important role the temple had in Judaism. Rather, they were against a defiled temple. Until the restored and purified temple was realised, they acted in the place of the temple. It seems best to conceive of this substitution as being an interim measure until such time when the temple is again purified and under the right administration.

4   Zion and Jewish revolutionary movements

We have been concentrating on literary documents and works. However, we now turn to movements which did not leave behind any literary documents but which have their history mediated to us through the writings of others. We have in mind particularly the many revolutionary movements which were so much part and parcel of second-temple Palestine. A consideration of these gives a broader picture of second-temple Judaism and prevents a skewed understanding of the influence of the Zion traditions on it.

The Maccabean revolt

The Hellenisation programme of the Seleucids, which culminated in the erection of an altar dedicated to Zeus Olympios in the temple by Antiochus Epiphanes (1 Macc. 1.41–64) in 168 BCE, precipitated the Maccabean revolt. These factors explain not only the cause of the revolt but also the rationale of the various actions taken by the revolters. Thus attention was centred on the sanctuary as it was desecrated. Once Judas Maccabeus managed to wrest control from the Seleucids, he immediately set about purifying the temple and reconsecrating it (1 Macc. 4.36). The narrator of 1 Maccabees describes the army as going up to Mt Zion (1 Macc. 4.37) and building high walls and strong towers around it to prevent pagans from defiling the place (1 Macc. 4.60).

It must not be forgotten that the nature of the revolt is predominantly religious in character. This can be seen in three ways. First, Mattathias' actions and speech revealed his zeal for the law (1 Macc. 2.24–7). Secondly, forced circumcision on boys conducted by Mattathias (1 Macc. 2.45) points unambiguously to the nature of the movement he fathered. Finally, as observed by Bockmuehl, the Hasmonean generals consciously engaged in the blowing of trumpets in the battlefield as a religious act in keeping with Numbers 10.9 (1 Macc. 3.53–4).[80] The religious (and not simply political) character of the Maccabean revolt must be sufficiently appreciated before one analyses the revolutionary movements around the time of Jesus.

Judas the Galilean

Hengel comments that anyone who fails to recognise the special religious character of the Jewish revolts against Rome – all of which had an eschatological and messianic aspect – and at the same time their uniqueness, will not be able to judge the events in Judaea between 6 and 70 CE in accordance with the facts.[81] Therefore, even though political and social factors have an important role to play in the armed revolts against Rome, it is religious tradition and theology which were the main causes.[82]

There are debates connected with the person of Judas the Galilean[83] and the movement he started,[84] called the 'fourth philosophy' by Josephus (BJ 2.118–19; AJ 18.23). Constraint of space dictates that such questions be bypassed. Although we are

---

[80] M. Bockmuehl, ' "The Trumpet Shall Sound": *Shofar* Symbolism and its Reception in Early Christianity' in W. Horbury (ed.), *Templum Amicitiae*, p. 206.

[81] M. Hengel, *The Zealots*, p. xv.

[82] But cf. the view of M. Goodman, *The Ruling Class of Judaea*, where he argues (p. 91) that there is one other important factor other than the religious and economic ones which caused the revolt of 66 CE, namely the decision of some factions of the Jewish ruling class to cut ties with Rome and seek power for themselves. Limitation of space does not allow us to discuss this in more detail. However, we do not discount factors other than the religious one, but view the latter as one of the most crucial.

[83] That is, whether Judas the Galilean is to be identified as Judas the son of Ezekias the bandit who instigated the revolt in Sepphoris *c.* 4 BCE, roughly ten years before another revolt in Galilee which was started in response to Quirinius' census in 6 CE (BJ 2.56; AJ 17.271–2). Scholars arguing for this identification include Hengel, *Zealots*, p. 331; Jeremias, *Jerusalem*, p. 73; B. Witherington III, *The Christology of Jesus*, p. 83. But for a contrary view, see R. H. Pfeiffer, *History of the New Testament Times*, p. 35 and R. A. Horsley, *Jesus and the Spiral of Violence*, pp. 20–120.

[84] That is, whether there is any connection between Judas and the movement explicitly named as 'zealots' by Josephus at the outbreak of the Jewish war. Defending this notion is Hengel's splendid appendix to his book, *Zealots*, pp. 380–404. But for a contrary view, see R. A. Horsley and J. S. Hanson, *Bandits, Prophets and Messiahs: Popular Movements in the Time of Jesus*, pp. 190–243; M. Smith, 'Zealots and Sicarii, their Origins and Relation', *HTR* 64 (1971), 1–19; T. L. Donaldson, 'Rural Bandits, City Mobs and the Zealots', *JSJ* 21 (1990), 19–40. But see also Witherington, *Christology*, pp. 84–7 for a spirited defence of Hengel's view together with a shrewd critique of the opposing view.

inclined towards the view of Hengel on these issues, similar results would still be obtained if one were to grant that Judas is not the son of Ezekias the bandit or that his movement is not related to the zealot movement at the outbreak of the Jewish war. As Smallwood observes:

> Even if the triple identification of Judas' sect, the terrorists [the Sicarii], and the Zealots of the war years cannot be proved definitely, the clear connection between the motives and beliefs of the three groups at any rate indicates a development of one group out of another. Even though the title Zealot was apparently not taken by Judas' sect or by the terrorists, the Zealots were inspired by the same attitude to the law, the same dream of the recovery of independence, and the same hostility to foreign domination and hence to Jewish collaboration with Rome, which was rooted in the tradition of Jewish nationalism going back to the days of the Maccabees.[85]

Hence, there is warrant to speak of similar tendencies[86] even if these Jewish movements originated differently.

According to Josephus, the uprising of Judas against the census of Quirinius was motivated by three principles (AJ 18.4–6, 23–5). First, Judas believed unequivocally that only God was to be the king and ruler of Israel. Secondly, freedom for the nation was to be at the top of the agenda of Judas' concerns. Thirdly, synergism was Judas' concept of how God's redemptive plan would be carried out. It must be emphasised that Judas was described as a σοφιστής by Josephus (BJ 2.118, 433) and had Saddok the priest as his aide (AJ 18.4–6). This observation is absolutely crucial in the assessment of the nature of the 'fourth philosophy' Judas started, for it shows that Judas' movement was not just motivated by political and social factors but was imbued with a pronounced theological character.

Although there is no explicit mention of Zion, Judas' reasons for the uprising can fall comfortably into the ambit of the Zion traditions. Indeed, when one bears in mind the impact of Zion on Jewish religious and eschatological thought of the second temple

---

[85] E. M. Smallwood, *The Jews under Roman Rule from Pompey to Diocletian*, p. 154.

[86] See C. Guignebert, *The Jewish World in the Time of Jesus*, pp. 170–1.

period, one may safely presume that the symbol may not be far from the thought horizon of Judas. This can be seen in a number of ways. First, the idea that God is the only king of Israel is explicitly sounded in the Zion traditions. God exercises his rule in Zion. Secondly, the concept of 'freedom' which Judas had was probably not primarily national independence but eschatological redemption by Yahweh[87] from the predicament that Israel was in. And such redemption and restoration of the nation were to be centred on Zion. Indeed, if one is allowed to identify Judas the Galilean with Judas the son of Ezekias the bandit, one can legitimately state that Judas made messianic claims.[88] Redemption of nation, God's kingship and the messianic king are all motifs related to the Zion traditions. And if one could further identify the movement started by Judas with the zealots and the Sicarii, the importance of the Zion traditions to Judas will be even more firmly established. This will be seen later.

The zealots and the Sicarii[89]

It must be emphasised at the outset that the main reasons for the revolt against Rome in 66 CE were theological in character.[90] This can be seen in a number of ways. Hengel insists correctly that such a war, which in human terms would be considered suicidal, could only take place because of religious motivation.[91] This appears even more clearly when one observes that the defence and occupation of the sanctuary took priority over the occupation of

---

[87] See Hengel, *Zealots*, p. 115.

[88] This can be seen in AJ 17.271–2 where Josephus narrates that Judas the son of Ezekias had zealous ambition for royal rank (καὶ ζηλώσει βασιλείου τιμῆς).

[89] For some recent discussions of their relationships see Smith, 'Zealots', 1–19; Donaldson, 'Rural Bandits', 19–40; and Hengel, *Zealots*, pp. 380–404. Many scholars understand Josephus to mean two different groups: the group which withdrew to Masada after the death of Menahem were the Sicarii (BJ 2.441–8; 7.253) while the group which defended the temple with John of Gischala were the zealots (BJ 5.248–50, 358; 6.92, 148). But such a view appears to be an oversimplification.

[90] But note Goodman's thesis in *Ruling Class*, p. 91. However, he does concede in principle that the religious reason might be primary in that the Jewish leaders sought to motivate the masses to join in the revolt on religious grounds. While this might mean that religion was being used as the vehicle for political ambitions, it must be remembered that religion and politics were most probably coexisting in a symbiotic relationship in second temple Jewry.

[91] Hengel, *Zealots*, p. xiv.

strategic locations.[92] Moreover, it is also possible to see the attack on the Antonia fortress as arising not from military considerations but from a religious concern: the purification of the temple.[93] In BJ 5.459 and Dio Cassius, *Roman History* 66:6, we have evidence that it was the temple which encouraged the belief that victory was imminent in spite of overwhelming odds. Finally, the speech of Eleazar ben Ari, which showed that freedom was the aim of the struggle (BJ 7.322–6), and the prophecies given just before the destruction of Jerusalem (BJ 5.459) both indicate unambiguously that it was religious considerations which led to such a suicidal revolt. In this case, it was the beliefs and eschatological expectations connected with the sanctuary which motivated such actions.

In the speech given by John of Gischala to Josephus in the shadow of defeat, we find an interesting statement: ὡς οὐκ ἂν πότε δεισείεν ἅλωσιν· θεοῦ γὰρ ὑπάρχειν τὴν πόλιν (BJ 6.98). This statement of John justifies our contention that the Zion traditions did have a motivating force in the revolt if Josephus' record of that speech is historically accurate. It was the belief that Jerusalem (not just the temple) was inviolable that caused John to refuse to surrender.

The clearest evidence we have for our contention comes from the coins minted after the temporarily successful capture of the city and temple. The bronze coins discovered which bore an amphora with a broad rim and two handles on their front, and, on their reverse side, a vine tendril with leaf and with the words, חרות ציון,[94] have been dated to the first revolt. Other coins discovered were silver shekels containing the words הקדשה ירושלים or ירושלים קדשה,[95] and bronze shekels – which have been incorrectly attributed to Simon the Maccabee[96] – carrying the inscription ציון לגאלת.[97] The numismatic evidence is significant in a number of ways. First, it may imply that the leaders of the revolt (Simon bar Giora and John of Gischala) who minted coins made messianic claims. This is made clear by the words חֵרוּת (*ḥerut*) and גְּאֻלָּה (*gĕʾullâh*), since they might point to the eschatological redemption

---

92 As observed by Hengel, *Zealots*, p. 221.
93 Hengel, *Zealots*, pp. 208–9.
94 Cf. A. Reifenberg, *Ancient Jewish Coins*, nos. 147–9. See also D. Hendin, *Guide to Biblical Coins*, pp. 94–5 (nos. 123, 126) and the discussion in Hengel, *Zealots*, p. 116.
95 See Hengel, *Zealots*, pp. 116–17 and the relevant literature he cites.
96 See L. Kadman, 'A Coin Find at Masada', *IEJ* 7 (1957), 61–5.
97 Hendin, *Coins*, pp. 96–7 (nos. 129–31).

which was awaited.[98] This same phenomenon can also be found in Bar Kokhba's revolt.[99]

Secondly, it is significant that it was Zion's or Jerusalem's liberation which was celebrated alongside Israel's[100] (the temple is not mentioned). The use of יְרוּשָׁלַיִם (*yĕrušālayim*) and צִיּוֹן (*siyyon*) points to their supreme significance in that they are used synecdochically for the nation and may further indicate that these revolutionaries believed the redemption of Israel *depended* on the redemption of Jerusalem.[101] As Rowland has observed, the concern of all these groups, whatever their origins and however loosely they may have been connected, was the redemption of Zion.[102]

In summary, it should be noted that Zion's redemption took paramount importance as on it depended the redemption of the nation. Zion needed to be liberated because it was occupied by the Romans and this occupation led to a continuous desecration of the sanctuary in Zion. The belief in the inviolability of Zion and the temple, an important tenet of the Zion traditions, led the revolutionary forces to conduct humanly suicidal wars against the Roman empire.

Other prophetic and messianic movements[103]

For want of a better term, we propose to follow Barnett in referring to those who led these movements as 'sign-prophets'.[104] These were mainly concerned with eschatological redemption, but with an emphasis on the wilderness as the place where such redemption was to be witnessed.[105] Two incidents deserve our attention.

The first is narrated in BJ 1.347. During the siege of Jerusalem by Sossius and Herod, we are told by Josephus that '[t]he feeble folk, *congregating around the temple*, indulged in transports of frenzy

---

[98] So Hengel, *Zealots*, pp. 117–18.
[99] See Hendin, *Coins*, pp. 102–4, 109 (nos. 135, 140–1, 162).
[100] See coins nos. 119, 121 in Hendin, *Coins*.
[101] As has also been observed by Hengel, *Zealots*, p. 118.
[102] C. C. Rowland, *Christian Origins*, p. 99.
[103] For a good discussion of these movements from a sociological point of view see Horsley and Hanson, *Bandits*.
[104] See P. W. Barnett, 'The Jewish Sign-Prophets – AD 40–70: Their Intention and Origin', *NTS* 27 (1980–1), 679–97.
[105] See BJ 2.258–9, 261; Acts 21.38. This may be due to the influence of Isa. 40, a text much used also by the Qumran community.

and fabricated numerous oracular utterances to fit the crisis'.[106] The second comes from the incident connected with the Egyptian who presumably led his followers into the desert and from there to the Mount of Olives (BJ 2.262). The express purpose was to make the walls of Jerusalem fall in order to gain access into the city to control it.[107]

Apart from these two incidents, the evidence at hand forbids one absolute certainty on whether these movements had the Zion traditions as one of their chief tenets.

The evidence from Luke

In the infancy narratives, Luke mentions the expectation among certain Jews of the redemption of Jerusalem (Luke 2.38). While one may find any purportedly historical incident in the infancy narratives to be suspect,[108] it must at least be conceded that such a view could not be an invention of Luke but represented Jewish hopes and piety of those times. Another passage, Luke 19.11, gives evidence that such a view was also found among Luke's readers, whether or not it is a true historical reminiscence. The interesting point to note is that in this passage, Jesus' going to Jerusalem was connected with Jewish expectation of the revelation of the kingdom of God by the crowds, something which, at the Lukan level, Jesus sought to correct.[109] The Lukan evidence shows once again the presence of the expectation of the redemption of Jerusalem during the second temple period.

5   Zion and the aftermath of the destruction of Jerusalem in 70 CE

With the sack of Jerusalem in 70 CE, one would have expected the Jews to have forsaken the use of Zion or Jerusalem as a symbol and focus of their national and eschatological hopes for another (e.g., the Torah). But this did not happen. In fact, the process of

---

[106] The translation is taken from H. St J. Thackeray, *Josephus. The Jewish War, Books I–III*, p. 163. Emphasis mine.

[107] But see Barnett, 'Sign-Prophets', 683, who has a very different view of the matter.

[108] For a splendid work on the infancy narratives which discusses exegetical, historical and theological issues, see R. E. Brown, *The Birth of the Messiah*.

[109] On this see I. H. Marshall, *The Gospel of Luke*, p. 700; and J. A. Fitzmyer, *The Gospel According to Luke* II, p. 1234. Note that in *Tg.Isa.* 31.4–5, Zion is affirmed to be the place where the kingdom of Yahweh will be revealed.

idealisation of Jerusalem continued apace culminating in a trans-cendentalisation of it.

In the apocalyptic literature which emanated from the period just after the destruction of Jerusalem, recourse is made to a heavenly Jerusalem to ameliorate the difficulties which have come about because of its destruction. In 4 Ezra 9.38–10.57, we have an extended allegory of a woman who actually represents a city. The interpretation of this passage has been disputed, primarily over the identification of the woman and the son. Rowland correctly observes, *contra* Myers,[110] that the woman and son do not stand for the heavenly and earthly Zion respectively. The son represents instead the period in which the first glorious temple was on Zion. The woman passes through two phases and this is an allegory of Zion passing through two phases: from an earthly Zion to a heavenly one.[111] Three points made in 4 Ezra 10 further indicate that the transformed woman represents the heavenly Jerusalem. First, the woman is said to have fled from the city and has no intention of going back (10.4). Secondly, the city is to be built on a site which has not been built upon before (10.51).[112] Finally, in 10.54 the explicit statement that 'no work of man's building could endure in a place where the city of the Most High was to be revealed' underlines the fact that this glorified city cannot be erected by any human agents and implies that its origin is heavenly. These three points serve to emphasise the discontinuity between the first city and the second.

In 2 Baruch 4.1–7, a clear distinction is made between the earthly and the heavenly Jerusalem. The necessity for the destruction of the earthly one is posited in 2.2–4. This arises from the notion that it is only through such a destruction that a new Zion could be built.

Finally, in the rabbinic literature,[113] one is able to witness the continued idealisation of Jerusalem. This takes place in many forms, from the ὄμφαλος myth[114] (*PRE* 11.20; *Num R.* 12.4; *Lam.*

---

[110] J. M. Myers, *I & II Esdras*, pp. 279–80.

[111] Rowland, 'Second Temple', p. 188.

[112] Davies in *Land*, p. 147 also supports our contention.

[113] For a good discussion of Zion in rabbinic thought see Donaldson, *Jesus*, pp. 54–62; Davies, *Land*, pp. 135–8, 148–50; and G. D. Cohen, 'Zion in Rabbinic Literature', in A. S. Halkim (ed.), *Zion in Jewish Literature*, pp. 38–64.

[114] For a good presentation of this myth, see A. J. Wensinck, *The Ideas of the Western Semites Concerning the Navel of the Earth*. See also R. Patai, *Man and Temple in Ancient Jewish Myth and Ritual*, pp. 54–104, especially p. 85; cf. J. D. Levenson, *Sinai and Zion*, pp. 115–20 and Chester, 'Sibyl', pp. 59–62.

R. 3.58–64 §9; such a myth was already present in Ezek. 5.5 and 38.12)[115] to the incredible idealisation found in *ARN* 35 where the idea that nothing untoward ever happened in Jerusalem was put forward. In the Shemoneh Esreh, especially benedictions 14 and 16, Jerusalem is to be remembered:

> [14] Be merciful, Lord our God, with thy great mercies, to Israel thy people and to Jerusalem thy city; and to Zion, the dwelling place of thy glory; and to thy temple and thy habitation; and to the kingship of David thy righteous messiah.
>
> [16] Be pleased, Lord our God and dwell in Zion; and may thy servants serve thee in Jerusalem.

This remembrance and veneration of Zion would continue to be ingrained upon the conscious and subconscious minds of subsequent generations. Hence, Zion cannot be forgotten. For the very symbol itself is evocative of God's promises and the nationhood of Israel. After the destruction of Jerusalem in 70 CE, 'Jerusalemless' Judaism continued with the expectancy of a renewed Zion. Alongside this expectancy is found the presence of the concept of a heavenly Jerusalem. The transcendentalising of Zion did not result in a distancing of the symbol Zion from its geographical home. It is therefore hardly surprising that the ideology which propelled modern Israel to seek a home in Palestine is also called 'Zionism'.

6   Conclusions

We see now that Zion was a tenacious and living national and eschatological symbol right from its inception (whenever this is to be dated) to the catastrophe of 70 CE and even beyond it. It survived in spite of the fact that the city was destroyed twice. We can thus gauge the importance the Zion traditions had for the Jews both in the first and second temple periods, and even beyond that. The influence of these traditions would explain the forms the different revolutionary movements and breakaway groups took during the second temple period. At the same time, it also creates the presumption that Jesus in his ministry had to interact with these traditions, and was, in turn, influenced by them.

The second result which arises from this study is that these

---

[115] Cf. L. Allen, *Ezekiel 20–48*, p. 206.

traditions were not static. Traditional elements were certainly retained, but there was also a continuous development in the veneration of Zion. The pinnacle of such developments can perhaps be said to be represented by Qumran's 'Apostrophe to Zion' (11QPs^a 22). There is also an implicit displacement of the temple in favour of Zion and the latter continued to attract to itself the hopes, both national and eschatological, of the Jews. Hence, in the development of Jewish thought concerning Zion, Zion can be seen to have absorbed to itself hopes which were not originally connected with it in the OT. In a very important sense, Zion became the symbol of the life, beliefs and hopes of all Jews. Thus, Zion was a focal point, attracting to itself not just theoretical speculations but also movements. It is in this light that one has to ask the all-important question, 'Why did Jesus go to Jerusalem?' If there was an expressed purpose, what was it, and to what extent was it influenced by the Zion traditions?

The third point to be noted is that it is in the realm of eschatology that Zion played a very important role and received the most creative reinterpretation and innovation. Interest in the present Jerusalem during the second temple period was slight when compared to interest in the eschatological Zion. This is unlike the strands of thought connected with Zion found in the Psalter. This may be due to the fact that eschatology loomed very large in the thought horizon of second-temple Jewry. As noted earlier, the prominence of Zion outstripped the prominence of the temple when it came to eschatology. And if one were to take into account the eschatological character of Jesus' ministry,[116] the study of Jesus *vis-à-vis* Jerusalem or Zion is of supreme importance. Once again, the question 'Why did Jesus go to Jerusalem?' cries out for an answer.

---

[116] This has been demonstrated convincingly by E. P. Sanders in his *Jesus and Judaism*, notwithstanding the attempt to argue for a different paradigm on the part of J. D. Crossan, *The Historical Jesus: The Life of a Mediterranean Jewish Peasant*.

PART II

The sayings

INTRODUCTION TO PART II

Part II will examine the sayings of Jesus to see whether there are data which shed light on the two questions posed at the outset of this study. There are some preliminary matters to be dealt with before we investigate the relevant sayings.

Word-statistics

The word 'Jerusalem' appears fifty-four times in the Synoptic gospels: twenty-five times as Ἱεροσόλυμα and twenty-nine times as Ἱερουσαλήμ.[1] The word Σιών appears once only in the Synoptic gospels (seven times in the whole of the NT).[2] The paucity of references to Zion in the NT is in stark contrast to the OT. Indeed, the one occurrence of Σιών in the Synoptic gospels is found in Matthew 21.5 as a fulfilment-formula quotation. The word Σιών is never put into the mouth of Jesus by any NT writer.

Of the references to 'Jerusalem' found in the Synoptic gospels, eight distinct instances are attributed to Jesus (Mark 10.33||Matt. 20.18||Luke 18.31; Matt. 5.35; Matt. 23.37||Luke 13.34; Luke 13.4; 13.33; 21.20; 23.28; 24.48). The interest of Luke in Jerusalem accounts for the higher number of references. Luke 13.4 can be taken out of consideration as it is irrelevant to the present discussion. Of the remaining seven instances, one is from the Markan strand of tradition, one from Q, one peculiar to Matthew and four peculiar to Luke. Not all of these references will be discussed in

---

[1] For attempts at explaining the presence of this phenomenon, especially in Luke, see J. K. Elliot, 'Jerusalem in Acts and the Gospels', *NTS* 23 (1977), 462–9; D. D. Sylva, 'Ierousalem and Hierosoluma in Luke–Acts', *ZNW* 74 (1983), 207–21; and L. Hartman, 'Ἱεροσόλυμα, Ἱερουσαλήμ', in H. Balz and G. Schneider (eds.), *Exegetical Dictionary of the New Testament* II, p. 177.

[2] Statistics are taken from K. Aland, *Vollständige Konkordanz zum Griechischen Neuen Testament* II.

detail but only the significant ones and those most promising in terms of authenticity.

Jesus and the land

A prominent idea associated with Zion or Jerusalem in the Jewish psyche of the second temple period is the land – אֶרֶץ יִשְׂרָאֵל (*'ereṣ yiśrǎel*).[3] Jerusalem is often viewed as the quintessence of the land.[4] Hence, any talk of Zion has to include the land. What is Jesus' attitude towards the land?

After a detailed and lengthy study, Davies concludes that Jesus, as far as one could gather, paid little attention to the relationship between Yahweh and the land.[5] The clearest possible reference that gives evidence of Jesus' awareness of the אֶרֶץ יִשְׂרָאֵל (*'ereṣ yiśrǎel*) is in Matthew 5.5, 'blessed are the meek for they shall inherit the earth (γῆ)'. But the authenticity of this beatitude is contested by many scholars. Even if one accepts its authenticity, γῆ is more likely to refer to the whole earth as it has acquired a cosmic significance even before the time of Jesus.[6]

The virtual neglect by Jesus of the Jewish doctrine of the land is glaring, especially in the context of Jewish aspirations for the land during the second temple period.[7] We shall attempt to account for this phenomenon in chapter 9.

[3] On the importance of the land in the OT, see W. Brueggemann, *The Land*.

[4] W. D. Davies, *The Gospel and the Land*, p. 131.

[5] Davies, *Land*, p. 65.

[6] See U. Luz, *Matthew 1–7*, p. 236. Cf. Davies, *Land*, pp. 359–62, where he mentions that γῆ may be spiritualised here.

[7] On this see D. Mendels, *The Land of Israel as a Political Concept in Hasmonean Literature*.

3

THE ATTRACTION OF JERUSALEM (I):
THE CITY WHERE PROPHETS DIE

Luke 13.31–3[1] purportedly concerns a report given by the Pharisees to Jesus about the intention of Herod to kill him and Jesus' significant response to that report. This pericope provides us with a window into the self-understanding of Jesus of his ministry, intention and destiny in relation to Jerusalem. Obviously, such results could be obtained only if Luke 13.31–3 is historically reliable and offers us at least the *ipsissima vox Jesu*. Hence, a large portion of this chapter will be devoted to the enquiry into the extent to which this pericope is historically reliable. Two other matters will also be dealt with: the meaning of Jesus' reply (vv. 32b–3); and the significance of this pericope for an understanding of how Jesus viewed his ministry *vis-à-vis* Jerusalem.

1 The authenticity of the incident

Fitzmyer writes that there is a consensus among commentators that the report of the Pharisees to Jesus about Herod's attitude towards him is a piece of authentic tradition.[2] Even Denaux, who views this pericope as Lukan, admits that there is an authentic kernel to it.[3] In other words, the authenticity of the incident is recognised although there may be disagreements regarding the authenticity and integrity of the two sayings (vv. 32–3). Older commentators have no problem in regarding this episode as substantially authentic. The reasons for such confidence are not difficult to find.

---

[1] This pericope has been assigned to 'L' by J. A. Fitzmyer, *The Gospel According to Luke X–XXIV*, p. 1028. Hereafter, 'L' is taken by us to mean those traditions which are peculiar to Luke. The use of the term does not prejudge the issue whether or not 'L' was a document.

[2] Fitzmyer, *Luke X–XXIV*, p. 1028.

[3] A. Denaux, 'L'hypocrisie des Pharisiens et le dessein de Dieu. Analyse de Lc, xiii, 31–33', in F. Neirynck (ed.), *L'evangile de Luc*, pp. 245–85.

First, the very obscurity of the episode speaks against its being a literary invention.[4] Why would such an incident be invented by the early church or Luke? Even the frequently sceptical Bultmann has some positive things to say about this pericope: 'there seems no ground for supposing that the scene is imaginary but rather for thinking that we have here in the strict sense a piece of biographical material'.[5] Such a conclusion is further strengthened by the observation that in this pericope we are not presented with any full-blown theologising which can be attributed to the early church or Luke.[6] In the assessment of Marshall, this incident makes good historical sense and satisfactory motives for inventing it have not been established.[7]

Secondly, Taylor regards this passage as having the freshness of originality which bespeaks authenticity, but judgments of this nature are often subjective.[8] However, the depiction of Herod given in this passage does correspond with historical evidence concerning him.[9]

Thirdly, it has been suggested that the picture of the Pharisees in this passage is markedly different from the generally denunciatory characterisation of them found in the gospels.[10] Indeed, Tyson regards this factor as the strongest attestation to the authenticity of the incident in that the Pharisees appear here not as antagonists of Jesus, but as friends.[11] But it must be said that it is not at all clear that the Pharisees are presented in this pericope as being friendly to Jesus. In fact, opposite conclusions have been drawn by two redactional critics, Denaux and Rese (who agreed with each other only in that the pericope is redactional). Denaux regards the Pharisees as being presented here as hostile,[12] whereas Rese comes to an

---

[4] As observed by I. H. Marshall, *The Gospel of Luke*, p. 569.

[5] R. Bultmann, *The History of the Synoptic Tradition*, p. 35.

[6] There is a possibility that Luke may have created this episode to suit his interest in depicting the necessity of the journey of Jesus to Jerusalem. But more of this later (see next major section).

[7] Marshall, *Gospel*, p. 570.

[8] V. Taylor, *The Formation of the Gospel Tradition*, p. 158.

[9] That is, the wily character of Herod (*Gen.R.* 25.20) and his dislike of any excitement in his realm (*AJ* 18.117–19). On 'fox' as depicting a wily character, see H. Hoehner, *Herod Antipas*, pp. 345–6. See also E. E. Ellis, *The Gospel of Luke*, p. 189; Fitzmyer, *Luke X–XXIV*, p. 1031; and J. Nolland, *Luke 9:21–18:34*, p. 740.

[10] E.g., Hoehner, *Herod*, p. 214; J. B. Tyson, 'Jesus and Herod Antipas', *JBL* 79 (1960), 245.

[11] Tyson, 'Herod', 245.   [12] Denaux, 'L'hypocrisie', pp. 263–8.

opposite conclusion.[13] Fitzmyer observes that Luke has a tendency to portray the Pharisees as friendly because, for Luke, Christianity in the long run is a logical sequel to Pharisaic Judaism (as found in Acts).[14] But Fitzmyer's observation may be tenuous in that he considers only the book of Acts.[15] In our opinion, the argument for the supposedly friendly picture of the Pharisees in this pericope is weak for it is unclear that the Pharisees are presented as friendly.[16] All that can be said from a reading of this passage is that the Pharisees receive no rebuke. Nothing is said concerning the motivation of the Pharisees and it is dangerous to read too much into it. Hence, this argument should not be regarded as the best attestation to the authenticity of the incident (*pace* Tyson).

In sum, the strongest attestation for the authenticity of the episode is its obscure nature and the improbability that such a pericope is created.

2   The authenticity and integrity of the sayings

Although most scholars would accept the authenticity of the incident (that is, there really was an incident where the Pharisees warned Jesus of the devious intention of Herod), not all would accept the two pronouncements attributed to Jesus in this passage as altogether authentic. Even scholars who defend the authenticity of the two pronouncements normally express doubts over their integrity. The problems which prevent a full acceptance of their authenticity and integrity are basically three: (a) the repetition of v. 32 in v. 33 (the literary problem);[17] (b) the Lukan vocabulary believed to be present pervasively in the two pronouncements; and (c) that the theology enshrined in them belongs to the church or Luke.

---

[13]   M. Rese, 'Einige Überlergungen zu Lukas xiii.31–33', in J. Dupont (ed.), *Jésus aux origines de la christologie*, pp. 209–12.

[14]   Fitzmyer, *Luke X–XXIV*, p. 1030. If Fitzmyer's observation is correct, then the argument from the friendly depiction of the Pharisees found in this pericope loses its force as this friendly depiction may be a result of Lukan redaction.

[15]   *Luke X–XXIV*, p. 1030. Hoehner observes that in the gospel of Luke (he does not consider Acts), wherever Luke has common material with Matthew and Mark, the Pharisees are always depicted in a bad light. Even in material peculiar to Luke, they may on the surface be presented as friendly but each episode ends with them being put in a bad light (11.53–12.2; 15.2; 16.14; 17.20–1; 18.9–14), with Luke 13.31–3 serving as an exception (*Herod*, p. 214 n. 4).

[16]   So also C. F. Evans, *Saint Luke*, p. 560.

[17]   Marshall, *Gospel*, p. 569.

The literary problem

The two pronouncements as they stand in Luke have one close resemblance: the temporal formulas (but note the slight difference: v. 32b has τῇ τρίτῃ for the 'third day' while v. 33 has τῇ ἐχομένῃ). The other elements, however, are not strictly parallel.[18] The close resemblance of the temporal formulas has led many scholars to regard them as repetitious and originally separate, and posit that they were brought together in the developing gospel tradition (or by Luke) by the catch-phrase link, σήμερον καὶ αὔριον καὶ τῇ τρίτῃ (or τῇ ἐχομένῃ).

Bultmann has suggested two possibilities to account for the history of the two pronouncements: either v. 33 was attached to an integral unit comprising vv. 31 and 32, or v. 32b (beginning with ἰδού to the end of the verse), including πλήν of v. 33, was added to an original unit comprising vv. 31 and 33 (without πλήν). In Bultmann's judgment, if the second possibility is correct, v. 32b and πλήν should be regarded as the creation of the church.[19] Many scholars, however, are less equivocal and they favour the first possibility suggested by Bultmann: that is, v. 33 is a secondary addition.[20]

There is one other suggestion to be dealt with regarding the 'literary problem' posed by these two pronouncements. As stated earlier, the other elements of the two pronouncements, other than the temporal formulas, are not parallel to one another and this lack of parallelism has caused some scholars to see contradictions between the two verses.[21] Verse 32 describes a 'two-day' event which comprises two actions followed by a climactic third day with

---

[18]   Verse 33 has only one action for the three days – πορεύεσθαι – while v. 32b has two actions for the first two days (exorcising and healing) followed by a climactic third day which is described by the verb τελειοῦμαι.

[19]   Bultmann, *History*, p. 35. Bultmann seems to imply that he has more difficulty accepting v. 32b as historical than v. 33 although he does not explicitly say so. Actually, Bultmann hesitates to give a decision on the whole matter.

[20]   Fitzmyer, *Luke X–XXIV*, p. 1028; Nolland, *Luke 9:21–18:34*, p. 739; J. Jeremias, 'Die Drei-Tage-Wörte der Evangelien', in G. Jeremias (ed.), *Tradition und Glaube*, pp. 221–9; perhaps also W. G. Kümmel, *Promise and Fulfilment*, pp. 71–2. Note that Kümmel is not at all clear whether he is in full agreement with the idea that v. 33 was an appended saying although he was cited to be so by Hoehner, *Herod*, p. 215. Kümmel actually prefaces his discussion of these verses with the words: 'Now it may only be a *conjecture* that v. 32 and 33 consist of two parallel sayings, of which the second did not belong here' (p. 71; emphasis mine).

[21]   E.g., J. M. Creed, *The Gospel According to St Luke*, p. 187.

the action described by τελειοῦμαι. But v. 33 has only one action for the three days, πορεύεσθαι. There is no explicit mention of any climactic day. The ὅτι clause of v. 33 is introduced not as a climactic fourth day but to explain the necessity (δεῖ) of the πορεύεσθαι. Moreover, as Creed has observed: 'if he [Jesus] works cures "today and tomorrow", how is it that he also "goes on his way" – that is what the Pharisees had advised – "today and tomorrow"?'[22] Clearly, the two verses cannot be construed to be parallel without some qualification. This inconcinnity has led some scholars to resort to textual emendation. Wellhausen proposes that καὶ τῇ τρίτῃ τελειοῦμαι should be deleted from v. 32 and σήμερον καὶ αὔριον καί from v. 33.[23] Such a suggestion would give a smoother reading of vv. 32–3 in that there is now only one temporal formula with a climactic third day of πορεύεσθαι followed by the ὅτι explanatory clause.[24] Black has proposed another form of textual emendation – through addition and not subtraction. On the basis of a reading found in the Peshitta, Black suggests that the verb 'work' is to be added after σήμερον καὶ αὔριον of v. 33 so that πορεύεσθαι would go with καὶ τῇ ἐχομένῃ and not with σήμερον καὶ αὔριον καὶ τῇ ἐχομένῃ. According to him, this would give an Aramaic parallelism in a two-line couplet:[25]

> Behold I cast out demons and I do cures day by day,
>> But one day soon I am perfected.
> But day by day I must needs work,
>> Then one day soon pass on.

But solutions involving textual emendation are always precarious especially when there is no evidence in the extant Greek manuscripts to support such an enterprise. Such solutions are often 'counsels of despair'. Furthermore, as we hope to demonstrate later, they blunt the force of the two pronouncements. It is hardly surprising that modern scholars have eschewed such a method of solving exegetical problems.

Is there a way out of this literary problem that we have been discussing? We believe there is and shall set it out here. Many

---

[22] Creed, *St Luke*, p. 187.
[23] J. Wellhausen, *Das Evangelium Lucae*, pp. 76–7. Creed is in favour of such a solution, see Creed, *St Luke*, p. 187.
[24] Thus giving the reading: ἰδοὺ ἐκβάλλω δαιμόνια καὶ ἰάσεις ἀποτελῶ σήμερον καὶ αὔριον. πλὴν δεῖ με τῇ ἐχομένῃ πορεύεσθαι κτλ.
[25] M. Black, *An Aramaic Approach to the Gospels and Acts*, pp. 206–7.

scholars regard v. 33 as being joined to an original nucleus comprising vv. 31–2. The typical explanation is that the *Stichwörte* σήμερον καὶ αὔριον καὶ τῇ τρίτῇ/τῇ ἐχομένῃ brought about the attachment. Unfortunately, such an explanation glosses over the differences between the two pronouncements (the *Stichwörte* in fact are not strictly alike) and misses the point of the answer which the two pronouncements have been designed to give. Assuming that both verses stem from Jesus, v. 33 could not have existed alone[26] without an introduction. If it is granted that v. 33 must have an introduction circulating with it right at the start, either Luke or an earlier tradent of the traditions of Jesus removed an original introduction and joined the pronouncement to vv. 31–2, *or* vv. 31–2 were the original introduction to the pronouncement. Both are possible. But the probability of the latter is further enhanced by the fact that v. 32 by itself is not a complete answer to the warning given by the Pharisees in v. 31[27] (this will be demonstrated in detail later).[28] Furthermore, the two pronouncements give a subtle word play[29] and a profound irony (this will be shown later).[30] In lieu of the incomplete nature of the reply of v. 32, and if both the pronouncements are accepted as authentic, it seems best to conclude that vv. 32–3 form an integral reply of Jesus.[31] Hoehner points out that if the addition of v. 33 results in making the text

---

[26] *Pace* Jeremias, 'Drei-Tage-Wörte', p. 223.

[27] As observed by Marshall, *Gospel*, p. 570.   [28] See below, section 3.

[29] Note the word play: πορεύου (v. 31), πορευθέντες (v. 32), πορεύεσθαι (v. 33). This word play was suggested long ago by Plummer although he did not subscribe to it: 'the repetition of πορεύεσθαι may be accidental' (*St Luke*, p. 300). We do not think that the repetition was accidental. Instead, it was intended. We hope to demonstrate this later.

[30] See below, section 3.

[31] It could perhaps also be argued that it was the incomplete nature of the reply of v. 32b that led Luke to look for another saying from the pool of Jesus' traditions (or perhaps to create one) in order to clarify Jesus' reply. But such an argument fails to take into account that a secondary explanation is added to clarify and not to mystify! Verse 33, as it stands in the text, is not perspicuous. It is improbable that an unclear answer is added later to accomplish the *raison d'être* of its addition – clarification. But it is perfectly understandable how the original author of the pronouncements could resort to an intended ambiguity in order to bring home certain points forcefully. Of course, it may be argued that Luke was the actual author of the pronouncements. But it is likely that Luke created clear sayings rather than obscure ones. The matter would be different if Luke was faithful to the traditions of Jesus which he received and such traditions only offered him an obscure reply at this juncture; a reply which is liable to be misunderstood even though through sustained scrutiny it is seen as the work of a master.

read more roughly, it is difficult to understand why it was inserted at all.[32] Hence, we conclude that the best explanation of the history of the pronouncements is that they were originally integral to one another. The apparent inconcinnity of the two pronouncements should not be regarded as a decisive refutation of their authenticity or integrity.

The alleged Lukan vocabulary

Do the two pronouncements contain Lukan vocabulary and would this mean that they are the evangelist's creation? It has been explained why it is improbable that Luke has created these sayings, whether one or both of them. But what of the alleged Lukan vocabulary? Marshall, aware of this problem, suggests that it is a case of redaction of tradition and that the presence of Lukan vocabulary throughout is no proof that a source has not been used.[33] But is the alleged Lukan vocabulary pervasive? This matter merits investigation.

(i) The vocabulary of verse 32

Goulder cites as Lukan vocabulary the following words: εἰπεῖν and πορεύεσθαι.[34] Another word normally attributed to Luke which Goulder does not mention is 'ἴασις.[35] The evidence for Lukanisms does not seem very impressive.

Εἰπεῖν and πορεύεσθαι, although frequently occurring in Luke, are not significant as they are both used rather frequently in the other gospels (although not as frequently as in Luke).[36]

Even if we grant that they are Lukan, they may simply have been a case of the use of a favourite word as a substitute for a synonymous word in the tradition.

More impressive is the case of 'ἴασις. Although from the point of

---

32 Hoehner, *Herod*, p. 215. Nolland has recently put forward the view that v. 33 is a Lukan creation which by reiteration accommodates v. 32 to the journey context of the travel narrative and bridges it to vv. 34–5, in his *Luke 9:21–18:34*, p. 739.

33 Marshall, *Gospel*, p. 570.

34 M. D. Goulder, *Luke, A New Paradigm*, p. 580.

35 This word occurs three times in the NT, all in the Luke–Acts corpus: twice in Acts (4.22, 30) and once here.

36 The number of occurrences of these two words is as follows. Εἰπεῖν: Matthew 182x, Mark 84x, Luke 294x, John 204x, Acts 124x, NT 925x; πορεύεσθαι: Matt. 29x, Mark 3x, Luke 51x, John 13x, Acts 37x, NT 150x.

view of word-statistics it is highly probable that 'ἴασις is Lukan, this is offset by the fact that the construction ἰάσεις ἀποτελῶ does not appear to be Lukan. Luke is fond of the verb ἰάομαι[37] and it is peculiar that he does not use ἰάομαι to describe the healings which were part of Jesus' ministry. Instead we have a rather obscure construction, ἰάσεις ἀποτελῶ. This may perhaps be explained by positing that Luke wants to give balance to his syntactical constructions.[38] Since ἐκβάλλω has an object, δαιμόνια, so Luke wanted to give a two-word structure to the second action: a verb (ἀποτελῶ) and an object (ἰάσεις). But the same result could be achieved by Luke's using his favourite ἰάομαι with an object perhaps like νόσος. Instead, we have an unusual verb, ἀποτελῶ, which occurs in the NT only here and at James 1.15. Interestingly, Schweizer regards ἀποτελῶ as Lukan.[39] But how does he come to such a conclusion? It is precarious to judge ἀποτελῶ as Lukan because it appears only once in Luke–Acts. Perhaps it is better to regard ἀποτελῶ as traditional and the phraseology, ἰάσεις ἀποτελῶ, as therefore traditional and not Lukan.[40]

It has often been thought that the temporal phrase, σήμερον καὶ αὔριον καὶ τῇ τρίτῃ, found in v. 32 was a Lukan borrowing from the Septuagint. It has been suggested that this temporal phrase has an equivalent in the LXX reading of Exodus 19.11.[41] But since the analogy between Exodus 19.11[42] and Luke 13.32 is highly remote,[43] the former could not have been the background of the latter, and

[37] Matt. 4x, Mark 1x, Luke 11x, John 3x, Acts 4x and NT 26x.
[38] We do not know of any scholar suggesting this explanation.
[39] E. Schweizer, *The Good News According to Luke*, p. 229. He does not explain how he comes to this conclusion.
[40] Fitzmyer is of the opinion that v. 32 comes from 'L', *Luke X–XXIV*, p. 1028.
[41] As proposed by W. Grimm, 'Eschatologischer Saul wider eschatologischen David. Eine Deutung von Lc. xiii 31ff', *NovT* 15 (1973), 114–33. Grimm further proposes that the appellation 'fox' alludes to King Saul (Hebrew שָׁאוּל, šā'ul; the Hebrew word for fox is שׁוּעָל, šu'āl) and the purpose of the appellation is that Jesus was contrasting the 'fox' (a pun on Saul) with the messianic 'lion' of the house of David (unstated). If this is correct, it would imply that Jesus was making an implicit messianic claim (114–17). But, as Marshall observes, in the absence of an *explicit* reference to the lion, this proposal is too speculative to be convincing (*Gospel*, p. 571). Hoehner's view which is akin to Grimm's is also subject to the same criticism (*Herod*, pp. 220–1).
[42] The text reads: καὶ ἔστωσαν ἕτοιμοι εἰς τὴν ἡμέραν τὴν τρίτην· τῇ γὰρ ἡμέρᾳ τῇ τρίτῃ καταβήσεται κύριος ἐπὶ τὸ ὄρος τὸ Σινα ἐναντίον παντὸς τοῦ λαοῦ.
[43] Exod. 19.10–19 describes a period of preparation/cleansing followed by a third day of revelation from God by fire. The connection between this passage and Luke 13.32 is remote and the temporal formulas of these two passages are vastly different. Cf. Marshall, *Gospel*, p. 571.

therefore it is unlikely that Luke has borrowed from it. It must also be said that the LXX of Hosea 6.2 cannot have been the exemplar of the temporal formula of Luke 13.32.[44] Since there is no possible LXX exemplar for the composition of the temporal formula found in Luke 13.32, it has to be concluded that Luke did not borrow from the LXX. In fact, Black has postulated that the Aramaic phrase, *yoma den wᵉyomaḥra* (i.e., 'day by day'), underlay the phraseology of the temporal formula of Luke 13.32 and that this formula is not to be traced to the LXX.[45] Furthermore, it must be pointed out that the temporal formula occurs only here and with a slight variation in v. 33, and nowhere else in the NT. In the light of all the preceding observations, we conclude that the temporal formula is not a Lukan borrowing from the LXX but is most probably to be regarded as traditional.

The significance of τελειοῦμαι is harder to assess. From word-statistics alone,[46] no firm conclusion can be drawn on whether τελειοῦμαι is Lukan or not.[47]

To sum up the discussion: there are no good reasons for assigning the pronouncement of v. 32b to Lukan redaction from the standpoint of vocabulary. Instead, there appear to be strong grounds for viewing the exact opposite – Luke received v. 32b from a source.

(ii) The vocabulary of verse 33

There are stronger grounds for viewing v. 33 as heavily Lukan in diction. The reasons are as follows:

  (a) πλήν[48] has often been regarded as Lukan;[49]

---

[44] The temporal phrase found in the LXX rendering of Hos. 6.2 reads: ... μετὰ δύο ἡμέρας ἐν τῇ ἡμέρα τῇ τρίτη.

[45] Black, *Aramaic*, pp. 205–6.

[46] Luke 2x, John 5x, Acts 1x, Heb. 9x.

[47] Black suggests that the Aramaic *ithkalᵉleth* lies behind τελειοῦμαι giving a word play with *shakhlᵉleth* which may lie behind ἀποτελῶ. If Black is right, then the possibility of τελειοῦμαι being Lukan is rendered more remote (*Aramaic*, p. 233).

[48] Matt. 5x, Mark 1x, Luke 15x, Acts 4x, NT 31x; Luke has more than 50 per cent of the NT usage.

[49] J. A. Fitzmyer, *Luke I–IX*, p. 111; Goulder, *Luke*, p. 580; H. J. Cadbury, *The Style and Literary Method of Luke*, p. 147. Cadbury cites three instances where Luke seems to have introduced πλήν to his sources: Matt. 6.33 has ζητεῖτε δέ, Luke 12.31 has πλὴν ζητεῖτε; Mark 14.21 has οὐαὶ δὲ τῷ ἀνθρώπῳ, Luke 22.22 has πλὴν οὐαὶ τῷ ἀνθρώπῳ; Mark 14.36 has ἀλλ᾽ οὐ τί ἐγὼ θέλω ἀλλὰ τί σύ, Luke 22.42 has πλὴν μὴ τὸ θέλημά μου ἀλλὰ τὸ σὸν γινέσθω.

(b) δεῖ[50] is typically Lukan;[51]

(c) πορεύεσθαι, used in a pregnant sense, is characteristically Lukan;[52] and

(d) Ἰερουσαλήμ plays a pivotal and significant role in Luke–Acts and hence Luke has a special interest in Ἰερουσαλήμ.[53]

This impressive array of evidence has led Fitzmyer to allow for the possibility that v. 33 did not stem from 'L' but from Lukan composition, as a sort of commentary on v. 32.[54] Yet, interestingly, Schweizer has stated that ἐνδέχεται[55] and Jesus' reference to himself as a prophet are 'unlukan'.[56] How are we to assess such a situation where there are arguments for both Lukan redaction and tradition? Marshall's proposal that this is a case of redaction of an earlier tradition[57] has most to commend it, and this would explain why there is evidence for both redaction and tradition.

Nevertheless, we believe that the supposed Lukan diction of these verses has been exaggerated. Luke does not have a monopoly of the use of δεῖ and πλήν. Although Luke shows greater interest in Jerusalem than do the other evangelists, Jerusalem could have been equally significant to Jesus. In this connection, it has to be

---

[50] Matt. 8x, Mark 6x, Luke 18x, John 10x, Acts 22x, NT 101x.

[51] Fitzmyer, *Luke I–IX*, p. 112, cf. *Luke X–XXIV*, p. 1032; Goulder, *Luke*, p. 580.

[52] Fitzmyer, *Luke I–IX*, p. 169. Fitzmyer cites the following as evincing a pregnant use of πορεύεσθαι: Luke 4.30; 9.51, 52, 53, 56, 57; 10.38; 17.11; 19.12 and the present verse under discussion, Luke 13.33. B. Lindars has pointed out in his *Jesus Son of Man*, p. 75, that 'The fact that we have here a genuine memory of Jesus' ironical use of "go" is supported by the fourth gospel, where it is used very effectively to express the passage of Jesus to the Father by way of the cross.'

[53] Fitzmyer, *Luke I–IX*, p. 168. Other scholars such as H. Conzelmann, *The Theology of St Luke*, p. 74; and J. T. Sanders, *The Jews in Luke-Acts*, pp. 24–36 also regard Ἰερουσαλήμ as playing a pivotal role in the Lukan understanding of salvation history. But it must be stressed that an interest in Jerusalem need not necessarily imply that Luke has created sayings about Jerusalem *de novo* in passages peculiar to him. Further, it must equally be stressed that Jerusalem would have been of interest to a Jew like Jesus who had a following.

[54] Fitzmyer, *Luke X–XXIV*, p. 1028. So also Nolland, *Luke 9:21–18:34*, p. 741.

[55] ἐνδέχεται is a *hapax legomenon* in the NT.

[56] Schweizer, *Luke*, p. 228. R. Stein observes that the designation of Jesus as a prophet would be rather unusual in a church creation in his *The Method and Message of Jesus' Teaching*, p. 170 n. 91. See also D. E. Aune, *Prophecy in Early Christianity and the Ancient Mediterranean World*, pp. 153–69. Although Fitzmyer is correct to think that the depiction of Jesus as a prophet in Luke's gospel may be a Lukan emphasis (*Luke X–XXIV*, p. 1030), this need not mean that the whole concept was invented by Luke.

[57] Marshall, *Gospel*, p. 570.

emphasised that Mark was equally interested in the 'way' of Jesus to Jerusalem.[58]

There is one other consideration for regarding v. 33 as substantially traditional other than the 'unlukan' elements highlighted above: Luke is unlikely to have created a saying to obscure rather than clarify v. 32. Therefore we conclude that the best explanation which accounts for all the evidence is that the pronouncement is substantially from Jesus, although there is a likelihood that Luke may have substituted or used certain of his favourite words.[59]

The theological motifs of verses 22-3

Already in the preceding discussion some attention has been given to theological motifs (e.g., 'prophet'). We propose now to deal with two other motifs which have led some to regard the pronouncements as stemming from the church: Jerusalem and the three-day motif.

At the outset, it should be emphasised that detecting a motif in the sayings of Jesus in line with the theology of the church does not necessarily mean that that motif or saying was the creation of the church. In principle, the church could create or collect materials in harmony with its theological outlook.

The Markan motif of three days found in the passion/resurrection predictions (Mark 8.31; 9.31; 10.33-4) has often been regarded as not stemming from Jesus but as reflecting the post-Easter community's belief.[60] But, clearly, the form of the three-day motif of the passion/resurrection predictions (we do not intend to discuss their authenticity here; on this see Bayer[61]) is different from that found in Luke 13.32-3.[62] It is highly improbable that τελειοῦμαι

---

58 Cf. Mark 8.27–10.45. Although πορεύεσθαι does not feature much in Mark's gospel, Mark is none the less interested in the way of Jesus. See E. Best, *Mark: The Gospel as Story*, pp. 84–92.

59 Cf. C. F. Evans, *Luke*, p. 560.

60 Kümmel, *Promise*, p. 86. Cf. Tyson, 'Herod', 245; G. Bornkamm, *Jesus of Nazareth*, p. 154.

61 H. F. Bayer, *Jesus' Predictions of Vindication and Resurrection*.

62 Luke 13.32 has σήμερον καὶ αὔριον καὶ τῇ τρίτῃ (τῇ ἐχομένῃ for v. 33) whereas Mark consistently has μετὰ τρεῖς ἡμέρας and Matthew and Luke consistently have τῇ τρίτῃ for parallels to Mark (except the second prediction in Luke in which there was no mention). The phrase σήμερον καὶ αὔριον is absent in the passion/resurrection predictions.

refers to the resurrection.[63] Verse 33 shows that the context is about death on the third day and not resurrection. Hence, the three-day motif does not reflect the usual three-day motif treasured by the post-Easter community as found in the passion/resurrection predictions. The difference is marked and this in itself may be an indication of authenticity.

We have already commented on the Jerusalem motif. Undoubtedly, Luke has a great interest in Jerusalem. Jerusalem is for Luke the place of Jesus' death and resurrection. It is also the place where the disciples receive the Holy Spirit, and from there the evangelisation of the world is to begin (Acts 1.8). Jerusalem would also have a significant place in the memory of the post-Easter community. This being so, there are strong grounds for viewing v. 33 as a church creation or, more probably, Luke's (since Luke has a greater interest in Jerusalem than do the rest of the evangelists). However, we are of the opinion that v. 33 goes back to Jesus because of the following reasons. As stated earlier, it is almost inescapable that Jesus who intentionally started a movement should have Jerusalem as a significant place in his mind. Secondly, the enigmatic quality and lack of perspicuity of the pronouncement hint at authenticity. Thirdly, as pointed out in the preceding discussion, there are many 'unlukan' elements in the pronouncements which make it unlikely that these traditions were created by Luke. Fourthly, the hyperbole,[64] introduced by the ὅτι clause, is part of the repertoire of Jesus' teaching methods. Fifthly, as we have seen, there are good grounds for viewing v. 33 as integral to vv. 31–2; since most scholars accept the authenticity of vv. 31–2, v. 33 would therefore be authentic too. In short, these strong indications of authenticity from v. 33 and the consideration that Jesus could have been strongly interested in Jerusalem demonstrate that the Jerusalem motif here need not be regarded as a Lukan creation.

---

[63] Hoehner: 'The third day probably does not have reference to his [Jesus'] resurrection, for in that case the first two days would be those of the crucifixion, whereas here Jesus is speaking of the preceding days as a period of casting out demons and performing cures' (*Herod*, p. 221).

[64] The hyperbole has a proverb-like ring around it and it is part of the characteristic of the teaching methods of Jesus (on this subject, see Stein, *Method*; R. Riesner, *Jesus als Lehrer*). Vermes boldly asserts without any supporting evidence that the hyperbole is an unattested Jewish proverb (G. Vermes, *Jesus the Jew*, p. 88)!

There is no doubt that Luke 13.31–3 is authentic.[65] Our discussion of authenticity has used the premise that the incident is historical as a starting-point. The first pronouncement found in v. 32b is accepted as stemming from Jesus. As v. 32b forms an incomplete reply, v. 33 is an integral part of Jesus' answer. Although v. 33 can possibly be seen to have passed through the redactional hand of Luke, it is none the less improbable that v. 33 has been created *de novo*. Luke 13.31–3 therefore offers us the *ipsissima vox Jesu*.

3 The meaning of the pronouncements (Luke 13.32–3)

We have noted earlier that the saying is a calculated ambiguity and that there is an intended imbalance in the two pronouncements. It is the concern of this section to demonstrate this and to discuss the interpretation of these two pronouncements.

Before we discuss the meaning of the pronouncements,[66] a brief review of the state of scholarship on these verses will be beneficial. As pointed out earlier, there is apparently an inconcinnity between the two pronouncements: they are not balanced in terms of formal structure and logical thought. Furthermore, the reply of Jesus is not at all clear: what was he trying to convey? These are the basic problems which vitiate the interpretation of the pronouncements.

As noted above, one solution popularly adopted made use of emendation.[67] What needs to be stated here is that it was the inconcinnity (both formal and logical) which led to proposals of textual emendation. In more recent commentaries, this inconcinnity is given surprisingly scant notice.[68] It seems that recent commentators are content just to note that the two pronouncements were originally separate. Hence, there is no serious attempt to understand the apparent inconcinnity in the two pronouncements.

Most scholars now accept that the temporal phrase, σήμερον καὶ αὔριον καὶ τῇ τρίτῃ/τῇ ἐχομένῃ (v. 33), is an Aramaism and that it

---

[65] Cf. Lindars, *Jesus*, pp. 70–1 and P. M. Casey, 'General, Generic and Indefinite: The Use of the "Son of Man" in Aramaic Sources in the Teaching of Jesus', *JSNT* 29 (1987), 44.

[66] We shall not deal with vv. 31–2a (the report of the Pharisees and the meaning of the appellation 'fox').

[67] Cf. the critique found earlier in this chapter, section 2.

[68] E.g., G. B. Caird, *St Luke*; Fitzmyer, *Luke X–XXIV*; Ellis, *Luke*; Schweizer, *Luke*; Nolland, *Luke 9:21–18:34*, have not dealt with it. One exception is Marshall, *Gospel*, pp. 572–3.

is not to be taken literally. Many would agree that the meaning of
the temporal formula is that a short indefinite period would be
followed by a certain climax or culmination.[69]

Black's suggestion that the Aramaic phrase *yoma den wᵉyomaḥra*
lies behind σήμερον καὶ αὔριον has not, to our knowledge, been
challenged. There is no reason why this consensus should be
questioned.

We shall now attempt to demonstrate that the intended irony
and ambiguity of the pronouncements, together with a word play,
have given rise to this apparent inconcinnity.[70]

The word play in Luke 13.31–3

Plummer has suggested that a word play is possible in Luke
13.31–3 although he himself does not subscribe to it. His reason is
that, as ἐξελθεῖν is not repeated, the repetition of πορεύεσθαι may
have been accidental.[71] But he has dismissed the possibility pre-
maturely.

The meaning of the Pharisees' warning and advice was essentially
that Jesus was to leave the territory of Herod as Herod desired to
kill him (v. 31). Jesus' answer began with the participle πορευθέντες which serves as an imperative; this verb is thrown back at
the Pharisees who also told Jesus to leave with two imperatives, one
of which was πορεύου.[72] Such a reply implies that the warning of
the Pharisees might not be heeded. Verse 33, the second pronouncement, also contains πορεύεσθαι and it gives the impression that the
advice would be followed after all, albeit for different reasons and
motives. It does not seem correct therefore to deny that a word play
is intended even though the word ἐξελθεῖν is not repeated. The
Pharisees' warning has as its core the verbs of motion. In the reply
of Jesus, a verb of motion is used twice and the usage of it does not
appear to be accidental. A calculated ambiguity and irony are

---

69   Hoehner, *Herod*, p. 221; Black, *Aramaic*, pp. 205–7; Marshall, *Gospel*, p. 571;
Bayer, *Predictions*, p. 144; Lindars, *Jesus*, pp. 70–1; Nolland, *Luke 9:21–18:34*,
p. 740.

70   Cf. J. D. M. Derrett, 'The Lucan Christ and Jerusalem: τελειοῦμαι (Luke 13.32)'
ZNW 75 (1984), 36–43 for an attempt to uncover puns in these sayings (which he
regards as an epigram) by positing a Hebrew(!) origin for them. His article is
replete with fanciful speculations with which we shall not interact because of
limitations of space.

71   A. Plummer, *St Luke*, p. 300.

72   This word play is also possible in Aramaic, *mutatis mutandis*.

probably intended. The sense could perhaps be put like this: instead of Jesus *going* away because of Herod, the Pharisees were told to *go* back to Herod, and yet Jesus will *go* for a different reason.[73] The recognition of this word play leads us to appreciate the masterful construction of the reply and also helps us to understand its meaning.

The intended ambiguity of the reply

Equally important is the recognition that there is a deliberate ambiguity in the reply; this is seen not just in the word play of πορεύεσθαι, but also in the use of the verb τελειοῦμαι. Jesus' response in v. 32b may be interpreted in two ways depending on the meaning assigned to τελειοῦμαι.[74] As observed by Marshall, it could refer either to the completion of Jesus' work of exorcism and healing,[75] whether in a temporal or a spatial[76] sense, or to the completion of his ministry in death.[77] Depending on the interpretation of τελειοῦμαι, the reply which forms the first pronouncement would suggest to the Pharisees that Jesus was either *conceding* (i.e., 'give me a little more time and my ministry of healing and exorcism would be completed') or *defiant* (i.e., 'I shall go on doing my work no matter what Herod says; only death can stop me!'). Such an ambiguity appears to be intended, and indicates that v. 32b by itself is not a complete reply but is meant to prepare the ground for the next pronouncement.[78]

---

[73] So also D. P. Moessner, *The Lord of the Banquet*, p. 116: 'Far from contradicting v. 32, the πορεύεσθαι of v. 33 graphically restates in spatial imagery the resolve expressed temporally in v. 32 as a crowning "on the third day". Jesus says in effect to the Pharisees, "Not I but you go away from here, for my course is already set by the One who has sent me."'

[74] We shall not discuss whether τελειοῦμαι is properly passive or middle. A decision on this matter does not really affect the present discussion, although we hold with many scholars that τελειοῦμαι is best read as a passive. But see J. Reiling and J. L. Swellengrebel, *A Translator's Handbook on the Gospel of Luke*, p. 571 for the view that τελειοῦμαι is middle in this instance.

[75] So T. W. Manson, *The Sayings of Jesus*, p. 276. Ellis has suggested that the word refers to the consecration of Jesus as high priest (*Luke*, p. 189) which appears to be oversubtle.

[76] The spatial sense is suggested by Fitzmyer (*Luke X–XXIV*, p. 1031), although he does not indicate whether he is in agreement with it. However, a reading of v. 33 with its strong overtones of death suggests that a spatial sense is probably not intended.

[77] Marshall, *Gospel*, p. 572. Marshall cites as evidence Wis. 4.13 for such a usage of the word. See also Lindars, *Jesus*, p. 70.

[78] As also observed by Marshall, *Gospel*, p. 570.

The irony in the second pronouncement

Jesus' reply, which forms the second pronouncement, is heavily ironical. Here irony is understood not in the narrow sense of the use of contrast between what is actually stated and what is wryly suggested, but in the broad sense of referring to an event or result that is opposite to what would normally be expected.[79]

If Jesus' reply in v. 33 is understood as an intended irony, the use of πλήν is easily explicable and can be given its strong adversative force.[80] The meaning would be something like this: 'Now, my work of healing and exorcising will continue for a little while, *but* (πλήν) I am actually doing what you Pharisees are suggesting, as these activities are part and parcel of my peripatetic ministry (πορεύ-εσθαι).' Jesus in his ministry of healing and exorcising is actually doing what the Pharisees suggested – 'go' (πορεύου).

The second pronouncement is ironical in another way too. The Pharisees told Jesus to leave because Herod wanted to kill him. This implies that if Jesus were to heed their advice, he would not be put to death.[81] But Jesus replied ironically that the reverse would actually be true. By his act of leaving Herod's territory, which the Pharisees advised, Jesus would meet his death. This is made clear by the ὅτι clause which explains that Jesus was going to meet his death, not at the hands of Herod, but in Jerusalem and this would be brought about because he would be 'going' (πορεύεσθαι), something which the Pharisees had advised. In fact, Jesus must 'go' (δεῖ ... πορεύεσθαι)!

Another intended irony can be found in the juxtaposition of προφήτης with Ἰερουσαλήμ. They are in a relationship of enmity.

---

[79] For such categories, see Stein, *Method*, p. 22.

[80] *Pace* Marshall, *Gospel*, p. 572 where he cites M. E. Thrall, *Greek Particles in the Greek New Testament*, pp. 20–1 but *wrongly*. On p. 21, Thrall indicates that πλήν in Luke 13.33 is to be understood in an adversative sense. The sense which Marshall hopes is supported by Thrall is found on p. 22 but Thrall's examples there offer him no support. Cf. C. F. Evans, *Luke*, p. 562.

[81] Interestingly, some commentators have understood that the Pharisees had an ulterior motive when they gave their warning to Jesus. L. L. Morris (*Luke*, p. 227) writes that the Pharisees co-operated with Herod in giving the warning so as to frighten Jesus 'into moving out of Perea into Judaea *where they had more power*'! (The emphasis is mine.) Akin to Morris' theory, Hoehner suggests that if Jesus were to be made to move to Judaea, 'then the Pharisees may have thought that the *Sanhedrin would take care of him*' in *Herod*, p. 220 (the emphasis is mine). This is reading too much into the Pharisees' intention and it may reflect the preconception that the Pharisees were always up to no good, a preconception which many scholars are trying today to correct.

Note the strong οὐκ ἐνδέχεται which makes the saying into a hyperbole. Jerusalem the holy city, the city of salvation, the city built for eternity, the city of Yahweh, the navel of the earth (Jub. 8.19), is now conceived by Jesus to be the city of the death of prophets (God's messengers) *par excellence*.

The inconcinnity of the two pronouncements

Once the above results are borne in mind, to a large extent the inconcinnity is alleviated. The logical imbalance[82] is resolved. Jesus intended his answer to be ironical and ambiguous. This need not cause any surprise as Jesus frequently made use of such communication techniques, as his parables and aphoristic sayings confirm. Jesus made use of a word play to bring out the characteristically peripatetic aspect of his ministry (πορεύεσθαι). While he was healing and exorcising, he was also 'moving' for he was under a divine compulsion to do so. This characterisation by Jesus of his own ministry as 'moving' (πορεύεσθαι) caused the inconcinnity. There is also irony in that what the Pharisees suggested was actually being followed, albeit not in the sense they intended.

The structural inconcinnity is slightly more difficult to deal with. In v. 32b, the temporal clause is divided into two parts. σήμερον καὶ αὔριον forms the first part, which contains the actions of exorcising and healing; the second part is expressed by καὶ τῇ τρίτῃ which is understood to be climactic. Whereas, in v. 33, the temporal formula is not broken down: it stands as one. Table 3.1 makes clear the structures of the two pronouncements.

In addition to the lack of a climactic nature, v. 33 states that 'going' is an imperative (δεῖ) for Jesus, giving it a much stronger force than the verbs of v. 32b.

As noted earlier, this structural inconcinnity caused Black to expect a verb to be sandwiched between σήμερον καὶ αὔριον and καὶ τῇ ἐχομένῃ so that there would be structural balance between v. 32b and v. 33.[83] It is our contention that such a structural imbalance is intended.[84] This structural imbalance is meant to show that Jesus' ministry of exorcising and healing and even his 'perfection' (on the climactic third day) are all part of his 'going' (way).

---

[82] As detected and expressed by Creed, *St Luke*, p. 187.
[83] Black, *Aramaic*, p. 206.
[84] Perhaps it can be said that the unexpectedness of such an imbalance points to authenticity.

Table 3.1. *The two pronouncements compared*

Verse 32b: the first pronouncement	
Duration	*Action*
1. σήμερον καὶ αὔριον	ἐκβάλλω δαιμόνια καὶ ἰάσεις ἀποτελῶ
2. καὶ τῇ τρίτῃ	τελειοῦμαι

Verse 33: the second pronouncement	
Duration	*Action*
1. σήμερον καὶ αὔριον καὶ τῇ εχομένη	δεῖ με . . . πορεύεσθαι

And his 'going' (way) is under a divine compulsion. There could not be any two-part structure to his 'going' (way) as everything which happens to him and everything that he does are part and parcel of the divinely appointed 'way'. Hence, we conclude that the temporal formula of v. 33 is meant to show that all the actions which are under the ambit of the temporal formula in v. 32b fall under the divinely appointed 'way' (πορεύεσθαι) of Jesus, and that this is a way that leads to death in Jerusalem.[85] Emending the text would result in a loss of what Jesus understood his whole ministry to be.[86]

The use of irony and ambiguity is characteristic of Jesus as a teacher.[87] Such a method would make his teaching memorable and its obliqueness would tease the hearers into active thought. Furthermore, by such a reply Jesus would concede nothing and yet at the same time leave Herod's territory to fulfil his divinely appointed destiny. Jesus will be going away from Galilee, not because of Herod's threat, but because this is what his ministry is all about – going in the divinely appointed way and on a path that would lead to his death, not at Herod's hands but at Jerusalem's 'hands'.[88]

---

[85] Marshall also regards the temporal phrase of v. 33 as corresponding to the whole of the three days in v. 32b (*Gospel*, p. 572).

[86] It is probable that it is this understanding on the part of Jesus of his own ministry which gave rise to Luke's and also to Mark's devoting a substantial portion of their gospels to show Jesus 'on the way' and also to expound the 'way of Jesus'. If this is correct, Luke's travel narrative, although not being chronologically structured, has its roots in the ministry of Jesus.

[87] Cf. Riesner, *Jesus*.   [88] Cf. Hoehner, *Herod*, p. 223.

4 The attraction of Jerusalem

If what we have been arguing is correct, certain conclusions can be drawn about how Jesus conceived his role and his ministry *vis-à-vis* Jerusalem. Such conclusions also serve as important data for the reconstruction of a very important phase of Jesus' ministry – Jesus in Jerusalem.

The first is that Jesus expected to die and he understood this dying as falling under the ambit of a divine necessity. That Jesus predicted his own death should not be surprising, as the execution of John the Baptist would have served as an ominous warning.[89] Moreover, it does not take supernatural prescience but merely ordinary insight of an intelligent person to discern that things are not working out as expected. In this light, the passion/resurrection predictions which have often been regarded as *vaticinia ex eventu*[90] ought to be reassessed. If Jesus expected to die, how then did he respond to this conviction of his? This question has immense implications for an understanding of the ministry and intentions of Jesus. This pericope reveals that Jesus believed his death fell under the ambit of divine necessity. To what extent did such a thought influence his actions in Jerusalem? Moreover, if Jesus perceived his forthcoming death to fall under the ambit of divine necessity, how did he interpret it? To what end was it? We hope to answer these questions in later chapters.

Secondly, Jesus understood that it was his appointed lot to die in Jerusalem. Note the hyperbole: οὐκ ἐνδέχεται προφήτην ἀπολέσθαι ἔξω 'Ιερουσαλήμ. Could the hyperbole be an unattested proverb?[91] No evidence has yet come to light to support this suggestion. Fitzmyer has commented that behind the hyperbole lies a traditional belief about the fate of various prophetic figures in the city of Jerusalem.[92] But the references cited by Fitzmyer only indicate that *some* prophets were killed in Jerusalem. The prophet Uriah was the only clear scriptural case (Jer. 26.20–3). There is a statement of Josephus to the effect that Manasseh filled Jerusalem

---

[89] As also observed by C. H. Dodd, *The Parables of the Kingdom*, p. 40. See also H. Schürmann, 'Wie hat Jesus seinen Tod bestanden und verstanden? Eine methodenkritische Besinnung' in his *Jesu ureigener Tod: Exegetische Besinnungen und Ausblick*, pp. 26–33.

[90] E.g., R. Bultmann, *Theology of the New Testament* I, p. 30.

[91] This is suggested by Vermes, *Jesus*, p. 88.

[92] See Fitzmyer, *Luke X–XXIV*, p. 1032.

with the blood of the prophets (AJ 10.38), but this information
does not appear in 2 Kings 21.16, which has 'innocent blood'
instead. Schweizer observes that although it is seldom[93] reported
that Jerusalem killed prophets, there are legends to that effect. He
cites Jeremiah 26.20–3; 2 Chronicles 24.21; 1 Kings 18.4, 13; 19.10,
14; but only Jeremiah 26.20–3 can be said to be evidence. He
observes further that Jewish confessions of sin looked upon such
killings as typical behaviour on the part of Israel.[94] Here he cites
Nehemiah 9.26, but it does not mention Jerusalem. Hence, with the
exception of Jeremiah 26.20–3 and AJ 10.38, all the evidence cited
by Fitzmyer and Schweizer shows only that the *nation* killed
prophets in the past as part of its hardness of heart and disobedience; the connection of the death of prophets with Jerusalem
is not made explicitly.[95] It seems that the locality of the death of the
prophets was of no concern in those texts. But in Luke 13.33 the
locality is highlighted and made significant. This implies that this
strong connection between the prophets' death and Jerusalem
could come only from two sources: Jesus or the church (because
Jerusalem was the city of Jesus' death). But we have ruled out the
church as the originator of v. 33. Therefore Jesus is logically the
originator of such an emphasis.

Perhaps an explanation comes readily to hand as to why
Jerusalem was not explicitly connected with the death of the
prophets in Jewish tradition. The grounds for this have been shown
in chapter 2. The upshot of all this is to make the statement of Jesus
even more significant and original:[96] it is impossible for a prophet
to perish outside Jerusalem. If Jesus held such an apparently
idiosyncratic view, what implications are there for our appreciation
of his motive for going there and his actions in Jerusalem?

Hence, this pericope offers evidence about Jesus' negative attitude towards Jerusalem. And this negativity is sharpened by the
hyperbole he used to describe that city. Would this mean that Jesus
rejected the Zion traditions and distanced himself from the use of

---

[93] Fitzmyer fails to recognise this (*Luke X–XXIV*, p. 1032).

[94] Schweizer, *Luke*, p. 230.

[95] R. J. Miller observes that the characterisation of Jerusalem as a city which kills
     prophets has no parallel in Judaism. But he suggests that 'it does correspond to
     the deuteronomistic characterisation of Israel (and it would be consistent with
     prophetic style to speak of Jerusalem in its role as representative of the whole
     nation)' in his 'The Rejection of the Prophets in Q', *JBL* 107 (1988), 234.

[96] Cf. S. Schulz, *Q – Die Spruchquelle der Evangelisten*, p. 351 and Miller, 'Reject-
     ion', 235.

Zion or Jerusalem as the symbol of God's reign and salvation? This negativity must be assessed in the light of other significant passages which offer evidence on Jesus' view of Jerusalem. To this we will turn in chapter 4.

However, it should also be pointed out, that in spite of the negativity expressed by Jesus, Jerusalem was also an attraction to him and his ministry. When v. 33 is read in conjunction with v. 32, Jerusalem is seen to be the place of Jesus' τέλος. As a result, he would not expect to be killed by Herod in his territory. But he would leave Herod's territory, not because of the advice of the Pharisees, but because of the pull from Jerusalem, which Jesus attributed as coming ultimately from God. What is the content of this τέλος? τελειοῦμαι could be interpreted as 'completion of ministry' (without involving the notion of death) or 'death' itself. We have suggested that a *double entendre* is intended. In Jerusalem, Jesus expected his ministry to be brought to a climax, and this climax would involve his prophetic death (v. 33). This climax could only be sought in Jerusalem. The specificity of the place was emphasised. His death was understood by him to be part and parcel of his ministry (πορεύεσθαι). In light of the fact that Jerusalem was a magnet for many Jewish movements and eschatological hopes, the fact that Jesus appreciated the attraction of Jerusalem is significant. The content of the climax he expected will be explored in later chapters. Hence, in spite of Jesus' negative statement about Jerusalem in v. 33, its importance for his ministry was also admitted by him.

And, finally, Jesus saw himself as a prophet who would perish in Jerusalem. The motif of the violent fate of the prophets has been much utilised by the early church (e.g., Acts 7.52; 1 Thess. 2.15) but what is novel here, and we reiterate, is that the death of a prophet is connected with Jerusalem (the anarthrous προφήτην of v. 33 is meant to be generic). If Jesus knew that he would die in Jerusalem as a prophet, should his actions in Jerusalem be understood as prophetic acts? We hope to answer these questions in Part III.

5 Corroboration from Mark 10.32–4

There is another strand of tradition, the Markan third passion prediction (Mark 10.32–4), which partially supports our insistence that Jesus expected to die in Jerusalem and nowhere else.

That there is a kernel of truth/historicity underlying the passion predictions (Mark 8.31–3 and parallels; Mark 9.30–2 and parallels; and Mark 10.32–4 and parallels) is increasingly being recognised.[97] It does not strain the imagination to conceive that Jesus predicted his own suffering and death. In view of the death of John the Baptist and in view of the fact that the motif of the violent fate of prophets was well known in first-century Judaism[98] and is attested in Jesus' teaching (Luke 13.31–3),[99] the plausibility of Jesus expecting a martyr's death is enhanced especially if he thought of himself as a prophet (see Mark 6.4; Luke 13.31–3). Hence, it is hardly defensible to attribute the passion predictions lock, stock and barrel to the creativity of the post-Easter community. By so arguing, we do not claim that there were no expansions or redactions of the predictions. Our main concern here is rather to point out that the recognition of the good possibility that Jesus predicted his death and communicated it to his disciples has led many to assign at least a kernel of authenticity to the passion predictions.

This recognition has led to much effort being spent on isolating the authentic core and tracing the relationships between the three predictions.[100] Were there actually three predictions? Or was there actually only one which was utilised to develop the other two? Most work of this nature tends to focus on the first and second predictions, with the third being often bypassed.[101] This is due to the fact that the third prediction is usually dismissed as an evidently *ex eventu* formulation because of its detailed nature. It is often claimed that the third prediction developed from the passion account.[102]

But the third passion prediction cannot be so easily dismissed. Recently, Bayer has argued cogently for the traditional nature of

---

[97] See, among many others, the recent works of Aune, *Prophecy*, p. 178; Lindars, *Jesus*, pp. 60, 74; Bayer, *Predictions*, pp. 214–21; Casey, 'General', 40–9; C. C. Caragounis, *The Son of Man*, pp. 193–201; Riesner, *Jesus*, p. 479; D. C. Allison, *The End of the Ages Has Come*, pp. 137–40.

[98] For the evidence of this, see H. A. Fischel, 'Martyr and Prophet (A Study in Jewish Literature)', *JQR* 37 (1946–7), 265–80; 363–86.

[99] So also Aune, *Prophecy*, pp. 157–9. See also O.H. Steck, *Israel und das gewaltsame Geschick der Propheten*, ad loc.

[100] E.g., Lindars, *Jesus*, pp. 60–81.

[101] For an exception, see R. McKinnis, 'An Analysis of Mark 10.32–34', *NovT* 18 (1976), 81–100.

[102] Even so conservative a scholar as V. Taylor accepts this in *The Gospel of Mark*, p. 437.

the third prediction.[103] A strong case for the independence of the third prediction from the passion narrative can be defended. This can be seen in a number of ways: (a) ἐμπαίζω introduces the string of abuses on Jesus in Mark 10.34 while it concludes that of 15.19–20;[104] (b) different terms are used for the beating as well as the death of Jesus (μαστιγόω in Mark 10.34 vs. φραγελλόω in 15.15; ἀποκτείνω in 10.34 vs. σταυρόω in 15.15, 24); and (c) Mark 10.34 suggests that the agents of the verb ἐμπαίζω are the Gentiles but, in the passion narrative, the action was performed by both Jews (14.65; 15.31) and Gentiles (15.19–20). Such inconsistencies militate against the claim that the third passion prediction is a summary of passages in the passion traditions.[105]

That there could be a passion prediction given at this juncture of Jesus' ministry, albeit in general terms, is also supported by Hooker.[106] Such an observation undermines Strecker's argument against Tödt's proposal[107] that the three predictions are all traditional. Strecker argues that 'such a proposal does not solve the problem of tradition history, but merely pushes it back to an older layer of tradition'.[108] What Strecker is really arguing is that during the oral tradition process, distinctions between the three predictions can hardly be recognised and that one grew from the other. But if Hooker's observation is correct, there is then a distinctive marker tagged on to the third prediction -- the location or context, namely 'the road to Jerusalem'. The same can be said for the first prediction – the confession of Peter.

Hence, the Markan third passion/resurrection prediction may offer another piece of evidence to show that Jesus expected death in Jerusalem and nowhere else.[109]

Jesus expected that his ministry would come to a climax in Jerusalem and that this would involve his death. This will have

---

[103] Bayer, *Predictions*, pp. 172–4, 216. We are indebted to his work in our discussion of this passage.

[104] Interestingly, G. Strecker recognises this although he comes to a negative conclusion about the traditional nature of the third prediction in his 'The Passion- and Resurrection Predictions in Mark's Gospel', *Int* 22 (1968), 435.

[105] R. H. Gundry adopts a similar line of argumentation in *Mark: A Commentary on His Apology for the Cross*, p. 575.

[106] M. D. Hooker, *The Son of Man in Mark*, p. 137.

[107] In H. E. Tödt, *The Son of Man in the Synoptic Tradition*, pp. 152–5.

[108] Strecker, 'Predictions', 433.

[109] Because of the limitations of space, we cannot discuss the meaning of the title 'Son of Man'. The bibliographical items on this topic are legion.

4

THE ATTRACTION OF JERUSALEM (II):
THE CITY OF THE GREAT KING

In Matthew 5.35, Matthew[1] attributes to Jesus a logion which purportedly indicates Jesus' attitude towards Jerusalem: πόλις ἐστὶν τοῦ μεγάλου βασιλέως. But is Matthew 5.35 dominical? Or is it a product of Matthean redaction, whether this involves Matthew's creating the saying *de novo* or his borrowing of a Jewish saying? It is the purpose of this chapter to investigate this logion to see to what extent it can be attributed to the historical Jesus. If the saying is dominical, its significance for research into Jesus' attitude towards Jerusalem and his intention to go there will then be set out.

1   The authenticity of Jesus' prohibition of swearing

We shall start with the consideration of whether there is an authentic core to the fourth antithesis as a whole. Obviously, if Jesus never forbade swearing, the whole fourth antithesis, including the logion under consideration, would be inauthentic.[2]

Matthew 5.35 occurs embedded in the fourth antithesis of the Sermon of the Mount, which elucidates Jesus' attitude towards swearing. Most scholars today hold that there is indeed an authentic kernel to the fourth antithesis.[3] The reasons for this confident outlook are two: Jesus' absolute prohibition of swearing goes beyond the many criticisms made by the Judaism of his time;[4]

---

[1]   The term used is conventional and does not imply any prejudgment on the issue of authorship.

[2]   The possibility of Matt. 5.35 being authentic on its own is remote as the logion is intricately linked to the whole matter of swearing.

[3]   E.g., G. Strecker, *The Sermon on the Mount*, pp. 78, 204 n. 7; U. Luz, *Matthew 1-7*, p. 313. But for an opposite view, cf. G. Dautzenberg, 'Ist das Schwurverbot Mt 5,33-7; Jak 5,12 ein Beispiel für die Torakritik Jesu?', *BZ* 25 (1981), 47-66. Dautzenberg rejects the authenticity of the whole of the fourth antithesis.

[4]   Strecker, *Sermon*, p. 78: 'an absolute prohibition against oaths is attested only for Jesus'. Similarly Luz, *Matthew 1-7*, p. 313.

and James 5.12, which is independent of Matthew 5.34–7, provides good collateral evidence.[5] In the opinion of Ito, the authenticity of the prohibition of swearing had not been really challenged until Dautzenberg's 1981 article.[6]

Dautzenberg argues against attributing the prohibition of swearing to Jesus and claims that the fourth antithesis actually goes back to a secondary Jewish-Christian tradition. His main arguments for the case are as follows.

(i) There are parallel materials contemporaneous with Jesus, which, on the basis of Exodus 20.7 and Leviticus 19.12, discourage swearing. Hence, the prohibition in Matthew 5.34 is not so radically different from some Jewish criticisms of oath-taking that it should be accepted as authentic Jesus tradition on the ground of the criterion of dissimilarity.[7]

(ii) There is a contradiction between the prohibition of swearing and the use of *die Beteuerungsformeln* (the Amen-sayings) in the Synoptic tradition.[8]

(iii) His third argument concerns the *Wirkungsgeschichte* of the prohibition in early Christianity, particularly as evinced in the letter of James and the writings of Paul. He argues that James was ignorant of the fact that such a tradition had stemmed from Jesus, and that he presented the prohibition as his own exhortation.[9] In addition, Paul's frequent recourse to 'God as witness' argues for his ignorance of such a logion.[10]

Luz is not convinced by Dautzenberg's first argument. He holds that Jesus' prohibition of oaths is radical, going beyond the Jewish criticism of oath-taking of his day.[11] His conclusion is inescapable when a comparison of Jesus' prohibition with the relevant Jewish

---

[5] For a good discussion on this particular point, see P. H. Davids, *The Epistle of James*, pp. 189–90. See also M. Dibelius and H. Greeven, *James*, p. 251.

[6] A. Ito, 'Matthew's Understanding of the Law with Special Reference to the Fourth Antithesis' (unpublished Ph.D. dissertation, CNAA, 1989), p. 21. Actually, in 1971, P. S. Minear had already raised objections to the authenticity of the fourth antithesis in his 'Yes or No: The Demand for Honesty in the Early Church', *NovT* 13 (1971), 1–13, but he did not present a comprehensive case for it.

[7] Dautzenberg, 'Schwurverbot', 56.   [8] 'Schwurverbot', 57–60.

[9] 'Schwurverbot', 61–3.   [10] 'Schwurverbot', 63–5.

[11] Luz, *Matthew 1–7*, pp. 313–16. On p. 313 n. 16, Luz writes that, in his opinion, this is a classical instance of the criterion of dissimilarity.

(or even secular Greek) texts is carried out.[12] Ito remarks that Dautzenberg fails to see a distinction, albeit fine, between Jesus' *prohibition* and Jewish *criticisms*. Jesus' prohibition appears to be more radical than the Jewish concern for the protection both of the institution of oath-taking and of the name of God from being taken in vain, a concern which gave rise to criticisms against the oft-abused practice.[13]

Hence, Dautzenberg's first argument loses its force in the light of these observations. For Dautzenberg's second argument to be valid, one must assume that Jesus could not contradict himself. Clearly, this is an a priori supposition. Hence, even if Dautzenberg is correct about the contradiction between Jesus' *Schwurverbot* and his *Beteuerungsformeln* found scattered in the Synoptic gospels, it does not entail that the *Schwurverbot* is inauthentic. In fact, if Dautzenberg is right about the contradiction, there would then be greater grounds for us to believe that the *Schwurverbot* is authentic, as it is highly unlikely that a saying which entails that Jesus contradicted himself would have been created in the early church. In other words, arguments against authenticity based on supposed contradictions are not decisive.

Nevertheless, Ito has shown quite convincingly that there is essentially no contradiction. He gives three main arguments. First, the ἀμήν sayings are not oath formulas in a strict sense. Secondly, ἀμήν corresponds to the 'yes, no' in Matthew 5.37. And finally, what may seem contradictory to us might not have been so for Jesus and his contemporaries.[14] Hence, from both perspectives, Dautzenberg's second argument collapses.

Dautzenberg's third argument is two-pronged. We shall deal with his discussion on the Pauline corpus first. Here, Dautzenberg's argument, if valid, constitutes a strong case for rejecting the authenticity of the fourth antithesis because it is highly improbable that Paul would contradict the teaching of one whom he called Lord. But, on this matter, two points may be made. Recently, Wenham has demonstrated the plausibility of Paul knowing the logion found in Matthew 5.37.[15] The grounds for such a conclusion

---

[12] See Luz's discussion of the parallel material in *Matthew 1–7*, pp. 314–15.

[13] Ito, 'Law', pp. 21–2. Ito does not spell out in what sense Jesus' prohibition was radical.

[14] Ito, 'Law', pp. 24–5.

[15] D. Wenham, '2 Corinthians 1.17,18: Echo of a Dominical Logion', *NovT* 28 (1986), 271–9. We are indebted to his study.

are the following. It is clear that there are characteristically common words shared by both passages: ναὶ ναί, οὖ οὖ (Matt. 5.37 and 2 Cor. 1.17).[16] In addition to this, it should be noted that the cumbersome repetition of the affirmative (ναί) and negative (οὖ) particles is peculiar in the light of the fact that in 2 Corinthians 1.18 there is no repetition. This redundancy is best explained by positing that Paul might be quoting from a source. τό may therefore serve as a particle to introduce the quotation (equivalent to quotation marks).[17] And, finally, Paul's use of the formula ναὶ ναί, οὖ οὖ is of a different nature from that envisaged in Matthew 5.37. The latter affirms plain speech but Paul is using it to claim that he is not a two-faced man. It has been suggested that this might constitute an objection to what we have been arguing, but a plausible explanation for this difference in usage can be given. Wenham suggests that this difference arose as a result of Paul's teaching of Jesus' prohibition of oaths being turned against him by the Corinthians.[18] Together, these arguments constitute a strong case for the supposition that Paul knew about such a logion in 2 Corinthians 1.17–20.[19]

Secondly, Paul's frequent recourse to calling on God as a witness is different from his contemporaries' oath formulas. There exists enough dissimilarity between Paul's locution and the typical oath formulas to posit that he might not be thinking that he was contravening the prohibition of Jesus. Furthermore, it must be noted that the prohibition in Matthew 5.35 is immediately followed by an attack on oath *formulas*, which may indicate (for Paul) that they should not be used.[20] Indeed, that the prohibition is placed

---

16 This has been observed by many commentators. E.g., C. K. Barrett, *The Second Epistle to the Corinthians*, p. 76.

17 *BAGD*, p. 552.

18 Wenham, 'Echo', 275–6.

19 On other aspects of Paul's indebtedness to the Jesus traditions, see D. C. Allison, 'The Pauline Epistles and the Synoptic Gospels: The Pattern of Tradition', *NTS* 28 (1982), 1–32; D. Wenham, 'Paul's Use of the Jesus Tradition', in D. Wenham (ed.), *Gospel Perspectives V: The Jesus Tradition Outside the Gospels*, pp. 7–37; T. Holz, 'Paul and the Oral Gospel Tradition', in H. Wansbrough (ed.), *Jesus and the Oral Gospel Tradition*, pp. 380–93; and J. D. G. Dunn, 'Jesus Tradition in Paul', in B. D. Chilton and C. A. Evans (eds.), *Studying the Historical Jesus: Evaluations of the State of Current Research*, pp. 155–78. For a generally negative view see D. L. Dungan, *The Sayings of Jesus in the Churches of Paul*; and F. Neirynck, 'Paul and the Sayings of Jesus', in A. Vanhoye (ed.), *L'apôtre Paul*, pp. 265–321.

20 A similar conclusion is arrived at by Ito although his argumentation is slightly different ('Law', pp. 26, 53–84). His explanation for the difference between

side by side with a castigation of oath formulas may indicate that the latter is to be used to understand the force and applicability of the former. If this is the case, calling on God as a witness might not have been regarded as an oath formula by Paul. However, even if a detailed analysis of the relevant material might lead to a conclusion from our modern standpoint that Paul had contradicted the *Schwurverbot* of Jesus, it is important to note that what seems contradictory to us may not have been so for first-century readers.[21]

Dautzenberg's appeal to the ignorance of James of the logion under consideration is misconceived, as he has failed to bear in mind the difference in genre between the two writings (gospel versus epistle). The fact that James did not attribute his exhortation to anyone may not be significant. Moreover, Davids has observed that James 'never cites anything as being from Jesus, despite his obvious closeness to the tradition. The readers may well have been expected to know the source.'[22]

In sum, Dautzenberg's assault against the authenticity of the prohibition of swearing does not stand up to scrutiny. There are

Pauline and Jewish usage on the grounds that Paul appeals to God over matters of divine origin (as compared to the lack of this in the Jewish ones) is unconvincing.

[21] If the members of the Qumran community are identified with the Essenes (see G. Vermes, *The Dead Sea Scrolls: Qumran in Perspective*, pp. 116–36 for an informed discussion), an interesting phenomenon arises from a consideration of the following texts: BJ 2.135; AJ 15.371; 1QS 5.8–11; CD 9.8–12, 15.3–4. Although they reject oaths, they swear an oath upon entering the community! Moreover, they are allowed to take an oath in a judicial court. This supports our argument that what to us may be a contradiction might not have been so for first-century Jews. This conclusion is circumvented only if the following are true: the Qumran community is not to be identified with the Essenes, or Josephus' description of Essenic practice is not accurate on this point.

[22] Davids, *James*, p. 190. Elsewhere, Davids has shown conclusively that James is in touch with the Jesus tradition: 'James and Jesus', Wenham (ed.) in *Gospel Perspectives V*, pp. 63–84. His statement that 'the readers may well have been expected to know the source' is justified in the light of the twin phenomena occurring in the epistle: numerous allusions to the Jesus tradition and the lack of formal citations (see his list on pp. 66–7). These twin phenomena would indicate that the Jesus tradition was accepted as authoritative and had become a basis for ethical instructions. As such, it is understandable why no formal citation is introduced as there would be no necessity for it. Dibelius and Greeven come to a similar conclusion, but their main reason for doing so is different: 'all paraenesis which is delivered by teachers who are considered bearers of the Spirit stems ultimately from the Lord, and therefore it possesses an even higher authenticity than a quotation formula' (in *James*, p. 251).

firm grounds (as set out earlier) for believing at least the *fact* that Jesus forbade swearing.

Although there are other interesting problems connected with the study of the fourth antithesis,[23] they will be bypassed as the interest of this chapter lies elsewhere: the reference to Jerusalem in v. 35. Therefore, the rest of this chapter will concentrate on the issue of the authenticity of the referents found in the oath formulas and the ὅτι clauses of vv. 34b–5, and the assessment of the significance of these verses for the enquiry into Jesus' attitude to Jerusalem.

2   The authenticity of Matthew 5.34b–5

The authenticity of the cited oath formulas[24]

After a detailed analysis, Brooks assigns Matthew 5.34b–5 to the 'M'[25] sayings and argues that there is a strong possibility that these verses form a pre-Matthean unity. There appears to be no good reason to contest such a claim.[26] Accepting Brooks' conclusions, we shall therefore leave v. 36 out of consideration.[27]

If Matthew 5.34b–5 forms a pre-Matthean unity, would not the probability of its being authentic be further enhanced? According to some scholars, this is not necessarily so. Davies and Allison argue that μὴ ὀμόσαι ὅλως of v. 34a makes vv. 34b–5 redundant and they suggest that the original unit to the fourth antithesis consisted of vv. 34a + 37a.[28] Strecker recognises that Matthew 5.34b–5 belong to pre-Matthean tradition on the basis of the parallel found in James 5.12. To Strecker, this shows that Jesus' prohibition against oaths was subject to a growth process.[29]

---

23 For example, the authenticity of the formulation (in the light of James' non-antithetical formulation) and the meaning of ὅρκος (v. 33).

24 By this we mean that Jesus did cite such oath formulas in order to deal with them. The issue of whether there was a significant differentiation between oaths (ὅρκος) and vows (εὐχή) in first-century Judaism will not be discussed. On this, see R. A. Guelich, *The Sermon on the Mount*, pp. 213–14.

25 'M' is taken by us to mean the traditions which are peculiar to Matthew. The use of the term does not prejudge the issue of whether or not 'M' was a document.

26 But cf. the recent article of D. C. Duling, ' "[Do not Swear ...] by Jerusalem because it is the City of the Great King" (Matthew 5.35)', *JBL* 110 (1991), 295–6. We shall interact with this later.

27 S. H. Brooks, *Matthew's Community: The Evidence of His Special Sayings Material*, p. 39.

28 W. D. Davies and D. C. Allison, *The Gospel According to Saint Matthew* I, pp. 533, 535.

29 Strecker, *Sermon*, p. 79.

Strecker does not fully explain how this took place but it is his view that the primitive tradition comprises vv. 33–4a only (which he regards as authentic).[30]

Although scholars are aware (and are in agreement) that James 5.12 offers valuable evidence for the reconstruction of the original logion of Jesus, they do not come to terms with it seriously enough. Luz accepts on the basis of James 5.12 that a basic part of vv. 34–5 may have belonged to the original saying. He states further that if the ὅτι clauses (which are, according to him, motivated by the OT) are regarded as secondary, 'then the prohibition part and the command part of the admonition as in James 5.12 would be approximately of equal length'.[31] In short, Luz is establishing his case by form-critical considerations. In this case, it is the *length* of the two clauses which constitutes decisive evidence. But this is not convincing, as there is no inherent reason why the two parts ought to be of equal length. In fact, there are important arguments which support the authenticity of the oath formulas. Before delineating them, we shall first deal with the objections noted above.

It is not at all clear why vv. 34b–5 should be redundant in the light of μὴ ὀμόσαι ὅλως of v. 34a. What Davies and Allison fail to see is that a radical statement like v. 34a would normally be expected to be followed by some explanation or application of it to a contemporary situation. Moreover, given the fact that oath formulas were a common occurrence in first-century Judaism,[32] would not Jesus also have dealt with them? Hence, it is perhaps more historically plausible for Jesus to expand on his prohibition (by exposition or explanation) than for him just to state a prohibition *simpliciter*. It therefore appears to us that viewing vv. 34b–5 as redundant represents an a priori stance (whether conscious or unconscious) that Jesus did not explain or apply his teachings, but left them enigmatic all the time; this is not based on good argumentation. Therefore, such an objection is hardly valid. This is not to say then that every element of vv. 34b–5 is authentic; whether it is so has to be demonstrated. Rather, there is naturally some sort of elaboration in view of the radical nature of the saying and the contemporaneous situation. What has just been set out are general considerations and they do not clinch our case. It has to be further substantiated.

[30] *Sermon*, p. 78.   [31] Luz, *Matthew 1–7*, p. 312.
[32] Cf. the evidence from Philo: *Leg. all.* 3.207; *Spec. leg.* 2.2; 2.8; 4.40; *Decal.* 84, 93. See also *m.Ned.* 1.3; *b.Ned.* 1.3; *b.Ber.* 33a. Cf. also Luz, *Matthew 1–7*, p. 314.

When a comparison is made between Matthew 5.34b–5 and James 5.12, it can be seen that even James includes oath formulas in his exhortation. James 5.12 has μήτε τὸν οὐρανὸν μήτε τὴν γῆν μήτε ἄλλον τινα ὅρκον. The two oath formulas found in James are found in Matthew too in the same order[33] and form. It is precisely due to this collateral evidence offered by James 5.12 that Gundry views the first two oath formulas as authentic sayings of Jesus.[34] Hence, by the invocation of the criterion of multiple attestation, the first two oath formulas can be claimed to be authentic.[35]

What about the third oath formula, 'by Jerusalem'? James 5.12 has μήτε ἄλλον τινὰ ὅρκον and it would seem to imply that James was aware of more oath formulas in the tradition which he received.[36] However, μήτε ἄλλον τινὰ ὅρκον could be James' own comment in that he intends to show the absolute nature of the command. Whether this is so remains to be seen. We must now, however, deal with some objections offered by Strecker and Duling against the authenticity of μήτε εἰς Ἱεροσόλυμα.

Strecker's main argument is that the Greek form, Ἱεροσόλυμα, is used instead of the Semitic, Ἱερουσαλήμ.[37] However, the complexity of the evangelists' use of the Greek and Semitic forms of Jerusalem should serve as a caution against the acceptance of this argument.[38] This being so, no firm conclusions should be drawn from it.[39] Moreover, why should the use of the Greek form of Jerusalem lead to the notion that the oath formula was inauthentic? If Jesus spoke Aramaic originally and his sayings were translated

---

[33] But note that nothing much can be claimed from the fact of identical order as it can be argued that οὐρανός and γῆ are expected to form a pair with οὐρανός preceding.

[34] R. H. Gundry, *Matthew: A Commentary on his Literary and Theological Art*, p. 92.

[35] We are here dealing with the authenticity of the oath formulas, leaving out of discussion the ὅτι clauses till later.

[36] Ito, 'Law', p. 113. Cf. the counter assertion of Gundry (*Matthew*, p. 92). Gundry suggests that the form of James may be earlier and original.

[37] G. Strecker, 'Die Antithesen der Bergpredigt (Mt 5.21–48 par.)', *ZNW* 69 (1978), 61. It must be said that Strecker does not deny that the third oath formula is derived from tradition although he insists that it is secondary (60). Luz offers a similar argument (*Matthew 1–7*, p. 312 n. 6).

[38] See J. K. Elliot, 'Jerusalem in Acts and the Gospels', *NTS* 23 (1977), 462–9; D. D. Sylva, 'Ierousalem and Hierosoluma in Luke–Acts', *ZNW* 74 (1983), 207–21 and L. Hartman, 'Ἱεροσόλυμα, Ἱερουσαλήμ', in H. Balz and G. Schneider (eds.), *Exegetical Dictionary of the New Testament* II, p. 177.

[39] Ito, 'Law', p. 114.

into Greek, it does not entail that the Semitic form of Jerusalem must be used during the process of translation.

Recently, Duling has argued that the third oath formula and the ὅτι clause which accompanies it are separate from the first two formulas. He bases his thesis on two main arguments. First, the Jewish parallels containing rejection of oaths show that the oath formulas found in the fourth antithesis are not conjoined but independent of each other. Secondly, the first two oath formulas use the preposition ἐν while the oath formula which refers to Jerusalem uses εἰς. From a form-critical perspective, the third oath formula should be considered as originally separate from the first two.[40]

Duling's first argument is weak in that we have here a summary treatment of oaths and therefore a citation of oaths one after another should not be surprising. Besides, the fact that they are conjoined in the text is evidence that someone has done so. Why should not the historical Jesus have done it?

Duling's second argument, which makes reference to the preposition in the oath formula, is unconvincing. Two possible alternative explanations may be given as to why εἰς is used here instead of ἐν. The first explanation is that it is simply a matter of style: εἰς can be considered as equivalent to ἐν.[41] The second is that the use of εἰς ('towards') may reflect the rabbinic distinction between swearing 'towards Jerusalem' and swearing 'by Jerusalem'.[42]

In contrast to Duling's and Strecker's sceptical attitude towards the third oath formula, the following considerations should be noted. If Jesus knew he was making a radical statement and if he intended to make himself intelligible to his contemporaries, then, in the light of the frequent use of Jerusalem in oath formulas,[43] the likelihood of Jesus referring to these oath formulas is conceivable.

Secondly, and this is often not noticed by scholars, if Matthew

---

[40] Duling, 'Jerusalem', 295–6.   [41] *BAGD*, pp. 230, 566.

[42] So Guelich, *Sermon*, p. 215. The relevant rabbinic texts are *m.Ned.* 1.3 and *t.Ned.* 1.3.

[43] The fact that the rabbis had to deal with the abuse of substitute oaths may indicate their pervasiveness especially when a whole tractate, *m.Seb.* was devoted to this issue (see also *m.Ned.* 1.3 and *t.Ned.* 1.3). Admittedly, the references are late but these points have to be borne in mind: (i) they could very well contain early traditions especially when it is noted that Jerusalem is being referred to (so Duling, 'Jerusalem', 295); (ii) such practices did not spring up overnight; (iii) Matthew may serve as evidence for the early nature of such practices to circumvent the name of God in oaths; and (iv) Philo deals with the issue too (see n. 32).

was written after the destruction of Jerusalem, the use of Jerusalem as an oath formula would have become a non-issue.[44] It is hard to posit a *Sitz im Leben* for this saying in the Matthean community. It seems improbable that Matthew would have to deal with people who swore using Jerusalem especially when it had recently been sacked. The only plausible answer as to why Matthew included it here is that he found it in the tradition. Stanton observes that Matthew usually follows his sources closely[45] and this would explain why Matthew included this oath formula, even though its applicability has been overtaken by events. But if Matthew could edit his source, Mark, and excise certain irrelevant features, why did he not do the same with the passage under consideration? We suggest that it is because the third formula is integral to the whole unit (in a profound way) and hence Matthew did not excise it even when it had, strictly speaking, become irrelevant.

What has just been set out forms a cumulative case. It starts with the observation that James might have known the third oath formula when he wrote μήτε ἄλλον τινὰ ὅρκον. It then proceeds to show that it is plausible that Jesus would have dealt with the common Jewish oath formulas of his day which made reference to Jerusalem, given the fact that, according to the rabbinic literature, they were pervasive. Following this, it was emphasised that if we accept the usual dating of the gospel of Matthew, the fact that Matthew included something which had become a non-issue in his day points to its authenticity. And if it is also borne in mind that Matthew 5.34b–5 probably form a pre-Matthean unity, our case is further strengthened.

The authenticity of the ὅτι clauses

We hope to have shown that the case for the authenticity of the oath formulas found in vv. 34b–5[46] can stand up to critical scrutiny. But are the ὅτι clauses which purportedly give Jesus' reasons for the rejection of such oath formulas authentic? To our knowledge, there is hardly a modern NT scholar who would defend their

---

[44] Minear mentions this point in his article, 'Yes and No', 6.

[45] G. N. Stanton, 'Matthew', in D. A. Carson and H. G. M. Williamson (eds.), *It is Written: Scripture Citing Scripture*, p. 213.

[46] It should be stated here that it is not our intention to defend the authenticity of v. 36 (containing the fourth oath formula) in this chapter as it is irrelevant to our present purposes.

authenticity.[47] Even so conservative a thesis as Ito's concludes that they were actually clarifying clauses from Matthew's hand.[48] What then are the reasons for such a pessimistic outlook?

One argument commonly used for the rejection of their authenticity is that James 5.12 does not attest to the presence of the ὅτι clauses.[49] Luz rejects them as secondary on this basis.[50] But this is an argument from silence and it is precarious to establish an entire case on it. Moreover, it is unreasonable to expect the NT writers to cite the materials they have *in toto*. So this argument is usually supported by others in order to clinch the case. The following have been argued.

(i) Matthew cites OT passages frequently and hence there is a presumption that the OT citations or allusions found in vv. 34b–5 are due to his hand.[51]

(ii) The idea of heaven as the throne of God (v. 34b) recurs in Matthew 23.22 and hence may be a Matthean motif.[52]

(iii) Verses 34b–5 are superfluous in the light of the absolute prohibition of v. 34a.[53]

(iv) Similar to (iii), it has been argued that the reason for enumerating these formulas was probably self-explanatory to Jesus' contemporaries[54] and hence Jesus would not have given such explanations.

(v) Luz makes the point that in wisdom admonitions there are normally no OT quotations.[55]

Argument (v) of Luz can easily be set aside. First and foremost, apart from the dubious category introduced to describe these logia,

[47] Cf. D. C. Duling, 'Against Oaths', *Forum* 6,2 (1990), 131 who surveys five prominent scholars and finds them all in agreement that these clauses are inauthentic. But S. Westerholm serves perhaps as an exception. See his book *Jesus and Scribal Authority*, p. 112 where he demonstrates the plausibility of their being authentic.

[48] Ito, 'Law', pp. 115, 117–18.

[49] Mention has also been made of the absence of these clauses from Justin Martyr's *Apologia* (I, 16, 5–7). See for example, Minear, 'Yes and No', 1. Although Minear rejects Sanders' explanation for the form in Justin (E. P. Sanders, *The Tendencies of the Synoptic Tradition*, pp. 57, 67) as quite unconvincing, it must be said that, none the less, Sanders' view that Justin gives the principles but not the particulars is a viable explanation of the phenomenon. What we wish to emphasise here is that the silence of Justin Martyr over these verses is not a decisive argument against authenticity.

[50] Luz, *Matthew 1–7*, p. 312. Cf. also Ito, 'Law', p. 117.

[51] Ito, 'Law', p. 117.   [52] Ito, 'Law', p. 117.

[53] Davies and Allison, *Matthew* I, p. 533. This problem has been discussed earlier.

[54] Ito, 'Law', pp. 117–18.   [55] Luz, *Matthew 1–7*, p. 312.

Luz's argument assumes a priori that wisdom admonitions 'normally' do not have OT quotations. Having set up this rule, any wisdom admonitions with OT quotations are then judged as 'normally' inauthentic. This is indeed arbitrary. Moreover, such an arbitrary categorisation ignores the frequent argumentative use of scripture in the NT corpus and writings of second-temple Judaism[56] to clinch a case or establish a halakhic point (cf. Matt. 9.13; 19.5; Mark 12.18–27). Furthermore, in Pauline admonitions scriptures are cited (e.g., 1 Cor. 5.13; 2 Cor. 6.1–2, 14–18).[57] It should also be noted that, for his argument to stand, it must be presupposed that everyone in antiquity followed this dubious rule, and that there was a special category of 'wisdom admonitions' in contrast to admonitions in general.

Arguments (i) and (ii) are similar in that they try to show that vv. 34b–5 are a product of Matthean redaction. It is true that Matthew frequently cites the OT, more than the other three gospels.[58] Here two methodological points must be emphasised. First, to insist that all OT quotations (apart from the fulfilment formulas) in Matthew's gospel stem from his hand is unreasonable. In the other gospels, Jesus is presented as citing OT texts. Hence, the presumption that Matthew's sources could not have OT quotations is questionable. Secondly, there are strong grounds to suppose that Jesus himself would have quoted scripture (cf. the pericope on divorce, Mark 10.5–15 and parallels).[59] Hence, although it may be a Matthean tendency to quote the OT, it is not his exclusive practice. Therefore, other factors must be considered in addition to this in order to suppose that the quotation is from Matthew. Such methodological observations would undermine argument (i).

Ito, who supports argument (ii), gives room for the possibility that such a reference was already found in the tradition.[60] As Matthew is more interested in the scribes than are the writers of the

---

[56] See A. Chester, 'Citing the Old Testament', in D. A. Carson and H. G. M. Williamson (eds.), *It is Written: Scripture Citing Scripture*, pp. 141–69 and also J. A. Fitzmyer, 'The Use of Explicit Old Testament Quotations in Qumran Literature and in the New Testament', *NTS* 7 (1960–1), 297–333 where examples of admonitions were supported by OT quotations (CD 10.16–17 = Deut. 5.12; CD 9.2 = Lev. 19.18; CD 16.6–7 = Deut. 23.24).

[57] On this see the recent work of B. S. Rosner, *Paul, Scripture and Ethics: A Study of 1 Corinthians 5–7*.

[58] See Stanton's discussion in 'Matthew', pp. 205–17.

[59] See especially the solid work of R. T. France, *Jesus and the Old Testament*.

[60] Ito, 'Law', p. 117.

other gospels,[61] he would be expected to be interested in such
casuistry normally indulged by scribes. This argument assumes that
a motif occurring in Matthew would imply that it was created by
the evangelist. This is possible but not necessary. We shall return to
this argument later.

Argument (iii) is misconceived and argument (iv) is a classic
example of prejudgment. Verses 34b–5 are not superfluous, as has
been shown earlier. In fact, we hope to show later that these verses
lead us into the heart of the reason as to why Jesus forbade
swearing. Nor can a scientific enquiry base itself on arguments such
as (iv). In language and communication, speakers often do mention
the things which they expect the audience to know. Moreover, if
Jesus is presenting something radical and is also at the same time
criticising the casuistry of scribal practices of swearing, it would be
expected of him to give reasons for so doing. In fact, the real issue
in the fourth antithesis has often been missed by commentators
because of an undue concentration on the apparently absolute
prohibition, with the result that a coherent explanation of Jesus'
purpose in the fourth antithesis is missed. By undue concentration
on v. 34a and v. 37a and a rejection of vv. 34b–5, Jesus has been
made out to be a rather unreasonable teacher.

Hence, most of the objections are weak, excepting perhaps (ii).
Against these objections we propose to set forth the case for
authenticity below, and in so doing to give an account of what the
real issue in the fourth antithesis is. We hope to show that the
underlying assumptions of the ὅτι clauses form a profound coherence with the main emphases in the teachings of Jesus.[62]

If our earlier arguments for the authenticity of the oath formulas
are correct, there is a prima facie case for concluding that Jesus
would have proceeded to explain the reasons for his prohibition of
such formulas. This appears even more plausible when one bears in
mind that these formulas are likely to have been prevalent at the

---

[61] For an exposition of the Matthean interest in scribes, see D. E. Orton, *The
Understanding Scribe*.

[62] Our method here would hence be quite akin to what J. A. Baird called the
principle of 'internal continuity' (in his *The Justice of God in the Teaching of
Jesus*, pp. 30–2). Baird makes the point that denying the implication of
authenticity from such consistency 'demands either a theory of apostolic agreement and deliberate concurrence beyond belief or a theory of verbal inspiration
that outdoes the literalists. The law of parsimony would seem to demand a
simpler answer: behind this unity stands Jesus of Nazareth, whose authentic
mind has come through the exigencies of Gospel formation reasonably intact'
(pp. 30–1).

time of Jesus. Hence, if Jesus meant to attack the whole system of oath-taking, there is a high probability that he would have dealt with these formulas and offered reasons for their rejection. Such a picture of Jesus is more credible and believable than the one which regards Jesus as forbidding oaths without explaining why.

The ὅτι clauses are essential to the true understanding of the whole issue: Jesus criticised the casuistry of the scribal practice of using circumventing oath formulas because ultimately they made reference back to God and impinged on his prerogatives. The oaths in question were conceived out of a pious intention to avoid profaning the name of God.[63] Although the rabbis are more concerned about the question of the validity of these oaths, Jesus' concern was something else altogether. His whole notion is that, good as these substitute oaths are in terms of intention, they none the less cannot be dissociated from God. Hence, there are thus no 'greater' or 'lesser' oaths. Every oath is an oath made before God.[64] Jesus is thus emphasising that such circumventing is not successful. If this interpretation is correct, a coherent trend of thought emerges from vv. 34–7.[65] The strong emphasis of μὴ ὀμόσαι ὅλως is meant to show that although the substitute formulas are probably conceived to avoid profaning God's name, they do, however, encroach on the name of God. And how this could come about is explained by the ὅτι clauses. Verse 37 would then be Jesus' strong recommendation or command which tacitly suggests that all oaths impinge on the sovereignty of God.

There is perhaps an important assumption behind the prohibition. And that is, because God's kingdom has drawn near, the time has now come to stop impinging on God's sovereignty: true speech without recourse to oaths should be enforced.[66] This heightened awareness of the presence of God in mundane affairs is a characteristic of Jesus' ministry: the kingdom has drawn near.[67] This bringing to bear of the nearness and reality of God to earthly

---

[63]   Davies and Allison observe that 'the unstated assumption behind Matt. 5.34b-6 is the Jewish conviction that God's name itself could not be named and that therefore, when one takes an oath, a substitute for God's name must be employed' in *Matthew* I, p. 536.

[64]   So Westerholm, *Jesus*, p. 111.

[65]   Davies and Allison write that the subtraction of v. 33b and vv. 34b–6 leaves a perfectly coherent piece (*Matthew* I, p. 533). We query the word 'coherent'. We suggest instead that if such substraction is to be done, what is left is not so much a coherent piece as a truncated and unbelievably naïve piece!

[66]   Cf. Strecker, *Sermon*, p. 79.

[67]   J. Jeremias, *New Testament Theology I: The Proclamation of Jesus*, pp. 96–7. See

matters is, we submit, an important presupposition behind the forbidding of oaths and the cause of the ὅτι clauses. If the truncated account as proposed by Davies and Allison[68] were accepted, Jesus would then be seen as offering no reason for such a prohibition.

In Matthew 23.16–22 a similar emphasis is seen. This passage represents an attack by Jesus on the casuistry of swearing by highlighting the anomaly introduced as a result of the casuistry of the scribes. A coherence of thought between it and Matthew 5.32–7 obtains. Jesus rejected the distinction drawn up by the scribes in the matter of oath-taking. There can be no circumventing God and, therefore, the disciples' speech must be 'Yes, yes' and 'No, no'. Such an emphasis, which went beyond the 'letter' and reaches into the 'inward',[69] is in harmony with the rest of the antitheses,[70] indeed with a large part of Jesus' attested teaching.[71]

In the words of Westerholm:

> It was thus not his intention to supply a set of rules which cover all situations, the careful observance of which might guarantee that a man does what is right before God; in fact, the observance of any set of rules may serve to blind its adherents to the fact that all is not as it should be, that God demands more. A heart submissive to the rule of God, a heart which draws back in horror from every infringement of the divine sovereignty and every suggestion of deceit, is alone capable of pleasing God. It is a heart of this kind, not the fulfilment of a new statute, which Jesus here required.[72]

In addition to all the considerations above, it should also be noted that the reason given for the prohibition of using the name Jerusalem is unlike the tenor of Matthew's gospel, which emanated from a community that had had some heated debates with the

also R. Schnackenburg, *God's Rule and Kingdom*; and G. R. Beasley-Murray, *Jesus and the Kingdom of God*.

[68] Davies and Allison, *Matthew* I, p. 533.
[69] Cf. Minear's study, 'Yes and No', 1–13.
[70] Especially the first, second and third antitheses.
[71] E.g., Jesus' teaching on the food laws (Mark 7.14–15). On this see J. D. G. Dunn, 'Jesus and Ritual Purity: A Study of the Tradition History in Mark 7,15', in F. Refoulé (ed.), *A cause de l'évangile: mélanges offerts a Dom Jacques Dupont*, pp. 251–76; R. P. Booth, *Jesus and the Laws of Purity: Tradition History and Legal History in Mark 7*.
[72] Westerholm, *Jesus*, p. 113.

synagogue.[73] Moreover, it is difficult to find a *Sitz im Leben* for the creation of such a clause, as the gospel of Matthew was written after the disastrous events of 70 CE.

Finally, we shall demonstrate the unity of the verses and show how they converge with an important aspect of Jesus' teachings. The connection of the three ὅτι clauses with the *kingship* of God often goes unnoticed. The first two ὅτι clauses, which are quoted from Isaiah 66.1, signify the *extent* of the realm in which the absolute kingship of God is exercised.[74] But the *locus* of God's reign on earth is none other than Jerusalem,[75] which is mentioned in the third ὅτι clause in a quotation taken from Psalm 47.3 (LXX).[76] In other words, the prevailing concept found in the three ὅτι clauses is that God is king. Such an observation enhances the authenticity of the three clauses when we bear in mind the characteristic message of Jesus' preaching: the kingdom of God. It is precisely the presence (or proximity) of the kingdom of God which necessitates that oath formulas are to be prohibited. There is thus a profound convergence of the thought of the three ὅτι clauses with the characteristic message of Jesus. Such a convergence of themes and underlying presuppositions is implicit and not explicit and therefore further provides a powerful indication of authenticity.

We shall now summarise our arguments regarding the authenticity of the ὅτι clauses. It is reasonable to believe that Jesus would have given some explanations in the light of his radical statement and the prevalent use of oath formulas in his day. Matthew probably did not tag Psalm 47.3 (LXX) to the oath formula involving the use of Jerusalem. The emphases of vv. 34b–5 are in profound harmony with Jesus' characteristic message (the criterion of coherence). We submit that the case for the authenticity of vv. 34b–5 is strong and this should override objection (ii) mentioned earlier. And if one bears in mind also that the other objections to their authenticity are tenuous, there are grounds for concluding that vv. 34b–5 are authentic.[77]

---

[73] See the survey of scholarship on this particular matter in G. N. Stanton, 'The Origin and Purpose of Matthew's Gospel: Matthean Scholarship from 1945 to 1980', *ANRW* 25.3, pp. 1911–16.

[74] Cf. J. C. de Young, *Jerusalem in the New Testament*, p. 31.

[75] See our previous discussions in chapter 2.

[76] On the text form of this quotation, see R. H. Gundry, *The Use of the Old Testament in St Matthew's Gospel*, p. 134.

[77] Duling has recently argued that Matt. 5.35 arose in the reign of king Agrippa I

3 Jesus and Jerusalem in the light of Matthew 5.34b–5

If what we have argued for in the foregoing pages is correct, this passage offers a further datum on Jesus' attitude towards Jerusalem. This datum is important in five respects.

First, this passage stems from 'M'. Since chapter 3 deals with an 'L' passage (Luke 13.31–3) and demonstrates that Jerusalem figures prominently there, it is of interest to note that further information for reconstructing Jesus' attitude towards Jerusalem is found in another strand of tradition. Hence, it is not just a Lukan concern to show the relationship between Jesus and Jerusalem.[78] Moreover, this attestation from multiple sources would help to establish our study on a firmer basis.

Second, in the light of the negative view of Jerusalem in Luke 13.31–3, this passage offers a counterbalance and explains why Jerusalem looms so large in Jesus' ministry. From Matthew 5.35 it can be gathered that Jerusalem was regarded by Jesus as sacred and that its status as the city of God made any swearing which referred to it sacrilegious. This would imply that Jesus sought to go to Jerusalem not just because it was a wicked city but because it had also an intrinsic importance which was not obliterated by its wicked deeds. It seems therefore incontrovertible to state that Jerusalem was important to the historical Jesus. Moreover, it should be noted that Jesus was a Jew and that years of tradition would instil in any Jew the importance and significance of Jerusalem in the plans and purposes of Yahweh. It is tempting to seek a developmental hypothesis to account for these seemingly contradictory stances. But this is precarious as we do not know which passage is chronologically prior (the establishment of which is important in any developmental hypothesis). Hence we cannot

who arrogated to himself the title 'the Great King' ('Jerusalem', 307–9). The logion was formulated as an ironical remark against him. Hence, Ps. 47.3 (LXX) is not the intended background to the third ὅτι clause. Three points in reply are in order. First, Duling's case is based on the premise that v. 35 was originally separate from v. 34b. If this premise is not accepted, the parallels he cites are irrelevant. Secondly, Ps. 47.3 (LXX) is ready to hand as the background of Matt. 5.35 in view of the fact that Jerusalem is the city mentioned in it. Thirdly, the ὅτι clauses in v. 34b refer to God's throne and footstool and this strengthens the presumption that the 'great king' in v. 35 refers also to God.

[78] The importance of Jerusalem to Luke has been studied by many scholars as evident in the following works: H. Conzelmann, *The Theology of St Luke*; C. H. Giblin, *The Destruction of Jerusalem According to Luke's Gospel: A Historical–Typological Moral*; J. T. Sanders, *The Jews in Luke–Acts*.

reconstruct any development in Jesus' attitude. Perhaps such a search is unnecessary as such contradictory stances may be more of the nature of a dialectical tension than true contradiction. Jesus could not distance himself from the conception of Jerusalem as religiously significant, nor could he escape from his belief that the Jerusalem of his day was not the city of peace but the city which killed prophets. This dialectical tension is seen in a clearer light in the next chapter.

Third, the emphasis that Jerusalem is the city of God recalls a very important aspect of the Zion traditions. God is acknowledged by Jews to be king of heaven and earth but it is especially in Jerusalem that God is to be enthroned as king. Jerusalem is the chosen city where God is pleased to dwell and exercise his kingship. This nexus of ideas is fundamentally related to the Zion traditions. From the context of the psalm (Ps. 47 LXX), the great king would be none other than Yahweh and not a Davidic king. It is also to be observed that the following context in the psalm speaks of Zion as 'the joy of the whole earth' (v. 3) and of the defeat of the kings of the nations (vv. 5–7). Whether such a nexus of meaning was in Jesus' mind cannot be deduced from Matthew 5.35 alone for it is tantalisingly brief. But if we were to juxtapose this verse with the *actions* of Jesus in Jerusalem during the final phase of his ministry, some significant results may arise. We shall do this in Part III. Suffice it to state here that Jerusalem is important and looms large in Jesus' ministry because, as explained by the third ὅτι clause, it is the city of the great king. One therefore must not swear by Jerusalem.[79] In this short explanatory clause a whole nexus of images has been conjured up.

Fourth, if Jesus' message is that the kingdom of God is near, and if the kingdom of God is understood in the abstract sense as 'reign', surely Matthew 5.35 implies that this reign of God must be established in Jerusalem since it is the city of the great king. It therefore seems probable that Jesus views Jerusalem as the place of the climax of his ministry whereby the confrontation between the kingship of God and Jerusalem is enacted. Once again, we find evidence for believing that Jerusalem exercised a pull on Jesus. As an important aspect of Jesus' message concerns the kingdom of

[79] It should be noted that in Ps. 47.3 (LXX) it is Zion that is the city of the great king. The change to Jerusalem may be due to the reason that the name Jerusalem is used in the oath formulas instead of Zion (Zion being a more evocative and spiritual symbol).

God, it is perfectly congruent that Jesus should seek to bring to a climax his ministry in Jerusalem. In other words, the status of Jerusalem as the city of the great king and the fundamental nature of Jesus' message would inexorably lead to a collision between the two. Matthew 5.35 thus allows us to affirm that the Zion traditions probably had a great impact on Jesus and his own conception of his ministry. The observations set out in this chapter explain why Jerusalem was to Jesus a magnet. This was intimated already in chapter 3, and we find here a significant convergence of it with Matthew 5.35. In chapter 5 we hope to confirm this further and to demonstrate that one very important aim of Jesus' ministry is most probably shaped by the Zion traditions.

Finally, it should be stressed that this chapter confirms that, for Jesus, religious or theological considerations take precedence over the sociological, political or other factors. This is not to deny that these considerations were also important to Jesus. But it is this concept that God is king in Jerusalem, and that therefore it is sacred, which becomes the fundamental and organising factor for these other aspects. This will have an important bearing on our study later.

5

'TO GATHER JERUSALEM' (Q 13.34–5)

The lament over Jerusalem found in the gospels both of Matthew (Matt. 23.37–9) and Luke (Luke 13.34–5), albeit in different contexts, offers valuable data for our study. The logia in both gospels exhibit considerable verbatim agreement[1] and, thus, the original source of Matthew and Luke can be recovered easily.

Although the potential of this passage for our present purposes is great, there are, however, certain difficulties. For instance, when and where did Jesus utter this lament, if he did utter it at all? As mentioned earlier, Matthew and Luke put it in different contexts. Whose context is historical or are both unhistorical? There are questions concerning the origin of these logia. Are they from Jesus,[2] Wisdom[3] or a Christian prophet speaking in the name of the risen Jesus?[4] Apart from these problems, there are a host of others connected with their interpretation. Clearly, it is not an overstatement to say that these logia bristle with difficulty at every level. But as they are a potential source of valuable data for our research, we cannot afford to ignore them. We propose to start our investigation by recovering the original text (Q). This will be followed by an assessment of their authenticity. Following this, we will look

---

[1] Interestingly, Matthew uses the Semitic Ἰερουσαλήμ only once and in this passage! He is fond of Ἰεροσόλυμα instead.
[2] W. G. Kümmel, *Promise and Fulfilment*, pp. 79–82; D. Hoffmann, *Studien zur Theologie der Logienquelle*, pp. 173–4; I. H. Marshall, *The Gospel of Luke*, p. 574; J. A. Fitzmyer, *The Gospel According to Luke X–XXIV*, p. 1035; D. Catchpole, *The Quest for Q*, p. 278.
[3] R. Bultmann, *History of the Synoptic Tradition*, pp. 114–15; O. H. Steck, *Israel und das gewaltsame Geschick der Propheten*, pp. 230–1; M. J. Suggs, *Wisdom, Christology and Law in Matthew's Gospel*, pp. 63–71; F. Christ, *Jesus Sophia*, pp. 136–52; G. Schneider, *Evangelium nach Lukas*, p. 310.
[4] This is the thesis of M. E. Boring, *The Sayings of the Risen Jesus*, pp. 171–3 and R. J. Miller, 'The Rejection of the Prophets in Q', *JBL* 107 (1988), 225–40. Cf. S. Schulz, *Q – Die Spruchquelle der Evangelisten*, pp. 346–60.

into their interpretation and their significance for our present
enquiry.

1   Isolating the Q text

The verbatim agreement between Luke 13.34–5 and Matthew
23.37–9 is remarkable. T. W. Manson notes that the degree of
agreement reaches a high 90 per cent.[5] As a result, the task of
recovering the Q text behind them is made appreciably easier. But
first, we shall tackle the textual problems found in both passages.

The text of Matthew

Apart from a few minor variants, the Matthean text is well
preserved. Here, only one significant variant reading need be
addressed. Some important manuscripts (B L) do not have ἔρημος
(Matt. 23.38). It can be argued then that ἔρημος was added in
conformity to Jeremiah 22.5. But this argument is offset by the fact
that ἔρημος is attested by a large number of early manuscripts
($\mathfrak{P}^{77vid}$ ℵ C D et al.) which give also a good geographical spread. It
is also to be noted that the LXX of Jeremiah 22.5 has εἰς ἐρήμωσιν
ἔσται ὁ ὁῖκος οὗτος which may not be a sufficient cause of the
alleged addition of ἔρημος. Moreover, it is better to regard ἔρημος
as being deleted in some manuscripts to avoid superfluity caused by
the presence of ἀφίεται.[6] As Garland observes, the sentence ἰδοὺ
ἀφίεται ὑμῖν ὁῖκος ὑμῶν ἔρημος does not make good Greek.[7]
Hence, it is concluded here that the original text of Matthew
23.37–9 is the same as the text given by NA[26].

The text of Luke

The Lukan text contains more significant textual variants than its
parallel in Matthew. ἔρημος (Luke 13.35), attested by D N Δ θ ψ
et al., is best regarded as an assimilation to the Matthean text.[8]
Note the preponderant weight of manuscript evidence against this
reading: $\mathfrak{P}^{75}$ ℵ A B K L R W Γ et al. The case of δέ (v. 35; NA[26]

---

[5]   T. W. Manson, *The Sayings of Jesus*, p. 102.
[6]   So B. M. Metzger on behalf of the Committee which is responsible for the
'Standard Text' in *A Textual Commentary on the New Testament*, p. 61.
[7]   D. E. Garland, *The Intention of Matthew 23*, p. 200 n. 120.
[8]   So also J. Nolland, *Luke 9:21–18:34*, p. 738.

encloses it in single brackets) is not as straightforward. The evidence for both its omission ($\mathfrak{P}^{45}$ ℵ* L) and inclusion ($\mathfrak{P}^{75}$ ℵ² A B *et al.*) is early and strong. It may have been added to avoid asyndeton or it could have been omitted because the clause following does not really contrast well with what precedes.[9] A decision on this matter is not crucial to our present enquiry, but we propose to follow the reading of NA²⁶.

Of more importance are the textual variants of ἕως ἥξει ὅτε εἴπητε. The case for the omission of ἥξει ὅτε is strong ($\mathfrak{P}^{75}$ B L *et al.*) and it is this factor which led to their bracketing (in single brackets) in NA²⁶. But it seems best to regard these words as original to the Lukan text for the following reasons: many manuscripts attest to their presence although some have an additional ἄν preceding them (A W 𝔐);[10] and the rarity of construing ὅτε with the subjunctive may have prompted scribes to drop it altogether with ἥξει.[11] Once again, our conclusions support the text of NA²⁶.

The text of Q

We propose that the Q text used by both Matthew and Luke is:

34. Ἰερουσαλὴμ Ἰερουσαλήμ,
    ἡ ἀποκτείνουσα τοὺς προφήτας καὶ λιθοβολοῦσα τοὺς
    ἀπεσταλμένους πρὸς αὐτήν,
    ποσάκις ἠθέλησα ἐπισυνάξαι τὰ τέκνα σου ὃν τρόπον
    ὄρνις
    ἐπισυνάγει τὰ νοσσιὰ αὐτῆς ὑπὸ τὰς πτέρυγας, καὶ οὐκ
    ἠθελήσατε.
35. ἰδοὺ ἀφίεται ὑμῖν ὁ οἶκος ὑμῶν.
    λέγω [δὲ/γὰρ] ὑμῖν,
    οὐ μὴ ἴδητέ με ἕως ἥξει ὅτε εἴπητε
    εὐλογημένος ὁ ἐρχόμενος ἐν ὀνόματι κυρίου.

The basis for our proposal is as follows.
    (i) ἐπισυνάξαι (Luke 13.34) is probably from Q as it is rarer than ἐπισυναγαγεῖν, the more usual second aorist infinitive.[12] Weinert observes that Luke usually uses the first

---

[9] Marshall, *Gospel*, p. 576.
[10] ἄν is probably to be regarded as an assimilation to the Matthean text.
[11] Metzger, *Commentary*, p. 163.   [12] Marshall, *Gospel*, p. 575.

aorist ἐπισυνάξαι with the passive and not the active (as found here) in line with Septuagintal usage.[13]

(ii) ἐπισυνάγει (Matt. 23.37) should probably be attributed to Q as the omission in Luke agrees with his general tendency to avoid excessive repetition.[14]

(iii) Matthew's τὰ νοσσία αὐτῆς should probably be attributed to Q as Luke provides sixteen of the twenty-two clear examples of the reflexive pronoun (ἑαυτῆς, v. 34) used with a noun in the Synoptic gospels.[15] However, it is difficult to decide between Matthew's τὰ νοσσία (plural) and Luke's τὴν νοσσιάν (singular) but, if our earlier observation is correct, it seems best to suppose that Luke has made the alteration here as well, probably in order to stress 'the flavour of personal intimacy in Jesus' metaphor'.[16]

(iv) Matthew's ἔρημος (v. 38) is probably not from Q. As Weinert observes: 'since Luke tends to keep or to add eremos, its absence in 13.35 suggests the influence of his source ...'[17] ἔρημος appears in Luke–Acts nineteen times out of a total of forty-seven attested in the NT.

(v) It is difficult to decide between Matthew's γάρ and Luke's δέ. Perhaps there was no connective in Q.[18]

(vi) The order of the two words, ἴδητε and μή, is different in the two gospels. A decision on this matter does not affect very much the sense of the text of Q. But, as μή occurring after the verb corresponds to the position of the Semitic pronominal verbal suffix, the Lukan ἴδητε μή is probably from Q.[19]

(vii) It is generally agreed that ἀπ' ἄρτι is Matthew's attempt to underscore the futurity of the event described.[20] Moreover, as Fitzmyer observes, Matthew is fond of ἀπ' ἄρτι.[21]

(viii) Luke's ἕως ἥξει ὅτε εἴπητε is to be regarded as stemming from his source as it is rare that ὅτε is followed by a subjunctive, as was noted earlier. It is thus unlikely that

---

[13] F. D. Weinert, 'Jesus' Saying About Jerusalem's Abandoned House', *CBQ* 44 (1982), 72.

[14] Weinert, 'Abandoned House', 72.   [15] Ibid.   [16] Ibid.

[17] 'Abandoned House', 73.

[18] But see C. M. Tuckett, *The Revival of the Griesbach Hypothesis*, pp. 163–4, where he writes that γάρ is from the redactional hand of Matthew and δέ is from Q.

[19] Weinert, 'Abandoned House', 74.

[20] G. R. Beasley-Murray, *Jesus and the Kingdom of God*, p. 408 n. 366.

[21] Fitzmyer, *Luke X–XXIV*, p. 1037.

such rare syntax came about through Luke's contribution. It is more probable that Matthew has simplified it to ἕως ἄν εἴπητε.[22]

The integrity of Q 13.34–5

There seem to be no valid grounds for objecting to the integrity of the passage as it stands in Q. The usual argument against its integrity is that Q 13.34–5a and Q 13.35b are originally separate sayings which were brought together at a later stage of transmission. In Haenchen's judgment, Q 13.35b is a Christian addition.[23] There is, however, no necessity for such a view. As Bayer observes, the argument of the later addition of Luke 13.35b loses its force when the integral literary structure of Luke 13.34–5 is adequately appreciated.[24] Miller writes that v. 35b serves as the interpretative conclusion to the larger saying.[25] It is therefore concluded that Q 13.34–5 forms an integral unit.

2   The authenticity of Q 13.34–5

The authenticity of Q 13.34–5 has often been dismissed but we believe that there are good grounds for accepting these sayings as words of Jesus. We shall set these out after interacting with the common objections to their authenticity. O. H. Steck has formulated the case for the rejection of the authenticity of this logion, and his view still commands the assent of many scholars today. He offers three main arguments.

(i) The words ποσάκις ἠθέλησα ἐπισυνάξαι envisage a broad understanding of time, reaching beyond the historical Jesus.[26] Bultmann actually intimates such an objection when he emphasised that 'the one making this statement must be a supra-historical entity'.[27] This form of argumentation is followed in the main by Suggs[28] and Boring.[29]

---

[22] So also Marshall, *Gospel*, p. 577.
[23] E. Haenchen, 'Matthäus 23', *ZTK* 48 (1951), 57. So also J. S. Kloppenborg, *The Formation of Q*, p. 228.
[24] H. F. Bayer, *Jesus' Predictions of Vindication and Resurrection*, p. 48; cf. Schulz, *Q*, p. 348.
[25] Miller, 'Rejection', 234.   [26] Steck, *Israel*, pp. 53–4.
[27] Bultmann, *History*, p. 114. Actually, Bultmann is open to the idea that Jesus may have quoted this logion which was originally a Jewish prophecy.
[28] Suggs, *Wisdom*, p. 66.   [29] Boring, *Sayings*, p. 171.

(ii) Verse 35a refers to the abandonment of Jerusalem by God and this event is not referred to elsewhere in Jesus' message.[30]

(iii) In v. 35b, Jesus speaks about his coming in the first person singular. This appears incredible on the lips of Jesus as he would not have spoken of his own parousia in such a manner.[31]

We shall now deal with Steck's arguments in detail. ποσάκις ἠθέλησα ἐπισυνάξαι need not necessarily envisage a supra-historical entity (although other aspects of the logion may, as will be seen later). This can be seen in a number of ways. John's gospel suggests that Jesus made several trips to Jerusalem. This is highly likely given that Jerusalem is the pilgrimage centre of a Jew. If this was the case, there would have been numerous occasions for Jesus to preach his message to the Jerusalemites.[32] But even this need not necessarily be assumed in order to defend the plausibility that ποσάκις came from the lips of Jesus. Fitzmyer writes that ποσάκις ἠθέλησα ἐπισυνάξαι reveals Jesus' untold desires, expressive of his abiding concern to spread the message of God's kingdom in Jerusalem.[33] From another angle, Dunn has suggested that the saying could simply be an appropriately poignant expression of Jesus' frustration and disappointment at his rejection by the religious authorities centred in Jerusalem.[34] Hence, it can be seen that there are at least three plausible explanations of the phrase ποσάκις ἠθέλησα ἐπισυνάξαι without recourse to seeing a supra-historical entity behind them. It has also been suggested that Sophia is the speaker behind the lament in vv. 34–5a.[35] Such a view argues that the background and the imagery used are sapiential but this is improbable as we shall see later.[36] Problems of interpreting and understanding the phrase ποσάκις ἠθέλησα ἐπισυνάξαι should not be the sole criterion for rejecting the authenticity of the logia in vv. 34–5. Steck's first argument presupposes a particular understanding of the phrase under discussion but there are other equally, or perhaps more, valid options of interpretation as have already been shown.

---

[30] Steck, *Israel*, pp. 54–5.   [31] Steck, *Israel*, p. 55.

[32] Cf. P. Stuhlmacher, 'Die Stellung Jesu und des Paulus zu Jerusalem', *ZTK* 86 (1989), 142, who holds this interpretation.

[33] Fitzmyer, *Luke X–XXIV*, p. 1036.

[34] J. D. G. Dunn, *Christology in the Making*, p. 203.

[35] So Steck, *Israel*, pp. 53–4, 230–2; Schulz, *Q*, p. 349 n. 94; R. A. Piper, *Wisdom in the Q Tradition*, p. 164.

[36] See below, section 3.

The second argument of Steck is hardly convincing. As temple and city are intimately connected in second-temple Judaism,[37] a judgment against the temple would strike at the heart of Jerusalem. There is evidence in the gospels that Jesus did prophesy the destruction of the temple (e.g., Mark 13.2 and parallels; Mark 14.57–8 and parallels[38]). As Catchpole observes, the abandonment of v. 35 is a variation of the Markan theme of the destruction of the temple.[39]

Concerning Steck's third argument, Bayer has observed 'that Jesus could not have spoken about his parousia in the first person singular is above all a postulate *e silentio* and is seriously weakened by the probability that Jesus referred to his parousia at least in the third person singular (Luke 12.8–9)'.[40] Moreover, as Marshall observes, the saying of v. 35b has a cryptic tone and this is consonant with Jesus' claims which are often cryptic in nature.[41] The implied temporary absence of Jesus found in v. 35b is paralleled in Mark 2.20. Furthermore, there are other considerations, which, when taken into account, will serve to ameliorate the difficulty of construing that Jesus spoke of his parousia. This will be discussed later.

Therefore it can be concluded that Steck's arguments against the authenticity of this logion are not decisive. In the course of the discussion, mention has been made of certain characteristics of this logion which point to authenticity: the cryptic nature of v. 35b and the possible prophetic character of the lament.

Since the work of Steck, much interest has been generated concerning the possibility of the creation of Jesus' sayings by early Christian prophets speaking in the name of the risen Jesus and their being mixed with the sayings of the earthly Jesus. This passage has often been attributed to the creative activity of such Christian prophets. Boring's case for regarding Q 13.34–5 as the prophetic speech of the Q prophets rests on this main argument: 'themes associated with, or even peculiar to, the Christian prophets permeate the saying'.[42]

Such a thesis is vitiated by the fact that there is good evidence

---

[37] See our previous discussion in chapter 2.
[38] So E. P. Sanders, *Jesus and Judaism*, pp. 71–5; D. E. Aune, *Prophecy in Early Christianity and the Ancient Mediterranean World*, pp. 173–7.
[39] Catchpole, *Quest*, p. 279.   [40] Bayer, *Predictions*, p. 47.
[41] Marshall, *Gospel*, p. 574. Cf. also Bayer, *Predictions*, p. 47.
[42] Boring, *Sayings*, p. 171.

indicating that the post-Easter community differentiated between the logia of the Jesus tradition and the sayings of the Christian prophets. Dunn argues that, in the light of the fact that the post-Easter community tested prophetic utterances, the incorporation of prophetic 'I' words into the Jesus tradition was by no means a large-scale affair.[43] He also observes that the lack of creation of any 'I' words on the issue of circumcision and food-laws is of great significance,[44] as these two controversies, judging from their prominence in the Pauline letters, were major issues for the post-Easter community. The lack of the creation of such sayings attests to the fact that the post-Easter community differentiated between the words of prophets and the logia of the historical Jesus. Hence, the confusing or fusing of them is highly improbable. Aune, who subjects this view to intense scrutiny, writes that 'the historical evidence in support of the theory lies largely in the imagination of scholars'.[45]

Thus far we have criticised attempts made by some scholars to reject the authenticity of the saying. There are, however, some strong indicators of authenticity found in these logia and to these we now turn.

The first is that the logia envision stoning for the speaker as a possibility.[46] The connective καί in the substantival clause ἡ ἀποκτείνουσα τοὺς προφήτας καὶ λιθοβολοῦσα τοὺς ἀπεσταλ-μένους πρὸς αὐτήν could be taken as an instance of synonymous parallelism, with the result that only one group of people is actually being referred to. If this is the case, then stoning is the means by which the agents of God, the prophets, are killed. Such a conclusion is further supported by two observations. The first is that only one specific type of 'killing' action is described in the logia. ἀποκ-τείνουσα refers to the general while λιθοβολοῦσα is a particular-ising of it. In Israel, the Jewish death penalty is usually meted out by stoning.[47] And if earlier traditions are enshrined in the tractate m.Sanh. 7.4, we could argue that Jesus probably regarded stoning

[43] J. D. G. Dunn, 'Prophetic "I" Sayings and the Jesus Tradition: The Importance of Testing Prophetic Utterances within Early Christianity', *NTS* 24 (1978), 175–98.

[44] Dunn, 'Prophetic "I" Sayings', 196.

[45] Aune, *Prophecy*, p. 245. See also D. Hill, *New Testament Prophecy*, pp. 160–85.

[46] D. C. Allison, 'Matt 23.39 = Luke 13.35b as a Conditional Prophecy', *JSNT* 18 (1983), 84 n. 26.

[47] See J. Blinzler, 'The Jewish Punishment of Stoning in the New Testament Period', in E. Bammel (ed.), *The Trial of Jesus*, p. 147.

as the main form of execution and may have expected to be executed summarily by it. There are reasons for us to posit this. According to *m.Sanh.* 7.4,[48] offences which carried the penalty of stoning include the practice of magic (cf. Jesus' miracles),[49] breaking the Sabbath (this is frequently attested to in the ministry of Jesus), blaspheming God (cf. Mark 2.1–12 and parallels) and, possibly, being a false prophet ('leading a whole town astray';[50] cf. Deut. 13.6–10). Perhaps it should also be pointed out that, just a few decades before Jesus' public ministry, Honi Ha-Meaggel, a Galilean charismatic, was stoned outside Jerusalem.[51] Therefore a tradition which may imply that Jesus expected death by stoning is probably authentic.[52] What is of importance is that crucifixion is not mentioned.[53] This may show that these logia were not created by the post-Easter community.

It has been mentioned earlier that the claim made by the speaker of the logia is cryptic, and that this is consistent with what we otherwise know of Jesus.[54] In addition, two aspects found in the logia are typical and compatible with the emphases of Jesus' ministry: the threat contained in the logia can be paralleled by Jesus' prediction of the end of the temple (Mark 13.2 and parallels); Jesus elsewhere spoke of the violent fate of the prophets (Luke 13.32–3; Luke 6.2‖Matt. 5.11–12; Luke 11.49–51‖Matt. 23.34–6). Hence, the characteristics of the logia converge with other aspects of Jesus' ministry.

Thirdly (and again, this observation is often ignored), the passage under consideration coheres very well with the prophetic

---

[48] Admittedly, the evidence is late, but there is no reason why *m.Sanh.* 7.4 should not enshrine earlier traditions given the fact that, in the OT, false prophets are probably stoned (Deut. 13.1–5, cf. vv. 6–10; 18.20).

[49] See G. N. Stanton, 'Jesus of Nazareth: A Magician and a False Prophet who Deceived God's People?', in J. B. Green and M. Turner (eds.), *Jesus of Nazareth: Lord and Christ*, pp. 178–9.

[50] Stanton observes that, in ancient Jewish polemic, the notion of deception is not necessarily linked to false prophecy but false prophecy, however, always involves deception in his 'Magician', pp. 166 n. 8, 180.

[51] See *m.Ta'an* 3.8, *y.Ta'an* 3.9[8], *b.Ta'an* 23a and especially AJ 14.22.

[52] Coming to a similar conclusion is J. H. Charlesworth, *Jesus Within Judaism*, pp. 144–5.

[53] The fact that crucifixion is not mentioned may be due to Jesus' describing here the violent fate of the prophets. Crucifixion is usually meted out to political offenders. See the discussion of E. Bammel, 'Crucifixion as a Punishment in Palestine', in E. Bammel (ed.), *The Trial of Jesus*, pp. 162–5, especially p. 165.

[54] Allison presents a similar point in 'Prophecy', 84 n. 26.

aspect of Jesus' ministry,[55] and also with the fact of Jesus' close association with John the Baptist. There is indeed an intimate connection between the city Jerusalem and the OT prophets. Beagley comments that prophetic 'accusations of evil and apostasy are hurled not simply at the nation as a whole, but frequently at the city of Jerusalem in particular, or at its inhabitants, or at both'.[56] Moreover, as Tiede observes, any Jewish prophet of the era of Jesus would have offered words of judgment or hope concerning the obvious peril of Jerusalem and Herod's temple within it.[57] The fact of the matter is that there were already protests against the leadership at Jerusalem during those times as is evident in the many movements which cropped up, especially brigandage.[58] We have tried to show above that there are good indications for the authenticity of these logia.[59]

3   The interpretation of Q 13.34–5

Demonstrating the authenticity of Q 13.34–5 is but the first step towards tapping data from it for a reconstruction of Jesus' stance *vis-à-vis* Jerusalem. In this section we intend to uncover the background of and the imagery behind the lament; the meaning of οἶκος; the meaning of the pronouncement in v. 35b; the referent of με in v. 35; and the context of Q 13.34–5. The ascertaining of these is of crucial importance to our study of the place of Jerusalem in Jesus' ministry. Therefore other important issues of interpretation will not be dealt with, such as the identity of ὁ ἐρχόμενος in v. 35b, as they do not contribute substantially to this study.

---

[55] Dodd has listed fifteen reasons why the category of 'prophet' could be applied to Jesus in his 'Jesus as Prophet and Teacher', in G. K. A. Bell and D. A. Deissmann (eds.), *Mysterium Christi*, pp. 53–66; cf. also Aune, *Prophecy*, pp. 153–63. It seems undeniable that Jesus was regarded by his contemporaries as a prophet and that he identified his own mission with that of the prophets of ancient Israel. If this is the case, it is hardly surprising that Jesus would address Jerusalem.

[56] J. A. Beagley, *The 'Sitz im Leben' of the Apocalypse with Particular Reference to the Role of the Church's Enemies*, p. 118.

[57] D. L. Tiede, 'Weeping for Jerusalem', in *Prophecy and History in Luke–Acts*, p. 67.

[58] On this particular point see R. A. Horsley and J. S. Hanson, *Bandits, Prophets and Messiahs: Popular Movements in the Time of Jesus.*

[59] The authenticity of these logia are supported by, among others, Aune, *Prophecy*, p. 175; Hoffmann, *Studien*, pp. 171–80; Schnider, *Jesus der Prophet*, pp. 142–7.

The imagery and the background

Some scholars have proposed that the background of the lament and the imagery employed are derived from a Wisdom myth.[60] The arguments given are usually the following:

(i) the imagery of a hen gathering its brood is a maternal image for divine being in 4(5) Ezra 1.30 and 2 Baruch 41.3–4, but it is also applied to Sophia in Sirach 1.15 and to the Shekinah;

(ii) the lament presupposes a supra-historical figure; and

(iii) the withdrawal of the speaker recalls 1 Enoch 42 or at least is a reworking of Sirach 24, both dealing with Sophia seeking a place to dwell (cf. also Prov. 1.28; Sir. 15.7).[61]

Here, a few points must be noted. First, as was shown earlier, ποσάκις need not presuppose a supra-historical figure. In fact, it is not ποσάκις, but the imagery used which may presuppose such a being.[62] Secondly, the idea of the withdrawal of Wisdom is found only in three texts: 1 Enoch 42; 4 Ezra 5.9–12; and Proverbs 1.20–33. Two of the texts are late: 1 Enoch 42[63] and 4 Ezra 5.9–12.[64] Proverbs 1.20–33 hardly speaks about Wisdom seeking a place to dwell; nor has Wisdom withdrawn herself in this passage. It is better to understand v. 28 as constituting a warning that there is a threshold, the crossing of which marks the point of no return. One could hardly read any myth depicting the withdrawal of Wisdom from Proverbs 1.28 without being first predisposed to do

---

[60] Bultmann, *History*, pp. 114–15; Steck, *Israel*, p. 237; Schulz, *Q*, pp. 346–60; Suggs, *Wisdom*, pp. 63–71; Kloppenborg, *Q*, p. 228; Piper, *Wisdom*, pp. 164–5; Christ, *Jesus*, pp. 136–50.

[61] These arguments are ably summarised by Piper, *Wisdom*, pp. 164–5.

[62] So Garland, perceptively: 'The imagery of sheltering wings ... suggests a trans-historical being', in *Intention*, p. 190 n. 90. Interestingly, Bultmann cites with approval Klostermann's observation that the OT usage of a bird signifies God(!). The same, Bultmann adds, is true of Judaism(!) in *History*, p. 114 n. 2.

[63] Although R. H. Charles dates the Similitudes of Enoch in the first century BCE ('1 Enoch' in R. H. Charles (ed.), *The Apocrypha and Pseudepigrapha of the Old Testament in English* II, p. 171), more recent opinion put them in the late first century CE, e.g., J. H. Charlesworth, '1 Enoch', *OTP* I, p. 7. Charlesworth's opinion reflects the consensus which came out of the SNTS Pseudepigrapha Seminar which met in 1977 and 1978 in Tübingen and Paris respectively. On this see, J. H. Charlesworth, 'The SNTS Pseudepigrapha Seminars at Tübingen and Paris and the Books of Enoch', *NTS* 25 (1978–9), 315–23; M. A. Knibb, 'The Date of the Parables of Enoch: A Critical Review', *NTS* 25 (1978–9), 345–59.

[64] 4 Ezra is indisputably late. B. M. Metzger assigns the non-interpolated sections (i.e., chapters 3–14) a date of 100–120 CE in 'The Fourth Book of Ezra', *OTP* I, p. 520.

it. There is therefore no evidence for a full-blown myth which describes the coming of Wisdom and her withdrawal before the time of Jesus.[65] Deutsch recognises this and cautions against speaking of Wisdom's myth or story without qualification.[66] Thirdly, the use of the hen imagery is not attested in any Jewish literature.[67] But the wing image is attested in the OT and is used as a powerful image (eagles' wings) to depict Yahweh's protection over Israel (Exod. 19.4; Deut. 32.11; cf. Isa. 31.5).[68] Hence, if anything, the imagery evokes the thought of Yahweh's protective care instead of Wisdom.[69] The use of the image of a hen's wings instead of an eagle's may be due to the desire on the part of Jesus to make the imagery congruent with the idea of tender protective care. Although some scholars have made recourse to the equation, Shekinah = Wisdom, for the purpose of co-opting the wing image into the domain of Wisdom,[70] Urbach has shown that 'in the theology of the Sages of the Talmud and the Midrash, the term "Shekinah" is not connected with "Wisdom", and the two are not identified'.[71] Therefore in the lament over Jerusalem we have Jesus' use of a powerful image to express Yahweh's love and concern for Jerusalem, his city. Not only is the image powerful, it is also evocative of tenderness and endearment. Indeed, the whole oracle

---

[65] Perhaps Prov. 1.28 may be the seed-bed out of which 1 En. 42 and 4 Ezra 5.9–12 develop their ideas.

[66] C. Deutsch, 'Wisdom in Matthew: Transformation of a Symbol', *NovT* 32 (1990), 30. In this article, Deutsch gives a good survey of the symbolic function of Wisdom in Jewish literature.

[67] Perhaps one may see here the unique contribution of Jesus in that he has transformed the bird symbol which is used for Yahweh as an image of power into a maternal one: i.e., from eagles' wings (Exod. 19.4; Deut. 32.11) into hen's wings.

[68] This is candidly observed by Miller, 'Rejection', 234 n. 33. Deutsch notes that Matt. 23.37–9 could well have represented a *prophetic* lament spoken in God's name although, on the Matthean level, the text refers to Wisdom ('Wisdom', 44–5). Stuhlmacher lists this as one possible connotation of the image in 'Stellung', 145.

[69] μετὰ ἀνθρώπων θεμέλιον αἰῶνος ἐνόσσευσεν of Sir. 1.15 can hardly be the background for the imagery found in Q 13.34. It speaks more of Wisdom 'tarrying' or 'nesting' (ἐνόσσευσεν may provide a contact point with νοσσιά). But the imagery of wings and protection is missing. It seems therefore that Sir. 1.15 is speaking of a totally different thing. Hence, the frequent recourse made by scholars to Sir. 1.15 as evidence that the use of the imagery found in Q 13.34 refers to Wisdom is mistaken.

[70] So Christ, *Jesus*, p. 141; F. W. Burnett, *The Testament of Jesus-Sophia: A Redactional-Critical Study of the Eschatological Discourse in Matthew*, pp. 68–75.

[71] E. E. Urbach, *The Sages – Their Concepts and Beliefs*, pp. 64–5. Such a conclusion is also followed by Garland, *Intention*, p. 191 n. 90.

closely resembles the prophetic oracles found scattered all over the OT. The tender imagery conceived by Jesus serves as a powerful message of the yearnings of Yahweh for an errant city and centre of Israel, and, at the same time, heightens its guilt.

There are many indications which point to the plausibility that the background to the lament is prophetic. The strongest indication arises from form-critical considerations. Steck observes that 'das Jerusalemwort gehört in die Gattungstradition des prophetischen Gerichtwortes' and he lists seven formal prophetic traits that are found in the *Jerusalemwort*: (i) ἰδού = הִנֵּה (*hineh*); (ii) the combination of *Scheltwort* and *Gerichtwort*; (iii) the repeated naming of the addressees; (iv) the use of participles to describe the conduct of the addressees; (v) the *Kontrastmotiv*; (vi) the use of metaphors for comparison; and (vii) the repetition of the introductory formula near the end of the oracle.[72] Beasley-Murray, who bases his analysis on the work of K. Koch,[73] observes that the lament resembles the prophecy of disaster.[74] The three parts of the prophecy of disaster may be found in vv. 34–5a: the indication of the situation or diatribe; the prediction of disaster or threat; and the concluding characterisation. Using this form as a framework, it can then be seen that the description of Jerusalem's sins corresponds to the first part. The prediction of disaster is found in the word beginning with ἰδού. Finally, the concluding characterisation is expressed in a double utterance: οὐ μὴ ἴδητέ με and ἕως ἥξει ὅτε εἴπητε κτλ. Hence, on form-critical considerations alone, Q 13.34–5 has its roots in the prophetic tradition and not Wisdom. And, as Evans has recently averred, 'to gather' is never used of the function of

---

[72] Steck, *Israel*, pp. 57–8. Boring is in agreement (*Sayings*, p. 171); cf. also Fitzmyer, *Luke X–XXIV*, p. 1034 and J. Neyrey, 'Jesus' Address to the Women of Jerusalem (Luke 23.27–31) – A Prophetic Judgment Oracle', *NTS* 29 (1983), 74–86. C. H. Giblin, however, disagrees chiefly on the grounds that prophetic judgment is 'unconditional' (does he mean by this term that it is irreversible?) and that οἶκος refers more to the leadership than the city or temple. Hence, the pronouncement of ἀφίεται is not a judgment but rather signifies the fact that the Jerusalemites are left to themselves, bereft of the parental care of Jesus. Giblin would categorise the oracle as prophetic altercation, adopting the *rîb* pattern (*The Destruction of Jerusalem According to Luke's Gospel: A Historical-Typological Moral*, pp. 37–43). Giblin is not convincing. It seems to us that there is no side-stepping the fact that ἰδοὺ ἀφίεται ὑμῖν ὁ οἶκος ὑμῶν is a pronouncement of judgment.

[73] K. Koch, *The Growth of the Biblical Tradition*, pp. 211–13.

[74] Beasley-Murray, *Jesus*, pp. 304–5.

Wisdom but is the regular word for the hope of God's restoration (Pss. 106.47; 147.2; Isa. 27.12; 52.12; Jer. 31.8–11; Zech. 2.6).[75]

We therefore conclude that the imagery used in Q 13.34–5 does not fit suitably with Wisdom. Indeed, the imagery has its roots in the OT and is often used for Yahweh. 'Wings' as an image for shelter and protection is used in the rabbinic literature for the Shekinah.[76] Although the use of the image of a hen gathering her chicks for Yahweh's tender care is not attested anywhere else, the wing image as a representation of Yahweh's care and protection in the OT is common (Deut. 32.11; Ruth 2.11; Pss. 17.8; 36.7; 57.1; 61.4; 63.7; 91.4; Isa. 31.5; cf. 2 Bar. 41.3–4). Especially relevant are the references found in the Psalms and Isaiah. The passages from Psalms (Pss. 17.8; 36.7; 57.1; 61.4; 63.7; 91.4) all speak of finding refuge under the wings of God, while Isaiah 31.5 has the imagery of a bird protecting Jerusalem. It follows then that the imagery suits Yahweh better than Wisdom. Hence, the lament is a prophetic utterance of Jesus and in it he conceived himself to be the one through whose prophetic ministry Jerusalem is to be gathered back to God.

The meaning of οἶκος

The prophetic pronouncement of judgment reads ἰδοὺ ἀφίεται ὑμῖν ὁ οἶκος ὑμῶν. How are we to understand ὁ οἶκος? It can possibly refer to four things: the city Jerusalem;[77] the temple;[78] the nation;[79] the Jerusalem leaders.[80]

There are two arguments in favour of understanding οἶκος as referring to the city itself. The first is that the lament is addressed

---

[75] C. F. Evans, Saint Luke, p. 564.   [76] See SB I.93.

[77] Some of the proponents of this view are Steck, Israel, p. 228; Hoffmann, Studien, p. 174; E. Klostermann, Das Matthäusevangelium, p. 191. Cf. Marshall, Gospel, p. 576; Nolland, Luke 9:21–18:34, p. 742.

[78] Some proponents: Manson, Sayings, p. 127; C. H. Dodd, The Parables of the Kingdom, pp. 44–5; Kümmel, Promise, p. 181; W. D. Davies, The Setting of the Sermon on the Mount, p. 198; H. van der Kwaak, 'Die Klage über Jerusalem (Matt 23.37–9)', NovT 8 (1965), 160; W. Grundmann, Das Evangelium nach Matthäus, p. 497; Christ, Jesus, p. 149 (both city and temple); J. Jeremias, The Parables of Jesus, p. 168; E. E. Ellis, The Gospel of Luke, p. 191; Schulz, Q, p. 356 n. 230.

[79] A handful of scholars hold this view: H. B. Green, The Gospel According to Matthew, p. 195; J. Schniewind, Das Evangelium nach Matthäus, p. 237.

[80] Some proponents: Weinert, 'Abandoned House', 75–6 (working on the Lukan level); D. L. Bock, Proclamation from Prophecy and Pattern, p. 326 n. 115; Fitzmyer, Luke X–XXIV, p. 1037; Bayer, Predictions, p. 46.

specifically to Jerusalem. Secondly, as Moessner has observed, abandonment (ἀφίεται) is a typical Deuteronomistic expression for Jerusalem's destruction; when God leaves the city, it falls preys to its enemies.[81]

In biblical literature, οἶκος is often used for the temple, more often than it is used for Jerusalem (1 Kings 9.1–9; 2 Chron. 7.19–22; Jer. 7.10–14; 26.4–6). Hence, the likelihood that Jesus is referring to the temple has to be reckoned with even though the lament is addressed to Jerusalem, for the pride of Jerusalem is the temple. SB asserts that 'house' with the plural suffix (i.e., ὁ οἶκος ... ὑμῶν) can never refer to the temple; to do that there should be no suffix at all but simply the articular ὁ οἶκος.[82] This is simply mistaken, for in Isaiah 64.10–11 we find exactly the reference which undermines SB's assertion: 'our ... house'. The strongest argument in favour of understanding οἶκος as referring to the temple is the OT citation at the end of the lament. The citation taken from Psalm 118.26 presupposes a setting in the temple, where the priests receive the pilgrims (royal?) with the pronouncement of blessing from out of the 'house', i.e., the temple.[83]

Another possible referent for οἶκος is the nation of Israel.[84] One argument which is often used to support such an understanding is that in Matthew 10.6 and 15.24 'house' refers to the nation.

And, finally, Weinert, working on the Lukan level and using Jeremiah 22:5 as the precursor of the pronouncement of judgment here, states that οἶκος 'does not refer primarily to the temple. Rather, it designates Israel's Judean leadership, and those who fall under their authority.'[85] Although Weinert is concerned primarily with the Lukan level, his arguments are of relevance to our present enquiry. Moreover, Jeremiah 22.5 seems to be the text on which the pronouncement of judgment drew.[86]

In the wake of the welter of opinions surveyed, some scholars counsel that a sharp distinction between the four options need not be made since city, temple, national life and leadership were all bound up together.[87] Such a counsel is wise and perhaps valid, but

[81] D. P. Moessner, *The Lord of the Banquet*, p. 235 n. 133. Moessner gives a detailed list of biblical references.

[82] SB I.943–4. SB is followed by Marshall, *Gospel*, p. 576.

[83] See H. J. Kraus, *Psalms 60–150. A Commentary*, p. 400.

[84] So C. F. Evans, *Luke*, p. 565.   [85] Weinert, 'Abandoned House', 76.

[86] The LXX of Jer. 22.5 reads ... ὅτι εἰς ἐρήμωσιν ἔσται ὁ οἶκος οὗτος.

[87] E.g., Garland, *Intention*, p. 199; and Catchpole, *Quest*, p. 271. Note that Garland does not list leadership as an option. This is an oversight on his part as the

it faces the danger of committing what Barr once called 'illegitimate totality transfer',[88] i.e., by οἶκος, a whole network of meaning is being referred to.[89] It is best to regard οἶκος as referring only to the temple. This is seen especially in the choice of the OT citation, Psalm 118.26. Moreover, Jeremiah 22.5 may not be the sole exemplar for the pronouncement of judgment here (as the important ἀφίεται is missing).[90] But as Davies has observed, '[Jewish] texts dealing with the temple always implicitly, and usually explicitly, implicate the city, just as Jerusalem became the quintessence of the land, so the temple became the quintessence of Jerusalem'.[91] Hence, to pronounce judgment against the temple affects the leadership, city and people[92] in succeeding concentric waves. Because of its opposition to the regathering overtures of Yahweh, Jerusalem will be judged and that judgment comes in the form of the abandonment of its very heart – the temple.[93] Hence, a judgment on the temple is especially relevant in the lament over Jerusalem's misdeeds.

The situation envisaged in Q 13.35b

Concerning this problem, Allison observes that solutions to it have generally followed one of two paths:[94] one either takes the statement of Q 13.35b as a declaration of unqualified judgment[95] or as offering hope for the conversion of the nation of Israel.[96] Perhaps it should be added that interpretations which follow the second track

Judaean leadership figured prominently in the last phase of Jesus' ministry. Cf. Allison, 'Prophecy', 82 n. 12.

[88] J. Barr, *The Semantics of Biblical Language*, p. 218.

[89] The word 'referred' is used deliberately here for it is possible in our judgment that a referent can carry a few inferents.

[90] It seems best to take the pronouncement as not referring to any one particular text.

[91] W. D. Davies, *The Gospel and the Land*, p. 152.

[92] Cf. D. R. Catchpole, 'Temple Traditions in Q', in W. Horbury (ed.), *Templum Amicitiae*, p. 319.

[93] Perhaps this explains why, according to the gospels, Jesus, upon entering Jerusalem, went to the temple first (Mark 11.11–17 and parallels).

[94] Allison, 'Prophecy', 75.

[95] The following scholars hold this view: J. Calvin, *A Harmony of the Gospels of Matthew, Mark and Luke* III, p. 71; Manson, *Sayings*, p. 128; Schulz, *Q*, p. 358; Gaston, *No Stone on Another*, p. 455; Garland, *Intention*, pp. 207–8 (on the Matthean level); Fitzmyer, *Luke X–XXIV*, pp. 1035–6 (on the Lukan level).

[96] Scholars who hold this view, amongst many others, are: J. Ernst, *Das Evangelium nach Lukas*, p. 433; E. Schweizer, *The Good News According to Matthew*, p. 445; Jeremias, *The Eucharistic Words of Jesus*, pp. 259–60; Kümmel, *Promise*, p. 81;

can themselves be divided into two further categories: one which takes the offer of salvation as conditional (the order could then be represented something like this: repentance → parousia/salvation[97]); the other as a prophecy of unconditional salvation (the order would then be: parousia → repentance/salvation).

The arguments for the first interpretation are essentially three. First, the pronouncement is set in a judgmental context: the lament over Jerusalem and the pronouncement of judgment on the temple. Therefore, it would only be natural to expect v. 35b to envisage a situation of unqualified judgment. This would then mean that there would come a time when Jerusalem or Israel will greet ὁ ἐρχόμενος with the pronouncement of blessing but then it would be too late because ὁ ἐρχόμενος comes as judge. Therefore the words εὐλογημένος ὁ ἐρχόμενος ἐν ὀνόματι κυρίου would actually be uttered grudgingly or out of fear, and not in jubilant exclamation. Secondly, it is argued that there is no other utterance of Jesus which anticipates Israel's repentance and redemption. Thirdly, Matthew 8.11–12‖Luke 13.28–9 may show that Jesus elsewhere regards salvation as being taken away from the Jews.

There are, however, problems connected with the view just outlined. First, as Allison observes, εὐλογεῖν and εὐλογημένος are not words of fear, nor are they typically voiced by the ignorant, the condemned or those in mourning. In the LXX, notably Psalm 117.26, which is cited in our text, and in the NT, εὐλογεῖν and εὐλογημένος (like the Hebrew בֶּרֶךְ, *berek*) are usually expressions of joy, and they consistently have a very positive connotation of 'to praise', 'to extol', 'to bless' and 'to greet'.[98] Hence, the OT citation does not envisage the nation of Israel confessing grudgingly, but fits the situation of rejoicing in the coming of ὁ ἐρχόμενος.

Secondly, there is no precedent in Jewish literature for the notion that the wicked or unbeliever will utter a blessing when the messiah comes.[99] It should be added that the argument from context is not convincing, as in many prophetic judgment oracles a 'lifeline' is

---

[97] There is almost a consensus that the parousia is being referred to in v. 35b. Luke may have a different understanding; we shall treat this later.

[98] Allison, 'Prophecy', 75. Cf. Kwaak, 'Klage', 165–6; W. Beyer, 'εὐλογεῖν κτλ', *TDNT* II, pp. 754–65; and J. Schaubert, 'בָּרַךְ (*brk*)', *TDOT* II, pp. 279–308.

[99] Allison, 'Prophecy', 76.

[100] See, for example, Jer. 13.15–17. Cf. G. N. Stanton, 'Aspects of Early Christian-

thrown out to the nation.[100] Again, the argument that Jesus had
nowhere else uttered words which anticipated the salvation of the
nation does not appear to be cogent when we take into account the
possibility that Jesus' ministry was directed at the nation of Israel,
principally for her restoration.[101] In fact, as Jeremias observes,
'Jesus is certain that the promise of God will be fulfilled and that
even in the blind and the obdurate city God will arouse a remnant
which will greet the coming one.'[102]

And, finally, Matthew 8.11–12‖Luke 13.28–9 need not necessarily refer to the ultimate rejection of the Jews. Beasley-Murray
points out that this saying is intended as a warning to the Jews
rather than as a revelation of the identity of the heirs of the
kingdom of God.[103]

The second interpretation takes the word of blessing as being
spoken jubilantly at the return of the messiah and, thus, v. 35b
offers a message of hope albeit joined to a grim picture of
judgment. In other words, at the coming of ὁ ἐρχόμενος, Jerusalem
or Israel will know salvation. The arguments for such a view are
many. First, this understanding of the matter accords well with the
spirit of Psalm 118.26 – a situation where joy is predominant.
Secondly, Psalm 118.26 has been interpreted messianically in the
context of eschatological salvation which is awaited by the Jews.[104]

The problem commonly cited against such a view is that it entails
setting two apparently contradicting statements side by side (i.e.,
the statement of judgment and the statement under discussion).[105]

But this objection is weak. As was pointed out earlier, the

---

[100] See, for example, Jer. 13.15–17. Cf. G. N. Stanton, 'Aspects of Early Christian-
Jewish Polemic and Apologetic', *NTS* 31 (1985), 385–90, where he proposes that
the Jewish Sin–Exile–Return (S–E–R) pattern may lie behind this pronouncement.

[101] On this see G. B. Caird, 'Jesus and Israel: The Starting Point for New Testament
Christology', in R. F. Berkey and S. A. Edwards (eds.), *Christological Perspectives*, pp. 58–68.

[102] Jeremias, *Words*, pp. 259–60.   [103] Beasley-Murray, *Jesus*, pp. 306–7.

[104] The midrash of Ps. 118.22 refers this final portion of the psalm to the day of
redemption. Such a text was used by Jews to express a future hope of deliverance.
Bock writes that, by the time of Jesus, the psalm itself has become part of the
Hallel psalms recited over the Passover meal and at the Feast of Tabernacles
(*Proclamation*, p. 118).

[105] Perhaps the discontiguous nature of these statements may indicate that they are
originally separate (e.g., Bultmann, *History*, p. 115). Such an explanation would
explain why the two statements are discontiguous but would founder on this
important observation: it does not explain why such discontiguous statements are
brought together. For what purpose would a tradent do this?

prophets often concluded their oracles of judgment with a message of hope. It seems best therefore to regard v. 35b as offering hope to Jerusalem and, by extension, to the whole of Israel.

However, it should be emphasised that v. 35b nowhere implies that such a salvation will come unconditionally. In fact, Allison has presented a strong case for viewing the offer of salvation as conditional, i.e., conditional on the repentance of Israel (the use of ἕως in v. 35b implies that), and such repentance will be evidenced by Jerusalem blessing ὁ ἐρχόμενος. Essentially, Allison's case is built on three arguments: (a) belief in the contingency of the time of the final redemption is well-attested in Jewish sources of the second century and later; (b) ἕως can indicate a contingent state in Greek; and (c) the structure of Q 13.35b is paralleled in many rabbinic texts and hence supports a conditional interpretation.[106] Jesus therefore, in pronouncing a judgment on Jerusalem's temple, offers a 'lifeline' for the nation in line with prophetic practice. God or Jesus[107] will be seen again by the city only if it blesses ὁ ἐρχόμενος. Such a vision would amount to salvation, for it would mean that the presence of God has been restored to the city again – hence, Jerusalem will 'see'.

The referent of με in verse 35

Limitation of space does not permit us to discuss in detail the issue of who the referent of με is in v. 35. This problem is exacerbated by the fact that if we posit Q 13.34–5 as originally separate from the contexts proffered by the gospels, no indication of who the speaker of these verses is is given. However, it is clear that the evangelists meant their readers to understand that the logia came from Jesus. We have demonstrated the plausibility of this. Hence, if vv. 34–5 are viewed as an integral unit, ποσάκις ἠθέλησα ἐπισυνάξαι κτλ (v. 34) and με (v. 35) would most likely refer to the same entity: that is, the one who seeks to gather Jerusalem is the same person whom Jerusalem will see if it blesses the one who comes in the name of the Lord. We have argued that the saying ποσάκις ἠθέλησα ἐπισυνάξαι κτλ (v. 34) comes from Jesus. If this is so, the

---

[106] Allison, 'Prophecy', 77–80; Allison's fourth argument will not be used by us as it appears to be more an exposition than an argument. M. J. Borg, *Conflict, Holiness and Politics in the Teachings of Jesus*, p. 183 and Beasley-Murray, *Jesus*, p. 307, hold a similar view although their argumentations are different.

[107] See later discussion on the referent of με of v. 35.

logical conclusion to draw is that the referent of με is Jesus of Nazareth. However, two further possibilities for the referent of με have been proposed in the history of scholarship: Sophia or Yahweh. We have earlier argued against attributing the logia of vv. 34–5 to Sophia and thus the viable alternatives which are left for considering the referent of με are Yahweh or Jesus.

Borg has made a strong case for interpreting με as referring to Yahweh.[108] One difficulty with this view is that the notion of seeing Yahweh is something of an oddity in Jewish tradition. Borg, however, argues that such a notion is found several times in the OT. Especially relevant is Isaiah 52.8, 'for with their own eyes they shall see Yahweh returning in pity to *Zion*'.[109] Furthermore, if the earlier clause, ἰδοὺ ἀφίεται ὑμῖν ὁ οἶκος ὑμῶν (Q 13.35a), refers to the abandonment of the temple (and we have argued that its most natural allusion is to the departure of the Shekinah), then it becomes probable that με is referring to Yahweh in that the departure of the Shekinah is to be answered by a return of the Shekinah. Hence, such an interpretation is eminently possible and Jesus would then be speaking as the mouthpiece of Yahweh.

It is also possible that Jesus is the referent of με. If this is the case, two possible lines of interpretation may follow and they depend to some extent on the contextual placement of these logia.[110] Either Jesus was designating the time he would next go to Jerusalem (following the Lukan placement) or he was referring to his parousia (following the Matthean placement). Both of these interpretations encounter difficulties. The former appears, in the words of Manson, to be 'a high falutin' way of conveying a very prosaic piece of information'.[111] Even on the Lukan level, the saying of v. 35b does not refer to the triumphal entry into Jerusalem (Luke 19.37–8) as it was the disciples and not Jerusalem who uttered the blessing of Psalm 118.26. Weinert's idea that the saying refers to a temporary respite for Jerusalem from the challenge of Jesus' ministry appears oversubtle and misguided.[112]

The other possible line of interpretation regards Jesus as speaking of his parousia and this is something which is met with scepticism on the part of many scholars. However, it should be pointed out that there are important arguments which serve to call

---

[108] Borg, *Conflict*, p. 183.   [109] Borg, *Conflict*, p. 183.
[110] On this particular question, see our later discussion on the context of Q 13.34–5.
[111] Manson, *Sayings*, p. 128.   [112] Weinert, 'Abandoned House', 73.

for a reconsideration of such scepticism. In addition to the arguments discussed earlier in section 1, the following should be noted. First, Jewish tradition provides a precedent for the belief that important historical figures might be translated to heaven in preparation for a future eschatological role. The translation of Elijah to heaven (2 Kings 2.11–12) and the anticipation of a future eschatological role for him (Mal. 4.5–6) is a case in point (cf. 4 Ezra 6.26).[113] Secondly, one saying attributed to Jesus by the Synoptic evangelists (Mark 14.25 and parallels) has good grounds for authenticity. This saying is accepted as authentic by many scholars.[114] The eschatological prospect of vindication and consummation cannot be denied whether one regards the first part of the utterance as referring to a vow of abstinence[115] or a prophecy of death.[116] This saying therefore offers evidence that Jesus expected to drink with the disciples at the consummation of the kingdom of God after an interval brought about by his death. As Kümmel has pointed out, Mark 14.25 corresponds with Luke 13.35 in that on both occasions 'Jesus counts on an absence which begins with his death and ends with the parousia.'[117] Finally, many prominent scholars have argued that at least some of the future Son-of-Man sayings are to be regarded as authentic although they may differ over whether Jesus identified himself with the future Son of Man.[118] In our view, Matthew 19.28 offers explicit evidence that Jesus identified himself with this future Son of Man. In that saying,

---

[113] Cf. the work of D. Zeller, 'Entrückung zur Ankunft als Menschensohn (Luke 13,34f; 11,29f.), in F. Refoulé (ed.), *A cause de l'évangile: mélanges offerts a Dom Jacques Dupont*, pp. 515–17. It is eminently possible that the Qumran community expected the return of Elijah. On this see the recent study of J. J. Collins, 'The Works of the Messiah', *Dead Sea Discoveries* 1,1 (1994), 102–6.

[114] Jeremias, *Words*, pp. 216–18; I. H. Marshall, *Last Supper and Lord's Supper*, pp. 53–6; Beasley-Murray, *Jesus*, pp. 261–3; R. H. Gundry, *Mark: A Commentary on His Apology for the Cross*, p. 834.

[115] So Jeremias, *Words*, pp. 207–9, 216–18.

[116] So Bayer, *Predictions*, pp. 43–4.   [117] Kümmel, *Promise*, pp. 81–2.

[118] R. Bultmann, *Theology of the New Testament* I; J. Jeremias, *New Testament Theology I: The Proclamation of Jesus*; F. Hahn, *The Titles of Jesus in Christology*; H. E. Tödt, *The Son of Man in the Synoptic Tradition*; A. J. B. Higgins, *Jesus and the Son of Man*; C. K. Barrett, *Jesus and the Gospel Tradition*; F. H. Borsch, *The Son of Man in Myth and History*; F. F. Bruce, *This is That*; L. Goppelt, 'Zum Problem des Menschensohns: Das Verhältnis von Leidens- und Parusieankündigung', in *Christologie und Ethik*; I. H. Marshall, 'The Synoptic Son of Man Sayings in Recent Discussion', *NTS* 12 (1966), 327–51; O. Cullmann, *The Christology of the New Testament*; C. C. Caragounis, *The Son of Man*; S. Kim, *The 'Son of Man' as the Son of God*; Beasley-Murray, *Jesus*; C. C. Rowland, *Christian Origins*.

Jesus promised his disciples thrones on which they would sit to judge Israel in the 'regeneration of the world' which most likely refers to the denouement of the kingdom of God. Taking this into consideration, it is inconceivable that Jesus did not consider himself as having a more major role in the kingdom than had the disciples. Thus, the Son of Man in Matthew 19.28 should be interpreted as referring to Jesus of Nazareth.[119] And if the saying of Mark 14.25 is regarded as authentic, as it has been by some scholars,[120] it will provide further evidence that Jesus identified himself with the future Son of Man. Thus, there is good evidence for us to conceive of Jesus as having referred to his parousia. It would therefore mean in the present context that the redemption of Jerusalem is intricately linked to a positive response to Jesus' person and message. Jesus would also have viewed himself as more than just a mere prophet.

As was argued earlier, it is more natural to take the logia of v. 34 and v. 35 as referring to the same person. The only difficulty in accepting this solution is that the possibility of Jesus ever referring to his parousia is met with scepticism on the part of many scholars. If such scepticism is unwarranted, nothing stands in the way of our accepting this interpretation. Thus, Jesus is most probably the referent of με.

The context of Q 13.34–5

Q 13.34–5 is preserved in contexts which are radically different in both gospels. Such a phenomenon raises the question of which gospel is preserving the correct Q order and historical context or whether they are both wrong. Admittedly, Q may be an unstructured document and, even if it is structured, the evidence we have on hand does not permit any confident reconstruction. Notwithstanding this, if the original Q order can be recovered, we are probably a step nearer the original context of the saying. The recovery of the context of the lament in Q can also perhaps provide us with vital clues to the historical context of the saying.

Suggs remarks that 'it is not certain that either evangelist has retained the Q setting of the saying. Both could have placed the passage in their contexts on the basis of mere "Stichwort"

---

[119] So Rowland, *Origins*, p. 184; and Sanders, *Jesus*, pp. 99, 308.
[120] Rowland, *Origins*, p. 184.

association.'[121] This observation forms a good introduction to this very difficult problem. We shall review the arguments given to support the various views.

The Matthean order is supported by many scholars, more so than the Lukan order.[122] There are basically two arguments in favour of it. The first is that there are thematic links between Q 13.34–5 and Matthew 23.29–36 (Q 11.47–51). The thematic words, ἀποστέλλω, προφῆται, ἀποκτείνω, appear in both passages. The second argument stresses the fact that the Lukan order is suspect and therefore the Matthean order ought to be original.[123] Obviously such an argument is weak for, if the Lukan order is 'manifestly' wrong, it does not follow that the Matthean order must be the correct one; both could very well be wrong. The first argument can cut both ways. The thematic links can point to the fact that the two passages were originally integral to one another or to the fact that, because of their shared themes, a redactional linkage was performed. But the serious problem confronting this solution is that of explaining Luke's purpose in moving the passage away from its original context to a manifestly inept context.

What about the Lukan order? As mentioned earlier, fewer scholars are prepared to accept it as the original order in Q. This arises from the fact that the context of the saying is manifestly artificial. It is therefore highly probable that Luke sutured Q 13.34–5 to Luke 13.31–3 by way of the Jerusalem *Stichwort* to provide a preview of the outcome of the journey to Jerusalem and also to set the tone for it.[124] But this argument can be double-edged. As was mentioned earlier, if the lament stood in the same position in Q as it does in Matthew, and Luke removed it from that context and placed it in a different context in his narrative, it would mean that Luke altered the original thrust of the lament with what can be only described as singularly *inept* results.[125] In other words, if the Matthean order is original, one is hard-pressed to account for such an inept manoeuvre by Luke. Garland argues that, in fact, the Lukan order is original, but Luke 13.31–3 have been spliced in

---

[121] Suggs, *Wisdom*, p. 64.

[122] Amongst many, the following scholars are proponents of this view: Bultmann, *History*, pp. 144–5; D. Lührmann, *Die Redaktion der Logienquelle*, pp. 45, 48; Suggs, *Wisdom*, pp. 64–6; W. Grundmann, *Das Evangelium nach Lukas*, p. 287; Schweizer, *Matthew*, p. 436; Marshall, *Gospel*, p. 573; Fitzmyer, *Luke X–XXIV*, p. 1034.

[123] Lührmann, *Logienquelle*, p. 45.

[124] Cf. Suggs, *Matthew*, p. 64.   [125] Garland, *Intention*, p. 192.

between Luke 13.22–30 and 13.34–5.[126] Matthew would then have moved Q 13.34–5 to a place appropriate to his redactional interests. This hypothesis is attractive as there are good grounds for seeing Q 11.47–51 and Q 13.34–5 as traditionally separate. Manson made the observation (whose significance has not been generally appreciated) that a word comparison between the passages would point to the fact that they were originally separate. His comments merit being quoted in full:

> Matt 23.34–6 contains (in Greek) 72 words, Luke 11.49–51 contains 58. The two versions of the saying agree in 22 words and partly agree in 7. Taking Luke's version as standard the amount of agreement between Matt and Luke is under 50 per cent. Now Matt 23.37–9 contains 56 words and Luke 13.34–5 53. There is agreement between the two in 45 words and partial agreement in 4. Again taking Luke as the standard, the amount of agreement between Matt and Luke is near 90 per cent. It is difficult to believe that this wide divergence followed by almost word for word agreement could have taken place in the quotation of a single short passage of little more than a hundred words.[127]

Therefore, it seems to us to be highly improbable that Q 13.34–5 is connected to Q 11.47–51. But again, the artificiality of the Lukan context still presents a problem, notwithstanding the solution offered by Garland. This is seen from the fact that certain standpoints presupposed in the lament do not fit Luke's context. The note of finality in Q 13.34–5 is pronounced. Moreover, the temple is judged.[128] Such sentiments are expected to have come during the last decisive conflicts between Jesus and the religious authorities and not as Luke's narrative implies.

We are thus led to conclude from the discussion above that Q 11.47–51 and Q 13.34–5 were originally separate and that Q 13.34–5 is a dominical tradition whose original context is not recoverable. The tradition is being used by both evangelists inde-

---

[126] Garland, *Intention*, p. 192. On p. 193 n. 99, Garland writes that, 'The lament over Jerusalem therefore comprises an apt and significant conclusion to the theme of rejection, which permeates the preceding verses, when vv. 31–3 are omitted.' Cf. also Kloppenborg, *Q*, p. 228.

[127] Manson, *Sayings*, p. 102.

[128] This argument does not pose insuperable problems to Garland's solution. But our explanation to be given later has more to commend it.

pendently of its context. It is also possible that this tradition was
passed on to the evangelists without any context.[129] However,
because of the finality of the tone of the lament, it seems plausible
that Q 13.34–5 came from the last phase of Jesus' ministry, possibly
after the 'temple-cleansing'. If what we suggest is correct, both
evangelists performed redactional suturing of this passage to their
narrative. Matthew provides the right historical context for the
saying, but his connection of this saying with the woes pronounced
over the Pharisees is probably not original.

Summary of interpretation

The lament is structured like a prophecy of disaster and it describes,
in the tradition of the prophets, the sins of Jerusalem. The
judgment, deserved by such behaviour, is hereby also pronounced.
Although some sapiential themes may be found in the lament, it is
best to understand the lament as being steeped in the prophetic
traditions. The words express the desire of one who is wanting to
gather the children of Jerusalem under his wings, as a hen gathers
her chicks. Such an image is unique in Jewish literature and we
have argued that it is conceived originally by Jesus to express the
tenderness of divine protection. (The OT frequently has eagles'
wings or just wings *simpliciter*.) The imagery serves to emphasise
the tender nature of God's overtures and, at the same time, the evil
posture of Jerusalem. But such overtures, expressed through the
ministry of Jesus, were rejected and, as a result, the quintessence of
Jerusalem, the temple, was judged. The judgment took the form of
the departure of the Shekinah from the temple. The present tense
ἀφίεται has the same force as the prophetic perfect and it signifies a
present and definite reality. Since the temple is abandoned, the city,
the leaders and the populace are all affected in turn, in succeeding
concentric waves. But hope is not totally absent. The redemption of
Israel which would result through the coming of ὁ ἐρχόμενος can
only come about when the city, the representative of the nation, is
prepared to bless ὁ ἐρχόμενος. It is further suggested that such a
lament, which contains elements of finality, is expressed during the

---

[129] Perhaps our view entails that Q and Mark are not the only documents Matthew
and Luke have in common. They also have tracts of material which were similar
but not part of Q. This theory would explain the unusually high degree of verbal
similarity between the two gospels over this passage. It is also possible that Q
may contain *tracts* of material and that it is not just a unitary document.

last phase of Jesus' public ministry while in Jerusalem, possibly just after the 'cleansing' of the temple. But on this we cannot be absolutely sure.

4   Q 13.34–5 and Jesus' intentions

In this section, we will draw the threads of our study together to explore and sketch its implications for our understanding and reconstruction of Jesus' intentions and his relationship to Jerusalem.

Jesus' conception of his role and the Zion traditions

Once it was popular to write about the self-consciousness of Jesus. This has almost disappeared now owing to many criticisms directed against such attempts. However, it is possible to speculate and have a fair measure of success at it when we come to ask about how Jesus viewed his own role *vis-à-vis* Israel. Hence, we shall try to draw some conclusions from this important passage about this matter, while recognising the limitations.

The first is the possibility that Jesus adopted the persona of a prophet. This can be seen in three ways: from the mention of the killing of the prophets (v. 34); from form-critical considerations of the oracle as a prophecy of disaster; and in the background to the lament, which we have taken to be prophetic. There are some other points in connection with this that are worth noting. Jesus' prophetic ministry is concerned primarily with Jerusalem. Prophetic judgment is pronounced on its unresponsiveness to the overtures of the one who desires to gather it. Such overtures ultimately stemmed from Yahweh, whether we conceive the subject of ἠθέλησα to be referring to Jesus or to Yahweh. The motif of regathering is especially significant and more so in that judgment is pronounced upon its refusal. The crucial importance of Jesus' ministry, which is highlighted by the fact that it is through Jesus that Yahweh seeks to restore Jerusalem (and, in this sense, the notion of fulfilment is present), may indicate that the prophetic category alone may not be adequate to describe what Jesus thinks of his own person. This is further supported if με refers to Jesus and not to Yahweh. But of this we cannot be absolutely sure. However, Part III (our study on Jesus' actions in Jerusalem) may have light to shed on this particular matter.

The second point to note is the imagery used. As is observed by Evans, 'to gather' is the regular word which evokes the hope of God's restoration.[130] This restoration does not mean just a return to Jerusalem's pristine glory but also the fulfilment of the eschatological glory promised to her as found in so many strands of Jewish thought of the second temple period.[131] It should also be noted that the image of avian wings suggests protection. In this connection, it is interesting to note that in Isaiah 31.5 the protection of Jerusalem in an avian manner is specifically mentioned. Such protection is mediated precisely through the ministry of Jesus. In this light, Luke 19.41–4, where the Lukan Jesus laments the ignorance of Jerusalem of τὰ πρὸς εἰρήνη (v. 42), carries a similar motif as found in this passage. And this leads to the third point – the restoration of Jerusalem as the intention of Jesus.

To understand the importance of this third point, the OT and Jewish backgrounds have to be taken into account. In chapter 2, we concluded that there was a yearning for the restoration of the nation and the city and that the latter had become the focus even of the former. If such an idea is borne in mind, Jesus' lament over Jerusalem in this passage signifies that the fulfilment of such a hope is to be brought about through his ministry and restorative message. Such an inference is not far-fetched, and it further implies that Jesus probably saw the restoration of Jerusalem as the crown of his intentions in his ministry. That this is eminently possible is supported by the results arrived at in chapter 3: Jesus understood Jerusalem as the τέλος of his ministry. The tone of finality in the saying in Q 13.35 (the pronouncement of abandonment) lends further support to the view that the 'gathering' of Jerusalem back to Yahweh was important to Jesus. These observations serve to highlight the congruence of Jesus' ministry with the important aspects of the Zion traditions where the restoration of Zion is the representation and crown of the restoration of the nation and the fulfilment of Yahweh's promises. Such congruence is further evident in the possibility that in this lament Jesus' presupposition was probably that Jerusalem was the mother of all Israelites; τὰ τέκνα (v. 34) probably refers not to Jerusalemites alone.[132] If this is correct, another aspect of the Zion traditions, in which Zion is the mother of Israelites, is seen to be part of Jesus' beliefs. The

[130] C. F. Evans, *Luke*, p. 564.
[131] See our previous discussion in chapter 2.   [132] So C. F. Evans, *Luke*, p. 564.

rejection of Yahweh's restoration through Jesus' ministry and preaching resulted in judgment – the departing of the Shekinah from the temple. This parallels the destruction of the first temple in 586 BCE. Hence, it would seem that the Zion traditions had greatly influenced Jesus' understanding of his intentions in his ministry.

However, in the light of the judgment pronouncement of Jesus over the temple, a question must be asked: what would this pronouncement of judgment on the part of Jesus reveal about his stance towards the Zion traditions? Did Jesus reject them? If Matthew 5.35 is authentic, we could at least say that there was a time that Jesus held to such traditions. But in view of the rejection he faced at Jerusalem, did he finally reject them?

It should be noted that, in the midst of judgment (Q 13.35b), hope is held out also to the nation. Jerusalem would see Jesus or Yahweh, and this would result in its salvation, if it was prepared to pronounce a blessing on ὁ ἐχόμενος. Until such time, the Shekinah would remain withdrawn from the temple and, by extension, also from the city itself. [133] Such a 'lifeline' would mean that, in spite of Israel's rejection of God's regathering overtures and the ensuing judgment which was pronounced, Israel was not rejected without any hope of future redemption. Jerusalem would still see ὁ ἐχόμενος if it became what it was meant to be: a place of blessing and a city ready to receive or bless him. Stuhlmacher is right: Jesus was convinced that Yahweh's promise of salvation for Jerusalem according to Isaiah 54.10 would ultimately be realised. [134] There is no ultimate rejection of the Zion traditions by Jesus.

Convergence

We saw that many elements of this passage converge with the chief aspects of Jesus' ministry and especially with our previous studies on Luke 13.31–3 and Matthew 5.35.

First, the data for concluding that Jerusalem had an important place in Jesus' ministry could be found in yet another strand of tradition, Q. [135] There is therefore evidence from three different strands of tradition which exhibits this phenomenon: 'L' (Luke

---

[133] Perhaps this hope is that from which the Petrine statement made in Acts 3.19–21 and the Pauline hope for Israel expressed in Rom. 11.26 derived their impetus.

[134] Stuhlmacher, 'Stellung', 146.

[135] By Q, we mean here the sayings material Luke and Matthew have in common. It does not imply that Q is a unitary document.

13.31–3), 'M' (Matt. 5.35) and Q (the present passage). This gives our study an even firmer base.

Secondly, it is interesting to note that Jesus adopted a prophetic persona *vis-à-vis* Jerusalem and here we find a convergence between this passage and Luke 13.31–3 (chapter 3). It must be pointed out that in the OT, many prophets are connected with Jerusalem (her fate, destiny, sin and salvation), whether in thought or deed. It should also be noted that in both passages (Luke 13.31–3; and 13.34–5) the death of prophets receives mention and this demonstrates that Jerusalem as the city which kills prophets is a typical characterisation by the historical Jesus. The pin-pointing of Jerusalem as the special city which kills prophets cuts across the usual Israelite's understanding of the significance of Jerusalem, its being the 'mother of every Israelite'[136] and the city of *salvation*.

Thirdly, the fact that Jesus understood Yahweh to be seeking to fulfil the restorative promises to Jerusalem through his own ministry offers another line of convergence with the results arrived at earlier in this study in chapter 4. Jerusalem was to Jesus the city of the great king and it is not surprising that its restoration to this great king should be sought by Jesus.

[136] Stuhlmacher, 'Stellung', 145.

CONCLUSIONS TO PART II

Part II is an intense probe into the sayings of Jesus and targets certain key sayings from diverse streams of tradition in order to answer the two questions posed at the outset of the study. The chronological and historical settings of the sayings studied have not been sought. Q 13.34–5 is an exception: we have proposed that it was uttered by Jesus in Jerusalem during the final days of his ministry. Also, a chronological and psychological development of Jesus' attitude towards Jerusalem has been eschewed: form critics rightly insist that the nature of the transmission of the sayings tradition pre-empts such an attempt.

Certain important results have been obtained. The first concerns the magnetic aspect of Jerusalem with regard to Jesus' ministry. Jerusalem is to be the place of Jesus' τέλος. There are two further important aspects under this head. The first is the prophetic aspect. Jesus adopted the persona of a prophet when speaking of Jerusalem as the τέλος of his ministry in Luke 13.31–3 (L). Such a phenomenon is also corroborated by evidence from Q 13.34–5. This outlook corresponds with many strands of prophetic tradition in the OT – the link between Jerusalem and the prophets. Hence, Jesus as a prophet is inexorably attracted to Jerusalem. The second is the aspect of the kingdom of God. Jesus regards Jerusalem as the city of Yahweh's kingship (Matt 5.35).

As Jesus' message concerns the establishment of Yahweh's reign on earth,[1] it would be legitimate to infer that he would be impelled by his very message to go to Jerusalem. Exactly such a phenomenon is attested by Q 13.34–5. In this passage, Jesus understands that Yahweh is seeking to 'gather' Jerusalem and her children through his ministry. Such a convergence between the two passages is perfectly understandable in that, if Jerusalem is the city of Yah-

---

[1] Whether this is interpreted in a futuristic and imminent sense, or in a realised sense is irrelevant for our purposes here.

weh's kingship, Jesus, who proclaims the message of this kingship, will seek to bring the city under Yahweh's kingship. Hence, the attraction of Jerusalem to Jesus' ministry is a very important consideration to bear in mind in any reconstruction of Jesus' intentions. It also facilitates the answering of the two questions posed at the outset in chapter 1. It should also be pointed out that this aligns very well with the results of chapter 2 where the restoration of Zion is shown to be of great importance in the second temple period.

The second result concerns the nature of the τέλος. Two important points ought to be noted under this head. The first is that Jesus understands his τέλος to involve his death (Luke 13.31–3). Although death may be a consequence expected by Jesus in his ministry in Jerusalem, he actually understands it to be the necessary culmination of his whole ministry. This observation has important repercussions for our understanding of Jesus' intentions in Jerusalem. The second is that the τέλος of his ministry involves also the fulfilment of Yahweh's restorative promises made to Jerusalem. This observation is developed from a conjunction of Luke 13.31–3 with Q 13.34–5. From the latter passage, we discover that Jesus' ministry concerns the fulfilment of such promises. In many strands of Jewish thought this forms the *climax* of the restoration programme of Yahweh for his covenant partner – Israel. Hence, Jesus' τέλος involves both the climactic fulfilment of the restoration promises to Zion and his death. How these two are related is not shown by the sayings tradition. Data have to be sought from Jesus' significant actions in Jerusalem (Part III of our study).

The third result concerns Jesus' appropriation of the Zion traditions. Although there is no evidence to point to a single utterance of the word 'Zion' by Jesus, it can be safely concluded that the Zion traditions play a significant role in Jesus' conception of his ministry. In this connection, it should be emphasised once again that these traditions are not a fixed and static entity but a conglomerate of motifs and themes which point to and guarantee the importance of Zion in the Jewish psyche. In this light, although it is quite often used in OT scholarship, the term 'Zion traditions' is a modern scholarly construct. Therefore, the lack of a particular and deliberate mention of the word 'Zion' by Jesus is not surprising. What is important instead is that Jesus' sayings are demonstrably congruent with many important aspects of these traditions. This implies that Jesus would probably have been significantly influenced by them. It is important to note that if what we are arguing for is correct, the theological and religious importance of Jerusalem is the main reason why Jesus went to Jerusalem: the social, economic and political factors have, no doubt, played a part. But these are not governing factors; they are only subsidiary.

The important data from Part II which allow us to suggest that the Zion traditions have been appropriated by Jesus for his ministry are the following. Zion attracts Jesus and he regards it as the place of the τέλος of his ministry. No other place is to have that function. Zion means for Jesus the city of the great king, Yahweh. Its sanctity is recognised and as such, and in the light of the coming of God's kingdom, oaths using the name of Jerusalem are banned. It is probable that Jesus also understands Zion to be the mother of Israelites (Q 13.34–5). Such a motif belongs to these traditions. Finally, the fulfilment of the restoration promises made to Zion is understood by Jesus as being effected through his ministry.

Although judgment is pronounced against the 'house' of Zion, Jesus does not ultimately reject her. In this light, it should be said that Jesus' attitude towards Jerusalem revolves around a tension between two poles: negativity and affirmation. It is negative in that Jesus castigates Jerusalem as the city which kills prophets. Yet, on the other hand, he affirms that, in spite of this, it has a unique place in Yahweh's relationship with his people.

It remains to be seen whether these results converge with a detailed study of Jesus' intentions in his significant actions in Jerusalem. To this we now turn.

PART III

The actions

INTRODUCTION TO PART III

The purpose of this part of our study is to probe into the significant actions of Jesus in Jerusalem so as to discover the intentions underlying them. Undue concentration on any one episode to the neglect of others would only lead to distortion and skewed results. Therefore, three important incidents are chosen: the 'triumphal' entry, the incident in the temple and the last supper. An enquiry into whether there is an underlying unity behind these actions will be conducted. This part of our study will also test whether the results obtained from the study of these actions dovetail with those in Part II.

6

JESUS IN JERUSALEM (I):
THE 'TRIUMPHAL' ENTRY

The 'triumphal' entry was prominent in earlier scholarly discussion of the intentions of Jesus. For example, Reimarus[1] and scholars who subscribe to the *putsch* theory of Jesus' intention have based their studies largely on this episode and the 'cleansing' of the temple.[2] More recently, however, this episode has largely been neglected in historical Jesus research.[3] We believe that this episode is extremely important for our understanding both of Jesus' intentions for going to Jerusalem and of his appropriation of the Zion traditions. We shall start by analysing the gospel traditions of this event (especially those offered by Mark and John) with a view to historical reconstruction. Next, we hope to draw out the significance and meaning of this incident in relation to Jesus' intentions and his indebtedness to the Zion traditions.

1 Historical reconstruction

The 'triumphal' entry is one of the few episodes which can be found in all four gospels (Matt. 21.1–9; Mark 11.1–10; Luke 19.28–40; John 12.12–19). Very probably, Luke and Matthew built their versions of this episode upon Mark.[4] John's version probably represents an independent tradition.[5] The agreement between these

---

[1] H. Reimarus in C. H. Talbert (ed.), *Reimarus: Fragments*, p. 146.
[2] For a good account of this trend in scholarship, see E. Bammel, 'The Revolution Theory from Reimarus to Brandon', in E. Bammel and C. F. D. Moule (eds.), *Jesus and the Politics of His Day*, pp. 11–68.
[3] Most recent books on the historical Jesus devote only a brief treatment to it. See, for example, E. P. Sanders, *Jesus and Judaism*, p. 306.
[4] Luke has some additional traditions; we shall attend to this later.
[5] On the issue of John's independence of Mark, there is still no consensus. See the excellent discussion in D. Moody Smith, *John Among the Gospels* and his recent essay, 'Historical Issues and the Problem of John and the Synoptics', in M. C. de Boer (ed.), *From Jesus to John: Essays on Jesus and New Testament Christology in Honour of Marinus de Jonge*, pp. 252–67.

four evangelists is close, although there are also interesting and significant variations, especially between Mark and John.[6] In this section, we shall first resolve the general question of the authenticity of the incident and then attempt to reconstruct the event. Regarding the question of authenticity, we propose to treat first the entry episode proper and after that the episode of the finding of the animal.[7]

The authenticity of the incident

It should be noted at the outset that there seems to be a consensus among scholars that at least the fact of Jesus' entering into Jerusalem with his disciples is historical, but with the proviso that the account has been overlaid with legends and coloured messianically.[8] Although some scholars may derive only 'attenuated' interpretations[9] from this episode, the majority are in agreement that there is at least a historical kernel to the accounts presented to us in the four gospels.[10]

There are three major reasons for this confidence. First, Harvey points out that the posture of Jesus' riding on an ass was in stark contrast to the usual mode of entry by pilgrims into Jerusalem – on foot.[11] Harvey comments, 'I find it impossible to believe that such an apparently gratuitous act of provocation to religious sensibilities could have been invented by the Christian tradition.'[12]

---

[6] Cf. the remark of C. H. Dodd: 'They differ in every point where it is possible to differ in relating the same incident', in his *Historical Tradition in the Fourth Gospel*, p. 155.

[7] In his 'Der Einzug Jesu in Jerusalem', *ZTK* 68 (1971), 1–26, H. Patsch distinguishes three elements in the Markan account: the story of the finding of the animal; the riding of the ass into the city as a fulfilment of Zech. 9.9; and the acclamation by the disciples. His attempt to separate what in our opinion is integral is unconvincing.

[8] See I. H. Marshall, *The Gospel of Luke*, p. 710.

[9] An example of what we mean by an 'attenuated' interpretation is presented by Sanders in his *Jesus*, p. 306: 'Perhaps the event took place but was a small occurrence which went unnoticed. Perhaps only a few disciples unostentatiously dropped their garments in front of the ass ... while only a few quietly murmured "Hosanna".'

[10] R. Pesch, *Das Markusevangelium* II, pp. 187–8; A. E. Harvey, *Jesus and the Constraints of History*, pp. 120–9; M. J. Borg, *Conflict, Holiness and Politics in the Teachings of Jesus*, pp. 170–1; C. C. Rowland, *Christian Origins*, pp. 180–2 and a host of others.

[11] In the earliest rabbinic sources, the infirm were explicitly exempted from the duty to make the pilgrimage on the grounds that they would be unable to accomplish it on foot (*m.Hag.* 1.1; *b.Hag.* 6a; *m.Ber.* 9.5).

[12] Harvey, *Constraints*, p. 121.

Secondly, it should be noted that there was no attested use of Zechariah to describe the coming messiah around the time of Jesus[13] and this may strengthen the case for authenticity. More in keeping with the ethos of Jesus' day may be the notion of the messiah on a war-horse, in line with the political and social undercurrents then.[14] In this regard, it is interesting to note that there was rabbinic embarrassment over the notion of a messiah entering Jerusalem on a lowly ass. In *b.Sanh.* 98a, rabbi Joshua ben Levi solves his own puzzle of why according to Jewish scriptures the messiah is said to come both with the clouds of heaven and also meek and sitting on an ass by pronouncing that 'if they [the Jews] are worthy, he will come with the clouds of heaven; if they are not worthy, meek and sitting on an ass'.[15] Admittedly, the text is late but it highlights the fact that such a notion of the messiah's entry into Jerusalem was not something easily congenial to Jewish minds. The foregoing demonstrates that the gospel account of Jesus' entry into Jerusalem may be dissimilar to Jewish expectations of that time.

Thirdly, at least one gospel account, Mark's (probably the most primitive of all the four gospels), does not support the idea that this episode is a post-Easter creation from Zechariah 9.9. He does not cite Zechariah 9.9 nor does he capitalise on the christological potential of this episode.[16] Such conservatism is difficult to explain if this is a creation of the post-Easter community. Concerning the other gospels, Carr observes that 'John and Matthew give a drastically truncated version of Zechariah 9.9. They both conflate it with other Scripture texts to avoid certain difficulties. Luke seems to make an attempt to divert the attention of his readers away from Zechariah 9.9, he does not cite the prophecy. It is difficult to

---

[13] The application of the prophecy of Zechariah to the coming messiah is not attested in the rabbinic tradition until the middle of the third century CE (*b.Sanh.* 98a; see Harvey, *Constraints*, p. 122). The reference to Zech. 13.7 in manuscript B of CD 19.5b–9 probably does not refer to the messiah as the shepherd but to a wicked ruler. On this see F. F. Bruce, 'The Book of Zechariah and the Passion Narrative', *BJRL* 43 (1960–1), 343; and M. A. Knibb, *The Qumran Community*, p. 59.

[14] On this see the illuminating essay of T. A. Idinopulos, 'Religious and National Factors in Israel's War with Rome', in S. Talmon (ed.), *Jewish Civilization in the Hellenistic Roman Period*, pp. 50–63.

[15] On this, see also J. Blenkinsopp, 'The Oracle of Judah and the Messianic Entry', *JBL* 80 (1961), 60.

[16] See V. Taylor, *The Gospel of Mark*, pp. 452–3; B. Witherington III, *The Christology of Jesus*, p. 105; and R. H. Gundry, *Mark: A Commentary on His Apology for the Cross*, p. 632.

explain these phenomena if the church created the tradition to prove that Jesus had fulfilled that prophecy.'[17] Nor should Genesis 49.10–11 be regarded as the substratum on which the present narrative is built.[18] There are too many significant differences between the two passages for such a theory to stand up to scrutiny. In Genesis 49.10–11 the animal is tied to a vine, while in Mark 11.4 it is tied to the door; the promised one *tethers* the animal in the Genesis passage while the disciples *loose* the animal in the gospel accounts (Matt. 21.2; Mark 11.2, 4; Luke 19.30, 33). The connection between the Genesis passage and the entry narrative is not explicitly made until much later (Justin, *1 Apol.* 32; Clem., *Paed.* 1.5.15).[19]

The foregoing may not amount to a full demonstration of the authenticity of the incident, but it does prevent one from attributing this episode to the presumed creative genius of the post-Easter community working on the substratum provided by Zechariah 9.9 or Genesis 49.10–11. The best explanation for the existence of such a story is that there was an incident which involved Jesus riding into Jerusalem on an ass. This should not be taken to imply that we disallow the possibility of christological expansions being made to this episode during the process of transmission. But whether this is so has to be closely investigated. Suffice it to point out here that there are good grounds for concluding that this incident is probably historical.

The greatest objection to the authenticity of this episode comes from the notion that any kind of public demonstration of a messianic nature would have led to police action. Since this did not happen, the episode could be fictional. Hence, to claim that it is historical, some scholars are driven to reduce the size and significance of the incident.[20]

But an objection along these lines is not strong. First, this incident could have been no noisier or more demonstrative than the arrival of any large group of pilgrims in Jerusalem at such a time of festival.[21] Moreover, it is unclear whether there was any messianic

[17] D. Carr, 'Jesus, the King of Zion: A Traditio-Historical Enquiry into the so-called "Triumphal Entry" of Jesus' (unpublished Ph.D. dissertation, University of London, 1980), p. 353.

[18] *Pace* Blenkinsopp, 'Oracle', 55–64.   [19] Cf. Gundry, *Mark*, p. 632.

[20] See, for example, Sanders, *Jesus*, p. 306.

[21] This is also observed by Marshall, *Gospel*, pp. 710–11; and Gundry, *Mark*, p. 32. Whether it was Passover or another festival does not concern us here. But see chapter 7 where we attempt to answer this question.

demonstration on the part of the crowds. One should not conclude from the acclamation of the crowds in the evangelists' narratives that a messianic demonstration was taking place. Police attention therefore would not be attracted or aroused.[22] Secondly, Bammel has pointed out in a different context that '[k]ingly claims outside Rome might be regarded with suspicion ... but they did not *ipso facto* clash with the established order of the day. Besides, the situation in Palestine was so complex, claims of a messianic character so common and, on the other hand, refuted already by part of the population, that it was a matter of good policy for the Romans to avoid involvement in these issues as far as possible.'[23] Hence, even if it is assumed that some of the crowd understood the procession as having a messianic character, it is unlikely that the Romans would have taken action unless it was accompanied by violent demonstrations.[24] In view of this, one must not allow the criticisms against the *putsch* theory to prevent one from reckoning with the possibility that the crowds were enthusiastically receiving Jesus. To such displays of enthusiasm, violent demonstrations need not be a necessary accompaniment. As to the lack of immediate action on the part of the Jewish aristocracy, it must be said that Jesus' action was not *explicitly* messianic. Nevertheless, it should be noted that the incidents which followed this episode in the gospels (Mark 11.18–19‖Luke 19.47–8; Mark 11.27–33 and parallels) in-dicate that sufficient interest was aroused on the part of the Jewish authorities. Such a phenomenon of Jewish authorities' interest on the one hand and the lack of direct action on the other is historically credible.

Even the recent attempt of Catchpole to mount a strong case for dismissing the Markan account as a post-Easter invention[25] does

---

[22] Cf. J. Nolland, *Luke 18:35–24:53*, p. 922.

[23] E. Bammel, 'The *Titulus*', in E. Bammel and C. F. D. Moule (eds.), *Jesus and the Politics of His Day*, p. 358. R. A. Horsley and J. D. Hanson have also pointed out that charismatic leaders among the Jewish peasants of the first century received the appellation 'king' from time to time even when they did not make explicit claims to be of royal lineage. This was done in the hope that they might liberate the people from foreign oppression (*Bandits, Prophets and Messiahs: Popular Movements in the Time of Jesus*, p. 115).

[24] Incidentally, the objection discussed here demonstrates that the *putsch* theory of Jesus' entry cannot stand up to scrutiny. For a sustained critique of the *putsch* theory see M. Hengel, *Was Jesus a Revolutionist?*

[25] D. R. Catchpole, 'The "Triumphal" Entry', in E. Bammel and C. F. D. Moule (eds.), *Jesus and the Politics of His Day*, pp. 319–34. Catchpole considers that, to all intents and purposes, the Markan account represents our best hope for mining a historical kernel of authenticity, see pp. 321–2.

not, in our opinion, stand up to scrutiny. Catchpole's case depends in part on his form-critical analysis of the episode and in part on his understanding of Markan redaction and compositional structure of his gospel. Regarding the former, Catchpole categorises the Markan 'triumphal' entry under a family of stories detailing the celebratory entry to a city by a hero-figure who has previously achieved his triumph.[26] Concerning the latter, Catchpole avers that the whole account is christologically determined and that the pre-entry activities could not be justifiably regarded as messianic.[27] Without attempting a detailed refutation of Catchpole's view, some general points will be noted here. First, Catchpole's implicit assumption that the conformity of an account to a certain genre of stories indicates inauthenticity is not necessarily true. Such a judgment is, in fact, a priori. It is eminently possible that a basically historical incident be redacted to conform to a certain pattern. Hence, a form-critical approach to this particular episode is not sufficient in itself to demonstrate authenticity or inauthenticity.[28]

Secondly, it is not clear that the Markan version of the 'triumphal' entry (Catchpole works on the basis of the Markan account) conforms to the genre of entry stories isolated by him. Catchpole is driven to regard the healing stories in Mark as the attainment of victory by Jesus prior to the entry in order to build a parallel between the Markan entry account and those he isolated. This seems forced.[29] In those stories Catchpole isolated, it was *military* victory which was mentioned. Hence, it is questionable whether the Markan entry story is derived from those entry stories. The significant differences have to be noted. Besides, there is a more viable background to explain the form of the Markan account which we will discuss later.

Finally, Catchpole is driven to dismiss the historicity of the Petrine confession (Mark 8.29) and the *titulus* (Mark 15.32) in order to support his point that Jesus could not be understood as the messiah apart from this account, since both of them provide evidence that Jesus was understood by others as claiming to be the

---

[26] Catchpole, 'Entry', pp. 319–23.   [27] 'Entry', p. 323.

[28] So also Witherington, *Christology*, p. 104; and B. F. Meyer, *The Aims of Jesus*, p. 199.

[29] Catchpole, 'Entry', p. 323. It is difficult to conceive Mark as having this in mind when he narrated the healing episodes. Moreover, the three passion predictions before the entry hardly prepare his readers to understand the entry as being 'triumphal'. Nolland makes a similar observation in another connection in his *Luke 18:35–24:53*, p. 923.

messiah.[30] On the contrary, they have both been amply demonstrated to be authentic by many scholars.[31]

Since there is no strong objection to the authenticity of the
incident and since there are good grounds for accepting the
contrary, one could therefore justifiably conclude that the account
of Jesus' entering Jerusalem on an ass amid the acclamation of the
festive crowd is historical. What follows is an attempt at reconstructing the whole event and this will form the basis for the
discussion on the significance of the incident and the meaning
intended by Jesus in the staging of this event.

Reconstructing the event from the gospel traditions

(i) The Markan tradition

It is usually held that Luke and Matthew derived their accounts of
the entry from Mark.[32] Luke does present some extra traditions
(especially Luke 19.38b and Luke 19.39–40) and they will be
discussed later. We shall work on the basis of the Markan account
and then compare it with the Johannine.

There has been a tendency to separate Mark's entry narrative
from the story of the requisition of the animal (Mark 11.1–6).[33]
The main reason behind such an expedient is that the latter is often
regarded as 'legendary' because of the presence of some 'unnatural'
elements, namely the foreknowledge of the animal on the part of
Jesus, the use of the word κύριος, and the uncanny ease with which
the disciples acquired the animal.[34] Nevertheless, Derrett has
offered a plausible account of the episode based on the custom of
impressment (ἀγγαρεία).[35] There is therefore no necessity to view
this episode as containing legendary elements. In many ways, the
apparently 'supernatural' elements connected with the requisition
story can be understood as a result of prearrangement.[36] Further-

---

[30] Catchpole, 'Entry', pp. 328, 330.
[31] The Petrine confession is defended by many scholars; a good summary of the
      case is offered by Marshall, *Gospel*, pp. 364–5. The authenticity of the *titulus* is
      recently defended by Bammel, 'The *Titulus*', pp. 353–64.
[32] Catchpole, 'Entry', pp. 321–2; see also Harvey, *Constraints*, p. 122.
[33] E.g., Patsch, 'Einzug', 1–26.
[34] R. Bultmann, *The History of the Synoptic Tradition*, p. 267.
[35] J. D. M. Derrett, 'Law in the New Testament: The Palm Sunday Colt', *NovT* 13
      (1971), 241–58.
[36] See Harvey, *Constraints*, pp. 122–3; Marshall, *Gospel*, p. 710.

more, from a literary point of view, the integrity of the two passages is evident.[37] It is therefore probable that the impressment narrative is historical and that it forms an integral part of the entry narrative.

In the Markan narrative, the quotation of Zechariah 9.9 is not mentioned although much space is devoted to recounting the requisition of the animal.[38] The failure to cite Zechariah 9.9 would in our opinion confirm the view that the Markan account is the most primitive of all the four gospels, and that the quotation was added later through christological reflection.[39]

Regarding the acclamation of the crowds, it is perhaps possible that they did not intend to hail the riding Jesus as king and that it was Mark who shaped his account of it in such a way as to give that impression: εὐλογημένη ἡ ἐρχομένη βασιλεία τοῦ πατρὸς ἡμῶν Δαυίδ (v. 10).[40] While it is difficult to demonstrate that these words were on the lips of the crowd, it may be going too far to suggest that, to the crowd, Jesus was just another pilgrim. If one could assume that Jesus' fame as a healer, exorcist and performer of miracles had spread, it is reasonable to suppose that, at least for some of the crowd, the question of whether Jesus was the messiah would have been aroused.[41] Moreover, as noted above, Jesus adopted a most provocative gesture by riding an animal into Jerusalem. Nevertheless, it is admitted that there is difficulty in ascertaining precisely what the crowd said and how they would have viewed Jesus.

The presence of the branches (στιβάδες) need not be doubted as they were plentiful around Jerusalem,[42] and the spreading of the garments is historically possible without invoking a christological understanding on the part of the crowd. Harvey makes mention of the possibility that the latter action could have a ritual significance, i.e., to prevent any unclean matter on the ground from rendering unclean a person who was about to enter the temple (*m.Zab.* 4.7).[43]

The question remains as to the actual scale of the whole procession. While not wanting to discount the possibility that post-

---

[37] Catchpole, 'Entry', p. 325.

[38] For some probable reasons as to why Mark gave a surprisingly large amount of space to narrating the requisition of the animal see Harvey, *Constraints*, pp. 123–4.

[39] So Witherington, *Christology*, p. 105.

[40] Harvey, *Constraints*, p. 127.   [41] So also Rowland, *Origins*, p. 182.

[42] See the discussion in D. A. Carson, *The Gospel According to John*, pp. 431–2; and Harvey, *Constraints*, p. 125.

[43] Harvey, *Constraints*, p. 125.

Easter reflection could have caused Mark to nuance and highlight certain aspects of the procession (πολλοί in v. 8; the acclamation in v. 10), it must also be said that such affairs were often noisy, being celebratory in nature. Hence, the Markan picture in vv. 8–9 should not be lightly dismissed.

(ii) The Markan account compared with the Johannine

It is clear that the Zechariah quotation (Zech. 9.9) was introduced into the Johannine and Matthean accounts through post-Easter reflection on the significance of the event (cf. John 12.16). Once this quotation is discounted, the only significant difference between the Johannine and Markan accounts is the *order* of the events of the procession into Jerusalem. Mark gives the impression that the riding of the animal was staged by Jesus with the effect that the *crowd* responded with their acclamation (especially evident in Mark's lengthy account of the requisition of the animal (Mark 11.1–6; cf. vv. 8–9)). But in John, the impression one receives is that *Jesus* responded to the crowd's acclamation by riding on an ass, with perhaps the intention of dampening the crowd's enthusiasm for a political liberator (as usually understood by many scholars),[44] and at the same time signifying that he was for peace. It has also been suggested that this was the actual order of events.[45]

It appears that too much weight has been placed on this supposed disagreement over the order of the events. As Beasley-Murray observes, this discrepancy may be an unintended result of the fourth evangelist's mode of description in vv. 12–13,[46] being summary in nature. Besides, as Barrett has noted, εὑρών could mean 'to find by the agency of others', and details insignificant to John are expurgated.[47]

Even if one grants that the Johannine account intended a different order of events over against Mark,[48] it would seem more probable that John, rather than Mark, was motivated by his own redactional interests to change it. The Johannine account of the

---

[44] So C. K. Barrett, *The Gospel According to St John*, p. 418; Carr, 'Jesus', p. 356; Carson, *John*, p. 433; G. R. Beasley-Murray, *John*, p. 210; Rowland, *Origins*, p. 181. See R. E. Brown, *The Gospel According to John I–XII*, pp. 462–3 for a slightly different interpretation.

[45] Carr, 'Jesus', p. 356.   [46] Beasley-Murray, *John*, p. 206.

[47] Barrett, *John*, p. 418.

[48] So Brown, *John I–XII*, p. 462, basing on the force of δέ in v. 14 which he regards as adversative.

response of Jesus to the crowd's reaction to make him king after the feeding of the five thousand (John 6.14–15) may be an intended precursor and parallel to the Johannine version of the entry.[49] In this light, John was concerned to portray Jesus not as a violent political liberator.[50] Moreover, it is harder to conceive that the animal just happened to be there coincidentally (v. 14). Hence, Mark has probably preserved an account which is closest to the original event.

(iii) The Lukan 'additions' (Luke 19.38, 39–40, 41–4)

There are some aspects unique to the Lukan account of the 'triumphal' entry. For the sake of simplicity, we shall call these 'additions'. The first 'addition' can be found in Luke 19.38 in the words ἐν οὐρανῷ εἰρήνη καὶ δόξα ἐν ὑψίστοις, which are usually regarded as redactional as they have an evident precursor in Luke 2.14: δόξα ἐν ὑψίστος θεῷ καὶ ἐπὶ γῆς εἰρήνη.[51] The second concerns the response of the Pharisees to the entry and Jesus' lamentation over Jerusalem. This can be further broken down into two parts, forming two logia of Jesus (Luke 19.39–40 and 19.41–4).

Luke 19.39–40 gives the impression that some of the Pharisees formed part of the procession and responded by asking Jesus to silence his elated and jubilant disciples (τινες τῶν φαρισαίων ἀπὸ τοῦ ὄχλου). But did this actually happen and did Luke place this episode in the correct chronological order? Parallels to this episode may perhaps be found in Matthew 21.14–16 and John 12.19, and this may show that a common tradition lies behind these accounts[52] and that this event probably happened around the time of the entry,[53] perhaps after and not during it. Because of the uncertainty over the precise location of this pericope, it is best to leave this account out of the discussion on the entry.

Regarding Luke 19.41–4, it is probable that these verses may have originally formed part of an apocalyptic discourse. Traces of this can be found in Luke 21.[54] Hence, these additional materials will not be utilised in the reconstruction of the event.

---

[49] This has been observed also by Beasley-Murray, *John*, p. 210.

[50] See Barrett, *John*, p. 418 for other plausible suggestions.

[51] See the extended discussion in Carr, 'Jesus', pp. 271–89, especially p. 289. Cf. H. Baarlink, 'Friede im Himmel: Die lukanische Redaktion von Lk 19,38 und ihre Deutung', *ZNW* 76 (1985), 170–86.

[52] Marshall, *Gospel*, p. 716.   [53] See Carr, 'Jesus', p. 290.

[54] Marshall, *Gospel*, p. 717. D. Wenham defends the authenticity of the logion, *The*

(iv) Reconstruction of the event

We can thus conclude from the discussion above that the Markan account of the entry is the most primitive version among the four extant accounts preserved in the gospels. As we have also regarded the story of the requisition of the animal as being in all likelihood authentic, it can thus be said that the Markan sequence of events is probably historical.

If the above conclusions are correct, one can thus see that the whole event was deliberately staged by Jesus. This can be seen in two ways: the deliberate arrangement for the requisition of the animal and the deliberately provocative posture adopted by the riding of an animal into Jerusalem. If this was a deliberate act, Jesus would have assigned some meaning to it.[55] What this meaning might be will be discussed later.[56] As to the actual scale of the event, one cannot be certain. But it seems justifiable to conclude that Sanders' view of the event as a small-scale affair involving only Jesus' disciples is incorrect[57] as this does not give proper weight to Jesus' fame as a healer, exorcist and miracle-worker. It is much harder to gauge whether the crowd saw in this event a deliberately symbolic and messianic act. Given the popularity that Jesus achieved in his peripatetic ministry, it would be far-fetched to conclude that no one in the crowd realised the import of this event.[58] But as there was no action from the Roman garrison, one would have to conclude that it was not an unruly or outwardly revolutionary demonstration.[59] The whole event would have enough ambiguity about it to forestall such actions from the crowd (as the book of Zechariah did not figure prominently as a source-book for messianic speculation then).[60] It is probable that Mark has given a christological thrust to the whole event by his redaction of the crowd's acclamation, but it must equally be said that such a redactional nuancing was done cautiously without much exploita-

    Rediscovery of Jesus' Eschatological Discourse, pp. 346–53. But cf. J. Neyrey, 'Jesus' Address to the Women of Jerusalem (Luke 23.27–31) – A Prophetic Judgment Oracle', *NTS* 29 (1983), 74–86 for a contrary view.

[55] Meyer, *Aims*, p. 199; Sanders, *Jesus*, p. 308; cf. also J. A. Sanders, 'A New Testament Hermeneutic Fabric: Psalm 118 in the Entrance Narrative', in C. A. Evans and W. F. Stinespring (eds.), *Early Jewish and Christian Exegesis*, p. 179.

[56] See discussion in next major section.

[57] Sanders, *Jesus*, p. 306; Nolland, *Luke 18:35 – 24:53*, p. 922.

[58] Cf. the keen observation of Rowland, *Origins*, p. 182.

[59] So Sanders, *Jesus*, p. 306.

[60] Bruce, 'Zechariah', 336–53; Harvey, *Constraints*, p. 122.

tion or embellishment.[61] The spreading of the garments on the ass and on the road and the leafy branches (palm? John = βαῖα, Mark = στιβάδες) need not be viewed as embellishments on the part of Mark.[62]

To conclude: Jesus made plans for the ass to be brought to him. It is possible that he walked part of the way without it (as suggested by Carson[63]) and only rode it into Jerusalem when his disciples met him along the way, with the animal. The crowds were jubilant and probably acclaimed him in traditional hymns and songs. While it is possible that some saw in this event a messianic significance, the evidence at hand does not lead to any firm conclusions. After the resurrection, the disciples understood the event to be christologically charged and brought out this significance by their various redactional thrusts.

2   The significance and meaning of the incident

The crux of the problem

'There is no recorded commentary by Jesus explaining his actions; such commentary as there is, is provided by the actions and words of the crowds...' These words, taken from Harvey,[64] lead us into the crux of the problem connected with the attempt to understand the meaning Jesus intended by the entry. Unless one holds that Luke 19.39–44 is connected with the incident, all four evangelists failed to record any commentary from Jesus.[65] Matthew and John sought to bring out the implicit meaning of the incident by citing scripture (Matthew has Zech. 9.9 and John has a conflated citation: Zech. 9.9 + Isa. 40.9[66] or Zeph. 3.16[67]). However, as noted earlier, there are strong grounds for concluding that the whole affair was deliberately managed. Three possible conclusions could be drawn from such a state of affairs. First, Jesus probably gave no commentary during the event; if there was a commentary, it would surely have been preserved by the post-Easter community. Secondly, the action may have been intended to be incomplete in itself, i.e., the

---

61 So also Witherington, *Christology*, p. 105.
62 Carr, 'Jesus', pp. 319–20, 360; cf. Harvey, *Constraints*, p. 125.
63 Carson, *John*, p. 433.   64 Harvey, *Constraints*, p. 125.
65 Perhaps this is an indication of the evangelists' faithfulness to the tradition they received.
66 So Barrett, *John*, pp. 418–19.   67 See the discussion in Carr, 'Jesus', p. 72.

meaning is only intimated but must be explained expressly by another event. In other words, the entry should not be interpreted on its own; it must be correlated and understood in the light of other episodes.[68] Thirdly, we can derive hints from the action since meaning is none the less intimated by the deliberate and planned nature of the event.[69] These points are to be borne in mind when interpreting the significance of this event.

The significance intended by Jesus

That the action is symbolic is clear from the intentional nature of the event and the lack of commentary on the part of the one who staged it.[70] But what is the symbolic content? Riding into Jerusalem on an animal during a festival would be tantamount on the part of Jesus to saying that he was an important figure. Of the entry accounts which Catchpole lists,[71] none explicitly mentions the riding of an animal in entries to Jerusalem.

(i) The background

Such a symbolic action would be meaningful only if there was an attested and accepted background to it. The place to start with in the search for this background is the Jewish traditions inherited by Jesus, especially the OT. To aid this search two important elements of the episode must be noted: the animal (an ass)[72] and the city (Jerusalem).

In 1 Kings 1.33, we are introduced to the royal animal, the mule, which Solomon would ride to Gihon in order to be proclaimed king. On two other occasions in the OT, the ass is used in a

---

[68] This is seldom noticed but see Meyer, *Aims*, pp. 168, 298 n. 132, where he seems to regard the entry and the 'cleansing' of the temple as constituting one continuous narrative which reflected a single, continuous event.

[69] All this leads to a further question: 'who was the intended audience of Jesus' action?' We shall tackle this question later, see pp. 153–4.

[70] That Jesus' action is meant to be parabolic or symbolical is recognised by many, e.g., Meyer, *Aims*, p. 199; Sanders, *Jesus*, pp. 235, 308; Borg, *Conflict*, p. 176.

[71] Catchpole, 'Entry', pp. 319–21.

[72] The Markan πῶλος designates simply a young animal without further specification. W. Bauer, 'The Colt of Palm Sunday (Der Palmesel)', *JBL* 72 (1953), 220–9, argues that in the 'triumphal' entry, πῶλος denotes a young horse. This is not necessary nor convincing as in the LXX, the word is used to denote an ass (Gen. 32.15; 49.11; Judg. 10.4; 12.14; Zech. 9.9). Moreover, the Matthean and Johannine accounts make it explicitly clear that an ass is being referred to (Matt. 21.7 = ὄνος; John 12.14 = ὀνάριον).

symbolic way: the oracle of Judah in Genesis 49.10–11[73] and the prophecy in Zechariah 9.9. It should be stressed here that the particular animal on which Jesus rode (an ass) does not in itself symbolise humility and peace.[74] Harvey has correctly noted that the fact that the mount was an ass rather than a horse does not in itself diminish the dignity of the rider,[75] since the ass has been associated with the royal traditions in the OT (1 Kings 1.33; Zech. 9.9). It may be difficult to ascertain which particular passage Jesus had in mind if one were to consider only the animal. The consideration of the particular city that Jesus was entering has also to be taken into account.

In 1 Kings 1.33, no entry into a city was envisaged. The proclamation of Solomon as king took place at Gihon and the procession to that place, which was probably outside the city, would have started from the palace. Such being the case, 1 Kings 1.33 is unlikely to have been the intended background. Zechariah 9.9 envisages an entry possibly by a vicegerent of Yahweh into Jerusalem on a mule to free Jerusalem.[76] The nations would be at peace with Jerusalem and warfare put to an end. Inasmuch as it is an entry into Jerusalem, Zechariah 9.9 provides the most plausible background to Jesus' entry. This conclusion is further confirmed by some indirect evidence. First, the use of Zechariah 13.7 by Jesus in Mark 14.27 would indicate that Jesus did use the book of Zechariah to describe his role.[77] This would suggest that Zechariah 9.9 might also have been appropriated by him in the present episode. Second, the evidence of the disciples' post-Easter understanding of the event supports this contention. Moreover, if the book of Zechariah does not feature as a source-book for messianic speculation among the Jews of Jesus' day,[78] it is possible to speculate that the later use of Zechariah for rabbinic messianic speculation was prompted by the Christian movement. An explanation, therefore, has to be given for the genesis of this phenomenon in the Christian movement at least. The most plausible explanation is that the impetus for such a usage

[73] See Blenkinsopp, 'Oracle', 55–64.   [74] See Derrett, 'Palm Sunday Colt', 255.

[75] Harvey, *Constraints*, p. 125 n. 20.

[76] See R. L. Smith, *Micah–Malachi*, p. 256.

[77] On the authenticity of this logion see D. J. Moo, *The Old Testament in the Gospel Passion Narratives*, p. 187 and the references he cites. See also the discussion in R. T. France, *Jesus and the Old Testament*, pp. 175–9, 183–4, 188–94, especially pp. 193–4.

[78] Carr, 'Jesus', pp. 9–10. See also Harvey, *Constraints*, p. 122.

of Zechariah came from Jesus himself. Zechariah 9.9 is probably the intended background of Jesus' action.

(ii) The intention of Jesus

Assuming that our understanding of the meaning and context of Zechariah 9.9 is correct, it could be said that in adopting this particular text as the background and hermeneutic for his action, Jesus probably intended to convey the idea that, with his entry, the reign of God is ushered into Jerusalem. In other words, God's promises of the restoration of Jerusalem are to be seen as fulfilled in Jesus' entry.[79] As the animal forms an important part of Zechariah 9.9, Jesus' mode of entry has the significance that he was the actual viceroy of Yahweh to fulfil these promises.[80] Implicit in this claim is a challenge issued to the Jewish authorities in Jerusalem, especially over the matter of the leadership of the nation. If Jesus' action implied that he was the chosen king and viceroy, the Jewish authorities in Jerusalem could no longer remain as leaders of the nation. Probably, they would also have to give an account to this coming king. What is noteworthy here is that in this incident, scripture was not cited but enacted. This enactment points to the fulfilment of the prophecy of Zechariah 9.9.

From the animal alone one cannot ascertain whether the notion of peace was in the mind of Jesus as the animal in itself does not signify humility or the desire to quest for peace; the mule can in many cases signify the royal animal and does not necessarily signify peace. Furthermore, to some Jews a messianic king may have signified war and the expulsion of Gentiles from Jerusalem (see Pss. Sol. 17.23–7). But if Jesus intended Zechariah 9.9 as the background and hermeneutic for his action, it then becomes plausible that he may have intended to convey the idea that an era of peace would be ushered in, even for the Gentiles.[81] Hence, it is not so much the particular animal chosen but the background which may indicate that Jesus may have conceived of his entry as ushering

---

[79] So Meyer, *Aims*, p. 199; Sanders, *Jesus*, p. 306, cf. p. 308; N. T. Wright, 'Jesus, Israel and the Cross', in K. Richards (ed.), *SBL 1985 Seminar Papers*, pp. 87–8.

[80] Cf. the suggestion of Sanders, 'Hermeneutic Fabric', p. 179.

[81] On the status of the Gentiles in Jesus' ministry, see the brief treatment of J. Jeremias, *Jesus' Promise to the Nations*. But cf. the negative conclusions of Sanders, *Jesus*, pp. 212–21. We hope to treat this issue in the next chapter.

peace into the city and for the Gentiles. Further evidence must be sought before this conclusion is drawn confidently.

(iii) The role of Jesus

We have intimated above the role Jesus conceived himself to be embodying in his symbolic action of entering Jerusalem on an ass. We have also eschewed the term 'messiah' when describing that role, as there is uncertainty over the meaning of it.[82] We have instead emphasised the 'kingly' aspect of the action. It is important that this is noted, as Jesus did not intend to convey the idea that he was only a prophet challenging Jerusalem with the impending irruption of the kingdom of God (cf. Luke 13.34–5).[83] As Wright has observed, the entry was a 'kingly' claim and was meant to signify the coming of the chosen king into the city.[84] Hence, this episode offers strong evidence that Jesus conceived his role to be more than that of a prophet.

The theory that Jesus conceived himself as having a kingly role can be supported by other evidence and considerations. As Rowland observes, 'It is inconceivable in the light of the eschatological character of Jesus' message, that the messianic issue would not have come up either for Jesus or his contemporaries.'[85] Furthermore, the *titulus* (Mark 15.26), which to all intents and purposes forms a firm piece of evidence,[86] suggests that Jesus was crucified as a messianic claimant. There must have been precedents in his ministry which would lead the authorities (whether Jewish or Roman) to raise this particular charge. Sanders highlights the fact that Jesus' giving of his disciples a role in the kingdom would imply that his own role could be summarised by the word 'king', as

---

[82] See in particular the essays in J. Neusner, W. S. Green and E. S. Frerichs (eds.), *Judaisms and their Messiahs at the Turn of the Christian Era*. But cf. A. Chester, 'Jewish Messianic Expectations and Mediatorial Figures and Pauline Christology', in M. Hengel and U. Heckel (eds.), *Paulus und das antike Judentum*, pp. 17–19.

[83] Cf. the suggestion of Sanders, 'Hermeneutic Fabric', p. 179: 'On the historical level, Jesus apparently went out of his way to demonstrate his claim to fulfilment of the ancient royal traditions.'

[84] Wright, 'Jesus', pp. 87–8.   [85] Rowland, *Origins*, p. 182.

[86] See the informed discussion in Bammel, 'The *Titulus*', pp. 353–64. J. Finegan, *Die Überlieferung der Leidens- und Auferstehungsgeschichte Jesu*, p. 78 offers a strong defence against the charge that the wording of the *titulus* has a Christian origin. See also N. A. Dahl, *The Crucified Messiah*, pp. 23–8.

obviously his role would be superior to theirs.[87] Indeed, the quibbling over whether Jesus did actually use the title 'messiah' to describe himself should not be allowed to obscure the fact that many of his sayings and this action in particular indicate that he viewed himself as having a kingly role. As Sanders shrewdly observes:

> The question of Jesus' self-claim has, to understate the case, vexed scholars – it seems to me unduly. Jesus taught about the *kingdom*; he was executed as would-be *king*, and his disciples, after his death, expected him to return to establish the *kingdom*. These points are indisputable. Almost equally indisputable is the fact that the disciples thought that they would have some role in the kingdom. We should, I think, accept the obvious: Jesus taught his disciples that he himself would play the principal role in the kingdom.[88]

But exactly what sort of kingly role Jesus viewed himself as embodying is another matter altogether and we shall attempt to answer this question after a study of Jesus' action in the temple in the next chapter.[89]

(iv) The audience

Who were the intended audience of Jesus' symbolic action? Some scholars[90] regard the disciples as the intended audience, while others suggest the people in Jerusalem.[91] Based on the evidence at hand, it is difficult to be certain. But there is no good reason why the two should be mutually exclusive. Indeed, Jesus may have intended this symbolic action also to have been seen by the Jewish authorities.[92] If Jesus intended his action to allude to Zechariah 9.9,

---

87 Sanders, *Jesus*, p. 307. Sanders has elsewhere in his book demonstrated convincingly the authenticity of the logia (especially Matt. 19.28) which offered a role to the disciples in the coming kingdom of God, see pp. 98–106.

88 Sanders, *Jesus*, p. 307 (italics his).

89 C. F. D. Moule interestingly suggests that Jesus' procession into the temple, which was next door to the Roman garrison, is meant to avoid a messianic uprising in his essay, 'On Defining the Messianic Secret in Mark', in E. E. Ellis and E. Grässer (eds.), *Jesus und Paulus*, p. 248. What is of interest here is that Moule saw the intimate connection in intention between the entry and Jesus' going into the temple, something which we hope to argue for and demonstrate.

90 E.g., Sanders, *Jesus*, p. 308.   91 E.g., Borg, *Conflict*, pp. 176–7.

92 So Wright, 'Jesus', p. 92.

it would most probably be meant for the entire nation. An interesting question remains as to why Jesus did not make things explicit. This may be due to the nature of the kingship which Jesus had in mind, a peaceful one albeit a fulfilment of Yahweh's promise to Jerusalem. It may also be that the intramural conflict with the Jewish authorities had to be resolved first and any explicitly revolutionary actions would have hindered that,[93] and thus were avoided.

(v) Summary

The action of Jesus, being symbolic, would in all probability have a background to it in order for it to be understood. We suggest that two factors have to be taken into account to ascertain this background: the choice of the animal and the city in which the procession terminates. Taking these two factors into consideration, Zechariah 9.9 forms the most plausible background. While one cannot be sure whether the whole context and meaning of Zechariah 9.9 was in the purview of Jesus when he planned the entry, one could at least conclude from the above two factors that Jesus signified by his action the fulfilment of Yahweh's promise to Jerusalem and his role in the realisation of it. The restoration promises made to Jerusalem are to be fulfilled and peace is to reign in it, and Jesus is to be the effecter of these. The plausibility of Jesus conceiving himself as having a kingly role is also supported by other evidence. While his lack of explicitness on this and the lack of revolutionary action on the part of the crowd may lead one to infer that Jesus' idea of kingship was different from that embodied by a warrior-king, the symbolic action alone does not lead to firm conclusions. Other evidence has to be brought in, especially when one realises that the action in itself may have been intended to be completed by other events or actions.

The entry and the Zion traditions

Meyer has observed that, according to the Synoptic tradition, a 'strain' on the messianic secret was characteristic of the last part of Jesus' ministry because of the urgent need to press Israel to decision

---

[93] Cf. Rowland's observation that Jesus rejected the bellicose connotations of the title 'Son of David' or 'messiah' in *Origins*, p. 182.

and to win it over for the reign of God. This urgency ignited flashes of self-revelation on the part of Jesus.[94] What is true for the Synoptic tradition is also true for the historical ministry of Jesus in so far as one can speak of a tendency on his part to keep his own conception of his kingly role a secret before this dramatic event.[95] Even so, one has to admit that in this demonstration charged with meaning and significance, implicitness and not explicitness was pronounced. In connection with this 'strain', two points are to be noted. The first is the telling change in profile and the second concerns the timing of the event.

(i) The change in profile

We have concluded in Part II that Jesus adopted the persona of a prophet in relation to Jerusalem (although, in Q 13.34–5, there is a possibility that he might view himself as more than a prophet). But, in the entry, he revealed instead that he was actually the king chosen by Yahweh for the task of restoring Jerusalem. It could thus be seen that a significant step had been taken by Jesus in terms of the revelation of his own understanding of his profile and role (from a prophet to a king). This change in profile probably implies that Jesus regarded his ministry to have reached a climax at this particular juncture.

(ii) The timing of the event

While this deliberate and significant revelation has often been noted, the question of why it was done at this particular time and place is seldom explored.[96] It has been surmised earlier that one reason for this change in profile on the part of Jesus is that he had viewed this particular phase of his ministry as the climax (Luke 13.31–3). But it is also significant to note the place of the climax – Jerusalem. This city was to be the τέλος of Jesus' 'journey'. He was not to die in Herod's territory, Galilee, although it was the scene of the major part of his peripatetic ministry. Instead, he was to die in God's chosen city – Jerusalem. If one were to adopt the notion

---

[94] Meyer, *Aims*, p. 199.

[95] See J. D. G. Dunn, 'The Messianic Secret in Mark', *TynB* 21 (1970), 92–117 for a demonstration that the idea of a messianic secret goes back to the historical Jesus and is not an invention of Mark.

[96] E.g., Witherington, *Christology*, p. 107.

(which in our view is correct) that Jesus had visited Jerusalem on numerous occasions before this dramatic entry of his,[97] then the question of timing becomes important. In other words, Jesus would have thought that the climax or τέλος of his ministry had arrived when he staged his entry into Jerusalem. If this was the case, it may mean that Jerusalem had never been far from the intention and scope of Jesus' ministry even when he was exercising it in Galilee. In other words, it could justifiably be said that his ministry prior to this event was meant to be only a preparation for his true vocation intimated in the entry. Hence, the climax of Jesus' ministry is to be seen in terms of both place and timing. Jerusalem was the place for this climax; this particular phase of his ministry was also understood by him as climactic. These two observations would then highlight the intimate connection between the entry and the Zion traditions. Zion is the place of climax for God's restorative programme for Israel. It is the microcosm and symbol of God's presence and kingship, and its restoration signifies the restoration of the nation. Moreover, in Jewish eschatological hopes, the schemes of restoration often culminate in the rebuilding and glorification of the temple and city. Hence, the restoration of Zion is also the climactic hour of the realisation of God's eschatological promises.

Once again, Jesus' intention in the entry is seen to be related to the Zion traditions and this time he was signifying through his action that he was the divinely appointed king who was to lay claim to his city to inaugurate the eschatological restoration.[98] The earlier announcements of the proximity of the kingdom (Mark 1.15) and the intimations that the kingdom of God was present in Jesus' ministry[99] led inevitably to Jesus' challenging Jerusalem with his message to recognise in him the divinely appointed agent of restoration (Q 13.34–5)[100] and in this particular hour, the time of restoration. Implicit in this demonstration is his challenge to the Jewish leaders in Jerusalem concerning the rightful heir(s) and destiny of the nation. Hence in the tiny compass of Jerusalem is played out the fate of the nation. This particular aspect can be seen

---

[97] Cf. the Johannine traditions which record several visits of Jesus to Jerusalem during his ministry.

[98] Cf. Marshall, *Gospel*, p. 711.

[99] See G. R. Beasley-Murray, *Jesus and the Kingdom of God*, pp. 144–6.

[100] This is demonstrated in chapter 5.

in full clarity in the incident in the temple which our next chapter will explore.

In the 'triumphal' entry, Jesus' own understanding of his role in God's eschatological restoration of Israel (Q 13.34–5) and his appropriation of the Zion traditions are seen revealed. Jerusalem was the τέλος of his ministry and he staged an action which signified the restorative overtures God was making through him as the divinely appointed agent and king to the city of Jerusalem. But as the episode was not commented on by Jesus, another episode (or other episodes) are needed to serve as further confirmation of what we have concluded thus far. The fact that such significance as there may be in the entry is demonstrated only implicitly may well imply that Jesus' view of kingship was very different from the prevailing ones (e.g., a mighty deliverer who would smite the Roman empire and set free the Jews; see Pss. Sol. 17.23–7). The context of Zechariah 9.9 suggests this. But whether this thesis is sustainable depends on further evidence, especially the evidence provided by the so-called 'cleansing' of the temple by Jesus.

7

JESUS IN JERUSALEM (II): THE INCIDENT IN THE TEMPLE

In as much as Zion is inseparable from the temple in the religious conception of most Jews of the second temple period,[1] the study of Jesus' action[2] in the temple (Mark 11.15–17 and parallels), traditionally called 'the cleansing of the temple', is of the utmost importance for our discussion of the impact of the Zion traditions on the ministry of Jesus and for determining the intentions of Jesus in Jerusalem. This episode is also of great importance in the modern effort to reconstruct the aims of Jesus and his relationship to the Judaism of his day.[3] Sanders' understanding of this relationship depends greatly on his reconstruction of this episode, as it forms the starting-point of his enquiry.[4] Moreover, many scholars today believe that the immediate cause of Jesus' death may be attributed to this particular action of his in the temple.[5]

As with so many actions of Jesus, there are interpretative problems. At present, there is a lack of a consensus over the interpretation of this episode. This state of affairs is largely attributable to the fact that scholars often take into account only a narrow range of evidence without giving consideration to other equally important evidence. We therefore propose to study this episode in detail, reviewing the different views which have been offered on its interpretation and advancing the state of scholarship a step further by highlighting some neglected aspects which are crucial for our understanding of Jesus' own conception of his role *vis-à-vis* his

---

[1] See our chapter 2.
[2] The word 'action' is used in order not to beg any questions in the light of the present uncertainty over the interpretation of its meaning.
[3] This episode forms an important component in the Reimarus–Brandon line of interpreting the aims of Jesus.
[4] E. P. Sanders, *Jesus and Judaism*, pp. 57–8, 61.
[5] Some prominent scholars who hold this view are: Sanders, *Jesus*, pp. 301–2; R. J. Bauckham, 'Jesus' Demonstration in the Temple', in B. Lindars (ed.), *Law and Religion*, pp. 88–9; J. D. G. Dunn, *The Partings of the Ways*, pp. 51–3.

people. We also hope to show that this action of Jesus is of a piece with his staging of his entry into Jerusalem.

1 The episode

The account of Jesus' action in the temple can be found in all four gospels. Variations between the Synoptic gospels are slight. Matthew and Luke have probably followed Mark in the main. John, however, does present some significant differences which prompt two questions: the relationship and priority between the Johannine and the Synoptic traditions, and also whether Jesus carried out two similar actions in his ministry. These questions will be dealt with in this section with other preliminary points before we move on to a discussion about the meaning of Jesus' action.

The historicity of the episode

That Jesus did disrupt the operations of the temple is regarded as a firm historical datum by most scholars today.[6] The main reason for this is that the conflict over the temple is deeply implanted in the Jesus traditions (cf. Mark 15.29–30; Matt. 27.39 and parallels; Acts 6.13–14, apart from the present episode we are now considering).[7]

As with many aspects of biblical studies, there are dissenting voices. Recently, Buchanan has attempted to mount a challenge against the consensus.[8] He bases his case on an oft-used argument of why Jesus was not arrested for the disturbance in the temple, given the fact that the Romans were especially vigilant and on the look-out for trouble-makers in it during the important festivals, especially the Passover (AJ 20.192). Arguing from this lack of intervention from the Roman garrison stationed at the Antonia fortress and the temple police, Buchanan allows for only two explanations: either that the incident was actually more violent than has been portrayed in the gospels (as Brandon has proposed[9])

---

[6] Sanders, *Jesus*, p. 61; Dunn, *Partings*, p. 47; B. F. Meyer, *The Aims of Jesus*, p. 170; M. J. Borg, *Conflict, Holiness and Politics in the Teachings of Jesus*, pp. 172–3, and many others.

[7] Sanders, *Jesus*, p. 61. B. Witherington III has also offered supplementary arguments in his *The Christology of Jesus*, pp. 109–10. Note that even the normally sceptical R. Bultmann allows for a kernel of authenticity for this episode in his *The History of the Synoptic Tradition*, pp. 36, 56.

[8] G. W. Buchanan, 'Symbolic Money-Changers in the Temple', *NTS* 37 (1991), 280–90.

[9] S. G. F. Brandon, *Jesus and the Zealots*, p. 333.

or that Jesus never performed that action in the temple.[10] Since he
distances himself from the Reimarus–Brandon line of interpretation
of this event, he opts for the second explanation: that such an act of
Jesus never really did happen, and that the gospel account was
originally a midrash which was written by 'some christian who
opposed the action of the zealots in Jerusalem ... using the Hebrew
texts [Isa. 56.7 and Jer. 7.11] to prove that the zealotic action was
wrong'.[11] An equally valid possibility of viewing Jesus' action as
being limited in time and space with the intention of making a
prophetic point was not even considered. Hardly any scholar today
understands this action of Jesus as being carried out on a large
scale. They usually judge as redactional the impression given by the
gospels that Jesus managed to put a total stop to temple operations.
Moreover, Buchanan ignores the point highlighted earlier that the
conflict over the temple is deeply embedded in the Jesus tradition.
Hence, his case is hardly persuasive and there is therefore no reason
why the consensus as defined earlier should be rejected.

The placement of the episode

The question of chronology is of special importance to our enquiry
as we hope to demonstrate that Jesus went into Jerusalem propelled
by his own understanding of the importance of the Zion traditions
and that he viewed the final phase of his ministry as the climactic
end whereby the ancient promises of the renewal of Jerusalem
would be fulfilled. But if the action in the temple was carried out
much earlier in his ministry, it would mean that the Zion traditions
might not have been of importance to Jesus as the climactic element
would have been lost.

As mentioned earlier, there are significant differences between
the Johannine and the Synoptic accounts of the action in the
temple, notably that of chronology. While most scholars today
would regard the Markan placement of the action in the final phase
of Jesus' ministry as authentic (over against the Johannine placement), there are some prominent scholars who opt for the Johannine scheme.[12] Their arguments have often been ignored. In this

---

[10] Buchanan, 'Money-Changers', 282–4.

[11] 'Money-Changers', 289. A team of scholars have recently shown that the idea of
gospel writers creating whole pericopae out of texts using the procedure of
midrash is questionable. See R. T. France and D. Wenham (eds.), *Gospel
Perspectives III. Studies in Midrash and Historiography*.

[12] Notably, J. A. T. Robinson, '"His Witness is True". A Test of the Johannine

section, we propose to discuss first the age-old question of whether there were one or two 'cleansings', and then to address the question of whose scheme is original if there was only one 'cleansing'.

(i) One or two cleansings?

Some conservative scholars claim that there were in fact two separate 'cleansings' in the temple, one performed at the beginning of Jesus' ministry and the other towards the end.[13] While not ruling this possibility out of court, such an interpretation appears to be misconceived as it fails to reckon with the linguistic similarity between the Johannine and the Markan accounts.[14] But the greatest objection to this hypothesis, as France has observed, rests with the *nature* of the act itself.[15] Once the act is recognised as a provocative demonstration (which its Jewish context demands), it is highly improbable that the authorities would not have taken action almost immediately. The delay of two to three years[16] in a reprisal presupposed by this hypothesis becomes incomprehensible. The theory of two 'cleansings' thus depends on a quite unrealistic minimising of the significance and impact of this action of Jesus.[17] It is more probable that there was only one 'cleansing'.

(ii) Whose chronology?

The recognition of the important significance of the action would tend to support the Synoptic placement as the historical one. There are other arguments which support this contention. First, such an act would probably have been carried out only after a prior prophetic career for its impact to be effective on the populace.[18] Second, as Barrett has observed, an 'act of overt rebellion against the authorities of the nation is more readily understandable at the

---

Claim', in E. Bammel and C. F. D. Moule (eds.), *Jesus and the Politics of His Day*, pp. 453–76; J. A. Fitzmyer, *The Gospel According to Luke X–XXIV*, p. 1265.

[13] E.g., L. L. Morris, *The Gospel According to John*, pp. 190–1; D. A. Carson, *The Gospel According to John*, pp. 177–8.

[14] As noted by Fitzmyer, *Luke X–XXIV*, p. 1264.

[15] R. T. France, 'Chronological Aspects of "Gospel Harmony"', *VE* 16 (1986), 41 (emphasis mine). Recent studies have highlighted the paramount significance this event has in the life and ministry of Jesus.

[16] Following traditional reckoning of the length of Jesus' ministry.

[17] France, 'Chronological Aspects', 41.

[18] This has been noted by Fitzmyer, *Luke X–XXIV*, p. 1264, although he opts for the Johannine scheme (p. 1265).

climax than at the beginning of the ministry'.[19] While it is premature to conclude at this juncture that this was an act of overt
rebellion, it can none the less be said that it was an indisputably
provocative action. Hence, Barrett's observation is still helpful in
this regard.

Scholars who support the Johannine placement usually regard
the Markan placement as being stylised, as he has room for only
one journey of Jesus to Jerusalem.[20] While not denying the stylised
character of the Markan presentation of Jesus' ministry, such a
consideration in and of itself does not negate the contention that
this action was probably performed towards the end of Jesus'
ministry. Notwithstanding the stylised character of the Markan
presentation, there is, however, an important reason for us to
conclude that the Johannine placement of this episode is redactional: John may be intending to give his readers not a chronological scheme of events but a theological one.[21] In the Johannine
scheme, the particular function of this episode is to apprise the
reader of the messianic authority of Jesus, and of the basic
challenge which he presents to established Judaism. Such a perspective is intended to guide him through the controversies of Jesus
with 'the Jews' which will be a prominent feature in his gospel.[22]
Thus, this episode is programmatic to the Johannine presentation
of the relationship between Jesus and Judaism.[23]

Although the Markan placement of this episode is probably
original, it does not follow that the Johannine account may not
have preserved the more authentic traditions of the elements of
Jesus' one action and the saying uttered during that incident.
Whether this is so will be discussed in due course.

The elements of the one action

In the Markan account, there are altogether four elements in the
provocative act of Jesus, explained by one saying. These four
elements are:

(i) driving out those who sold and bought (ἐκβάλλειν τοὺς
πωλοῦντας καὶ τοὺς ἀγοράζοντας);

[19] C. K. Barrett, *The Gospel According to St John*, p. 195.
[20] For scholars of this persuasion, see n. 13.   [21] Barrett, *John*, p. 195.
[22] France, 'Chronological Aspects', 42. See also G. R. Beasley-Murray, *John*, pp.
38–9.
[23] A similar phenomenon is found in Luke 4.16–30.

(ii) overturning the tables of the money-changers (τὰς τρα-πέζας τῶν κολλυβιστῶν ... κατέστρεψεν);

(iii) overturning the seats of those who sold pigeons (τὰς καθέδρας τῶν πωλούντων τὰς περιστερὰς κατέστρεψεν); and

(iv) prohibiting anyone from carrying a σκεῦος through the temple.[24]

John's account is quite similar to Mark except that he does not have element (iv) and provides additional details to element (i). The animals which were being traded are described (sheep and oxen) and John has the additional detail of Jesus making a whip of cords to drive out the animals (John 2.14–15).[25] Significantly, the saying of Jesus in John (John 2.16) is different from that in Mark (Mark 11.17) and is directed against the dove-sellers (again, different from Mark where the targets of Jesus' saying are left quite unspecified).

From a comparison of these two accounts, it seems plausible that the Markan account of the action is in the main supported by the Johannine. Points (i) to (iii) receive mention in John although point (i) has been expanded. If one takes into account that John has probably preserved an independent tradition, by invoking the criterion of multiple attestation, one can quite safely say that these three elements are authentic. Element (iv) is most probably authentic as it is difficult to explain how such an obscure reference which does not serve to clarify the meaning of the event was included if it was not authentic.[26] It is of great importance that the interpretation of the meaning of this episode should take into account all the elements of the action. Failure to do this may lead to skewed results.

That something was said during the incident is also probable. Although John has a different saying, he agrees with Mark in writing that something was said. But this is complicated by the fact that a saying lying behind Mark 14.58‖Matthew 26.61 has also been proposed as the original saying.[27] The determination of which

---

24 Luke has only one element – driving out those who sold – while Matthew follows Mark in the main except that element (iv) has been omitted probably because its significance was lost or obscure to him.

25 The impression one receives from John is that Jesus was driving out only those who sold but not those who bought, unlike in Mark. Also, in the Synoptic accounts, no mention was made of other sacrificial animals except the dove. This may be significant; see the discussion in the next section.

26 This is accepted as authentic by many scholars, e.g., Bauckham, 'Demonstration', pp. 77–8; W. R. Telford, *The Barren Temple and the Withered Tree*, p. 83.

27 See for instance Sanders, *Jesus*, pp. 72–5.

saying was original has repercussions for the interpretation of this
episode as will be seen later.

2   Meaning and significance

Three things have been established in the earlier section. First, that
the incident has very good claims to historicity. Second, that the
Markan chronological placement of this event is reliable. And
third, that all the elements of the action as found in Mark are
probably authentic (although there is doubt over the saying). We
now come to the important question, 'What was intended by Jesus
when he performed this provocative action in the temple?'

A revolutionary act

The fact that Jesus was not arrested immediately by the authorities
after causing a disruption in so important an institution and
symbol of nationalism as the temple presents a puzzle. The
Reimarus–Brandon line of interpretation attempts to solve this
puzzle by arguing that this particular act of Jesus was revolutionary
and was accompanied by much violence.[28] Jesus managed to wrest
control of the temple from the authorities and intended to incite the
crowd to rebellion. The violent nature of this act was significantly
reduced by the evangelist Mark in order to depoliticise Jesus.[29]

This theory has been examined critically and shown to be
tenuous in the extreme.[30] If Jesus' action was intended to be
revolutionary, there would have been an immediate and decisive
response from the Roman troops. Even if we assume that these
troops failed to wrest control of the temple back from Jesus on the
very day itself, they would have called for reinforcements and a
large-scale battle would have ensued.[31] That this did not happen
and that Jesus was not arrested immediately are detrimental to this
view. One has to assume too much (that Jesus had with him a large

---

[28] H. Reimarus, in C. H. Talbert (ed.), *Reimarus: Fragments*, pp. 66, 126, 146;
      Brandon, *Jesus*, p. 333.
[29] Brandon, *Jesus*, pp. 322–4.
[30] The decisive refutation of it can be found in the volume of essays edited by
      Bammel and Moule, *Jesus and the Politics of His Day*. See also the masterly
      refutation by M. Hengel, *Was Jesus a Revolutionist?*
[31] For evidence that such a course of action was to be expected on the part of the
      Romans, see AJ 20.98–9, 169–72. Moreover, the destruction of Jerusalem in
      70 CE by the Romans would be conclusive evidence that they were prepared to
      take drastic action to quell any rebellion.

band of followers and managed to wrest control of the temple) and disregard too much (the consistent evidence of the gospels that he was not arrested immediately and that there was no military clash between Jesus and the Romans) in order to espouse such a view.[32] Moreover, the fact that Jesus' disciples were not rounded up and executed may present an intractable problem to such a thesis, since the disciples of Theudas and the Egyptian (shortly after the time of Jesus) were.[33] It is not without reason that most scholars consider this theory to be untenable.

A prophetic or symbolic act

Given the fact that the temple's outer courtyard[34] was extremely large (measuring about 450 yards in length and 300 yards in width[35]) and that Jesus was not arrested immediately, one has to draw the conclusion that the scale of the action was indeed small and that Jesus did not intend to stop all temple operations altogether. Hence, most scholars today view Jesus as engaging in a prophetic or symbolic action. Although these two categories are often taken as synonymous, due consideration should be given to the distinction between them. A prophetic act, although often symbolic, may be intended simply as a protest against or denunciation of certain practices (in the spirit of the classical prophets, e.g.,

[32] This has been observed by J. Sweet, 'The Zealots and Jesus', in Bammel and Moule (eds.), *Jesus and the Politics of His Day*, p. 9.

[33] The procurator Cuspius Fadus sent a squadron of calvary against Theudas and his followers. Theudas was executed and many of his followers were either killed or taken prisoner (AJ 20.98–9). In the other instance, it is instructive to note that the Egyptian did not disrupt temple operations but simply gathered his followers on the Mount of Olives with perhaps a revolutionary intent. Felix's response was swift. He set out from Jerusalem with a *large* force of calvary and infantry (μετὰ πολλῶν ἱππέων τε καὶ πεζῶν) and slew four hundred of the Egyptian's followers and took two hundred prisoners. The Egyptian managed to escape (AJ 20.169–72). Such evidence indicates that the Romans were poised to use *great* force to quell any armed rebellion.

[34] It was in the form of an enclosure with colonnades, see W. H. Mare, *An Archaeology of the Jerusalem Area*, pp. 145–6.

[35] See the discussions in A. Parrot, *The Temple in Jerusalem*, pp. 76–100 and E. P. Sanders, *Judaism: Practice and Belief*, p. 57. Finegan estimates that the area of the whole temple mount might be about thirty-five acres (see his *Archaeology of the New Testament*, p. 118). Interestingly, the measurements given by Josephus in AJ 15.400 are different from that found in *m.Mid.* 2.1. Josephus envisaged the length of each side to be one *stade* (about 585–600 feet?) but the description in *m.Mid.* 2.1 has 500 cubits to each side (about 850 feet?). Although we cannot be sure as to its actual size, we can at least infer from these figures that it was indeed very large.

Neh. 13.8–9) without the intention of symbolising anything, while a symbolic act may not be prophetic at all (e.g., Ruth 3.7). To regard all prophetic acts as symbolic is unwarranted.

Given that the scope of Jesus' action was small, what was he trying to convey? We will test the various proposals which have been given by scholars and see whether they take into account the four elements of the action isolated earlier.

(i) The contribution of Sanders: an act symbolising destruction

Sanders' provocative thesis proposes that Jesus' action symbolises the destruction of the temple and destruction in turn looks to restoration.[36] It must be noted at the outset that according to Sanders' interpretation, this destruction was brought about not by anything unworthy which was going on in the temple but because destruction of the old must logically take place before a new temple could be erected.[37] Therefore, if one were to carry Sanders' logic to its conclusion, Jesus' action was a portent not of judgment but of *hope*. For it announces the *replacement* of the old temple (by destruction) with the new.[38]

It is instructive to note how Sanders arrives at this interpretation. First, Sanders asserts that there is no hard evidence for the view that the temple establishment was financially corrupt.[39] Secondly, the arrangements in the temple were necessary for its proper function.[40] Suitable sacrificial victims have to be sold (at least for the convenience of the populace) and money-changing facilities were necessary in order for Jews from all over the Roman world to pay the temple tax in a standard coinage (the Tyrian στατήρ) acceptable by the temple.[41] It is reasonable to expect that a small profit should be taken in order for these facilities to be economically viable. Thirdly, destruction is the most obvious meaning of the action of overturning the tables of the money-changers.[42] Fourthly, Sanders views the saying in Mark 11.17 as inauthentic and argues

---

[36] Sanders, *Jesus*, pp. 69, 71.   [37] *Jesus*, pp. 71, 75.

[38] This has been observed also by Bauckham, 'Demonstration', p. 87: 'The point is not really the destruction so much as the *replacement* of the temple.' Emphasis his.

[39] Sanders, *Jesus*, pp. 66, 367 n. 39.   [40] *Jesus*, pp. 63–5.

[41] The Tyrian coinage was preferred probably because of its choice silver. See the discussion in I. Abrahams, *Studies in Pharisaism and the Gospels* I, pp. 83–4.

[42] Sanders, *Jesus*, p. 70.

instead that something similar to Mark 14.58 was said during the incident.[43] The evangelist Mark was embarrassed by this saying which contains an accusation against Jesus of threatening to destroy the temple and hence substituted it with a conflated citation taken from Isaiah 56.7 and Jeremiah 7.11. To summarise Sanders' understanding of the meaning of Jesus' gesture in the temple, the diagram below would serve adequately:

> Overturning of tables → Destruction of temple → Erection of the new temple

This chain of actions, argues Sanders, is understandable in the Jewish context of Jesus' day. This being so, the people gathered in the temple would have understood the symbolism of Jesus' action.[44]

It can be seen from the above summary of Sanders' arguments that he focuses on only one element of the action of Jesus in the temple: the overturning of the money-changers' tables. The other elements are glossed over. This constitutes a severe weakness in Sanders' thesis, as a proper interpretation of this important action of Jesus has to take into account all the elements of that action. Moreover, as many have noted, there is a lack of perspicuity in the action of overturning the tables.[45] This particular action is not an entirely self-evident symbol of destruction.[46] As Moule has observed, a better symbolic action was ready to hand which has a precedent in the OT: the breaking of a pot (Jer. 19.10).[47] Hence, a major peg of Sanders' thesis is found to be weak. None the less, it must be stressed here that in the light of the importance of the temple tax to second-temple Judaism, the overturning of the money-changers' tables was indeed a very provocative act on the

---

[43] *Jesus*, pp. 66–7, 73–4. Sanders is not too concerned to recover the original form of the saying (p. 74).

[44] *Jesus*, pp. 77–90.

[45] E.g., Dunn, *Partings*, p. 48. Cf. his review of Sanders' book in *JTS* 37 (1986), 512.

[46] And when this particular action is interpreted in tandem with the other elements isolated earlier, it is scarcely conceivable that they all symbolise destruction. Does the action of driving out those who bought and sold and the prohibition of anyone from carrying a σκεῦος signify destruction? This is scarcely possible.

[47] Sanders is aware of Moule's suggestion and hence he writes that his view 'depends . . . on further considerations' (*Jesus*, p. 70). His 'further considerations' are chiefly two: the Jewish expectation for a new temple and a threat saying against the temple similar to the one in Mark 14.58 which he believes was uttered during the incident.

part of Jesus.[48] A discussion of the origins of this institution and its reception by the ordinary Jew would be necessary to shed light on the meaning of this action. This will be done later in the chapter but suffice it now to point out that the overturning of the money-changers' tables is not a self-evident symbol of destruction.

The weakness of Sanders' case does not just consist in what was pointed out above. Sanders' insistence that there was no corruption (of a financial nature) of the priesthood in the second temple period does not square with the evidence.[49] The Qumran community were highly critical of the temple establishment and some of their criticisms concerned financial corruption. In 1QpHab, the high priest is accused of robbing the people, including the poor (8.12; 9.5; 10.1); of amassing wealth (8.8–12; 9.4–5); and of defiling the sanctuary of Yahweh (12.10). Although these criticisms were probably directed at Jonathan,[50] it is not unreasonable for us to imagine that during the first century, the men of the Qumran community did not hold a substantially different view of the Jerusalem priesthood then, given their distancing from it.[51] Similarly, we find in 4QpNah 1.11 reference being made to the riches which were amassed by the priests of Jerusalem. Although most of these riches came from the spoils of war, it would not be surprising if the Qumranians, contemporaneous with Jesus, would attribute the riches of the temple to corruption on the part of the priests. That this suggestion is eminently possible is seen from the fact that these writings (1QpHab and 4QpNah) would have been read by the Qumranians contemporaneous with Jesus. What we want to establish here is that, although such criticisms were not originally

---

[48] The Tosefta (*t.Shek.* 1.6) explains that the half-shekel tax was exacted so as to make all Israelites responsible for the daily whole-offerings which were understood to atone for the sins of Israel. This is an interpretation based on a proof-text, Exod. 30.16. Although the Tosefta was compiled at about 300 CE, the reference here is probably an accurate presentation of the beliefs of first-century Jewry especially when it was based on a proof-text. Such an idea would then be current and the Jews would have grasped the *raison d'être* of the presence of the money-changers. See J. Neusner, 'Money-changers in the Temple: The Mishnah's Explanation', *NTS* 35 (1989), 287–90.

[49] In a later work, Sanders concedes reluctantly that 'of the high priests during the period 6–66 CE, some were corrupt' in his *Judaism: Practice and Belief*, p. 323. However, he does not relate this to the episode of Jesus' action in the temple (pp. 86–92). Even his most recent and more popular work, *The Historical Figure of Jesus*, does not take this into account (pp. 225–60).

[50] See M. A. Knibb, *The Qumran Community*, pp. 238–9.

[51] See C. A. Evans, 'Jesus' Action in the Temple: Cleansing or Portent of Destruction', *CBQ* 51 (1989), 260–1.

directed against the temple establishment of Jesus' day, these references serve to show that there was a precedent to encourage a Jew of Jesus' day to hold such a view and that this view was probably taken by the Qumran community contemporaneous with Jesus.

Josephus provides indirect evidence of the corruption of the temple establishment before 70 CE. From AJ 14.110, we may gather that the temple has amassed to itself great wealth through the contributions of the diaspora Jews.[52] The families of the high priests also possessed great wealth and this can be seen in a number of ways: First, great sums were paid as dowries (*b.Ketub.* 66b). Second, the widows of the high priests were beneficiaries of extremely generous pensions which were paid out of the temple treasury (*b.Ketub.* 65a; *Lam.R.* 1.50–1 (on 1.16)). Third, at least one high priest (Ananias) was able to enhance his reputation by bribery (AJ 20.213; cf. *b.Yebam.* 61a; *b.Yoma* 18a). Obviously, the mere fact of wealth does not prove the existence of corruption, but it may be an indication of it.[53] To prove this, corroborating evidence has to be sought.

The first may perhaps be found in BJ 2.426–7: the records of debts were burnt once the temple was captured by the zealots. This may be indicative of the economic oppression suffered by the poor.[54] Secondly, Josephus mentions that shortly before the Jewish war with Rome, tithes were forcibly extracted from the people (AJ 20.181, 206–7) but he, presenting himself as virtuous, refrained from taking these tithes which were his due (*Vita* 80). Thirdly, there are explicit references in the rabbinic literature which point unmistakably to corruption on the part of the temple establishment before 70 CE. Granted that such writings are late, they cannot be ignored as some of them may enshrine authentic pre-70 CE traditions (some even may date from the time of Jesus). The outstanding example is found in *b.Pesh.* 57a, which reads:

> Woe unto me because of the house of Baithos [Boethus];
> woe unto me for their lances [or 'evil-speaking']!

---

[52] There is also evidence that the temple served as a bank. See N. Q. Hamilton, 'Temple Cleansing and Temple Bank', *JBL* 83 (1964), 365–72.

[53] For indications from other Jewish writings, see C. A. Evans, 'Jesus' Action in the Temple and Evidence of Corruption in the First-Century Temple', in D. J. Lull (ed.), *SBL 1989 Seminar Papers*, pp. 522–39.

[54] See R. A. Horsley, *Jesus and the Spiral of Violence*, pp. 252–3.

> Woe unto me because of the house of Hanin,[55]
>   woe unto me for their whisperings [or 'calumnies']!
> Woe unto me because of the house of Qathros[56]
>   woe unto me because of their reed pens!
> Woe unto me because of the house of Ishmael b. Phiabi,
>   woe unto me because of their fist![57]
> For they are high priests and their sons are treasurers
>   and their sons-in-law are temple overseers,
>   and their servants smite the people with sticks.[58]

That this lament contains authentic traditions is probable enough. The four families mentioned supplied most of the high priests from the reign of Herod the Great to the fall of Jerusalem.[59] As Bauckham observes, the fact that the house of Ishmael b. Phiabi is placed last may indicate that the lament dates from the time of the second high priest (the first was high priest *c*. 15–16 CE) of that name (i.e., *c*. 59–61 CE). And since the house of Qathros (or Kantheras), who was also the son of Boethus, is counted separately from the latter's house, the first line of the lament refers to the period before 6 CE.[60] Thus this lament refers to the period 6–61 CE. Greed, nepotism, oppression and violence, according to this rabbinic tradition, characterised the leading aristocratic priestly families before 70 CE. It should also be noted that the summary statement of the lament highlights that these various forms of abuses exercised by these families were possible because of their dominance over the fiscal and administrative affairs of the temple. Hence, *t.Men.* 13.22 may not be biased when it records R. Yohanan b. Torta as saying, 'As to Jerusalem's first building, on what account was it destroyed? Because of idolatry and licentiousness and bloodshed which was in it. But [as to] the latter [building] we know that they devoted themselves to Torah and were meticulous about tithes. On what account did they go into exile? Because they *love money* and hate[61]

---

55 Hanin was Annas (NT) or Ananus (Josephus).
56 Qathros was Kantheras.
57 This line is missing in *t.Men.* 13.31 which offers a parallel to this passage.
58 This translation is taken from J. Jeremias, *Jerusalem in the Time of Jesus*, pp. 196–7.
59 See E. Schürer, *The History of the Jewish People in the Age of Jesus Christ* II, p. 234; Jeremias, *Jerusalem*, pp. 194–5.
60 See Bauckham, 'Demonstration', pp. 79–80.
61 This description probably refers to the internecine warfare between different Jewish groups during the first revolt.

one another.'[62] This rabbinic tradition dovetails with that discussed earlier.

The conclusion to be drawn from the above discussion is that even if exaggeration and bias have been allowed for, there is no reason to regard the above rabbinic passages as wholesale fabrication without any grain of authentic information. Besides, such data comport well with the evidence from Josephus and Qumran, and demonstrate that the possibility of corruption on the part of the temple establishment has to be taken seriously.[63]

Sanders' case is further vitiated by the fact that he does not want to view Jesus' action as a portent of judgment but that it was simply symbolising the end of the present temple in order that a new one may be erected (presumably by Yahweh) as a replacement. While Sanders is right that the expectation of a new temple is prevalent in second-temple Judaism,[64] he fails to see that in most texts concerning the new temple, the old is usually destroyed because of *judgment* either directly by Yahweh or through the hostile nations.[65] It would not make sense to a Jew for an eschatological figure (whether messiah or prophet) to threaten to destroy the temple in order to bring in a new one.[66] Announcements of the destruction of the temple were normally made in the context of the divine judgment which was about to fall (Mic. 3.12; Jer. 7; Sib. Or. 3.265–81; 4.115–18; 2 Bar. 1–8; 4 Ezra 1–4; 1 En. 90.28 (cf. 1 En. 89.73 which is critical of the temple and thus provides the cause of its destruction and replacement)). Even 11QT 29.8–10,[67] which may appear to support Sanders' case, seems only to imply the removal of the old temple. It could be argued, however, that 11QT 29.8–10 might attest to a notion similar to that which propelled Jesus to carry out his provocative action: the old

---

[62] The translation is taken from J. Neusner (tr.), *The Tosefta* V, p. 162. Emphasis mine.

[63] See Evans, 'Evidence', pp. 522–39 for other possible evidence of corruption.

[64] See the evidence he cites in *Jesus*, pp. 79–86.

[65] According to Jewish theology, the Shekinah of God must depart from the temple before the temple can be destroyed as it is the dwelling-place of God. The Shekinah departing from the temple would mean judgment. See Jer. 12.7; 22.5 and Ezek. 10.18.

[66] Chester has made the same observations in another connection, see his 'The Sibyl and the Temple', in W. Horbury (ed.), *Templum Amicitiae*, p. 55.

[67] The translation from Y. Yadin (ed.), *The Temple Scroll* II, pp. 128–9 reads:
> [8]...and I will consecrate my [t]emple by my glory, (the temple) on which I will settle [9]my glory, until the day of blessing on which I will create my temple [10]and establish it for myself for all times, according to the covenant which I have made with Jacob at Bethel ...

was not corrupt and was acceptable to Yahweh, but the time had
come for it to be replaced by the eschatological one and, thus, its
destruction was announced. Even so, it has to be conceded that it is
Yahweh who does the removal in 11QT 29.8–10. Moreover, it
should be emphasised that the four elements of the action of Jesus
formed a very odd way of conveying that message. More probably,
Jesus' contemporaries would naturally have interpreted his actions
as a denunciation of what was going on in the temple and as an
implicit challenge to the authority of the priestly aristocracy instead
of (following Sanders' logic) interpreting Jesus' action as actually
announcing a message of hope! In other words, on Sanders' view,
one has to assume that Jesus' action was not only ill conceived, but
foolish in the extreme. Not that this is historically impossible, but a
highly implausible assumption has to be made in order for Sanders'
case to stand.

Finally, it remains to be pointed out that Sanders rejects the
authenticity of the saying in Mark 11.17 and opts instead for a
saying similar to Mark 14.58 (although he is not concerned to
recover its original form). If Mark 11.17 is authentic, Sanders' case
would be further weakened. We hope to show that Mark 11.17 has
good claims to authenticity.

Hence, it can be seen that Sanders' interpretation of the temple
episode is tenuous in the extreme. But he is to be thanked for
criticising views which impose a modern-day presupposition on
first-century beliefs and sources.

(ii) An act of symbolic cleansing

Notwithstanding Sanders' trenchant criticism of the 'cleansing'
view,[68] some prominent scholars (who are acquainted with
Sanders' work) have been attracted to it.[69] J. D. G. Dunn[70] and
several other scholars[71] argue that this cleansing was eschatological
in nature, performed with the conviction that the temple had to be

---

[68] Sanders, *Jesus*, pp. 61–8.
[69] Dunn, *Partings*, p. 48; B. D. Chilton, '[ὡς] φραγέλλιον ἐκ σχονίον (John 2.15)',
in W. Horbury (ed.), *Templum Amicitiae*, p. 34; Witherington, *Christology*, p.
115; Evans, 'Cleansing', 237–70. But Evans seems to have modified his position
in 'Evidence', p. 528, where he says, 'In my view, Jesus' action in the temple
should be understood as a criticism of the Temple establishment (whether or not
it should be called a "cleansing").'
[70] Dunn, *Partings*, p. 48.
[71] E.g., Evans, 'Cleansing', 269–70; Witherington, *Christology*, p. 115.

made ready for its eschatological function in a renewed Zion. Defenders of this view usually argue that there was an expectation that the messiah or God's chosen agent would cleanse and sanctify the sanctuary.[72] The passages which are usually cited to support such a position are: Malachi 3.1–4; Jubilees 4.26; Psalms of Solomon 17.30.

However, Gaston has argued that the motif of the cleansing of the temple stems from *historical* profanations rather than from eschatological hopes.[73] If Gaston is correct, there is then no historical precedent for the belief that a person would cleanse the temple to prepare it for the eschatological denouement. It should also be pointed out that, with the possible exception of Psalms of Solomon 17.30, the texts cited earlier do not explicitly state that it is the task of the messiah to cleanse the sanctuary. The passage from Malachi 3.1–4 refers to the cleansing of the Levites, not the temple, in order that pure agents might bring acceptable sacrifices to God. Jubilees 4.26 does, however, mention the purification of Zion but it makes no reference to the messiah. In Psalms of Solomon 17.30, it is mentioned that Jerusalem is to be purged; the temple is not mentioned. While it is possible that mention of Jerusalem could also imply the temple, the purging specified in 17.30 could be interpreted as the expulsion of Gentiles. That this is eminently probable can be seen from the context. Verse 45 mentions the uncleanness of enemies while verse 22 mentions the cleansing of Jerusalem from nations that trample her. Hence, it is probable that the cleansing of Jerusalem is connected to the uncleanness of enemies and thus it refers to the expulsion of the Gentiles, who were the source of uncleanness in Jerusalem. If our interpretation of the 'cleansing' in 17.30 is cogent, it could be seen that the passage refers to cleansing of profanation and this is more congenial to Gaston's view than to Dunn's. In any case, the cleansing in 17.30 refers to Jerusalem's cleansing and this probably means the expulsion of the Gentiles from the city.

Another difficulty faced by this interpretation concerns the scope of the action. Modern proponents of this view usually concede that the scope of the action was small as it was meant to be a symbolic cleansing. But what does a symbolic cleansing mean? Does it mean that after Jesus' action, the temple is accounted by Jesus (and God) to be clean? If so, why did Jesus predict its destruction later on

---

[72] Dunn, *Partings*, p. 48.   [73] L. Gaston, *No Stone on Another*, p. 119.

(Mark 13.2)? It will not do to dismiss the possibility that Jesus did predict the destruction of the temple, for it has been embedded deeply in the tradition.[74] Furthermore, how is this symbolic cleansing to be understood in its Jewish context? That Jesus' action in overturning some tables, driving out some who sold and bought, and forbidding anyone from carrying a σκεῦος through the temple symbolised the cleansing of the whole sanctuary? All the recorded cleansings of the Jewish temple are thorough cleansings, not symbolic at all. If Jesus meant to perform a symbolic cleansing, the officiating priests and the inner sanctuary would logically have been the targets.[75]

We conclude that the cleansing view is improbable. The action of Jesus does not symbolise a cleansing, for the idea of a symbolical cleansing does not make sense in the light of the historical precedents and in the light of the fact that Jesus did predict its destruction. Moreover, we have tried to show that the very idea itself is not credible and that the elements of the action of Jesus do not cohere very well with such an understanding. Furthermore, there is no explicit evidence that the Jews were looking for an eschatological figure to cleanse the sanctuary.

(iii) A prophetic protest

In rejecting both Sanders' and the 'cleansing' views, we have emphasised the need to take into account all the elements of Jesus' action and the historical background in order that a valid interpretation may emerge. We propose to do this in this section.

a. The overturning of the tables of the money-changers. The money-changers were required in the temple in order to change diverse coinage into the Tyrian silver στατήρ required for the temple tax. According to *m.Shek.* 1.3, the tables of the money-changers were set up on the 25th of Adar (i.e., three weeks before the Passover) and presumably remained there until the 1st of Nisan, the date by which payment was supposed to be made (*m.Shek.* 3.1–3 seems to imply this).[76] The payment of this tax was

---

[74] Sanders, *Jesus*, p. 61. This has also been amply shown by D. E. Aune, *Prophecy in Early Christianity and the Ancient Mediterranean World*, pp. 173–5.

[75] See the instances of Hezekiah (2 Chron. 29), Josiah (2 Kings 23) and Judas Maccabeus (1 Macc. 4.36–59).

[76] Cf. W. L. Lane, *The Gospel According to Mark*, p. 405.

not voluntary (*pace* Sanders[77]) but was voluntary only for those not legally obliged to pay (women, slaves, minors and priests).

Such an institution probably originated in the late post-exilic period,[78] although, according to first-century Jewish interpretation, its legitimacy was derived from Moses, based on a proof-text (Exod. 30.11–16). The rationale for the tax was to make provision for the daily whole-offering which atoned for the sins of Israel.[79] Thus the tax not only enabled Jews to participate in the daily sacrificial worship, but also enabled atonement to be made for the nation. According to Exodus 30.11–16, the occasion for the payment was a census; there was no suggestion of it being understood as an annual tax. How this came about later is lost in antiquity.[80] Even though it became a tax, one has to reckon with the idealism of the Mishnah which states that Jews paid this tax readily (*m.Shek.* 1.3; cf. 3.1–3). Hence, we do not know how it was enforced and whether it was wholeheartedly accepted by all the people. Indeed, Horbury has demonstrated that Palestinian Jews were not beyond reproach in paying the tax.[81] Such a state of affairs would explain why the question whether Jesus paid this tax was directed at Peter (Matt. 17.24), suggesting that it was not taken for granted that everybody would pay.

The above background information helps us to understand the intention of Jesus when he overturned the money-changers' tables.[82] We have seen that this particular action does not self-evidently symbolise the destruction of the temple. A better interpretation might be that Jesus was rejecting this whole institution of the temple tax to pay for the daily whole-offerings. Such would be

---

[77] Sanders, *Jesus*, p. 64. The mishnaic passage he cites (*m.Shek.* 1.3) does not support his case. The text mentions expressly that it is a tax.

[78] See W. Horbury's study, 'The Temple Tax', in Bammel and Moule (eds.), *Jesus and the Politics of His Day*, pp. 265–86. Horbury points out that this particular tax is not mentioned in certain texts which do mention offerings in the temple (Tob. 1.6–8; *Aristeas*; Jubilees). He cites especially 4Q159 where payment of this tax is limited to a single event in a person's life. Finally he shows from rabbinic literature that this tax was not totally welcome (pp. 277–82). For a different view see N. J. McEleney, 'Matthew 17.24–27 – Who Paid the Temple Tax? A Lesson in Avoidance of Scandal', *CBQ* 38 (1976), 179–80.

[79] According to *t.Shek.* 1.6.

[80] Schürer suggests that 'a levy of this sort did not exist before the exile because until then the expenses of public sacrifice were defrayed by the king (Ezek. 45.17ff.)', *History* II, p. 271.

[81] Horbury, 'Temple Tax', pp. 261–7.

[82] It also helps us to situate this action in time, that is, it was performed two to three weeks before Passover.

the most obvious way of understanding Jesus' action. But could it also imply that Jesus was announcing the end of the need for atoning sacrifices to be made on behalf of Israel?[83] This is possible although neither necessary nor convincing.[84] If we take into account that this tax was not totally welcome in Palestine, it may be that Jesus was opposed to the idea of a tax itself but not the function which the tax was understood to fulfil.

The pericope on the temple tax (Matt. 17.24–7) can shed further light on our present discussion. Bauckham has drawn attention to it to show that Jesus was opposed to the principle of the tax.[85] What we can gather from the saying in Matthew 17.25–6 is that theocratic taxation, even though levied in God's name, is inappropriate in view of God's fatherhood.[86] Jesus therefore was not implying that money-changing was not allowed in the temple and that it could go on elsewhere. Nor was he implying that money-changing, a convenient facility, was wrong. Rather, he was against the tax in a radical manner based on his understanding of God's fatherhood:[87] that is, since God is Father to his people, he does not exact taxes from his own children (Matt. 17.25–6).[88] Hence, Jesus rejected the very idea of an annual tax for the upkeep of the temple (going against the grain of the understanding of the priestly aristocracy). It could well be that he was for free-will offerings for such a purpose (see Mark 12.41–4). This radical objection to the tax itself would probably lead Jesus to regard it as being oppressive. This is further exacerbated by the fact that a Palestinian Jew had many taxes to pay in addition to this particular one.[89]

It should also be noted that money-changing was not a piece of

---

83 So Neusner, 'Money-changers', 287–90.

84 See the discussion in Dunn, *Partings*, pp. 53–5.

85 R. J. Bauckham, 'The Coin in the Fish Mouth', in C. L. Blomberg and D. Wenham (eds.), *Gospel Perspectives VI: The Miracles of Jesus*, pp. 219–52. He has also demonstrated quite convincingly the authenticity of the Jesus saying in vv. 25–6. We are indebted to this insight of Bauckham that the overturning of the money-changers' tables in the temple can be understood in connection with the pericope on the temple tax.

86 Bauckham, 'Coin', p. 223.

87 That God's fatherhood was an important part of Jesus' message has been shown by J. Jeremias, *Abba: Studien zur neutestamentlichen Theologie und Zeitsgeschichte*. Cf. Bauckham, 'Coin', pp. 232–3. Cf. also G. Vermes, *The Gospel of Jesus the Jew*, pp. 19–37 from a Jewish perspective.

88 This connection is also perceived by Horbury, 'Temple Tax', p. 283.

89 For such evidence, see T. Rajak, *Josephus: The Historian and His Society*, pp. 22–4, 122–3. See also P. Perkins, 'Taxes in the New Testament', *JRelEth* 12 (1984), 195.

private enterprise but a facility organised by the temple authorities.[90] This would mean that the assumed financial corruption of the temple establishment held in some circles, as demonstrated earlier, was also probably regarded as being connected to the very facility of money-changing, providing an additional reason for Jesus to view it as oppressive. Conversely, an attack on the tax itself by the overturning of the money-changers' tables also amounted to a challenge to the priestly aristocracy. This particular aspect of Jesus' action will be highlighted later.

Hence, Jesus overturned the tables of the money-changers because he was objecting to the tax in principle. This principle is informed by a theological point. Jesus understood God as the Father of Israel, his own people, and, therefore, the idea of an annual tax for the upkeep of his Father's house would contradict the concept of God's fatherhood. This could only mean that, for Jesus, the temple tax was oppressive to him and his people. Apart from this theological principle which Jesus held, his action might also have been motivated by some socio-economic factors. We shall discuss this aspect later. In order to test this proposed interpretation, we have to look at the other elements of Jesus' action to see whether they cohere with it.[91]

> *b. The overturning of the seats of the dove-sellers.* What might this particular action mean? A recourse to the historical background is necessary in order that a proper understanding of it may be derived.

The dove was a poor man's offering. Only in three cases were dove-offerings obligatory: for the cleansing of a man (Lev. 15.14) or a woman (Lev. 15.29), both from ceremonial uncleanness caused by bodily discharges, and for the cleansing of a Nazirite (Num. 6.10). In all other instances, the dove was an alternative sacrificial animal for those who could not afford the more expensive ones (e.g., Lev. 12.6–8).[92]

---

[90] See Abrahams, *Studies* I, p. 86.

[91] Recently, B. D. Chilton has proposed that Jesus' action of overturning the money-changers' tables was a fiction of Christian *haggadah*, designed to make it more comprehensive and attractive, in his *The Temple of Jesus: His Sacrificial Program within a Cultural History of Sacrifice*, pp. 101–3. This is groundless in that this particular action has an excellent *Sitz im Leben Jesu*. Moreover, the creation of this Christian *haggadah* would be pointless as it does not appear to meet any need of the post-Easter community.

[92] Apart from the OT references, see also *m.Ker.* 6.8 and AJ 3.230.

Two further points should also be noted. First, the requirements which had to be satisfied in order for the bird to be accepted as a valid sacrifice were so stringent[93] that there was an officer appointed to oversee this particular offering (*m.Shek.* 5.1).[94] Such stringency can easily lead to high prices. Secondly, from *m.Ker.* 1.7 we have evidence that the prices of the doves could be made exorbitantly high. One could perhaps conjecture that the temple establishment may have had vested interests in the sale of the birds.[95]

When this background is taken into consideration, it is possible that Jesus overturned the dove-sellers' seats because he viewed the whole enterprise as being profiteering and oppressive. This can be seen from the fact that dove-offerings were normally cheaper alternatives for the poorer man. Thus we can see that this particular action of Jesus is consistent with his overturning of the money-changers' tables. Jesus was against the oppression caused by the temple authorities against the people of God, especially the poor ones. He was not against the cult *per se* but protested against the oppressive regime set up by the priestly aristocracy in God's name.

     c. Driving out those who bought and sold.   Who were those who bought and sold (τοὺς πωλοῦντας καὶ τοὺς ἀγοράζοντας, Mark 11.15)? Two interpretations of these words are possible. They may refer to the people who were selling their wares (presumably sacrificial animals, cf. John 2.15) and the common people who were buying them.[96] Therefore if Jesus drove out both the traders and the populace who were buying from them, the impression one

---

93 See *m.Hul.* 1.5; *m.Me'ila* 3.4 and especially *m.Kin.*, the whole tractate.

94 Bauckham opines that 'the notorious complexity of the laws on bird offerings (*m.'Abot.* 3.19) probably explains the comment in *m.Shek.* 5.1 about the special skills of Petahiah, the temple-treasurer in charge of bird offerings', in his 'Demonstration', p. 172 n. 24. He also suggests that the rearing and sale of doves for the temple probably took place under the auspices of the temple treasurer (p. 176).

95 Sanders is correct to insist that very little is known about how the sale of doves was managed (*Judaism: Practice and Belief*, pp. 85–6). While there is no evidence which demonstrates that the establishment had a monopoly over this particular trade, the following considerations may indicate that it had vested interests in it: (1) These animals were sold in the temple precincts and hence control over the prices and the management of the trade could be exercised by the establishment. (2) The stringency of the regulations connected with such a sacrifice could easily lead to the establishment setting up its own trade in these animals. (3) The amassed wealth of the high priests discussed earlier is most easily explicable by the conjecture that they were probably involved in this trade.

96 So V. Taylor, *The Gospel of Mark*, p. 462 and C. S. Mann, *Mark*, p. 448.

receives is that he intended to stop the sale of sacrificial animals,[97] and, perhaps, even sacrifice itself (or else why should he drive out those who were buying?).[98] Or, more plausibly, the phrase may refer to the people who were trading with the temple staff. Hence they would be people selling supplies to the temple staff and merchants who were buying valuable items which the people had donated to the temple (*m.Shek.* 5.6).[99]

It is therefore possible that it was the merchants that Jesus drove out and perhaps also the staff employed by the temple to oversee such affairs. But they were not the common people who had come for sacrifice.

One datum from Mark may serve to show that our proposal here is not misconceived. According to Mark 11.18, the high priests did not arrest Jesus immediately because they feared the *people* for they were amazed at Jesus' teaching (presumably his action and the saying which gave the rationale for the former). If Mark is reliable at this point, Jesus could not possibly have driven out the people who came to sacrifice. For in so doing, he would have lost popular support and it was precisely this support which according to the gospel tradition[100] prevented his immediate arrest by the temple establishment. But an action directed at the establishment and people who were involved in the trade which was going on (i.e., the merchants) would have gained such support, especially if there was disaffection with the establishment.

d. Forbidding anyone from carrying a σκεῦος through the temple (Mark 11.16). This action was not mentioned by Matthew and Luke, probably because of its obscurity. Two questions

---

[97] Sanders avers that it was highly unlikely for quadrupeds to be sold in the temple precincts, *Judaism: Practice and Belief*, pp. 87–8. But he is wrong. The rabbinic literature does attest to the availability of sacrificial quadrupeds on the temple mount (*t.Hag.* 2.11; *y.Betz.* 2.4, 61c13–16). Sanders' argument is based mainly on the assumption that the excrement from the quadrupeds would defile the temple. He fails to note that actually numerous Passover lambs and other animals had to be sacrificed during festivals and a queue of animals was to be expected! In other words, arrangements would have been made to offset this problem. The Solomon Stables, under the Royal Portico, could possibly provide an example of such an arrangement.

[98] So Telford, *Temple*, p. 93 n. 102.

[99] Cf. the observation of Bauckham, 'Demonstration', p. 78. He seems to intimate that the temple staff were also targets of Jesus' action.

[100] See Mark 12.12||Matt. 21.46||Luke 20.19. There is no reason why this should not be reliable.

immediately emerge: What is a σκεῦος? Why did Jesus prohibit people from carrying one διὰ τοῦ ἱεροῦ?

The usual explanation is that Jesus was reinstating a standing rule which prohibited the use of the temple precincts as a thoroughfare.[101] This interpretation bases itself on two passages: one taken from the Mishnah (*m.Ber.* 9.5) and the other from Josephus (*Ap.* 2.106). The σκεῦος would therefore refer to any variety of domestic utensils or goods whose transport is made more convenient by using the temple as a short cut. However, this view is untenable for the following reasons. No mention of the carrying of vessels is made in the mishnaic passage.[102] Moreover, *Ap.* 2.106 does not envisage the use of the sacred precincts as a thoroughfare but refers only to the prohibition against the carrying of any vessel into the *inner* sanctuary itself.[103] It is incredible, as Bauckham has observed, that Jesus could have encountered people who were trying to do precisely that.[104]

A connection with Zechariah 14.21 has been suggested. According to this view, Jesus was trying to commandeer all vessels brought into the temple for sacred purposes.[105] However, in Mark 11.16, Jesus was prohibiting vessels from being brought διὰ τοῦ ἱεροῦ! Nor is Ford's argument that σκεῦος could be understood as a money-bag linguistically convincing.[106]

One is compelled to agree with Telford that the most natural meaning of σκεῦος is a sacred vessel for the carriage of materials used for the offering.[107] But we disagree with Telford when he infers from this action that Jesus was forbidding sacrifice. In line with our understanding of the other elements of his action in the

---

[101] So J. Lightfoot, *Horae Hebraicae et Talmudicae* II, p. 432; J. Jeremias, *New Testament Theology I: The Proclamation of Jesus*, p. 145 n. 1; Abrahams, *Studies* I, p. 84.

[102] The relevant line from *m.Ber.* 9.5 reads, 'he may not enter into the temple mount with his staff or his sandal or his wallet, or with the dust upon his feet, nor may he make of it a short by-path; still less may he spit there' (translation taken from H. Danby (tr.), *The Mishnah*, p. 102).

[103] This is suggested by its context: 'no vessel whatever might be carried into the temple, the only objects in which were an altar, a table, a censer, and a lampstand'. All these items were found in the *inner* sanctuary. The translation is taken from H. St J. Thackeray (ed.), *Josephus* I, p. 335.

[104] Bauckham, 'Demonstration', p. 172 n. 30.

[105] C. Roth, 'The Cleansing of the Temple and Zechariah xiv.21', *NovT* 4 (1960), 177–8.

[106] J. M. Ford, 'Money "bags" in the Temple (Mark 11.16)', *Bib* 57 (1975), 249–53.

[107] Telford, *Temple*, p. 93 n. 102. He points out that more than one-third of the references to σκεῦος in the LXX are to the sacred cult objects of the tabernacle, altar or temple and also that such a usage is common in Josephus.

temple, we believe a case can be made for understanding the prohibition as an attempt to stop the carriage with these sacred vessels διὰ τοῦ ἱεροῦ into the storehouses in the Court of Women[108] by the temple staff of sacred supplies (flour, oil and wine), which would later be sold to the populace when they came for sacrifice.[109] That the temple sold these items is clear from *m.Shek.* 4.3; 5.4. Thus Jesus was once again directing his attack at the temple establishment and this time it was against the probably profiteering racket which was going on in the sacred precincts. If our interpretation of this obscure reference of Mark 11.16 is correct, it can be seen then that all the elements of Jesus' action do cohere very well. Jesus was protesting against the temple establishment for turning the sacrificial system into an oppressive profit-making industry.

    e. The saying. That something was said by Jesus during the incident cannot be denied. In the OT, prophetic symbolical gestures were usually accompanied by explanation (e.g., Isa. 8.1–4; Jer. 13; 19; 27; 32; Ezek. 4; 12). Indeed, as Borg observes, 'odd gestures had as their *raison d'être* the pronouncement which followed'.[110] Moreover, Daube has pointed out that in the rabbinic tradition, there often exists a tripartite form of instruction consisting of gesture, question and pronouncement.[111] All these observations support the presumption that something was said to explain the provocative action of Jesus. But what exactly was said?

Mark records a conflated quotation taken from Isaiah 56.7 and Jeremiah 7.11 as being said by Jesus after the demonstration (Mark 11.17). The authenticity of this saying has come under heavy fire especially from Harvey and Sanders.[112] Sanders proposes instead that a saying similar to Mark 14.58 was originally expressed during the incident.[113] It must be pointed out that Sanders' case is built out of inference as such a saying was not attributed to Jesus by the evangelists, with the possible exception of John (John 2.19). Two other things must be said in this connection. First, it is hazardous to opt for a saying whose form is irrecoverable unless Mark 11.17 is shown to be inauthentic. Second, even if a nebulous saying as

---

[108] See *m.Mid.* 2.5.   [109] So Bauckham, 'Demonstration', p. 78.

[110] Borg, *Conflict*, p. 173.

[111] D. Daube, *New Testament and Rabbinic Judaism*, pp. 175–81. In this instance, the middle element is missing (the question, but this could be implicit).

[112] Sanders, *Jesus*, p. 66; A. E. Harvey, *Jesus and the Constraints of History*, p. 132.

[113] Sanders, *Jesus*, pp. 66–7, 73–4.

proposed by Sanders was said at this juncture, it in no wise proves that Mark 11.17 was not said. In other words, there is no necessity to view the two sayings as mutually exclusive. Mark could have left out the other owing to redactional reasons.[114] What is crucial, then, is the authenticity of Mark 11.17.

The saying in Mark 11.17 is prefaced with the words καὶ ἐδίδασκεν καὶ ἔλεγεν αὐτοῖς. Some scholars have assumed that this phrase is redactional and may therefore introduce a saying which is redactional (if it is dominical, the placement of it may be redactional).[115] But even if we grant that the phrase is redactional, it does not follow that the saying which follows is redactional.[116] Indeed, Bauckham strongly avers that the elaborate Markan introduction to the saying can tell us nothing about whether Mark found the saying already connected to vv. 15b–6 in his source.[117] Therefore the case for the authenticity (or inauthenticity) of Mark 11.17 depends on other considerations.

Harvey has argued that the phrase ὁ οἶκος μου οἶκος προσευχῆς κληθήσεται πᾶσιν τοῖς ἔθνεσιν cannot be extracted from the Hebrew original which Jesus would have used.[118] But this argument cannot stand up to scrutiny. For, in the first place, the words in question can be extracted from the Hebrew of Isaiah 56.7![119] The LXX of this verse which is found in Mark 11.17 is a literal translation of the Hebrew text.[120] Moreover, a reading of Isaiah 56 will show clearly that vv. 6–7 were addressed to foreigners (proselytes) and that these foreigners were obviously from the 'nations' (τὰ ἔθνη). Therefore, even if Jesus used the Hebrew text, it would

---

[114] We concede that a saying behind the accusation of Mark 14.58 has good grounds for being viewed as being authentic but its recovery is difficult in view of the fact that the origins of such a charge are obscure.

[115] J. Roloff, *Das Kerygma und irdischen Jesu*, p. 91. He is followed by Sanders, *Jesus*, p. 66.

[116] For example, Mark 9.1 is prefaced by the words καὶ ἔλεγεν αὐτοῖς but is dominical, as shown convincingly by B. D. Chilton, *God in Strength*, pp. 251–74. R. P. Booth makes a strong case for the authenticity of the logia in Mark 7.20–2 which are prefaced by the words ἔλεγεν δέ in his *Jesus and the Laws of Purity: Tradition History and Legal History in Mark 7*, pp. 96–114.

[117] Bauckham, 'Demonstration', p. 81. He suggests that Mark will have introduced the formula to make the incident the introduction to the theme of Jesus' teaching in the temple.

[118] Harvey, *Constraints*, p. 132.

[119] כִּי בֵיתִי בֵית־תְּפִלָּה יִקָּרֵא לְכָל־הָעַמִּים (*ki beti bet-tĕpillâh yiqqāre' lĕkâl hā'ammim*).

[120] Indeed, Hooker has justifiably retorted, 'But what Hebrew version is *Harvey* using? For the words in question are there in *my* Hebrew text' (emphasis hers) in 'Traditions About the Temple in the Sayings of Jesus', *BJRL* 71 (1988), 18.

make no difference either to the interpretation of the saying or to its authenticity, as the LXX quoted in Mark 11.17 translates accurately the Hebrew original.

Another common objection to the authenticity of Mark 11.17 has to do with the second half of the saying which is taken from Jeremiah 7.11. It is argued that the word λῃστής is inappropriate to describe the people who carried out those activities described earlier.[121] λῃστής does not mean thief but brigand, a violent raider or even a guerrilla fighter.[122] The money-changers and those involved in the temple trade could not be described as violent men. Buchanan therefore proposes that Mark 11.17 is a saying which was composed after the fall of Jerusalem (in view of the fact that Josephus called the zealots λῃσταί) with reference to the occupation of the temple by the zealots in 68–70 CE.[123]

Is this objection insurmountable? Hooker argues that scholars who regard the term λῃστής as inappropriately used here miss the significance of the quotation.[124] The description of the temple as a den of robbers in Jeremiah 7.11 is metaphorical since the crimes described are not just limited to violent ones. The sense in Jeremiah 7.11 is that people who are guilty of the worst crimes regard the temple as a safe refuge. Because of the belief in the invulnerability of the temple (Jer. 7.4), they think they can commit crimes with impunity, like brigands retreating to the security of their caves after every raid. If it is borne in mind that the usage of the term is metaphorical in Jeremiah 7.11, there appears to be no good reason to doubt the appropriateness of its citation in the temple incident. Jesus was using scripture in a creative manner and his point was that the temple establishment, by virtue of their unassailable authority and privilege (similar to a brigand in his cave),[125] were abusing their position to plunder the people of God and oppress

---

[121] Gaston, *No Stone*, p. 85; Harvey, *Constraints*, p. 132; Sanders, *Jesus*, p. 66; G. W. Buchanan, 'Mark 11.15–19: Brigands in the Temple', *HUCA* 30 (1959), 169–77; C. K. Barrett, 'The House of Prayer and the Den of Thieves', in E. E. Ellis and E. Grässer (eds.), *Jesus und Paulus*, pp. 13–20.

[122] It is this consideration that drives Borg to give this saying a rather odd interpretation. To Borg, the word refers to the temple establishment, who, because of their ideology of exclusivism, made use of the temple as a symbol of political resistance against Rome (*Conflict*, p. 174). We do not find this explanation convincing as there is evidence that the establishment was viewed by the people as being in collusion with Rome! See M. Hengel, *The Zealots*, pp. 213, 364. See also BJ 2.441.

[123] Buchanan, 'Brigands', 176–7.   [124] Hooker, 'Traditions', 18.

[125] Interestingly, the temple is also described as the seat of robbery by the Qumran community. See 1QpHab 10.1 (its beams were laid in robbery) and 4QpNah 1.11

them.[126] Hence, the term ληστής in Mark 11.17 does not owe its origin to the zealot movement but in all likelihood to a creative use of Jeremiah 7.11 by Jesus.[127]

But what about John 2.16? Many scholars have sought to show that this was the actual saying and not Mark 11.17.[128] It is usually supposed that an allusion to Zechariah 14.21 is made in this saying.[129] Hence, according to this view, Jesus was scandalised by the use of the temple courts for the selling of animals (or trading)[130] and, by performing the demonstration, he was signifying that 'he was bringing in that final holy time when there would be no longer any trader in the house of the Lord'.[131] But a strong case can be made for viewing John 2.16 as a redactional paraphrase of the logion found in Mark 11.17. In John, the first part of the saying (about the temple being a house of prayer) was probably suppressed, in line with John's tendency *vis-à-vis* the cult (cf. John 4.21). Moreover, Mark 11.17 (especially the words πᾶσιν τοῖς ἔθνεσιν) would probably be a source of difficulty for the early church in view of the events that transpired which seemed to imply the lack of fulfilment of this saying[132] and in view of the fact that the members of the Christian community regarded themselves as the true temple.[133] The second part was paraphrased as μὴ ποιεῖτε τὸν οἶκον τοῦ πατρός μου οἶκον ἐμπορίου. That this Johannine saying was congenial to his account of the temple episode can be seen from the fact that the Johannine Jesus directed his attack on the sellers (the buyers are not mentioned, unlike in Mark).

(referring to the amassing of wealth by the priests which God would judge one day).

[126] Recently, W. R. Herzog III has suggested that 'Jesus was declaring that the true social bandits were not the deviants operating out of caves in the Judean desert but the prominent officials of the Temple built over the sacred cave of the Temple Mount through their exploitative and oppressive domination of the Jews in Palestine', in his article, 'Temple Cleansing', in J. B. Green, S. McKnight and I. H. Marshall (eds.), *Dictionary of Jesus and the Gospels*, p. 820.

[127] *Pace* Buchanan, 'Brigands', 169–77.

[128] Witherington, *Christology*, p. 114; cf. Bultmann, *History*, p. 36.

[129] Harvey, *Constraints*, p. 133; Witherington, *Christology*, p. 114; C. H. Dodd, *Historical Tradition in the Fourth Gospel*, pp. 159–60; B. Lindars, *The Gospel of John*, p. 139; R. E. Brown, *The Gospel According to John I–XII*, p. 121.

[130] There may be good evidence that the practice of selling sacrificial animals (sheep and oxen) on the temple mount may have been a recent innovation. See the discussion in Chilton, 'φραγέλλιον', pp. 335–7.

[131] Witherington, *Christology*, p. 114.

[132] As also observed by I. H. Marshall, *The Gospel of Luke*, p. 721.

[133] This is amply attested in the Pauline corpus. On this topic see R. J. McKelvey, *The New Temple*.

Hence, it is more probable that Mark retained the original form of the saying and the later evangelists redacted it than vice versa. As there are no strong objections to its authenticity, it is here proposed that Mark 11.17 is authentic and serves the very important function of explaining the motivation behind Jesus' action.[134]

(iv) Summary

We propose that Jesus intended his action in the temple to be a prophetic protest against the mismanagement of the temple by the priestly aristocracy.[135] That it is an action performed in order to make a protest can be seen from its scale. It was not intended to put a stop to all the operations in the temple.

Regarding the meaning of the action, we propose that it was not meant to symbolise the cleansing of the temple by an eschatological agent of God. Nor does it symbolise its destruction. Rather, it was a protest, carried out in the spirit of the OT prophets against the oppression and corrupt profiteering of the temple establishment.[136] It is possible that Jesus did not object to the services which these commercial activities were providing, in so far as they provided worshippers with convenient victims and money-changing facilities. And thus what he was actually against was the exploitation of these facilities by the powerful temple establishment for their lucrative gain. That this conclusion is plausible can be seen from our

---

[134] A short word on the saying about the destruction of the temple (whether threat or prediction) is in order here. We have earlier intimated that a saying behind the charge of Mark 14.58 has good support for its authenticity. But in view of the fact that we have proposed that Mark 11.17 was the saying that was uttered at the demonstration, where are we then to situate the saying which lies behind Mark 14.58? In other words, Mark 14.58 is in need of a setting. It is to be noted at the outset that the sayings against the temple (Mark 13.2 and parallels; Mark 14.58‖Matt. 26.60–1; Mark 15.29‖Matt. 27.40; John 2.19; Acts 6.14) are in two forms: prediction (Mark 13.2 and parallels; John 2.19) and threat. The questions which then arise are: 'Are these two separate sayings or did one derive itself from the other?' and 'If the latter is true, which one is prior?' The issues are too complex to be discussed here but we would none the less offer our proposal. The prediction of the destruction of the temple was given after the whole incident, but was used against Jesus in the form of a threat saying, either through misunderstanding or out of a malicious intent.

[135] So also Hengel, *Revolutionist*, pp. 16–17.

[136] On the topic of the OT prophets as social and religious reformers, see the brief and introductory treatment by J. F. A. Sawyer, *Prophecy and the Prophets in the Old Testament*, pp. 40–4. For more detailed treatments, see D. L. Petersen, *The Roles of Israel's Prophets*; P. D. Miller, *Sin and Judgment in the Prophets*.

interpretation of the different elements of the one action of Jesus and the saying which was spoken during that occasion. We have found that they are all of a piece.

Of course, a prophetic protest can carry implications that the temple, because of its mismanagement by the establishment, is rejected and condemned. Whether this is so cannot be gathered explicitly from the episode itself, although there are hints. The fact that part of the saying of Jesus in Mark 11.17 was taken from Jeremiah 7.11 may well imply that Jesus was equating the priests of his generation with those of Jeremiah's and that he understood the doom of the temple as certain. That this is a plausible reading of the intention of Jesus can be seen from the fact that Mark records Jesus as predicting the destruction of the temple after and not before the incident (Mark 13.2).[137] Hence, Sanders may not be totally wrong when he opines that the destruction of the temple was somehow connected to this action of Jesus, although his whole procedure is wrong and his interpretation of the incident is questionable in the extreme.[138] The destruction of the temple is only implied and is a logical outworking of the protest against the mismanagement of it. And this came about not through any action of Jesus, but simply through the fact that the temple has failed in its function as the house of prayer for all nations. That such a description of the temple is usually found in an eschatological context[139] has important implications for our enquiry and this will be explored later.

The prophetic protest was directed against the establishment who ran the affairs not just of the temple, but also of the city, under the auspices of the Roman empire. They also had the temple police under their charge. Why was there no immediate action against Jesus from the Roman garrison or the temple police if his action was clearly a challenge to their authority? The following is probably the explanation.

First, as was pointed out earlier, the scale of the action was small. It was a demonstration in protest at some practices in the temple. Such being the case, it is not surprising that the Roman garrison stationed in the Antonia fortress[140] did not take action.

---

[137] Q 13.34–5, which is relevant, is situated *after* the incident in Matthew (Matt. 23.37–9) although in Luke it is before. We have argued for the Matthean placement, see our chapter 5.

[138] Sanders, *Jesus*, pp. 69, 71.   [139] See our chapter 2.

[140] AJ 20.192.

For it is usually the policy of Rome to leave these small affairs to the national leaders.[141] But why was there no action from the temple police? This leads us to the second point.

The populace at large (perhaps particularly those from Galilee[142]) probably sympathised with this action of Jesus. We have shown that the temple tax was not wholeheartedly welcome in Palestine. We have also adduced evidence to show that not a few considered the temple establishment to be oppressive and corrupt. Theissen may well be correct to suggest that there were tensions between those who dwelt in the city of Jerusalem, many of whom depended on the temple for their livelihood, and those who dwelt elsewhere in the land, especially Galilee.[143] Although the ongoing activities in the temple brought about economic benefits[144] and social relief, such benefits were felt only in Jerusalem.[145] In addition to this consideration, we have highlighted the fact that the heavy burden of taxation was felt throughout the land and resented. This was made worse by the contributions demanded by Herod for the building of the second temple and also, perhaps, the temple tax.[146] Hence, people from the provinces experienced the temple not only as worshippers but also as taxpayers with the suspicion that they were perhaps fleeced. Therefore, Jesus' action (which would not have been obscure to his contemporaries) would have received an implicit approval from them. The temple establishment would have thought it expedient to await an opportune moment to arrest him.

Thus it can be seen that such a prophetic demonstration is also implicitly a challenge to the political–economic base in Jerusalem.[147] While this is one plausible angle for looking at the motivation behind Jesus' action, there is, however, a more important motivation. And to this we now turn.

---

[141] See E. Bammel, 'The *Titulus*', in Bammel and Moule (eds.), *Jesus and the Politics of His Day*, p. 358.

[142] See Bauckham, 'Demonstration', p. 88.

[143] G. Theissen, 'Die Tempelweissagung Jesu: Prophetie und Spannungsfeld von Stadt und Land', *TZ* 32 (1976), 144–58.

[144] It must be remembered that the temple was a vast economic enterprise. For evidence see Schürer, *History* II, pp. 280–1; Jeremias, *Jerusalem*, pp. 27–8, 56–7; and Hamilton, 'Bank', 365–72.

[145] See R. A. Horsley, 'Popular Prophetic Movements at the Time of Jesus: Their Principal Features and Social Origins', *JSNT* 26 (1986), 29.

[146] See Borg, *Conflict*, pp. 31–6; Rajak, *Josephus*, pp. 122–3; Perkins, 'Taxes', 195; D. E. Oakman, *Jesus and the Economic Questions of His Day*, especially p. 211; Horsley, *Spiral*.

[147] This is also observed by C. C. Rowland, 'The Second Temple: Focus of Ideological Struggle?', in W. Horbury (ed.), *Templum Amicitiae*, pp. 197–8.

3   The temple incident and the Zion traditions (Mark 11.17)

What theological presupposition or motivation, if there was any, led Jesus to perform this audacious and provocative action? Jesus' action can be interpreted from sociological,[148] political,[149] or economic[150] angles, but we believe that his main motivation was theological. This is not to say that we want to separate Jesus' theology from his sociological, political and economic views, for, in Jewish life and thought, theology shapes praxis and praxis in turn influences theology.[151] Rather, it is to say that Jesus' actions cannot be separated from his understanding of God's programme which was coming to expression through his ministry, the role he had in this programme, and the crucial 'hour' of this programme. That this is a plausible explanation of the motivation behind Jesus' action can be seen from a careful consideration of Mark 11.17 as it gives the theological rationale for it.

Mark 11.17 is composed of two parts with one part being antithetical to the other. The fundamental contrast is between the two descriptions of the temple: one, the eschatological ideal (οἶκος προσευχῆς ... πᾶσιν τοῖς ἔθνεσιν); the other, the present abuse (σπήλαιον λῃστῶν). Although some have doubted the authenticity of the phrase πᾶσιν τοῖς ἔθνεσιν (since both Matthew and Luke agree in omitting it),[152] there is actually a strong argument in favour of its authenticity. Events during 70 CE probably led Matthew and Luke to omit it either because it had become irrelevant, or because it might be construed as an unfulfilled prophecy by their readers.[153]

In Jesus' eyes, what the priestly aristocracy had done with the temple was manifestly wrong and this evoked the description of it as a σπήλαιον λῃστῶν. What the temple should be instead, at this particular juncture of God's restoration programme, is οἶκος προσευχῆς ... πᾶσιν τοῖς ἔθνεσιν. What was envisaged by these words taken from Isaiah 56.7 was usually understood in second-

---

[148] E.g., Theissen, 'Tempelweissagung', 144–58.
[149] E.g., Borg, *Conflict.*   [150] E.g., Oakman, *Jesus.*
[151] See Hengel, *Zealots*, where he tried to show how these two elements (with a bias towards theology) shaped the zealot movement. Cf. M. Goodman, *The Ruling Class of Judaea*, for a different account of the uprising.
[152] E.g., B. Gärtner, *The Temple and the Community in Qumran and the New Testament*, pp. 110–11; R. H. Hiers, 'Purification of the Temple: Preparation for the Kingdom of God', *JBL* 90 (1971), 89.
[153] So Borg, *Conflict*, p. 175; Bauckham, 'Demonstration', p. 83.

temple Jewry to refer to the eschatological temple; when such a temple is erected, there would be an influx of Gentile proselytes to Zion to worship Yahweh. And thus would be fulfilled the prophecy that the temple would be a house of prayer for all nations (Ps. 22.27; Isa. 2.2–3; Zeph. 3.9–10; Tob. 13.11; Pss. Sol. 17.30, 33; Sib. Or. 3.702–18, 772–6; T. Ben. 9.2).[154] That the temple of Jesus' day was understood not to have fulfilled such an eschatological function can be seen from the fact that access into the temple was strictly forbidden to Gentiles[155] and that there was no real effort to proselytise Gentiles and admit them to the temple.[156] Second-temple Jewry looked for a restored temple on a restored Zion.

Against the grain of scholarship, Bauckham writes that Jesus was not referring to the eschatological temple when the saying was uttered. Instead, Jesus was saying that what was to be realised in the messianic age – the pilgrimage of the nations to Zion – has been Yahweh's intention for the temple all along.[157] His reason for such a view is that the temple establishment could not be accused of contradicting a divine intention which was meant to be fulfilled only with the eschatological temple.[158]

But such a view ignores the abundant evidence which shows the connection between the pilgrimage of the Gentiles to Zion and the *eschatological* temple.[159] That is, the common understanding of Jesus' contemporaries was that the Gentiles, if they were not already annihilated, would come to Zion only when the eschatological temple was set up. There was no expectation of an influx of Gentiles before such a temple was set up.

In this light, Bauckham's view is fraught with the same difficulty he is trying to obviate in that the temple establishment should not be faulted for not knowing it was Yahweh's intention that the temple should function as a house of prayer for all nations all along. Bauckham fails to see that for his view to be tenable he must sever the intimate connection between the pilgrimage of the Gentiles and the eschatological temple which is abundantly attested

---

[154] Dunn, *Partings*, p. 48.   [155] See the evidence in AJ 15.417.

[156] Borg, *Conflict*, pp. 175–6; see also D. R. Schwartz, 'On Sacrifices by Gentiles in the Temple', in his *Studies in the Jewish Background of Christianity*, pp. 102–16, where he argues that it was only with the greatest reserve that Gentiles were allowed to sacrifice in the temple. For a most recent discussion of this matter, see now L. H. Feldman, *Jew and Gentile in the Ancient World: Attitudes and Interactions from Alexander to Justinian*; and M. Goodman, *Mission and Conversion: Proselytizing in the Religious History of the Roman Empire*.

[157] Bauckham, 'Demonstration', p. 85.

[158] Ibid.   [159] See our chapter 2.

to in the extant Jewish literature from the second temple period (Tob. 13.11; Pss. Sol. 17.30, 33; T. Ben. 9.2; Sib. Or. 3.702–18, 772–6).

As a matter of fact, Bauckham's main consideration which led him to adopt his peculiar view serves to highlight the self-understanding of Jesus when he uttered that saying. We agree with Bauckham that the temple establishment should not be faulted for something which is attainable only in the eschaton. But the fact that they were faulted and had a saying spoken against them which was usually understood as referring to the eschatological temple shows that Jesus understood that his presence in Jerusalem and the actions he performed (the entry and the present one under consideration) amounted to the fulfilling of these eschatological promises. It is plausible that Jesus was saying through these actions that the time for the eschatological renewal of Zion had arrived. But the temple as it stood then was found to be wanting and unworthy to be the temple of the eschaton because of the abuses of the priestly aristocracy. Thus, the temple establishment would be faulted for their mismanagement of the temple and for their failure to recognise in Jesus' ministry the dawn of the eschatological fulfilment promised by Yahweh. Hence, instead of a renewal of the temple, it is sentenced to be destroyed. Whether Jesus held out the promise that there would be a new temple to replace the one destroyed is another matter.[160] If our interpretation of the significance of Mark 11.17 is correct, we can see that Jesus viewed this particular phase of his ministry not only as the climax of his vocation but also as the fulfilment of what Yahweh had promised regarding the temple on Zion through the prophets. In this light, the presence and activities of Jesus in Jerusalem could be said to be a *hinge* moment in the eschatological scenario.[161] Because it was the hinge moment, the temple when found wanting has to be condemned and judged, and this would explain why Jesus predicted the destruction of the temple shortly after (Mark 13.2) and lamented for Jerusalem (Q 13.34–5).[162]

---

[160] It must be borne in mind that according to Jewish eschatology, it was not necessary for the old temple to be destroyed before the new could be erected (see 11QT 29.8–10). Indeed, as J. Riches has observed, the many Jewish texts (with the exception of 1 En. 90.28–9) which refer to the erection of the new temple (Tob. 14.5; Jub. 1.15–17) do not explicitly mention the destruction of the old. See his 'Apocalyptic – Strangely Relevant', in W. Horbury (ed.), *Templum Amicitiae*, p. 247.

[161] To use the phraseology of Meyer, *Aims*, p. 198.   [162] See our chapter 5.

Hence, Mark 11.17, by virtue of its reference to the eschatological temple and by virtue of the fact that it records that Jesus demanded that the temple should fulfil that eschatological role, gives evidence of how great an impact the Zion traditions had on Jesus. That Jesus understood his presence in Jerusalem to be the hinge moment in the eschatological drama had its basis in these traditions.

While it is difficult to speak of Jesus' concern for the Gentiles in his ministry without a thorough engagement with Sanders,[163] Mark 11.17 may encourage one to think that he was positive towards them. However, it must be stressed here that to view Jesus' action as being motivated by his desire to include the Gentiles in the kingdom[164] is not the only possible reading here. It is more arguable that Jesus was more taken up with the fulfilment of the promises made to Zion than that he was specially concerned for the Gentiles when those words were uttered. The mention of the Gentiles served only as a foil to highlight the crucial moment in God's programme which was coming to pass with Jesus' presence in Jerusalem. This may explain why the post-Easter community did not make explicit overtures to the Gentiles immediately.[165] None the less, the fact that a verse about the pilgrimage of Gentiles is cited may yet show that Jesus was not indifferent to the participation of Gentiles in the eschatological blessings.

Nor was Jesus clearing an 'eschatological' space for the Gentiles in the temple.[166] That such a conception is unlikely can be seen in two ways. Firstly, such a theory often highlights the point that the action was performed in the Court of the Gentiles. But the appellation 'Court of the Gentiles' is a modern one. There is no evidence that the outer court was thought of positively as the place where Gentiles could worship. Instead, it was conceived negatively as the limit beyond which Gentiles should not pass.[167] Secondly, such an understanding would make Jesus' action a rather impotent one. As Borg observes, this implies that the outer court was where the Gentiles belonged while Israel continued to enjoy a fuller service in the inner courts; this is definitely not what Isaiah 56.7

---

[163] Sanders, *Jesus*, pp. 218–21.

[164] E.g., Borg, *Conflict*, p. 175; W. D. Davies, *The Gospel and the Land*, pp. 350–1.

[165] That there was a significant delay in the Gentile mission has been taken as strong evidence that Jesus did not make any positive gesture towards the Gentiles in his ministry. See, e.g., Sanders, *Jesus*, p. 221.

[166] E.g., Davies, *Land*, pp. 350–1.   [167] Bauckham, 'Demonstration', p. 85.

meant.[168] Therefore, if the spatial aspect of the action is emphasised, it would contradict the intention of Isaiah 56.7 which was
cited.

To summarise: Jesus' theological motivation for his action in the
temple is informed thoroughly by the Zion traditions. Some
significant results follow from this.

First, the eschatological character of Jesus' visit to Jerusalem
(and especially the temple) is prominent. The fact that it was
demanded of the second temple to be the house of prayer for all
nations, a function realisable only in the eschaton, shows clearly
that Jesus' visit to the temple was eschatological through and
through. In other words, according to Jesus, the renewal of Zion
has been set in motion in his visit to Jerusalem.

Second, as a corollary of the first point, the fulfilment character
of Jesus' presence in Jerusalem has to be mentioned. The promises
made by Yahweh to Israel are to be fulfilled at its heart (Jerusalem)
through the ministry of Jesus in Jerusalem. Once again, we see the
theological and eschatological attraction Jerusalem had for Jesus.
He began his ministry preaching in Galilee that the kingdom of
God was at hand (Mark 1.15). That message must be preached and
its content fulfilled in the heart of Jewry, Zion itself.

Finally, the conflict with the establishment becomes more significant. It was not just a class struggle waged by a Galilean
peasant against the aristocracy. Rather, Jesus' presence in Jerusalem represents the confrontation of the kingdom of God with the
authorities who had been given the task of running the heart of
Jewry, Jerusalem. Through the presence of Jesus, the leaders were
confronted with their very king, Yahweh.

4   The action in the temple and the entry into Jerusalem

In the Synoptic gospels, the entry is placed cheek by jowl with the
incident in the temple.[169] Undoubtedly, the Synoptic evangelists
wish their readers to see a connection between the two episodes. We
propose to explore this connection here.

---

[168] Borg, *Conflict*, p. 175.
[169] Mark intercalates the incident in the temple with the cursing of the fig-tree
episode (Mark 11.12–25).

A thematic unity[170]

We have suggested in chapter 6 that, through his entry into Jerusalem, Jesus was signifying that he was the divinely appointed king laying claim to his city in order to inaugurate the eschatological renewal of Zion. In the incident in the temple, the basic theological motivation for Jesus' provocative protest comes from his understanding that the hour has come whereby the temple is brought into an encounter with the eschatological restorative programme of God. It needs to be pointed out that the themes of the two episodes can be seen to be a unity. What is this unity? It will be going too far to claim that, in the demonstration in the temple, Jesus was adopting a messianic profile and therefore entered it as its lord.[171] Nor is the question of the status of the Gentiles and the issue of peace the thematic unity.[172]

The thematic unity can be fully appreciated only when it is seen in the light of both their backgrounds in the Zion traditions and the timing of events in Jesus' own perception of the course of his ministry. Jesus understood his presence in Jerusalem as the climax of his ministry and the hinge moment of God's programme for his people. It was with this conviction that he made the fateful trip to Jerusalem. The kingdom of God has to be brought into a decisive encounter with the heart of Jewry: the city and the temple in it. For Jerusalem was not only the political and religious centre of Jewry, it was also the focus of God's eschatological promises for his people. In this encounter, the city and the temple had to recognise this decisive hour. Such an encounter would inexorably result in a challenge to the priestly aristocracy, whose task was to look after Yahweh's city and temple. The entry was a symbolical event; it was also a challenge to both the city and the leaders. While the protest in the temple has relatively less symbolical content, it was also a challenge to the leaders and the temple. The motivation behind the latter challenge is identical with the symbolical content of the entry. But in the action in the temple, the plot is advanced a stage further. The leaders' mismanagement of the temple was exposed. In Jewish thought, the city and temple partake in the vices of the leaders and

---

[170] That there might be a thematic unity between the two episodes has been noted by scholars although, unfortunately, it is seldom spelt out. See Meyer, *Aims*, pp. 168, 170; Borg, *Conflict*, pp. 176–7; Witherington, *Christology*, p. 115.

[171] E.g., Gärtner, *Temple*, p. 107. Cf. also E. Lohmeyer, *Das Evangelium nach Mätthaus*, p. 299.

[172] E.g., Borg, *Conflict*, pp. 176–7.

the people, even though they are symbols of God's presence.[173] Therefore, the disobedience of the leaders would involve judgment not only on them but also on the temple and city.

It has been pointed out earlier that the pilgrimage of the Gentiles is a motif connected with the Zion traditions. This particular motif may be present in both episodes. We have suggested in chapter 6 that the conceptual background behind Jesus' staging of the entry comes from Zechariah 9.9. In this passage, the king, after entering Zion, went on to make peace with the nations. A similar concern for the Gentiles could be detected in the saying of Mark 11.17 -- the temple was to be the house of prayer for all nations. While the entry may implicitly indicate that Jesus had in mind the participation of the Gentiles in the eschatological kingdom of God in Zion, the saying of Mark 11.17 is more explicit on this matter.

The chronology

While the thematic unity of the two episodes is clear, their chronological proximity is less certain. We have seen that the action in the temple took place about two to three weeks before Passover (the presence of the money-changers is indicative of this).[174] What about the entry? Was there a significant time lapse between the two events?

According to traditional understanding, the entry was staged during the time the Jews made their pilgrimage to Jerusalem for the Passover. This being so, the time lapse between the two episodes is hardly significant; one took place almost immediately after the other. Such a view is not unreasonable as the Synoptic evangelists do give such an impression. If one were to read only Matthew and Luke, the impression received would be that the goal of Jesus' journey to Jerusalem was the temple and the action was performed immediately. This corresponds with the practice of most Jews: their pilgrimage to Jerusalem has the temple as its goal.[175] Even for

---

[173] The OT prophetic indictments against the city and the temple were actually against the people and the leaders (religious and national). Nevertheless, the city and the temple were implicated (e.g., Jer. 7). See the discussion in G. Fohrer and E. Lohse, 'Σιών', *TDNT* VII, pp. 308–9.

[174] *m.Shek.* 1.3 (cf. also 3.1–3). The tables of the money-changers were set up in the provinces on 15 Adar and in the temple forecourt on 25 Adar. The tax was due on 1 Nisan, which was five days after 25 Adar and two weeks before the Passover.

[175] See Jeremias, *Jerusalem*, p. 29.

Mark, there is no significant time lapse. Jesus went into the temple after the entry for an initial inspection (καὶ περιβλεψάμενος πάντα, Mark 11.11);[176] if Mark 11.15 is informed by the time note of Mark 11.12, the action took place a day later.

However, some scholars have argued that the entry actually took place during Sukkoth.[177] If this view is correct, an intolerable strain would be put on our explanation of the thematic unity between the two episodes by virtue of the significant time lapse between the two. Such a case is often constructed from the reference to the βαΐα in John (John 12.13) and the στιβάδες of Mark (Mark 11.8), for it is assumed that palm fronds were a tell-tale sign that it was Sukkoth.[178] Two points have to be made in this connection. First, that palm fronds were used during the entry is an impression that is derived from the Johannine account, not the Markan. The Markan στιβάδες need not signify that. In fact, it simply means leaves or leafy branches.[179] Secondly, even if we view the Johannine term as the more precise one, it has to be noted that, during the time of Jesus, the waving of palm fronds was no longer associated solely with Sukkoth.[180] Instead, the palm had become a nationalistic symbol by that time (cf. 1 Macc. 13.51). In this connection, it is instructive to note that palms were also used for Hanukkah (2 Macc. 10.7)![181] Hence, there is no compelling reason to reject the Passover dating of the entry and posit a six-month gap between it and the action in the temple (the time lapse between Sukkoth and Passover).

The chronological proximity of these two episodes would lend further support to the thematic unity for which we are arguing. And this raises the question whether the temple episode was intended to be an explanation of the meaning of the entry as there was no comment from Jesus' lips to explain the latter. This is certainly possible as the temple episode shows that a challenge (implicit in the entry) was directed at the temple establishment and not the Roman empire. In other words, it could be that the inaugurating of God's kingdom in the heart of Jewry necessitated,

---

[176] Lane, *Mark*, p. 398; R. Pesch, *Das Markusevangelium* II, p. 186.

[177] So T. W. Manson, 'The Cleansing of the Temple', *BJRL* 33 (1950–1), 272–98.

[178] In the OT, the Israelites were commanded to take palm fronds for the celebration of Sukkoth (Lev. 23.40); such a command was not given for the Passover.

[179] See *BAGD*, p. 768. Cf. Lane, *Mark*, p. 392 n. 6 and R. H. Gundry, *Mark: A Commentary on His Apology for the Cross*, p. 629.

[180] See 1 Macc. 13.51; 2 Macc. 10.7.

[181] See the discussion in Carson, *John*, p. 432.

first and foremost, a challenge to God's own people and city. Its effect on the Roman authorities was left unmentioned by Jesus. Thus, the bellicose ideas usually associated with God's restoration of Israel in the theology current at that time were avoided and perhaps even rejected.[182]

Would the condemnation of the old temple lead to the erection of the new in the understanding of Jesus? This episode does not provide clear evidence. But if one assumes that Jesus' eschatology has some continuity with the common Jewish one, one would expect him to look for a new temple. It is also possible that Jesus could have adopted a similar idea to that found in the Qumran community where the community functioned as the 'interim' temple because the standing one was judged to be corrupt.[183] Would Jesus proceed to form his own community with a view that this community were to be the temple (interim or otherwise) of God's dwelling? In other words, would Jesus take remedying actions for the sake of his own people? Would Jesus found an eschatological community of God that would be the bearer of God's eschatological blessings and programme? Would the founding of a new community within Judaism entail a covenant-establishing action? That such a trend of thought is possible is supported by the fact that a similar phenomenon took place in the Qumran community.[184] Such important questions do not receive answers from this episode although they are prompted by it. But one is driven along inexorably in the quest for an answer to the last important action of Jesus in Jerusalem – the last supper.

[182] So Meyer, *Aims*, p. 170; cf. also the observations of C. C. Rowland, *Christian Origins*, pp. 181–2.

[183] See 1QS 8.1–10. Nickelsburg has observed that, 'In the light of the statements ... about the defilement of the temple, [the] cultic language suggests that the community and its pious conduct are understood to be a substitute for the Jerusalem cult.' See his *Jewish Literature between the Bible and the Mishnah*, p. 133. See also Gärtner, *Temple*, pp. 22–4.

[184] See the brief discussions in G. Vermes, *The Dead Sea Scrolls in English*, pp. 36–57. (See 1QS 8.10; 9.7–9; CD 2.2; 6.11b; 8.1.)

8

THE LAST SUPPER: RESTORATION, COVENANT AND PEOPLE

1 Introduction

The study of the last supper accounts (Mark 14.22–5 and parallels) is of immense importance in our quest to understand Jesus' intentions in Jerusalem. This can be seen in two ways: first, they purportedly preserve Jesus' own understanding of what his death signified and meant. If what they recount is accurate, further light is shed on the results gathered in chapter 3.

Secondly, a question could legitimately be asked about the relationship of the last supper meal to the two provocative actions studied earlier (chapters 6 and 7). Both of these actions have to do with challenging the city to heed his message in the context of the climactic fulfilment of the restorative promises made by Yahweh to Jerusalem. But since the Jewish leadership in Jerusalem and the temple had failed to be ready for the restorative message given through Jesus, they were both judged. However, in the light of the utterly significant and climactic character of Jesus' ministry in Jerusalem (in Jesus' own understanding), one would presumably expect him to take counter actions against the failure mentioned earlier, in the manner of OT prophets (e.g., Elijah discipling Elisha; Jeremiah entrusting his prophecies to Baruch). We posed some pertinent questions at the end of our previous chapter which ask whether, in the light of the Qumran community's reaction against a temple which they deemed to be defiled, Jesus would do the same, given the similar milieu they were in.

The above considerations impel one to probe seriously into the last supper narratives. While these narratives have an important place in the life-of-Jesus research, we are also confronted with unwelcome problems posed by them. Issues ranging from authenticity, the earliest recoverable form of the sayings, to the type of meal presupposed have been keenly debated by able scholars. We shall not delve into all these debates; we shall discuss only the issues which are relevant to us, focusing particular attention on the covenant motif of the cup-saying. This obviously involves a prior discussion on the authenticity of the incident and also of the cup-saying. The argument of this chapter is that from the covenant motif of the cup-saying Jesus intended to ratify a 'new' covenant for a 'new' people of God through the shedding of his blood. In other words, the last supper is proleptic and signifies the *definitive* constitution of the eschatological people of God to be the bearers of God's eschatological and restorative blessings. We shall also try to demonstrate that, in all probability, the Zion traditions have caused Jesus to perform this covenant-establishing action in Jerusalem.

2   The authenticity of the incident

That Jesus had a last meal with his disciples in the sense that, in retrospect, this particular meal was recognised as having been the last one shared by him and his twelve disciples amounts to stating something obvious and trite.[1] Rather, what we are interested to ascertain in this section is whether Jesus understood this particular meal to be his last and held it accordingly.

Most scholars today are confident that the above question can be answered in the affirmative. Sanders regards the historicity of the incident as almost equally certain[2] as the incident in the temple, although he does not explain the reasons for such confidence. Like Sanders, many scholars also do not see a need to defend the authenticity of the incident when they deal with the more difficult issues related to the sayings.[3] However, one major objection which has been raised against its authenticity has to be dealt with.

H. Braun writes that the last supper 'might be a reading back into Jesus' last days of the Lord's supper celebrated in Hellenistic Christian congregations'.[4] His reasons for such a suggestion are that on the one hand, the meal bears the stamp of Hellenistic sacramental piety and, on the other, 'it is hard to square with

---

[1] Such is the interpretation of J. D. Crossan, *The Historical Jesus: The Life of a Mediterranean Jewish Peasant*, p. 361.

[2] E. P. Sanders, *Jesus and Judaism*, p. 307.

[3] E.g., C. C. Rowland, *Christian Origins*, pp. 176–7; J. D. G. Dunn, *The Partings of the Ways*, p. 55.

[4] H. Braun, *Jesus of Nazareth: The Man and His Time*, p. 34.

religious thought in Palestine, including Qumran'.[5] This form of argumentation was anticipated by R. Bultmann who, in turn, based his view on the works of A. Eichhorn and W. Heitmüller.[6] He argues that the last supper account arose in Hellenistic Christianity as an aetiological cult-narrative for the purpose of celebrating a cultic meal in memory of the death of the Kyrios.[7]

It should be emphasised at the outset that an aetiological aspect to the Synoptic accounts of the last supper may well be admitted in that the evangelists sought to anchor their communities' celebration of the Lord's supper in the ministry of the historical Jesus.[8] The more important issue is whether the evangelists' portrayal of the meal as having its *Sitz im Leben* in the ministry of Jesus is historical.

On critical analysis, the objections raised by Bultmann and Braun are untenable. The claim that the narratives arose in Hellenistic Christian circles is demonstrably false in the light of the presence of Semitisms in Mark's account,[9] which is held by many to be the most primitive form of the tradition.[10] Moreover, there is hardly a shred of evidence for identifying the celebration of the Lord's supper with the cultic meals of the mystery religions.[11] It should be pointed out that the cultic meals of the mystery religions were usually celebrated on the birthday of the person in honour of whom they were held and were not meant to commemorate the death of the founder.[12] There is, however, no evidence of any meal celebrated on the anniversary of the birthday of Jesus by the early churches. Hence, the confusing of one type of meal with the other is grossly mistaken. Thus, we conclude that the main objection described earlier is untenable.

There are, however, several positive considerations which lend

---

[5] Braun, *Jesus*, p. 34.
[6] See R. Bultmann, *The History of the Synoptic Tradition*, p. 265.
[7] Bultmann, *History*, p. 265 and see also his *Theology of the New Testament* I, p. 148.
[8] This has also been observed by J. A. Fitzmyer, *The Gospel According to Luke X–XXIV*, p. 1387.
[9] See J. Jeremias, *The Eucharistic Words of Jesus*, p. 196.
[10] E.g., Jeremias, *Words*, pp. 173–86; R. Pesch, *Das Abendmahl und Jesu Todesverständnis*, pp. 21–53, 69–89. Recently, Pesch has attempted to answer his critics in his 'Das Evangelium in Jerusalem: Mark 14,12–25 als ältestes Überlieferungsgut der Urgemeinde', in P. Stuhlmacher (ed.), *Das Evangelium und die Evangelien*, pp. 113–55.
[11] See H. Patsch, *Abendmahl und historischer Jesu*, §3.
[12] Jeremias, *Words*, pp. 239–43.

support to the case for authenticity. The Pauline evidence (1 Cor.
11.23–5) indicates that, as early as 52–3 CE, the celebration of the
Lord's supper was already a normative event and was understood
by the early church to have its roots in the last meal of Jesus with
his disciples.[13] This indicates that a time-gap of only about twenty
years had elapsed between the event in question and the first
attested evidence of its normative celebration. That its celebration
is normative can be seen from the words παρέλαβον ... καὶ
παρέδωκα (1 Cor. 11.23) which indicate the process of receipt and
transmission of a tradition.[14]

The early attestation of its normativeness, its dissimilarity from
other pagan cultic meals, and the untenability of the objection
usually raised against it give strong grounds for us to view the
accounts of the last supper as having their *Sitz im Leben* in Jesus'
ministry. This does not, however, prejudge the issue of whether
later interpretations and reflections on the part of the early church
were added to the original account.[15] The possibility and extent of
this phenomenon can be determined only through a thorough
analysis of the evidence coming from all sources: Mark, Luke and
Paul.[16]

3   The cup-saying and the covenant theme

Having established the high probability that the last supper has its
basis in the ministry of the historical Jesus, we shall move straight
on to discuss the cup-saying and the covenant theme which it
evokes, bypassing issues related to the bread-saying, the type of
meal and the vexed question of the precise chronology of the

---

[13] On the dating of 1 Corinthians, see the discussion in C. K. Barrett, *A Commentary on the First Epistle to the Corinthians*, pp. 5–6.

[14] That this idiom represents technical language for the receipt and transmission of traditions has been recognised by many commentators, e.g., H. Conzelmann, *1 Corinthians*, pp. 195–6; Barrett, *First Epistle to the Corinthians*, pp. 264–5. The words ἀπὸ τοῦ κυρίου need not imply Paul's independence of tradition (*pace* Conzelmann) but that Paul received the factual tradition by human means although the basis of interpretation comes directly from ὁ κύριος (see Barrett, *First Epistle to the Corinthians*, p. 265). The absence of the mention of 'revelation' supports such a case. See also the discussion in G. D. Fee, *1 Corinthians*, p. 548.

[15] H. Maccoby, for all his scepticism over these narratives, allows for the authenticity of the incident, 'Paul and the Eucharist', *NTS* 37 (1991), 247–67, esp. 262.

[16] It is usually and with good reasons assumed that Matthew has followed Mark closely in his last supper account.

incident itself.[17] There are two reasons for doing this. First, the cup-saying is most explicit about Jesus' understanding of what the last supper was intended by him to signify. It can perhaps be said that the full significance of the bread-saying only becomes clear in the light of the cup-saying. And even though the saying of abstinence and eschatological anticipation (Mark 14.25; Luke 22.16–18)[18] helps us to appreciate who Jesus understood himself to be, we are primarily interested in how Jesus viewed his death. Secondly, the cup-saying contains the covenant motif. This is something which this chapter is primarily concerned with, and we hope to show how this covenant theme ties in with Jesus' other significant actions in Jerusalem (chapters 6 and 7).

The cup-saying is found in all three Synoptic gospels (Mark 14.24; Matt. 26.28; Luke 22.20[19]) and in Paul (1 Cor. 11.25). Most scholars identify two separate strands of tradition behind our attested sources: the Markan and the Lukan/Pauline;[20] the Matthean form is usually regarded as being derived from Mark and the additional words, εἰς ἄφεσιν ἁμαρτιῶν, as an editorial expansion. Two questions arise from this state of affairs: the question of whether the cup-saying in its multiply attested forms is authentic, and the question of priority between the strands.

---

[17] On this particular issue, see the discussions in Jeremias, *Words*, pp. 15–88; I. H. Marshall, *Last Supper and Lord's Supper*, pp. 57–75; and R. T. France, 'Chronological Aspects of "Gospel Harmony"', *VE* 16 (1986), 43–54.

[18] For a recent and judicious discussion on this, see G. R. Beasley-Murray, *Jesus and the Kingdom of God*, pp. 261–3.

[19] We assume here that the longer text is original. But even if this assumption is wrong, the Pauline strand has to be reckoned with in our study, and this strand is quite similar to these disputed verses (Luke 22.19b–20). Hence our discussion of the cup-saying need not be hampered by this issue. None the less, there are good grounds for us to view this assumption as sound. (1) Although the shorter text may appear to be the 'harder' reading, the manuscript evidence for it is extremely poor (only one Greek manuscript, D, and some Latin versions). The idiosyncratic nature of D has also to be borne in mind. Moreover, as B. M. Metzger has pointed out, other witnesses of the Western text type (of which D is a member) support the longer reading (*A Textual Commentary on the New Testament*, p. 174). This forms the strongest objection against the originality of the shorter text. (2) It is possible that the longer text is not based on Paul but comes from a primitive source. See the recent discussion in J. B. Green, *The Death of Jesus*, pp. 38–42. (3) Without vv. 19b–20, Luke's narrative becomes extremely abrupt to the point of breaking down. Note how incongruous verses 19a and 21 become without the intervening vv. 19b–20.

[20] E.g., Marshall, *Supper*, pp. 38–40. See also Pesch, *Abendmahl*, pp. 26–34. Even if one views the Lukan form as not being derived from Mark or Paul, its similarity with Paul justifies the category Lukan/Pauline.

The question of authenticity

That the cup-saying is probably authentic is evident in a number of ways. In the past, objections have been raised against the Markan form of the cup-saying (although not the Lukan or the Pauline) because it was believed that it could not be retroverted into Aramaic.[21] But this objection is fallacious as can be seen from the following arguments. First, the apparent impossibility of retranslation need not imply that there was not an Aramaic substratum to the Greek form of the saying, for, in the process of translation, a formal method may not have been used.[22] As has been pointed out by Casey, words have semantic areas, and neither semantic areas nor syntax nor word order are the same in Aramaic and Greek.[23] Therefore too rigid an approach is unwarranted. Secondly, different attempts have been made to demonstrate that it is indeed possible to retranslate the Markan cup-saying into Aramaic.[24] Of course, the difficulty which we have been disproving lies only with Mark and not with Luke and Paul and, therefore, the objection, even if valid, is not detrimental to the case for the authenticity of the cup-saying.

Another consideration to bear in mind is the originality of the saying in both form and content. The mode of referring to the contents of the cup as the blood of an individual is unexampled.[25] The interpretation given to the contents of the cup is significantly different both in meaning and in form to the words said over the

---

[21] This argument was classically formulated by J. Jeremias, 'The Last Supper', *JTS* (old series) 50 (1949), 7: 'The words τὸ αἷμά μου τῆς διαθήκης cannot be retranslated into Aramaic, for in Aramaic a noun with a personal pronoun τὸ αἷμά μου cannot be followed by a genitive. So τῆς διαθήκης may be an interpretive expansion from the first decade after Jesus' death.' See also his *Words*, pp. 193–6.

[22] See also the observations of Marshall, *Supper*, p. 91.

[23] P. M. Casey, 'The Original Aramaic Form of Jesus' Interpretation of the Cup', *JTS* 41 (1990), 11. See also the instructive comments, appertaining to this issue, of L. D. Hurst, 'The Neglected Role of Semantics in the Search for the Aramaic Words of Jesus', *JSNT* 28 (1986), 63–80.

[24] See the contributions of J. A. Emerton, 'The Aramaic Underlying τὸ αἷμά μου τῆς διαθήκης in Mk XIV.24', *JTS* 6 (1955), 238–40; 'ΤΟ ΑΙΜΑ ΜΟΥ ΤΗΣ ΔΙΑΘΗΚΗΣ: The Evidence of the Syriac Versions', *JTS* 13 (1962), 111–7; 'Mark XIV.24 and the Targum to the Psalter', *JTS* 15 (1964), 58–9; and more recently, Casey, 'Aramaic Form', 1–12. It is instructive to note that this particular problem was considered solved by G. D. Kilpatrick, *The Eucharist in Bible and Liturgy*, p. 24.

[25] So B. F. Meyer, *The Aims of Jesus*, p. 311 n. 132.

cup in Jewish meals.[26] Furthermore, the cup-saying gives the impression that the disciples were drinking blood (at least from the Markan form of the saying)[27] and this would be repulsive to Jews or early Jewish-Christians. That such words could shock the Jews can be seen from John 6.53–6. Although this passage may imply that the early Christians had no compunction about such language, it should be noted that the language was none the less unusual, perhaps even shocking, as can be seen from the context of that passage.[28] The fact that, in spite of its shocking nature, the early Christians did not refrain from using it was due probably to their belief that their Master had provided them with the precedent.

Finally, there seems to be a consensus that the cup-sayings as attested by Mark and Luke/Paul are from independent strands of tradition.[29] If this emerging consensus is correct, the probability of the saying being authentic is increased by the invocation of the criterion of multiple attestation.

The question of priority

Regarding the question of priority between the different strands of tradition, prominent scholars take opposing sides.[30] It appears that this debate has been fought to a draw. However, we are not interested in ascertaining the earliest form of the saying, a difficult if not a well-nigh impossible task. Instead, we want to highlight the fact that there are many important common elements between the strands: the αἷμα word which is said to be Jesus' blood qualified by the first person singular pronoun but in different cases; the διαθήκη word (whether this should be viewed as referring to the new

---

26 This includes also the Passover liturgy where the *haggadah* based on Exod. 12 was recited before the drinking of the second cup of wine.

27 It is also implicit in Luke and Paul.

28 See the discussion in Marshall, *Supper*, p. 47.

29 Pesch, *Abendmahl*, pp. 31–4 (even though he denies the independence of the Lukan saying); Marshall, *Supper*, pp. 36–40; Beasley-Murray, *Jesus*, p. 260; Green, *Death*, pp. 28–42.

30 Supporters of the priority (by this we mean the more primitive form) of the Markan form include Jeremias, *Words*, pp. 138–203; Patsch, *Abendmahl*, pp. 59–105; Pesch, *Abendmahl*, pp. 34–51; A. J. B. Higgins, *The Lord's Supper in the New Testament*, pp. 24–44. Supporters of the priority of the Pauline form: J. Behm, 'κλάω κτλ', *TDNT* III, pp. 730–2; W. Marxsen, *The Lord's Supper as a Christological Problem*, pp. 4–8; G. Bornkamm, *Early Christian Experience*, pp. 134–8; E. Schweizer, *The Lord's Supper According to the New Testament*, pp. 10–17. Supporters of the Lukan form: H. Schürmann, *Der Einsetzungsbericht Lk 22,19–20*; Marshall, *Gospel*, pp. 799–807.

covenant of Jer. 31.31 is a matter to be resolved later); and perhaps also the ὑπέρ formula. These common elements are set out in table 8.1.

Table 8.1. *Traditions associated with the cup-saying*

	Mark	Luke	Paul
(1) The αἷμα word	τὸ αἷμα μου	ἐν τῷ αἷματι μου	ἐν τῷ ἐμῷ αἷματι
(2) The διαθήκη word	τῆς διαθήκης	ἡ καινὴ διαθήκη	ἡ καινὴ διαθήκη
(3) The ὑπέρ formula	τὸ ἐκχυννόμενον ὑπὲρ πολλῶν	τὸ ὑπὲρ ὑμῶν εκχυννόμενον	——

From these common elements one can reconstruct the *ipsissima vox Jesu* and his intended meaning of the saying without the need to ascertain the *ipsissima verba Jesu* or the earliest form of the saying. We shall now demonstrate this.

From the diagram it can be seen that, in the αἷμα word, a qualifier is attached to the noun in all three instances specifying the source of the αἷμα. Mark and Luke have the first person genitive pronoun, while Paul uses the dative ἐμῷ as an adjective (the dative is used because of the preposition ἐν). Mark does not have the preposition ἐν, unlike Luke and Paul. While it is difficult to discern whether the presence of the preposition ἐν results in a different meaning from that attested in Mark, it should be noted that, in the αἷμα word, all three writers attest that it is Jesus' blood with which the saying is concerned and that this blood becomes the effective means of the second word group under consideration: the διαθήκη word.

It is over the διαθήκη word that sharp disagreement has been generated. Mark has διαθήκη *simpliciter* while Luke and Paul have the additional adjective καινή. Beasley-Murray suggests that the significant difference between these two forms is the difference in the OT associations which they evoke.[31] Mark's idiom recalls the ratification of the covenant at Sinai (Exod. 24.8) while the primary passage Luke and Paul refer to is Jeremiah 31.31, the prophecy of the new covenant. The question which then arises is, which form is

---

[31]   Beasley-Murray, *Jesus*, p. 264.

original? Is the difference as stark as Beasley-Murray views it? Since the Markan form may suggest that the covenant at Sinai was being renewed,[32] did Jesus therefore intend to renew an old covenant and not institute a new one? Beasley-Murray also mentions that Mark's idiom is oriented towards the cult while the Lukan/Pauline idiom is fundamentally eschatological.[33]

We believe that the distinctions as conceived by Beasley-Murray are misguided and misleading. For one thing, the new covenant in Luke/Paul is linked to the blood of Jesus and this aspect is definitely cultic! Moreover, as will be demonstrated later, the Markan idiom may also be eschatologically oriented.

More importantly, it should be noted that the difference between a new covenant and a renewed one may be insignificant in the theological outlook of first- and second-temple Judaism. In order to substantiate this statement, recourse will be made to the Jewish literature of this period. This background also serves as a very important pointer to what Jesus meant when the cup-saying was uttered.

4   Covenant in the OT prophetic corpus and the inter-testamental literature

That the concept of a covenant has an important place in the religion of the OT and especially in the prophetic corpus is undeniable.[34] The prophetic charges that Israel and Judah had broken the covenant with the consequent entailment of a divine punishment raised yearnings and hopes for a 'new' covenant. This section will be devoted to exploring the Jewish expectation of a 'new' or renewed covenant and the ideas usually associated with it. The words 'new covenant' occur only in Jeremiah 31.31 in the whole of the OT.

---

[32] It is also possible that a new covenant is meant in that a ratification by blood is envisaged and not simply a renewal ceremony. For most covenant-renewal ceremonies in the OT, no ratification by blood was envisaged. See Josh. 24; Ezra 10.3; Neh. 9–10. Moreover, the blood to be used is from a man, Jesus, and not any other sacrificial victim.

[33] Beasley-Murray, *Jesus*, p. 265.

[34] For a good survey of scholarship on this particular aspect of Israel's religion see E. W. Nicholson, *God and His People: Covenant and Theology in the Old Testament*, pp. 3–117.

The covenant in Jeremiah 31.31

In what sense is the covenant new in Jeremiah 31.31?[35] In other words, does Jeremiah 31.31 envisage a covenant new in quality or time (the latter would imply that a renewed covenant is being envisaged)? Scholars have observed that in the new covenant of Jeremiah 31.31 there are elements of continuity and discontinuity with the Sinaitic covenant.[36] The parties of the covenant remain the same: it is to be a covenant between Yahweh and Israel. No new party is envisaged.[37] Moreover, it is quite clear that the Mosaic Torah is not rejected or done away with; it does not envisage a new Torah.[38] Hence, the elements of continuity are clear. However, it can be said that there is at least a new element in the covenant of Jeremiah 31.31 and this has to do with the interiorisation of the Torah in the hearts of the people of Israel.[39] Dumbrell's statement will serve as a good summary of the meaning of the new covenant in Jeremiah 31.31: this covenant will not be new 'because of new conditions which Yahweh will attach to it, nor because it is the product of a new historical epoch, nor because it will contain different promises for indeed those attached to the Sinai covenant could hardly have been more comprehensive but what will make it new is that in the new age *both* partners will keep it. In that age, there will be no possibility of the new arrangement being breached unilaterally.'[40] One could see how this idea (the invulnerability from being breached) is also presupposed in the 'everlasting' covenant in other prophets.[41]

From the above discussion, it can be seen that the new covenant in Jeremiah 31.31 cannot be said to be totally new. There is a harking back to the traditions at Sinai and, by implication, the

---

[35] On the question of authorship, see W. L. Holladay, *Jeremiah 2*, pp. 164–5, 197; and R. P. Carroll, *Jeremiah*, p. 613.

[36] P. M. van Buren goes to the extreme extent of asserting that there is no discontinuity whatsoever in *A Christian Theology of the People of Israel II: A Theology of the Jewish-Christian Reality*, p. 155.

[37] W. Brueggemann, *To Build and to Plant: A Commentary on Jeremiah 26–52*, p. 70.

[38] See J. Mejia, 'La problématique de l'ancienne et de la nouvelle alliance dans Jeremie xxi 31–34 et quelques autres textes', in J. A. Emerton (ed.), *Congress Volume: Vienna 1980*, p. 272.

[39] Carroll, *Jeremiah*, p. 610.

[40] W. J. Dumbrell, *Covenant and Creation: An Old Testament Covenantal Theology*, p. 178.

[41] This receives frequent mention: Isa. 55.3; 61.8; Jer. 32.40; 50.5; Ezek. 16.60; 37.26.

Sinaitic covenant. In other words, the new covenant in Jeremiah 31.31 has significant elements of a covenant renewal albeit in a different epoch and with different results. Thus, the addition of חָדָשׁ (*ḥādāš*) to qualify בְּרִית (*běrit*) may not be more radical than the other covenant renewals envisaged by other prophets which we will consider later. That this is probably true can be seen from the fact that the new covenant of Jer. 31.31 was hardly referred to in the inter-testamental literature (this will be shown later). In other words, it appears that Jewish thought during the period with which we are dealing did not look forward to a radically new covenant and, perhaps, did not understand Jeremiah 31.31 to be such either.

It is important also to note that this covenant-ratification is performed cheek by jowl with the restoration of the people of Israel to their land and as the people of God. In Jeremiah 31.23–5, Jeremiah envisages not only that the Israelites would be restored to the land but also that they would also be reconstituted as the people of God. Interestingly, the words of blessing which the people of this envisaged epoch would use make reference to the 'sacred mountain' (Jeremiah 31.23). This could only refer to the temple mount in Jerusalem. The concept of restoration is also closely connected to covenant renewal in other prophetic and inter-testamental passages.

Covenant renewal in the other OT prophets

The connection between restoration and the renewal of the covenant receives mention in the prophetic corpus. These prophetic passages presuppose a rupture in the relationship between God and his people which resulted from the breaking of the covenant by Israel. The message of hope offered by them is that the covenant would be renewed (and with very special terms, cf. the 'everlasting' covenant of Isa. 55.3) after the restoration of the Israelites to the land. A few prophetic passages will be considered below to demonstrate this point.

In Hosea 2.14–23, the prophet declares that Yahweh will lead the Israelites through another wilderness experience (v. 14) in order for restoration to be possible (v. 15).[42] A covenant will be made in that day (v. 18). While this covenant is directly concerned with the

---

[42] See the discussion in D. Stuart, *Hosea–Jonah*, pp. 53–4.

beasts of the field (and what is actually involved is not very clear),[43] it would also involve the restoration of the relationship between God and the Israelites (v. 23). Hence, restoration and renewal of the status of people of God for the Israelites are two very important motifs connected with the covenant in Hosea 2.14–23.

In Ezekiel 16.59–63, Yahweh promised through the prophet that even though the original covenant was broken by the Israelites, he would remember them and make an 'everlasting' covenant for them.[44] Interestingly, in this passage the covenant renewal also involves atonement (v. 63). The mention of atonement would presumably imply the restoration of the relationship between Yahweh and his people. In this sense, the ideas of restoration and people are implicit. Ezekiel probably envisages a renewal of the covenant (v. 60), which would be permanent in nature, although Brownlee has understood it to be a 'new' covenant.[45]

Our final survey of the prophetic corpus will fall on Isaiah. In Isaiah 55.3, an 'everlasting' covenant is mentioned, similar to Ezekiel 16.59–63. Unfortunately, what this really involves is not clear. But, in Isaiah 59.21, the covenant involves the words of Yahweh being put into the mouths of the people permanently (cf. Jer. 31.31). And this covenant comes about because of the coming of the Redeemer to Zion which in Jewish thought involves restoration. Again, in Isaiah 61.8, an 'everlasting' covenant is referred to and the connection with the restoration of the nation is made in vv. 4–7.

We now summarise our findings from the prophetic corpus. The prophets looked for a future ratification of a covenant and they described this covenant using different adjectives and from different perspectives. Perhaps attention should be focused not on the adjectives, but on the motif of the restoration of Israel to be the people of God, through a ratification of a covenant in the future.

---

[43] Stuart observes that two parallel restoration blessings are predicted: freedom from harm via the animal kingdom because of Yahweh's covenant with fauna and freedom from harm via humans. Both of these blessings 'are manifestations of the general blessing of *covenant renewal* (... as in Lev 26.45 and Deut 4.31)' in his *Hosea–Jonah*, p. 58. The emphasis is mine.

[44] The final phrase of v. 61, וְלֹא מִבְּרִיתֵךְ (*wĕlo' mibbĕritek*), has posed problems for interpretation. The difficulty lies chiefly with how one should understand the pre- position מִן (*min*). The suggestions which have been given are: 'but not by your covenant', 'but not because of your covenant', or 'but not outside your covenant'. See the discussion in W. H. Brownlee, *Ezekiel 1–19*, pp. 251–2.

[45] Brownlee, *Ezekiel 1–19*, p. 252.

The connection between covenant, restoration and people should not be missed.

Covenant in inter-testamental literature

While the yearning for an eschatological restoration is rife in the inter-testamental period,[46] the idea of a new or renewed covenant is, surprisingly, hardly mentioned, if the Qumran literature is not taken into account.[47] Lehne has observed that 'there seems to be a studious avoidance of Jeremiah's phrase ברית חדשה or its Greek equivalent καινὴ διαθήκη. In fact, even the word "covenant" seems to appear less frequently than in the Hebrew scriptures.'[48] But word studies conducted in isolation from motifs, themes and theological presumptions can be very deceptive.[49] Even if the word 'covenant' does not appear frequently in the Jewish literature of this period, the *idea* is very much alive as a concept in Israel's self-definition.[50] Hence, one must proceed with caution as the lack of mention of a new or renewed covenant may not imply that such an idea was not important during that period.

To our knowledge, there is only one passage which is relevant to our discussion – Baruch 2.30–5.[51] Schreiber has attempted to show that two other passages (Jub. 1.16–25 and 4 Ezra 6.26b–8) betray knowledge of the new covenant of Jeremiah 31.31,[52] but unconvincingly in our opinion: there is no mention of the word 'covenant' at all in these two passages. Most probably, even the notion itself is not present.[53]

In Baruch 2.34–5 an 'everlasting' covenant is mentioned (cf. Ezek. 16.60–3; Isa. 55.3; 61.8):

---

[46] As can be seen from the Jewish literature emanating from it. See Sanders, *Jesus*, pp. 77–90, especially pp. 87, 95–8.

[47] This will be considered later.

[48] S. Lehne, *The New Covenant in Hebrews*, p. 35.

[49] This is demonstrated by E. P. Sanders, *Paul and Palestinian Judaism*, concerning the idea of the covenant in second-temple Jewish literature.

[50] In addition to the work mentioned in the above note, see A. Jaubert, *La notion d'alliance dans le Judaisme aux abords de l'ène chrétienne*.

[51] Baruch was written before 116 BCE, following the dating of G. W. E. Nickelsburg, *Jewish Literature between the Bible and Mishnah*, p. 113.

[52] R. Schreiber, 'Der Neue Bund im Spätjudentum und Urchristentum' (unpublished Th.D. dissertation, Eberhard-Karls-Universität, Tübingen, 1954), pp. 24–32.

[53] See Sanders, *Paul*, pp. 372–4 on Jub. 1.16–25 and Lehne, *Covenant*, pp. 40–2 on 4 Ezra 6.26b–8.

> ³⁴Then I will bring them back to the land I promised on
> oath to Abraham, Isaac and Jacob, and make them
> masters in it. I will increase their number: they shall not
> dwindle.
> ³⁵And I will make an everlasting covenant with them; I
> will be their God and they shall be my people. And I will
> never again drive my people Israel out of the land that I
> have given them.

This passage probably envisages the restoration of a prior covenantal relationship established in the Sinaitic covenant[54] as can be
seen from the mention of Moses and the law in vv. 27–9. But the
important points to note are that the writer looks forward to a still
future restoration, in spite of the fact that the Israelites have
already returned from their exile in Babylon, and that the making
of the 'everlasting' covenant is connected with restoration and the
reconstitution of the people of God (vv. 34–5).

To summarise: the new-covenant terminology and any explicit
quotation of Jeremiah 31.31 in Jewish literature of the second
temple period, other than the Dead Sea Scrolls, are absent, and this
may point to the fact that the idea of a wholly 'new' covenant was
not envisaged at all by most Jews of this period. This phenomenon
may further imply that the covenant in Jeremiah 31.31 is understood as being similar to the other prophetic passages about
covenantal renewal.[55]

Covenant at Qumran

The frequent mention of the word בְּרִית (*bĕrit*) in the literature
emanating from the Qumran community represents a stark contrast
to the other inter-testamental writings. Indeed, the covenant
concept is fundamental to the community.[56] While it is true to say
that, in this, the community were simply appropriating to themselves a basic OT idea, the stark contrast highlighted earlier

---

[54] See Lehne, *Covenant*, p. 38 for a detailed treatment.
[55] It will be noticed by now that, statistically speaking, the 'everlasting' covenant
receives more emphasis than the 'new' covenant in the OT and inter-testamental
literature (Bar. 2.34–5). Perhaps the idea of permanence suggested by the word
'everlasting' was more attractive to the Jews during a period where uncertainty
(politically or otherwise) reigned. They longed for a covenant which could never
be breached by either party.
[56] M. A. Knibb, *The Qumran Community*, p. 84.

deserves an explanation. There may be two reasons for this: the eschatological outlook of the community[57] and their sectarian nature.[58] The frequent mention of a covenant may be prompted by a polemic which serves to define the community over against Jewish orthodoxy in Jerusalem.

The words הַבְּרִית חֲדָשָׁה (*habbĕrit hădåšåh*) occur in their writings, and this constitutes an unparalleled phenomenon in second-temple Jewish literature. The occurrence of this terminology may come about as a result of the community's eschatological outlook.[59]

One other point should be noted before the relevant passages are studied. In the passages discussed earlier, the new or renewed covenant is considered as still future. The same is not true for the Qumran community. They believed that they were already the people of a 'new' covenant (CD 6.19; 8.21b‖19.33b–4a; 20.12; 1QpHab 1.16–20a). Yet interestingly, they also looked forward to a renewal of the covenant in the future (1Q34 2.5–6; 1QSb 3.25–6; 5.21–2). An explanation will be posited for this phenomenon at the end of the discussion of these passages.

(i) The new covenant at Qumran

An analysis of the word-statistics on the verb חָדָשׁ (*hådaš*) and the adjective חָדָשׁ (*hådåš*) in the Qumran literature reveals an interesting point. The verb appears five times altogether, twice for the self-renewal of the sectaries (1QS 10.4; 1QH 11.13) and three times in a covenantal context (1QSb 3.26; 5.21; 1Q34 2.5, 6). The adjective occurs seven times altogether: twice in the context of the new creation (1QS 4.25; 1QH 13.12) and five times in passages referring to the new covenant.[60] In other words, these words occur chiefly in covenantal contexts.

There are altogether four 'new covenant' passages in CD: 6.19a; 8.21b; 19.33b–4a (from manuscript B, possibly a parallel to 8.21b of manuscript A) and 20.12. This covenant is described as 'the new

---

[57] On this see H. Ringgren, *The Faith of Qumran*, pp. 152–66. See also L. Schiffmann, *The Eschatological Community of the Dead Sea Scrolls*, especially the concluding chapter, pp. 68–71.

[58] See especially the writings CD and 1QS.

[59] See G. Vermes, *The Dead Sea Scrolls in English*, pp. 37–8.

[60] The statistics are taken from K. G. Kuhn, *Konkordanz zu den Qumrantexten*, pp. 67–8. His reference to 1QSb 5.5 (in connection with the verb חָדָשׁ, *hådaš*) cannot be located.

covenant in the land of Damascus'. How did the sectaries understand this 'new covenant'?

The new-covenant terminology in CD occurs in passages which
are highly polemical in nature: polemic is made against apostates
(19.34) and those who reject God's commands (8.19), especially the
'men of scoffing' (20.11).[61] It is also possible that CD 6.18–19 may
have a polemical element in that the mention of keeping the
Sabbath and other holy days according to the finding of the
members of this new covenant may imply an implicit distancing of
the community from the views of the Jerusalem priesthood.[62]
Hence, it is incontrovertible that the new-covenant terminology
serves a polemical function at Qumran. But did the community also
understand their new-covenant terminology according to Jeremiah
31.31? In other words, was the terminology used eschatologically?

P. R. Davies argues that the reference to the 'new Damascus
covenant' comes from the literary activity of a later community and
is introduced to distance this community (which believed that they
were the faithful adherents of the teachings of the Teacher of
Righteousness) from the earlier parent body.[63] His idea is built on
the probable gloss found in 20.11–12, הוּא בְּרִית הַחֲדָשָׁה (*hu' běrit
hahădāšāh*). But, as Callaway observes, 'his exegetical and historical
inferences therefrom seem to stray from the textual evidence'.[64] A
better explanation for the genesis of this gloss is that a later guide
wanted to harmonise 20.11–12 with the other passages which made
mention of the 'new covenant in the land of Damascus'.

Since it is highly probable that 8.21b is parallel to 19.33b–4a,[65]
the community might have understood the new covenant as being
identical to the one in Jeremiah 31.31, for 8.20 mentions Jeremiah
speaking to Baruch (this is not found in manuscript B). But this is
by no means certain, as the Jeremiah reference may be related to a
different passage.[66] However, given the fact that the new-covenant
terminology occurs only in Jeremiah 31.31, it is arguable that such
a connection was made.[67] But the more important question to
pursue is, 'In what sense was the covenant "new" at Qumran?' We

---

61 See Knibb, *Qumran*, p. 73 for a possible identification of the men of scoffing.
62 Knibb, *Qumran*, p. 54.   63 P. R. Davies, *The Damascus Covenant*, p. 177.
64 P. R. Callaway, *The History of the Qumran Community*, p. 125.
65 So Vermes, *Scrolls*, p. 90. See also S. A. White, 'A Comparison of the "A" and
    "B" Manuscripts of the Damascus Document', *RevQum* 48 (1987), 537–53,
    where she attempts to prove that both manuscripts stem from one original.
66 See Knibb, *Qumran*, p. 69; he suggests Jer. 45.3–5.
67 See the discussion in Callaway, *History*, p. 126.

shall try to answer this after a quick survey of the other relevant passages.

In 1QpHab 2.3 a lacuna is found after the word 'new'. This poses a problem as to whether a new covenant is referred to in the passage. However, in the light of the context, which is heavily covenantal in nature, it is virtually certain that a new covenant is being referred to. Again, the new covenant is here used in a passage which is also strongly polemical in nature – against the apostates.

In 1QSb, there is an expectation of the renewal of covenants in the future (3.25–6 and 5.21–2). The plural is used because it is quite likely that two distinct covenants are envisaged: the covenant of the ('everlasting') priesthood (3.26) and the covenant of the community (5.21–2). Whether this latter covenant is related to the new covenant in CD is a moot point. Suffice it to point out here that a still future renewal of covenants is expected by the community. However, in 1Q34 2.5–6, the renewal of the community's covenant is an action conceived as having taken place in the past! This is indeed an interesting phenomenon but could be explained thus: it is probable that the future renewing of the covenant envisaged in 1QSb 5.21–2 is of a different (but climactic) nature from that of 1Q34 2.5–6 in that the 'prince of the congregation' is involved, a figure who is expected to come. Probably, with the coming of this figure, the eschatological denouement would take place. Hence, after the actualisation of the new covenant, another 'new' covenant was also expected by the Qumran community. It should also be noted that in the preceding context of 1Q34 2.5–6 the motif of the true people of God is found.

It is now time to give a synthesis of the Qumranic understanding of the 'new' covenant, if a synthesis is at all possible. Mention must be made of the fact that the community represent a movement of renewal and repristination and that their goal is to return to the true intentions of the Sinaitic covenant.[68] As Sanders has pointed out, 'returning to the law of Moses' in CD 15.5–11 is equivalent to joining the new covenant.[69] In this sense, there is a profound sense of continuity of their understanding of the new covenant with the Sinaitic one.

On the other hand, elements of newness cannot be denied. First, there is the element of new revelation and it is this belief of the community which sets them apart from other reform movements of

---

[68] So Lehne, *Covenant*, p. 50.   [69] Sanders, *Paul*, p. 241.

the second temple period.[70] The community claim that secrets contained in the Mosaic covenant have been revealed recently and only to them.[71] While it is true to say that these newly found secrets are ultimately derived from the old covenant, 'the sectarian covenant also supposes a new initiative on the part of God in revealing the "hidden things" and "mysteries" (CD 3.10–14 and 1QpHab 7.4f. . .)'.[72] It is also fair to say that the sectaries are convinced that they alone possess a new key for unlocking the secret oracles of scripture and for interpreting history accordingly. This makes it legitimate for us to take the view that they understood their covenant as a new one in distinction to the old Mosaic revelation.[73]

The second element of newness consists in the eschatological character of the community's outlook. The community view themselves as participating in some sense in the eschatological time of the 'last generation' (CD 1.12). The belief that the Holy Spirit is present in their midst (CD 5.11; 7.14) testifies to their belief that their community are experiencing the new age. Hence, the covenant that they were in partook of an eschatological character. And, in this sense, the 'renewal' of the covenant has already been carried out (1Q34 2.5–6).

(ii) Summary

There are elements of repristination (continuity) and eschatological newness (discontinuity) in the Qumranic understanding of the new covenant. This is similar to the outlook of the OT prophets. But unlike the OT prophets and the author of Baruch, the community believed that the new or renewed covenant had already been ratified. Having said that, there is evidence to show that they were also looking for a renewed covenant in the future to be ratified between God and the 'prince of the congregation' (1QSb 5.21–2). However, it should be emphasised that the Qumran community did not understand their new covenant as totally and radically new. It seems therefore only correct to conclude that the difference between a new and a renewed covenant is anachronistic. The expectation of a renewal of the covenant includes new elements and

---

[70]   Lehne, *Covenant*, p. 51.
[71]   CD 3.10–14; cf. 1QS 5.11–12 and 1QpHab 7.4–5. See the discussion in Sanders, *Paul*, p. 241.
[72]   Sanders, *Paul*, p. 242.   [73]   Lehne, *Covenant*, p. 51.

a new situation while the new covenant has elements which are profoundly connected with the Sinaitic one.

Although the new-covenant terminology was used, there was no explicit quotation of Jeremiah 31.31 or any *pesher* done on it by the Qumran community. This is highly significant when account is being taken of the fact that the covenantal idea was very important to the sectaries for their self-understanding. This may indicate that Jeremiah 31.31 was not understood as the future covenant *par excellence* as opposed to other prophetic passages about a future covenant renewal. It seems true to say that there appears to be no significant difference between a new and a renewed covenant at Qumran and that the sectaries were not striving for terminological precision. Hence, one term could easily slide into the other.

It should be noted that the covenantal terminology is used in the service of polemic at Qumran and this polemic serves to point out that the community were indeed the true people of God over against other Jews and especially against the hierarchy at Jerusalem and the apostates. It should also be noted that the belief that they were the true people of God and that in some sense the eschaton has dawned upon them points to the fulfilment of God's restorative blessings. Hence, covenant is once again associated with restoration and people.

5   The intention of Jesus in the cup-saying

The material surveyed earlier has important consequences for our understanding of the intentions of Jesus in the cup-saying. On the one hand, the perspectives of the Markan and the Lukan/Pauline forms of the διαθήκη word cannot be too woodenly distinguished in the manner of Beasley-Murray.[74] This appears to be correct from the following considerations: the Lukan/Pauline idiom mentions the blood of Jesus as the effective instrument of the ratification of the new covenant and this aspect is cultic. However, the word 'blood' does not occur in Jeremiah 31.31. Therefore the appearance of this word in the Lukan/Pauline idiom could also imply that an implicit reference is made to Exodus 24.8.[75] Secondly, the Markan idiom can be said to be eschatological if one bears in mind that, in second-temple Judaism, a renewal of the covenant

[74] Beasley-Murray, *Jesus*, p. 265.
[75] Cf. the comments of Marshall, *Supper*, p. 92.

can also be eschatological. Thirdly, the Markan idiom envisages a new ratification of the covenant with a new element – Jesus' blood. Although the Markan form may hark back to Exodus 24.8 as the primary background, the Lukan/Pauline idiom may not be divorced from this either. It should also be noted that the new covenant in Jeremiah 31.31 harks back to the Sinaitic one. Fourthly, if one assumes that Luke and Paul have preserved the original idiom of Jesus' διαθήκη word, it is still highly probable that Jesus understood the new covenant in Jeremiah 31.31 not to be wholly new, given the Jewish understanding of Jeremiah 31.31 in the second temple period. Hence, the difference in notion that is often perceived in the two different idioms is misleading. Therefore, we contend that there is no necessity to determine the original form of the διαθήκη word spoken by Jesus as both forms have a similar meaning. In short, whether one opts for one form or the other, the element of newness is present (discontinuity) and the reference of blood may hark back to Exodus 24.8 in both forms (continuity). Hence, by the διαθήκη word, Jesus is communicating to the disciples that something significantly new is being initiated by God. Yet this new element is not totally divorced from the acts of God in the past for Israel.

A further conclusion could be drawn from the preceding discussion. It was emphasised earlier that the notion of covenant renewal or a new covenant is closely connected to the motifs of restoration and people. Such ideas were also probably present in the farewell meal of Jesus with his disciples. This can be seen especially in the διαθήκη word. Hence, in making the disciples participants in this covenant which he was ratifying, Jesus may also be pointing to the fact that the longed-for restoration of the nation of Israel has come about albeit in a very confined compass – his followers. They would form the nucleus of the people on whom the eschatological restorative blessings of God would be bestowed.

It was mentioned earlier that there is an element of newness in the ratification ceremony for it was the blood of Jesus and not any sacrificial victim which was used for the ratification. Whether one understands this as something vicarious or that Jesus' death represented the death of a martyr (or the suffering servant) for the people of God is of great importance, but not for the purposes of this study. What we want to point out here is that the cup-saying signifies that it is only through the blood of Jesus that such a covenant is to be ratified. Hence, it is through Jesus' giving of himself to the disciples in sacrifice that the constitution of the new people of God can be achieved.[76] This is further corroborated by the bread-saying whose authenticity has been supported by many prominent scholars.[77] In the light of this self-giving and sacrifice, one can understand why Matthew added the redactional phrase εἰς ἄφεσιν ἁμαρτιῶν (Matt. 26.28), for sins could only be removed through a blood sacrifice. Moreover, in Ezekiel 16.60–3 atonement is closely connected to the ratification of the 'everlasting' covenant.[78] Hence, Jesus did charge with meaning the death which he expected to die. Jesus understood that it was for the sake of the ratification of the covenant which God would be sealing with his nucleus people, Jesus' followers, that he was to shed his blood. It was only through his death that the new relationship into which God was entering with his people, in the context of the fulfilment of the eschatological restoration, was made possible.

Our conclusions have ramifications for two important aspects of Jesus' ministry: his choosing of the twelve; his distancing of himself from the corrupt temple establishment.

Sanders has ably defended the historicity of the choosing of the twelve.[79] It is likely that the number twelve symbolises the twelve tribes of Israel.[80] Hence, the twelve disciples were probably looked upon by Jesus as the nucleus of the restored people of God in an eschatological sense. The choosing of the twelve took place during Jesus' Galilean ministry. The interesting point to note now is that the *definitive* constitution of this new people of God *in nuce* was done in a proleptic manner at the last supper.[81] This ratification was done proleptically since it involved Jesus' death. It was Jesus' death which was the actual moment of the ratification of the

---

[76] It is interesting to note that at Qumran there is no cultic form of ratification for their covenant. This may be due to the fact that they have distanced themselves from the Jerusalem temple. Instead, the covenant ceremony is ratified by an oath-taking on the part of new members (CD 15.7–10). See Knibb, *Qumran*, p. 121.

[77] E.g., Jeremias, *Words*, pp. 201–3; Marshall, *Supper*, pp. 85–90; Beasley-Murray, *Jesus*, pp. 267–73.

[78] As has been pointed out by Pesch, the Targum on Exod. 24.7–8 stresses the atoning effect of the blood which was thrown against the altar of Moses. Hence, in the understanding of some Jews, the covenant blood which was sprinkled during the ratification of the Sinaitic covenant is seen to have atoning power. (Pesch, *Abendmahl*, pp. 95–6.)

[79] Sanders, *Jesus*, pp. 98–106.

[80] This has also been noted by Rowland, *Origins*, pp. 152–3.

[81] It should also be noted that the covenant at Sinai has to do with the constitution of the people of God.

covenant. By drinking from the same cup,[82] the disciples were given a share in the covenant, and thus were made the new people of God.[83] Hence, what was indicated in a symbolical manner during the Galilean ministry of Jesus was ratified definitively at the last supper.

We have seen in chapter 2 that, according to the common Jewish understanding of that time, the restoration of Zion is indispensable for the restoration of the people of Israel. In the restoration of Zion, a covenant is normally expected to be ratified and this ratification would lead to the constitution of the true people of God (e.g., Isa. 59.20–1; 61.3, 8). Hence, the motif of the restoration of Zion implicitly conjures up the notions of restoration, covenant-ratification and the constitution of the true people of God. Hence, it is not inconceivable that Jesus believed that the ratification of a 'new' covenant has to be done on Zion. Stuhlmacher has suggested that Zion remains for Jesus the central place of salvation in spite of judgment on the temple and on Jerusalem.[84] This would explain why a symbolical call of the twelve was followed by a definitive ratification of their call to be the people of God in Jerusalem.

In chapter 7, we suggested that the rejection of the temple (through Jesus' prophecy of its destruction) could have led to Jesus' erecting a different temple formed by the members of his community, whether interim or otherwise, who would be the recipients and bearers of God's eschatological blessings. What is of importance here is that the sectaries of Qumran, who conceived of their community as forming the 'interim' temple, regarded the covenant idea as vital to the existence of the community. Moreover, this covenant idea was employed in a polemical manner to indicate that they were the true people of God in receipt of his eschatological blessings. The covenant-ratification ceremony which was proleptically conducted by Jesus in the last supper may have served a similar function.

---

[82] Whether Jesus' action of sharing his cup with his disciples is an unparalleled action is debated. See H. Schürmann, 'Wie hat Jesus seinen Tod bestanden und verstanden? Eine methodenkritische Besinnung', in his *Jesu ureigener Tod: Exegetische Besinnungen und Ausblick*, pp. 76–7; but cf. Marshall, *Supper*, p. 92.

[83] Much has been written on the meaning of the actions of giving (on the part of Jesus) and receiving (on the part of the disciples). See the discussions in Jeremias, *Words*, pp. 231–7; Marshall, *Supper*, pp. 83–5; L. Goppelt, *Theology of the New Testament* I, pp. 217–20.

[84] P. Stuhlmacher, 'Die Stellung Jesu und des Paulus zu Jerusalem', *ZTK* 86 (1989), 146.

We suggest that the failure of the temple to be the temple of the eschaton led Jesus to constitute definitively the restored people of God through a covenant-ratification ceremony so that this community would serve as recipients and bearers of God's eschatological blessings. In other words, the failure of Jerusalem and its temple to heed the message of repentance and restoration brought by Jesus[85] resulted in the blessings being bestowed on a people obedient to that message who would also be the bearers of these blessings. Hence, the fulfilment of God's restoration blessings on Israel was localised in this community. The covenant-ratification ceremony served to confirm this in a definitive manner. Restoration indeed had come about; but it was not Jerusalem or the temple but the followers of Jesus partaking of the cup with Jesus at the last supper who were the recipients of this eschatological restoration.[86]

6 Conclusions

In this chapter, we have not attempted to deal with all the issues related to the study of the last supper narratives. Instead we have concentrated on the cup-saying which contains the covenant motif. We conclude that, at the last supper, Jesus thought of his impending death as the effective means to the ratification of a covenant whereby God would enter into a new relationship with his restored people. The disciples who partook of the cup offered by Jesus comprised this restored people *in nuce*. It is the ratification of this 'new' covenant and the constitution of the new and restored people of God, in the context of the restoration of Zion, that Jesus understood his death to signify. Hence, in the last supper, motifs of restoration, covenant and people are prominent and intertwined.

Once this is recognised, the thread linking the three important events in Jerusalem which involved Jesus could be discerned. The thread may be termed 'the restoration thread' in the context of the restoration of Israel and Zion. In the 'triumphal' entry, Jesus signified that the longed-for messianic king has entered the city, ushering in, and, at the same time, confronting the city with, the

---

[85] See our chapter 5.

[86] Perhaps the increasing use of the terminology ἡ καινὴ διαθήκη in the NT (e.g., 2 Cor. 3.6; Heb. 8–9) may reflect a polemical tendency similar to that which obtained at Qumran. If this is the case, the Markan form of the διαθήκη word would appear to be more primitive than the Lukan/Pauline one.

restorative message of God. Zion is to be restored as promised and it is now coming to pass through Jesus' entry into Jerusalem. But the temple was found to be unfit to function as the temple of the eschaton. The Jewish leadership was also found to be unworthy. Hence city, temple and leaders were judged. Jerusalem and her temple had forfeited these eschatological blessings of God and so those blessings were communicated to the newly constituted people of God. This was brought about by Jesus' ratification of the covenant between his disciples and Yahweh, a ratification which involved the shedding of his blood. The members of the newly constituted community would be the recipients and bearers of these blessings. Fulfilment of the restorative blessings of God has indeed come about but not on the city or her temple, but for a small group of Jews who partook of the cup during the last supper.

Excursus: Did Jesus expect a post-mortem role?

The chief purpose of this book is to explore the extent to which the Zion traditions had impacted on and informed Jesus *vis-à-vis* the understanding and aims of his ministry. However, in the course of our study on this intriguing matter, a hiatus has become apparent which calls for a resolution. It was stated in chapter 6 that Jesus understood his entry into Jerusalem on an animal to signify that the prophecy of Zechariah 9.9 was fulfilled. The promises of restoration that Yahweh had made to Zion had come to pass as the promised king had entered the city. It was also stated that, at the last supper, Jesus signified by the cup-saying that his impending death would be the means for the ratification of the new covenant. How are these two strands of thought to be brought together: the strand about his fulfilling the Zion promises as the king of the city and the strand regarding his death as ratification of the new covenant? In particular, how did he understand his kingship in view of the fact that he also expected to die? Did he understand his kingship to be temporary, lasting between the entry and the crucifixion?

One possible way of resolving the problem is to regard Jesus as not expecting any important post-mortem role for himself. He might have believed that together with the band of faithful Israelites, he would be resurrected at the last day to inherit the kingdom of God. If this is the case, Jesus would probably have understood his death as the death of a martyr, perhaps in the same vein as the notion attributed to the Maccabean martyrs (2 Macc. 6, 7).[87] His martyrdom would then signify his unswerving faithfulness to Yahweh's calling (similar to the prophets) and that the climax of his vocation was his death to ratify the new covenant. But this involves envisaging Jesus as understanding his kingship to be a temporary or truncated one: between the entry and the crucifixion, which is rather peculiar.

Another possibility is to regard Jesus as expecting to play a post-mortem role which was crucial to the future establishment of the kingdom of God. Jesus might have viewed his death as ratifying the new covenant (hence, his death would be deemed as necessary) but that death would not signal the end of his ministry. He would have looked for vindication and restoration by Yahweh to his appointed role as king. If this line of resolution is accepted, the hiatus is to a large extent obviated. But is there evidence that Jesus expected a post-mortem role for himself through vindication by Yahweh? And was such an expectation conceivable in those times?

The complete answer to these questions is inevitably linked to the resolution of another complex problem which concerns the sayings on the resurrection and parousia attributed to Jesus by the evangelists. We cannot hope to solve this problem within the short compass of this excursus. There are, none the less, good arguments to show it is plausible that Jesus expected to play a post-mortem role *vis-à-vis* the kingdom of God.

First, it must be said that it is entirely conceivable that a Jew during the time of Jesus might believe in the parousia of great prophets and servants of God. There is an OT expectation of the parousia of Elijah (Mal. 4.5). In 4 Ezra 6.26, we find the belief that there were men who were exalted to heaven without tasting death and that such men would one day return. Testament of Zebulun 10.2–3 offers us another interesting datum.[88] In this passage, which does not bear the marks of Christian interpolation, Zebulun consoles his children with the promise that he will rise again and be a leader of the tribe yet again. Thus, Zebulun was regarded by some

[87] See the discussiion in M. de Jonge, *Jesus, the Servant-Messiah*, pp. 45–8.
[88] We follow here the dating of H. C. Kee of the Twelve Patriarchs in the second century BCE in his 'Testaments of the Twelve Patriarchs', *OTP* I, pp. 777–8 *contra* de Jonge's in his *The Testaments of the Twelve Patriarchs: A Study of Their Text, Composition and Origin*. De Jonge has since changed his mind, cf. his 'The Testaments of the Twelve Patriarchs: Christian and Jewish', in *Jewish Eschatology, Early Christian Christology and the Testaments of the Twelve Patriarchs*, p. 234.

circles of Jews to have a post-mortem role after the resurrection, and that role would be the headship of the tribe. The expectation of restoration and rescue in Psalm 16 and in Isaiah 53 provides further evidence of such a background. Thus, it can be concluded that the belief that a prominent servant or prophet of Yahweh would one day return to carry out an important role is not inconceivable for a Palestinian Jew of the first century.

Secondly, the post-Easter community recognised that Jesus of Nazareth would be coming back after his death to usher in the end. Such a belief is multiply attested in the different writings of the NT,[89] signifying that the belief was widely held. Admittedly, this evidence could be double-edged. It could mean that it was the post-Easter community who created the sayings on the resurrection and the parousia in line with their belief or it could mean that the prevalence of this belief came about as a result of its having its roots in the teaching of Jesus of Nazareth. Scholarship, unfortunately, often shows bias against the latter and, thus, opts for the former without giving due consideration to evidence that might support the latter. Such a bias should not be allowed to pre-empt serious consideration of the possibility that Jesus might have *expected* a post-mortem vindication and role.

Thirdly, it must be recognised that the only effective means of circumventing our proposal is to deny the historicity of all the sayings on the resurrection and the parousia which are attributed to Jesus by the evangelists. Such a course of action amounts to denying too much material which has good indications of authenticity.[90] Barrett has pointed out that if Jesus did predict and interpret his approaching passion, although the forms of these sayings may not be fully recoverable, such interpretation must have included the prediction of some kind of vindication beyond the passion and, thus, it is inconceivable that Jesus simply predicted the complete and final failure of his mission.[91] Moreover, we have argued earlier (chapter 5) that Q 13.34–5 is authentic and that Jesus probably expected his parousia to take place when Jerusalem was penitent and ready to 'bless the coming one'. The saying of abstinence at the last supper (Mark 14.25) is patient of being

---

[89]   For a treatment on this, see P. Perkins, *Resurrection: New Testament Witness and Contemporary Reflection*, pp. 37–69.

[90]   See especially the work of H. F. Bayer, *Jesus' Predictions of Vindication and Resurrection*, on this issue.

[91]   C. K. Barrett, *Jesus and the Gospel Tradition*, p. 76.

understood in terms of Jesus' expectation of a post-mortem role: his being the host at the great feast of the kingdom of God.[92]

Fourthly, the saying in Matthew 19.28 offers strong support for our argument for the historical plausibility of Jesus' expecting a post-mortem role. This saying has a parallel in Luke 22.30b and has been thus often regarded as part of Q. Allowing for certain redactional elements which have been introduced by Matthew,[93] the substance of the saying may be said to be traditional notwithstanding the influential view of Bultmann which posits that the saying is a creation of the church.[94] In fact, a rigorous defence of the saying's authenticity has recently been mounted by E. P. Sanders. He argues that the number 'twelve' in the saying was not a post-Easter creation and that, after Judas' betrayal of Jesus, it was inconceivable for the post-Easter community to create a saying which seemingly included him in the promise of great authority.[95] Furthermore, Kümmel has rightly pointed out that the saying comports well with other authentic material of Jesus which envisions a coming eschatological judgment linked with the present (cf. Mark 8.38).[96] Dupont also points out that the role of judgment over Israel envisaged for the twelve in the saying is an archaism, and this supports the view that the saying could not have been created by the church but is most probably authentic.[97] Finally, the presence of the word παλιγγενεσία[98] must not be allowed to preempt one from seriously considering the probability of the saying's being authentic, as the word does not appear in the Lukan parallel and, moreover, a formal method of translation from the Hebrew or

---

[92] See Bayer, *Predictions*, p. 52.

[93] E.g., the phrase 'the Son of Man' and the term παλιγγενεσία.

[94] Bultmann, *History*, pp. 158–9; cf. also F. W. Beare, *The Gospel According to Matthew*, p. 400.

[95] Sanders, *Jesus*, p. 99. So also T. W. Manson, *The Sayings of Jesus*, p. 217. Cf. also the confident assessment of the historicity of this saying in Fitzmyer, *Luke X–XXIV*, p. 1414; Beasley-Murray, *Jesus*, p. 277; Rowland, *Christian Origins*, p. 184.

[96] W. G. Kümmel, *Promise and Fulfilment*, pp. 47–8.

[97] J. Dupont, 'Le logion des douze trônes (Mt 19,28; Lc 22,28–30)', *Bib* 45 (1964), 388.

[98] This word is chiefly used in Jewish literature in contexts which describe the restoration of Israel and the renewal of the world; see F. Büchsel, 'παλιγγενεσία', *TDNT* I, pp. 686–9. That there is no exact equivalent for this term in Hebrew or Aramaic is readily conceded by scholars. However, the term could be a possible translation for the Hebrew *concept* of restoration. In this light, it is instructive to note that an equivalent new creation language may be found in 1QS 4.25: עשות חדשה! Cf. Dupont, 'Le logion', 365; and Nolland, *Luke 18:35–24:53*, p. 1064.

the Aramaic need not be have been followed. What is significant and needs to be pointed out here is that if this saying is accepted as authentic and if therefore thrones were promised to the disciples in the 'regeneration' (παλιγγενεσία), *by Jesus*, it would be inconceivable that he would have expected anything less.[99] In all probability, he would have expected to have a role greater than that of the disciples in the new world since he was the master of his disciples during his earthly ministry. Thus, it is highly probable that Jesus did not view his death as an end of his vocation but that he expected a post-mortem role greater than the one he had on earth.

All the foregoing serves to show the plausibility of Jesus' expecting a post-mortem role for himself with regard to the kingdom of God. If this is accepted, what, according to him, was precisely the content of such a role? Here, Matthew 19.28 and our discussion in the earlier chapters would be relevant. Let us outline this briefly.

   (i) Jesus promised his disciples thrones in the new world and thus he would most probably have expected a greater role for himself.

  (ii) This role could be in continuity with the one he signified by his entry into Jerusalem: the king of Zion. If there is any grain of authenticity in the resurrection and parousia sayings, Jesus believed that death did not amount to failure but expected vindication from Yahweh and restoration to his role as king.

 (iii) The probably authentic three-day motif used in the resurrection sayings shows that Jesus expected only a short duration to transpire between his death and his resurrection.

 (iv) Whether Jesus expected a *Zwischenzeit* between his resurrection and his parousia is something we cannot answer confidently from this study.

The inevitable question which arises from the discussion concerns Jesus' expectation of his own death. Did he regard it as preordained and fixed regardless of Israel's response to his message? Or is the expectation of death entertained only as a response to adverse reactions to his ministry? To put it differently, would Jesus have expected to die if his ministry was well received by the nation and especially by Jerusalem? Here we come to a great puzzle which demands an abundance of data for its resolution but, unfortu-

---

[99] So also Rowland, *Christian Origins*, p. 184.

nately, such data are unavailable. Wright has valiantly tried to work in the notion of atonement in his depiction of Jesus' own understanding of his aims.[100] Jesus' death was conceived by Wright to effect an atonement for the sins of Israel centred in her rebellious stance towards Rome. Such an interpretation appears forced and quaint. However, there are indications in the NT that Jesus' death was understood by the earliest Christian communities to be an atonement for sins without any explicit connection with the political situation obtaining then. The evangelist Matthew redacted the cup-saying by adding the words εἰς ἄφεσιν (Matt. 26.28), thus indicating that, to him, Jesus' death was an atonement for sins. In Mark 10.45, whether or not this saying is to be regarded as authentic,[101] the Son of Man (probably Jesus, as understood by the evangelist)[102] would offer his life as a ransom. The Johannine saying on the lips of John the Baptist describes Jesus as the Lamb of God offered for the sins of the world (John 1.29).[103] It would be superfluous to cite the many passages in Paul to illustrate the prominence of this concept in the earliest Christian communities.[104] The prevalence of this interpretation of Jesus' death in these communities might be due precisely to the plausibility that it had its origins in the teaching of Jesus of Nazareth. It should also be pointed out that the accounts of the deaths of the Maccabean martyrs in 2 Maccabees 6–7 (especially 7.37–8) contain strains of atonement theology in that a martyr's death could cause Yahweh to avert his anger and show mercy to Israel. If all this is accepted, we are perhaps correct to opine that Jesus might have deemed his death as leading to an averting of Yahweh's wrath and securing his mercy.[105] Hence, he would probably not have deemed his death to be necessary if Israel, and especially Jerusalem, responded positively to his ministry. The course of history would then be quite

---

[100] N. T. Wright, 'Jesus, Israel and the Cross' in K. Richards (ed.), *SBL 1985 Seminar Papers*, pp. 75–95, especially pp. 90, 93; cf. the proposal of A. Schweitzer in his *The Quest of the Historical Jesus*, pp. 387–9.

[101] See the discussion in S. H. T. Page, 'The Authenticity of the Ransom Logion (Mark 10:45b)', in R. T. France and D. Wenham (eds.), *Gospel Perspectives I: Studies of History and Tradition in the Four Gospels*, pp. 137–61.

[102] See the discussion in R. H. Gundry, *Mark: A Commentary on His Apology for the Cross*, pp. 581, 587–93.

[103] For further discussion on the presence of the concept of atonement in John, see M. Turner, 'Atonement and the Death of Jesus in John: Some Questions to Bultmann and Forestell', *EQ* 62 (1990), 99–122.

[104] See further discussion in de Jonge, *Jesus*, pp. 42–4.

[105] See the brilliant work of M. Hengel, *The Atonement*.

different and, needless to say, the shape and direction of historical Jesus research would also be quite different.

The many issues just discussed warrant a book-length treatment in order to do justice to them. As this is not possible here, we have attempted to highlight only the important questions and their possible resolutions, and offered arguments for our preferred approach to overcoming the hiatus. Jesus expected an important post-mortem role for himself with regard to the kingdom of God. Death would therefore not be an end to his vocation. Instead, Jesus looked beyond death to vindication and restoration by Yahweh. Such vindication and restoration could have been understood as taking the form of resurrection and parousia. This belief is not incredible for a Jew in Jesus' time as there were already Jewish precedents for it. Whether this would mean that the traditional Christian belief that Jesus was historically raised from the dead and appeared to his disciples is true is a matter that this book is not equipped to answer.

Conclusions

9

JESUS AND THE ZION TRADITIONS

1 Summary of results

At the outset, two related questions were posed for our study: 'What intentions did Jesus have when he made that final trip to Jerusalem?' and 'Did Jesus appropriate the Zion traditions for his ministry?' Our study has attempted to look for a unifying hypothesis which would explain Jesus' significant actions in Jerusalem (the 'triumphal' entry, the temple incident and the last supper). We have also considered whether or not the Zion traditions informed the theological motivations behind Jesus' actions in Jerusalem, and perhaps also his whole ministry.

That it is reasonable to ask the second question is shown in chapter 2. Zion was an important symbol and place for Jewish national and theological hopes of the first century. It was a magnet which progressively attracted to itself other eschatological themes which were not originally conjoined with it. It became the *focus* of national and eschatological hopes. Yearnings for the redemption of Zion (also commonly called the 'restoration of Zion' in both second-temple Jewish literature and OT scholarship) were expressed by writings and movements of the second temple period. Given such a milieu, the question whether Jesus was affected by these traditions is a reasonable and significant one.

To ascertain whether Jesus was affected by this stream of tradition, our study proceeded to probe the sayings traditions first, without paying particular attention to their chronological settings (chapters 3–5). Such a procedure is adopted in recognition of the form-critical insight that the pericopae in the gospels may not have been arranged chronologically. Luke 13.31–3 (L) offers significant evidence to show that Jesus viewed Jerusalem as the terminus or goal of his ministry (chapter 3). It would be in that particular place that his work would be completed and this would involve his death.

His death was understood by him to be part and parcel of his peripatetic ministry (πορεύεσθαι; Luke 13.33). Jerusalem, however, was viewed in a negative light by him in that it was described as the city where prophets were killed. This exaggerated characterisation of Jerusalem is not paralleled elsewhere in Jewish literature and is thus significant for our understanding of Jesus' view of Jerusalem. However, it should also be noted that, in spite of this negative comment, the attraction of Jerusalem for Jesus in his own conception of his ministry is highlighted. This is further supported by Mark 10.32–4. In that passage is also found the datum that Jesus expected to die in Jerusalem. In short, Jesus understood that the necessity of his death in Jerusalem did not arise from human initiative.

Chapter 4 warns us to take the negative view of Jerusalem in Luke 13.31–3 with caution, for in Matthew 5.35 (M) Jesus recognises the importance of Jerusalem to Yahweh. Jesus forbade the use of Jerusalem in oath formulas because πόλις ἐστὶν τοῦ μεγάλου βασιλέως. Common to Jerusalem and Jesus' message is the kingship of God which is itself the important aspect of Jesus' message. This saying, while giving evidence on the one hand of Jesus' positive assessment of the theological role of Jerusalem, also suggests that Jesus would be drawn inexorably to Jerusalem (cf. Luke 13.31–3), for it is there that the kingship of God is exercised in a decisive manner. And the intimate connection between the kingship of God and Jerusalem is part and parcel of the Zion traditions. The ambivalence in the attitude of Jesus towards Jerusalem is not surprising. A similar phenomenon is also found at Qumran. What may be ambivalent on the formal level may be seen to be consistent on a deeper level.

But are there other reasons why a Galilean itinerant preacher like Jesus would be inexorably drawn to Jerusalem? Q 13.34–5 (chapter 5) provides a positive answer. Jesus understood that, through his ministry, Yahweh was seeking to 'gather' (ἐπισυνάξαι; following Luke who was probably preserving the original reading of Q) Jerusalem. Motifs connected with the Zion traditions are found in the saying: the 'sheltering' of Jerusalem by Yahweh (Isa. 31.5); the promise of Yahweh to restore Zion. Hence, the 'restoration' of Jerusalem to be the city of Yahweh's kingship was the goal of Jesus. Here one can see the convergence of Matthew 5.35 with Q 13.34–5, in that, if Jerusalem was the city of the great king (πόλις τοῦ μεγάλου βασιλέως), Jesus would seek to 'restore' Jerusalem to the kingship of God, for the kingship of God was the main ingredient of his message. One important point to note is that such a restoration overture on the part of Yahweh through Jesus (as Jesus conceived it) was regarded as crucial in that a rejection of this overture on the part of the city would lead to the abandoning of the divine presence (the Shekinah) from the temple and city, leaving both condemned to destruction. The precise chronological placement of this logion is difficult, but we have suggested that it occurred after the incident in the temple. However, the precise chronological placement of this saying does not affect our study very much, as it is sufficient to ascertain that the restoration of Jerusalem was an important goal for Jesus, if not the primary one.

Hence, the sayings traditions confirm that Zion was to Jesus a magnet and τέλος of his ministry. It was understood by him to be the city of God's kingship and he sought the restoration of it to that kingship. In spite of his expectation of death in that city, Jerusalem remained for Jesus the central place of God's kingship and redemption. As a result, the level of appropriation of the Zion traditions by Jesus can be said to be fundamental, as the goal of his main message and intention were informed by them.

Can the results gathered from the study of the sayings traditions be confirmed by a detailed study of Jesus' significant actions in Jerusalem? That is, do these actions show the impact of the Zion traditions on Jesus? And do these traditions shed light on the intentions of Jesus in his performance of those actions and thus provide us with the possibility of a unifying hypothesis for them? Part III is devoted to these questions (chapters 6–8).

The mode of entry into Jerusalem (chapter 6) was deliberate on the part of Jesus. The posture he adopted by riding on an ass in the entry is provocative, as the ass was often regarded as a royal animal in Jewish writings. This was probably meant by Jesus to symbolise the fulfilment of the promises of Yahweh made to Zion in Zechariah 9.9. Jesus' action further suggests that the city of God's kingship is being confronted with the kingship of God through the entrance of the promised messianic king. This would further imply a challenge to the Jewish authorities in charge of the city. Although no comment was forthcoming from the lips of Jesus, we suggest that he intended this event to be interpreted by one closely following it – the incident in the temple.

In chapter 7, we have tried to demonstrate that the action in the temple was a protest by Jesus, carried out in the spirit of the classical prophets, against the oppressive and profiteering regime run by the establishment under the cloak of the temple cult. We based this conclusion on an interpretation which takes into account all the authentic elements of that one action. But the quotation from Isaiah 56.7 shows that the motivation behind Jesus' action was more than just social, economic or political. Rather, he understood that the restoration of Zion had been set in motion, and hence expected the temple to fulfil its eschatological role as the οἶκος προσευχῆς ... πᾶσιν τοῖς ἔθνεσιν (Mark 11.17). This motivation recalls an important motif in the Zion traditions: the pilgrimage of the Gentiles to Jerusalem to worship Yahweh in the temple. The failure of the temple at such a decisive hour led to the temple and the city being judged. (Here, one can see an important convergence between Q 13.34–5 and this pericope.) From the temple incident, it can also be seen that the challenge issued by Jesus in the entry (chapter 6) was directed at the Jewish nation and not the Romans (*pace* Reimarus). It was an intramural conflict and not an extramural one. Some further suggestions were given as to why Jesus did not comment on the significance of the entry.

In chapter 8, attention was focused on the cup-saying of the last supper narrative. We argued that the total significance of the event can be defined by the cup-saying. The cup-saying signifies that Jesus intended to ratify a covenant (whether the qualifier 'new' or 'renewed' is attached does not amount to any significant difference) with his disciples who partook of the cup and were thus constituted as the restored or new people of God *in nuce*. We suggested that the restorative blessings of Yahweh have been transferred from the city and the temple onto the disciples. In one sense, the restoration programme which Jesus understood himself to be bringing about was reinterpreted, in that Yahweh's restorative programme for Israel was not stalled by the intransigence of the city and temple, but has shifted its locus onto Jesus' disciples. A similar phenomenon could also be found at Qumran.

There is therefore a thematic unity which runs through and links the three significant actions of Jesus in Jerusalem. We have termed this 'the restorative thread'. Hence, the common denominator between these actions is the word 'restoration' and this restoration is carried out in the context of the appropriation by Jesus of the Zion traditions. Israel was to be restored (and this would entail the constitution of the restored people of God), but this has to take place definitively in Jerusalem.

Hence, in this light, the ratification of the renewed covenant has to be carried out in Jerusalem even though in the choosing of the twelve Jesus signified that they were the restored twelve tribes *in nuce*. Viewing the three actions from the standpoint of the Zion traditions allows one to see their thematic unity. Thus, the results gathered in Part II are confirmed in Part III.

That Jesus understood his ministry in Jerusalem, which commenced with the entry, to be his τέλος can be deduced from the nature of the actions he performed in Jerusalem. The provocative nature of Jesus' actions in the entry and the temple incident would result in a situation where no turning back was possible. Either the city and its authorities were to accept his message, or they would have to repudiate him and find a way to silence him. It was in that city that the restorative programme of God's kingdom was fought out. Moreover, the celebration of the last supper by Jesus affords a further confirmation that Jesus understood Jerusalem as the city of his τέλος.

2 Thesis

Our thesis is simple. The Zion traditions were appropriated by Jesus in his ministry and they help us to understand the unifying aim behind his actions in Jerusalem. Jesus went to Jerusalem to bring his ministry and God's restorative programme to a climax. This involves the fulfilment of the restorative promises made to Zion and the constitution of a new people restored to a new relationship with Yahweh.

Jesus therefore would have disagreed with one possible strand of Jewish thought which viewed Israel's exile as being already ended (cf. 1 Macc. 5.53–4)[1] and the restoration of its fortunes, promised by the prophets, already fulfilled. He would hold instead the contrary viewpoint, expressed in many Jewish writings and movements of the second temple period, that Israel was still, to some extent, in a state of exile[2] and that, therefore, restoration was still pending. However, he also understood that with his ministry, the restorative programme promised long ago by Yahweh would begin, and he placed this restoration in an eschatological framework. That

---

[1] See the comments of J. Goldstein, *1 Maccabees*, p. 304.
[2] Cf. the recent work of N. T. Wright, *The New Testament and the People of God*, pp. 268–71.

is, the great and final restoration promised by Yahweh was to be fulfilled through him, and, in this restoration, eschatological blessings would be channelled to the new people of Yahweh, with whom a new covenant was made. It is probable that, in the light of the intransigence and hostility of the Jewish leadership in Jerusalem, Jesus would have expected to have a decisive post-mortem role to achieve the culmination of the restoration programme already begun with his disciples.

Schweitzer's either-or dictum[3] is thus seen to be misleading. Jesus did not go to Jerusalem simply to die. To regard this as his only goal would not make much sense out of his actions in Jerusalem (especially the entry and the temple incident) unless one were to regard them as performed simply to provoke the authorities to put him to death. Moreover, the symbolic quality of the entry would have been lost sight of. Nor should Jesus be regarded as going to Jerusalem simply to 'work' (Schweitzer's term) or to challenge the city with his message.[4] This also fails to take into account the fulfilment quality of the entry and Jesus' express understanding that the climax of his ministry must include his death (the last supper and Luke 13.31–3). It would seem that *both* clauses of Schweitzer's dictum explain Jesus' intentions in going to Jerusalem. Meyer suggests that one model for understanding how Jesus regarded his death in Jerusalem in the context of his work there is that Jesus did not seek to die but sought to *charge with meaning* the death he expected to die.[5] This, although helpful, is still questionable in that Jesus might have understood his death to be already charged with meaning by his sense of vocation from Yahweh, and might simply have submitted to what he thought was necessary in his vocation (cf. Luke 13.31–3 and the last supper).

Reimarus, while sensitive to the possibility that there was a unifying motivation on the part of Jesus behind the entry and the temple incident, errs in arguing that Jesus intended to stage a revolutionary coup.[6] Jesus' reticence in the entry and his action of protest against the Jewish authorities and not against the Romans in the temple incident would suggest that his motivations behind

---

[3] '[O]ne might use ... as a principle of division ... to clarify the lives of Jesus, whether they make him go to Jerusalem to work or to die' (A. Schweitzer, *The Quest of the Historical Jesus*, p. 389 n. 1).
[4] Cf. G. Bornkamm, *Jesus of Nazareth*, pp. 154–5.
[5] B. F. Meyer, *The Aims of Jesus*, p. 218.
[6] H. Reimarus, in C. H. Talbert (ed.), *Reimarus: Fragments*, p. 146.

these actions were far from an intended coup. Instead, he was motivated by his understanding that God's restorative programme for Zion had dawned. The question of how the Romans were to be dealt with in the context of God's restoration was not directly addressed by those actions[7] but they do not suggest that Jesus intended the liberation of Jerusalem from the Romans, at least not in a revolutionary way. Perhaps this would explain why, while being profoundly informed by the Zion traditions in his own conception of his ministry, Jesus was not too concerned about the doctrine of the land, אֶרֶץ יִשְׂרָאֵל (*'erɛṣ yiśrâel*; see the introduction to Part II), which is often connected to the Zion traditions. This would probably indicate that the theological symbolism of Jerusalem was more important to Jesus than the political one. However, we have no wish to dichotomise the two. Our study only suggests that the theological aspect is more prominent when compared to the other.

One crucial result of our thesis is that an important strand of Jewish traditions – the Zion traditions – is brought into a fruitful dialogue with Jesus' ministry. These traditions were appropriated by Jesus in a very significant way. This helps us to understand another important aspect of the Jewishness of Jesus and to show how an individual Jew could creatively appropriate his heritage in his own ministry. The window provided by this dialogue allows us to understand that the provocative actions of Jesus in Jerusalem were not performed in a moment of impulse: they stemmed from a unified motivation. More importantly, Jesus' appropriation of the Zion traditions explains why he understood that the climax of his ministry and his death had to take place nowhere else except in Jerusalem.

Such conclusions unmask the weaknesses of some recent treatments of the intentions of the historical Jesus. Thus, Sanders' picture of a Jesus without any definite plans[8] collapses in the light of our thesis. So do the scholarly reconstructions which characterise Jesus as primarily a rabbi or teacher. Vermes' picture of Jesus as a Galilean *ḥasid* is misleading, especially since it does not reckon seriously with the question why Jesus went to Jerusalem. It should also be pointed out that Jesus' aims should not be conceived in

---

[7] Although some see in these actions an implicit universalism. See M. J. Borg, *Conflict, Holiness and Politics in the Teachings of Jesus*, pp. 175–7.

[8] E. P. Sanders, *Jesus and Judaism*, pp. 226, 235.

merely moral terms (e.g., 'he went about doing good') for this would not explain his significant actions in Jerusalem nor the *raison d'être* behind his 'doing good'.[9]

3   Some implications for historical Jesus research

Our thesis has utilised an intense probe into a particular but important motivation of Jesus. It focuses on selected but significant passages to verify the hypothesis assumed at the outset: i.e., the interrelatedness of the Zion traditions and Jesus' intentions in Jerusalem. Because of its narrow focus, other aspects of the study of the historical Jesus have not been considered. Therefore we shall attempt here a brief sketch of the implications for historical Jesus research which arise from our thesis.

The recent 'portraits' of Jesus

We have already discussed the weaknesses of certain scholarly reconstructions of Jesus appertaining to the topic of the intentions of Jesus. We now move on to other aspects of Jesus research which recent works have highlighted.

Borg's recent article on North American scholarship on the historical Jesus suggests that two questions central to 'the renaissance of Jesus research' concern Jesus' eschatology and his relationship to the social world.[10] According to him, it is the weight assigned to these questions which separates the works of the five scholars he was reviewing.[11] Our thesis does not engage itself directly with these questions. However, since we have shown that the Zion traditions were an important factor which had influenced Jesus' conceptions of his intentions and that it was the eschatological and theological aspects of these traditions which attracted him to Jerusalem, our thesis lends support to portraits of Jesus which picture him as working in a predominantly eschatological framework.[12] The importance of Jesus' relationship to his social world is

---

[9] So Meyer, *Aims*, pp. 220–1.

[10] M. J. Borg 'Portraits of Jesus in Contemporary North American Scholarship', *HTR* 84:1 (1991), 1–22. For another useful survey of the American scene see P. Hollenbach, 'The Historical Jesus Question in North America Today', *BTB* 19 (1989), 11–22.

[11] Borg, 'Portraits', 19. The five scholars surveyed are E. P. Sanders, B. Mack, E. S. Fiorenza, M. J. Borg and R. A. Horsley.

[12] Thus, Sanders' reconstructed framework of Jesus' ministry is supported by

not denied, but we would want to emphasise that, for Jesus, theology overrides societal constraints and informs his relationship to the social world. Hence, many aspects of his ministry are religious first even though they certainly have social roots. We hope to have demonstrated in chapter 2 that this is also true for some of Jesus' contemporaries.

There has been an increasing tendency on the part of certain American scholars to view Jesus as a wisdom teacher or a cynic.[13] Interestingly, such a view is linked to the increased veneration of the Gospel of Thomas and Q (where the actions of Jesus do not receive significant mention) on the part of these scholars. Such portraits may be misleading in that they are derived principally from the sayings of Jesus without due regard to the actions and without reckoning with the intentions of Jesus in Jerusalem. Jesus had aims which engaged with the destiny of Israel. He was not simply a wisdom teacher.

Jesus and Israel

How should one describe the relationship of Jesus to the nation of Israel? From the conclusions derived from our study, it would follow that Jesus was concerned for the fulfilment of the restorative promises of God to Israel. These were to be made concrete by the constitution of a restored relationship between Yahweh and his people. Meyer has attempted to interpret the career of Jesus from this vantage point.[14] And from this vantage point, Jesus' career becomes intelligible as a unity. While we cannot explore the relationship of Jesus' intentions in Jerusalem to his aims in his career prior to that, Meyer's thesis offers a fruitful way of viewing

---

us. However, the problem of what is meant by 'eschatological' has to be dealt with in the light of the slippery use of the term. On this, see the excellent discussions in I. H. Marshall, 'Slippery Words I: Eschatology', *ExpT* 89 (1977–8), 264–9 and G. B. Caird, *The Language and Imagery of the Bible*, pp. 243–4. As the word has become part and parcel of the language used in biblical studies, the call for its expurgation would be futile. Generally, the word is taken to mean a reference to the future without further specifying whether this future involves an apocalyptic end of the world. See also S. Talmon, *Eschatology and History in Biblical Judaism*, where he attempts to show that, for biblical Judaism (i.e., the OT), the promises of the future are realised in a this-worldly context (pp. 33–4).

13 Chief of which is J. D. Crossan, *The Historical Jesus: The Life of a Mediterranean Jewish Peasant*. See also F. G. Downing (British), *Jesus and the Threat of Freedom*, especially pp. 126–60.

14 *Aims*, p. 221.

it. Both phases have to do with the matter of restoration in the context of the imminent reign of God. Indeed, the one (Jesus' ministry in Jerusalem) can be said to be the crown and climax of the other.

A question which is often posed is whether Jesus intended to found a sect. According to our study, the answer should be no, even though it is admitted that some sect-like qualities may be present in Jesus' understanding of his career (see chapter 8). But this is a feature which every movement shares if it differs from the general or official ethos. Jesus' action in the temple and his lament over Jerusalem (Q 13.34–5) need not imply the rejection of the nation *in toto* (the Q saying implies that a lifeline is held out to the nation even in judgment). Nor should the constitution of the new people of God by the ratification of a new covenant through Jesus' blood imply his desire to found a sect. By partaking of the contents of the cup, the disciples were constituted the restored people of God *in nuce* with a mission of reaching out to the whole of Israel (the evidence provided by Acts). It would seem that the idea of 'remnant theology'[15] would be a better word to describe this phenomenon than the term 'sect ideology'. To borrow the terms of Meyer, Israel was probably viewed by Jesus as *massa salvanda* and not *massa damnata*, although the failure to heed his message would lead to judgment from God.

Jesus' attitude towards Jerusalem

What was Jesus' attitude towards Jerusalem? Did Jesus reject[16] or affirm[17] the central importance of Jerusalem as the place of God's reign and restoration? From our study, it would seem that a neat synthetic picture is not available, as there are elements of both rejection and affirmation. On the one hand, Jesus made the unparalleled statement that Jerusalem was the city of death for prophets *par excellence* (Luke 13.33). Moreover, judgment upon the temple and city was also pronounced (Q 13.34–5). On the other hand, Jesus affirmed the central importance of Jerusalem as the city

---

[15] On remnant theology in the OT see G. F. Hasel, *The Remnant: The History and Theology of the Remnant Idea from Genesis to Isaiah*. On the possibility that Jesus would have appropriated this theology see Meyer, *Aims*, pp. 220–2.

[16] J. C. de Young, *Jerusalem in the New Testament*, pp. 75–102.

[17] P. Stuhlmacher, 'Die Stellung Jesu und des Paulus zu Jerusalem', *ZTK* 86 (1989), 140–56.

of God's kingship and sought to bring about the fulfilment of the restorative promises made to it. Such a picture is reminiscent of the stance of many OT prophets towards Jerusalem: condemnation for its sins but promises of its future restoration when the period of punishment is over. This 'ambiguity' could also be found in the Qumran community (chapter 2). If a synthesis is to be proposed at all, it is perhaps this: Jesus accepted the legitimacy of Jerusalem as serving the symbolic reality of God's reign, but that did not tie him to any historical Jerusalem. The OT prophets and Jesus sought to bridge the gap between the historical Jerusalem and the ideal one. In this light, Stuhlmacher's statement of the attitude of Jesus towards Jerusalem is probably correct: depite Jesus' pronouncement of judgment over Jerusalem and the earthly temple, Zion remained for him the future centre of the restored divine community.[18]

4 Prospects for further research

The Zion traditions in the early church

It will be fruitful to study how different aspects of the life and theology of the early church were related to these traditions.

(i) The origins of the Gentile mission

The tentative steps that the post-Easter community took in the Gentile mission (and after much hesitation) have often been read as casting doubt on the link between the historical Jesus and such a mission.[19] Paul has often been given the responsibility for the genesis of such a mission. The issues are complex, but we suggest that viewing the Gentile mission in the light of the Zion traditions may help. Our conclusions in chapter 7 show that Jesus probably was aware of the motif of the pilgrimage of the Gentiles in the eschaton. Perhaps it was the centripetal aspect of the conversion of the Gentiles and not the centrifugal aspect of a mission to the Gentiles which caused the post-Easter community to be hesitant in taking steps to start such a mission.[20] Could it be that the historic-

---

[18] 'Stellung', 146.
[19] E.g., Sanders, *Jesus*, p. 221. See also A. Harnack, *The Mission and Expansion of Christianity* I, pp. 36–43.
[20] Cf. J. D. G. Dunn, *The Partings of the Ways*, p. 118.

ally probable limitation by Jesus of the mission of the disciples to Israel (Matt. 10.5–6) might be explained in the light of the Zion traditions, i.e., Zion was not yet restored and, therefore, any mission to the Gentiles was premature? If this speculation is correct, this helps us to see that Jesus' limitation of his disciples' mission to Israel and his expectation that the Gentiles would stream into the kingdom (Matt. 8.11‖Luke 13.29)[21] are probably consistent and not contradictory.[22]

(ii) The origins of the Jerusalem church

It is surprising that the city which killed the founder of the post-Easter community soon became the community's headquarters and had an important place in the infant Christian movement (before the destruction of Jerusalem in 70 CE). Why was this community's headquarters established in the very city where Jesus was killed, when, logically, it would be safer to establish it elsewhere without being exposed to unnecessary perils? Given the fact that Galilee was the prominent locus of Jesus' ministry, would not a town in Galilee (e.g., Capernaum) be more suitable for such headquarters? Was the theological and eschatological importance of Jerusalem part of the reason which led to the establishment of a Christian community there? Furthermore, how did this church become prominent even when other centres were already established before 70 CE? Were the Zion traditions influential? Are there grounds for linking the cause of the importance of the Jerusalem community with the words of the risen Jesus in Luke 24.47 and Acts 1.4? Such questions prompt further research.

Jesus and his career

Our thesis has concentrated on the last events of Jesus' ministry and his intentions behind them. But a very fruitful and necessary step from here is to relate our conclusions to the intentions of Jesus in his ministry prior to the period we have been considering.

---

[21] The authenticity of this logion is strong. See J. Jeremias, *Jesus' Promise to the Nations*, pp. 55–63.

[22] For a recent discussion of the origins of the Gentile mission see C. H. H. Scobie, 'Jesus or Paul? The Origin of the Universal Mission of the Christian Church', in P. Richardson and J. C. Hurd (eds.), *From Jesus to Paul*, pp. 47–60. See also S. G. Wilson, *The Gentiles and the Gentile Mission in Luke–Acts*, pp. 1–28.

Murphy-O'Connor has attempted to reconstruct Jesus' earlier career before the death of the Baptist and to show how that death led to a change in the direction of his ministry.[23] This sort of study ought to be expanded to take in Jesus' entire career. Are we then advocating a return to writing the 'lives' of Jesus which was such a popular pastime in the nineteenth century? The data available are not adequate for a full biographical approach. None the less, certain broad pictures of Jesus' life could in principle be drawn, bearing in mind the limitation of the NT.[24] Perhaps the Synoptic evangelists' stylised presentation of the career of Jesus (the narration of only one trip made by Jesus to Jerusalem) serves to capture the development of Jesus' own conception of his ministry. That is, the Synoptic evangelists want to show the theological progression of Jesus' ministry instead of the geographical one, with geography being used in the service of theology.

[23] J. Murphy-O'Connor, 'John the Baptist and Jesus: History and Hypotheses', *NTS* 36 (1990), 359–74.

[24] In one sense, the recent works on the historical Jesus could be seen as attempts to write the 'lives' of Jesus albeit on a narrow scale.

BIBLIOGRAPHY

Books and articles on historical Jesus research are legion. The following list is restricted only to those cited in the text and notes.

1 Primary sources

Cary, E. (ed. and tr.). *Dio's Roman History*, 9 vols., Cambridge, MA: Harvard University Press, 1914–27.
Charles, R. H. (ed.). *The Apocrypha and Pseudepigrapha of the Old Testament in English*, 2 vols., Oxford: Clarendon Press, 1913.
Charlesworth, J. H. (ed.). *The Old Testament Pseudepigrapha*, 2 vols., New York: Doubleday, 1983, 1985.
Danby, H. (tr.). *The Mishnah*, Oxford: Clarendon Press, 1933.
Neusner, J. (tr.). *The Tosefta*, 6 vols., New York: Ktav, 1977–86.
Rahlfs, A. (ed.). *Septuaginta*, Stuttgart: Württembergische Bibelanstalt Stuttgart, 1935.
Sanders, J. A. *The Psalm Scrolls of Qumran Cave 11 (11QPsᵃ)*, Oxford: Clarendon Press, 1965.
Thackeray, H. St J., Marcus, R. and Feldman, L. H. (eds. and trs.). *Josephus*, 10 vols., Cambridge, MA: Harvard University Press, 1926–65.
Vermes, G. *The Dead Sea Scrolls in English*, London: Penguin Books, ³1987.
Yadin, Y. (ed.). *The Scroll of the War of the Sons of Light Against the Sons of Darkness*, Oxford: Oxford University Press, 1962.
  The Temple Scroll, 3 vols., Jerusalem: Israel Exploration Society, 1983.

2 Secondary literature

Abrahams, I. *Studies in Pharisaism and the Gospels*, 2 vols., Cambridge: Cambridge University Press, 1917.
Aland, K. *Vollständige Konkordanz zum Griechischen Neuen Testament*, 3 vols., Berlin: de Gruyter, 1978.
Allen, L. *Ezekiel 20–48*, Dallas: Word Books, 1990.
Allison, D. C. 'The Pauline Epistles and the Synoptic Gospels: The Pattern of Tradition', *NTS* 28 (1982), 1–32.
  'Matt 23.39 = Luke 13.35b as a Conditional Prophecy', *JSNT* 18 (1983), 75–84.

The End of the Ages Has Come, Edinburgh: T & T Clark, 1988.

Alt, A. *Kleine Schriften zur Geschichte des Volkes Israel*, Munich: C. H. Beck'sche, 1959.

Aune, D. E. *Prophecy in Early Christianity and the Ancient Mediterranean World*, Grand Rapids: Eerdmans, 1983.

Baarlink, H. 'Friede im Himmel: Die lukanische Redaktion von Lk 19,38 und ihre Deutung', *ZNW* 76 (1985), 170–86.

Baird, J. A. *The Justice of God in the Teaching of Jesus*, London: SCM, 1963.

Bammel, E. 'Crucifixion as a Punishment in Palestine', in E. Bammel (ed.), *The Trial of Jesus*, London: SCM, 1970, pp. 162–5.

'The Revolutionary Theory from Reimarus to Brandon', in E. Bammel and C. F. D. Moule (eds.), *Jesus and the Politics of His Day*, Cambridge: Cambridge University Press, 1984, pp. 11–68.

'The *Titulus*', in E. Bammel and C. F. D. Moule (eds.), *Jesus and the Politics of His Day*, Cambridge: Cambridge University Press, 1984, pp. 353–64.

Bammel, E. and Moule, C. F. D. (eds.). *Jesus and the Politics of His Day*, Cambridge: Cambridge University Press, 1984.

Barnett, P. W. 'The Jewish Sign-Prophets – AD 40–70: Their Intention and Origin', *NTS* 27 (1980–1), 679–97.

Barr, J. *The Semantics of Biblical Language*, Oxford: Clarendon Press, 1961.

Barrett, C. K. *Jesus and the Gospel Tradition*, London: SPCK, 1967.

A Commentary on the First Epistle to the Corinthians, London: A & C Black, 1968.

The Second Epistle to the Corinthians, London: A & C Black, 1973.

'The House of Prayer and the Den of Thieves', in E. E. Ellis and E. Grässer (eds.), *Jesus und Paulus*, Göttingen: Vandenhoeck & Ruprecht, 1975, pp. 13–20.

The Gospel According to St John, London: SPCK, ²1978.

Bauckham, R. J. 'The Coin in the Fish Mouth', in C. L. Blomberg and D. Wenham (eds.), *Gospel Perspectives VI: The Miracles of Jesus*, Sheffield: JSOT Press 1986, pp. 219–52.

'Jesus' Demonstration in the Temple', in B. Lindars (ed.), *Law and Religion*, Cambridge: James Clarke, 1988, pp. 72–89.

Bauer, W. 'The Colt of Palm Sunday (Der Palmesel)', *JBL* 72 (1953), 220–9.

Bayer, H. F. *Jesus' Predictions of Vindication and Resurrection*, Tübingen: Mohr & Siebeck, 1986.

Beagley, J. A. *The 'Sitz im Leben' of the Apocalypse with Particular Reference to the Role of the Church's Enemies*, Berlin: de Gruyter, 1987.

Beare, F. W. *The Gospel According to Matthew*, Oxford: Blackwell, 1981.

Beasley-Murray, G. R. *Jesus and the Kingdom of God*, Exeter: Paternoster, 1986.

John, Waco: Word Books, 1987.

Behm, J. 'κλάω κτλ', *TDNT* III, pp. 726–43.

Best, E. *Mark: The Gospel as Story*, Edinburgh: T & T Clark, 1983.

Betz, O. and Riesner, R. *Jesus, Qumran and the Vatican*, London: SCM, 1994.

Beyer, W. 'εὐλογεῖν κτλ', *TDNT* III, pp. 754–65.

Black, M. *An Aramaic Approach to the Gospels and Acts*, Oxford: Clarendon Press, ³1967.

Blenkinsopp, J. 'The Oracle of Judah and the Messianic Entry', *JBL* 80 (1961), 55–64.

Blinzler, J. 'The Jewish Punishment of Stoning in the New Testament Period', in E. Bammel (ed.), *The Trial of Jesus*, London: SCM, 1970, pp. 157–61.

Bock, D. L. *Proclamation from Prophecy and Pattern*, Sheffield: JSOT Press, 1987.

Bockmuehl, M. N. '"The Trumpet Shall Sound": *Shofar* Symbolism and its Reception in Early Christianity', in W. Horbury (ed.), *Templum Amicitiae*, Sheffield: JSOT Press, 1991, pp. 199–225.

This Jesus: Martyr, Lord, Messiah, Edinburgh: T & T Clark, 1994.

Booth, R. P. *Jesus and the Laws of Purity: Tradition History and Legal History in Mark 7*, Sheffield: JSOT Press 1986.

Borg, M. J. *Conflict, Holiness and Politics in the Teachings of Jesus*, New York: Edwin Mellen, 1984.

Jesus: A New Vision, New York: Harper & Row, 1987.

'An Orthodoxy Reconsidered: The End-of-the-World Jesus', in L. D. Hurst and N. T. Wright (eds.), *The Glory of Christ in the New Testament: Studies in Christology in Memory of George Bradford Caird*, Oxford: Clarendon Press, 1987, pp. 207–17.

'Portraits of Jesus in Contemporary North American Scholarship', *HTR* 84:1 (1991), 1–22.

Boring, M. E. *The Sayings of the Risen Jesus*, Cambridge: Cambridge University Press, 1982.

'Criteria of Authenticity: The Lucan Beatitudes as a Test Case', *Forum* 1,4 (1985), 3–38.

Bornkamm, G. *Jesus of Nazareth*, London: Hodder & Stoughton, 1960.

Early Christian Experience, London: SCM, 1969.

Borsch, F. H. *The Son of Man in Myth and History*, London: SCM, 1967.

Brandon, S. G. F. *Jesus and the Zealots*, Manchester: Manchester University Press, 1967.

Braun, H. *Jesus of Nazareth: The Man and His Time*, Philadelphia: Fortress, 1979.

Brooks, S. H. *Matthew's Community: The Evidence of His Special Sayings Material*, Sheffield: JSOT Press, 1987.

Brown, R. E. *The Gospel According to John*, 2 vols., New York: Doubleday, 1966–70.

The Birth of the Messiah, London: Doubleday, 1977.

Brownlee, W. H. *Ezekiel 1–19*, Waco: Word Books, 1986.

Bruce, F. F. 'The Book of Zechariah and the Passion Narrative', *BJRL* 43 (1960–1), 336–53.

This is That, Exeter: Paternoster, 1968.

Brueggemann, W. *The Land*, Philadelphia: Fortress, 1977.

To Build and to Plant. A Commentary on Jeremiah 26–52, Grand Rapids: Eerdmans, 1991.

Buchanan, G. W. 'Mark 11.15–19. Brigands in the Temple', *HUCA* 30 (1959), 169–77.

Jesus: The King and His Kingdom, Macon: Mercer University Press, 1984.

'Symbolic Money-Changers in the Temple', *NTS* 37 (1991), 280–90.

Büchsel, F. 'παλιγγενεσία', *TDNT* I, pp. 686–9.

Bultmann, R. *Theology of the New Testament*, 2 vols., London: SCM, 1952, 1955.

The History of the Synoptic Tradition, Oxford: Blackwell, ²1968.

The Gospel of John, Oxford: Blackwell, 1971.

Buren, P. M. van. *A Christian Theology of the People of Israel II: A Theology of the Jewish-Christian Reality*, San Francisco: Harper & Row, 1983.

Burnett, F. W. *The Testament of Jesus-Sophia. A Redactional-Critical Study of the Eschatological Discourse in Matthew*, Washington DC: University Press of America, 1981.

Cadbury, H. J. *The Style and Literary Method of Luke*, Cambridge, MA: Harvard University Press, 1920.

Caird, G. B. *St Luke*, Harmondsworth: Penguin Books, 1963.

The Language and Imagery of the Bible, London: Duckworth, 1980.

'Jesus and Israel: The Starting Point for New Testament Christology', in R. F. Berkey and S. A. Edwards (eds.), *Christological Perspectives*, New York: Pilgrim's Press, 1982, pp. 58–68.

Callaway, P. R. *The History of the Qumran Community*, Sheffield: JSOT Press, 1988.

Calvin, J. *A Harmony of the Gospels of Matthew, Mark and Luke* III, Edinburgh: T & T Clark, 1972.

Caragounis, C. C. *The Son of Man*, Tübingen: Mohr & Siebeck, 1986.

Carr, D. 'Jesus, the King of Zion: A Traditio-Historical Enquiry into the so-called "Triumphal" Entry of Jesus' (unpublished Ph.D. dissertation, University of London, 1980).

Carroll, R. P. *Jeremiah*, London: SCM, 1986.

Carson, D. A. *The Gospel According to John*, Leicester: Inter-Varsity Press, 1991.

Casey, P. M. 'General, Generic and Indefinite: The Use of the "Son of Man" in Aramaic Sources in the Teaching of Jesus', *JSNT* 29 (1987), 21–56.

'The Original Aramaic Form of Jesus' Interpretation of the Cup', *JTS* 41 (1990), 1–12.

Catchpole, D. R. 'The "Triumphal" Entry', in E. Bammel and C. F. D. Moule (eds.), *Jesus and the Politics of His Day*, Cambridge: Cambridge University Press, 1984, pp. 319–34.

'Temple Traditions in Q', in W. Horbury (ed.), *Templum Amicitiae*, Sheffield: JSOT Press, 1991, pp. 305–29.

The Quest for Q, Edinburgh: T & T Clark, 1993.

Causse, A. 'Le mythe de la nouvelle Jerusalem du Deutero-Esaire a la IIIᵉ Sibylle', *RHPR* 18 (1938), 397.

Charlesworth, J. H. 'The SNTS Pseudepigrapha Seminars at Tübingen and Paris and the Books of Enoch', *NTS* 25 (1978–9), 315–23.
  Jesus Within Judaism, London: SPCK, 1988.
Chester, A. 'Citing the Old Testament', in D. A. Carson and H. G. M. Williamson (eds.), *It is Written: Scripture Citing Scripture*, Cambridge: Cambridge University Press, 1988, pp. 141–69.
  'Jewish Messianic Expectations and Mediatorial Figures and Pauline Christology', in M. Hengel and U. Heckel (eds.), *Paulus und das antike Judentum*, Tübingen: Mohr & Siebeck, 1991, pp. 17–89.
  'The Sibyl and the Temple', in W. Horbury (ed.), *Templum Amicitiae*, Sheffield: JSOT Press, 1991, pp. 37–69.
Chilton, B. D. *God in Strength*, Sheffield: JSOT Press, 1987.
  '[ὡς] φραγέλλιον ἐκ σχονίων (John 2.15)', in W. Horbury (ed.), *Templum Amicitiae*, Sheffield: JSOT Press, 1991, pp. 330–44.
  The Temple of Jesus: His Sacrificial Program within a Cultural History of Sacrifice, Pennsylvania: Pennsylvania State Press, 1992.
Chilton, B. D. and Evans, C. A. (eds.). *Studying the Historical Jesus: Evaluations of the State of Current Research*, Leiden: E. J. Brill, 1994.
Christ, F. *Jesus Sophia*, Zürich: Zwingli, 1970.
Clements, R. E. *God and Temple*, Oxford: Blackwell, 1965.
  Isaiah and the Deliverance of Jerusalem, Sheffield: JSOT Press, 1980.
Cohen, G. D. 'Zion in Rabbinic Literature', in A. S. Halkim (ed.), *Zion in Jewish Literature*, Lanham: University Press of America, 1988, pp. 38–64.
Collins, J. J. 'The Works of the Messiah', *Dead Sea Discoveries* 1,1 (1994), 98–112.
Conzelmann, H. *The Theology of St Luke*, London: Faber & Faber, 1960.
  1 Corinthians, Philadelphia: Fortress, 1975.
Craigie, P. C. *Psalms 1–50*, Waco: Word Books, 1983.
Creed, J. M. *The Gospel According to St. Luke*, London: Macmillan, 1957.
Crossan, J. D. *The Historical Jesus: The Life of a Mediterranean Jewish Peasant*, Edinburgh: T & T Clark, 1991.
Cullmann, O. *The Christology of the New Testament*, London: SCM, 1959.
Dahl, N. A. *The Crucified Messiah*, Minneapolis: Augsburg, 1974.
Daube, D. *New Testament and Rabbinic Judaism*, London: Athlone Press, 1956.
Dautzenberg, G. 'Ist das Schwurverbot Mt 5,33–37; Jak 5,12 ein Beispiel für die Torakritik Jesu?', *BZ* 25 (1981), 47–66.
Davids, P. H. *The Epistle of James*, Exeter: Paternoster, 1982.
  'James and Jesus', in D. Wenham (ed.), *Gospel Perspectives V: The Jesus Tradition Outside the Gospels*, Sheffield: JSOT Press, 1985, pp. 63–84.
Davies, P. R. *The Damascus Covenant*, Sheffield: JSOT Press, 1982.
Davies, W. D. *The Setting of the Sermon on the Mount*, Cambridge: Cambridge University Press, 1964.
  The Gospel and the Land, Berkeley: University of California Press, 1974.
Davies, W. D. and Allison, D. C. *The Gospel According to Saint Matthew* I, Edinburgh: T & T Clark, 1988.
Day, J. *Psalms*, Sheffield: JSOT Press, 1990.

Denaux, A. 'L'hypocrisie des Pharisiens et le dessein de Dieu. Analyse de Lc, xiii, 31–33', in F. Neirynck (ed.), *L'évangile de Luc: problèmes littéraires et théologiques*, Gembloux: J. Duculot, 1973, pp. 245–85.

Derrett, J. D. M. 'Law in the New Testament: The Palm Sunday Colt', *NovT* 13 (1971), 241–58.

'The Lucan Christ and Jerusalem: τελειοῦμαι (Luke 13:32)', *ZNW* 75 (1984), 36–43.

Deutsch, C. 'Wisdom in Matthew: Transformation of a Symbol', *NovT* 32 (1990), 13–47.

Dibelius, M. and Greeven, H. *James*, Philadelphia: Fortress, 1975.

Dodd, C. H. 'Jesus as Prophet and Teacher', in G. K. A. Bell and D. A. Deissmann (eds.), *Mysterium Christi*, London: Longmans, Green & Co., 1930, pp. 53–66.

Historical Tradition in the Fourth Gospel, Cambridge: Cambridge University Press, 1953.

The Parables of the Kingdom, London: Fontana, 1961.

The Founder of Christianity, London: Fontana, 1971.

Donaldson, T. L. *Jesus on the Mountain*, Sheffield: JSOT Press, 1985.

'Rural Bandits, City Mobs and the Zealots', *JSJ* 21 (1990), 19–40.

Downing, F. G. *Jesus and the Threat of Freedom*, London: SCM, 1987.

Christ and the Cynics: Jesus and Other Radical Preachers in First-Century Tradition, Sheffield: Sheffield Academic Press, 1988.

Draper, J. A. 'Korah and the Second Temple', in W. Horbury (ed.), *Templum Amicitiae*, Sheffield: JSOT Press, 1991, pp. 150–74.

Drury, J. *The Parables in the Gospels*, London: SPCK, 1985.

Duling, D. C. 'Against Oaths', *Forum* 6,2 (1990), 99–138.

'"[Do not Swear...] by Jerusalem because it is the City of the Great King" (Matthew 5:35)', *JBL* 110 (1991), 291–309.

Dumbrell, W. J. *Covenant and Creation. An Old Testament Covenantal Theology*, Exeter: Paternoster, 1984.

Dungan, D. L. *The Sayings of Jesus in the Churches of Paul*, Oxford: 1971.

Dunn, J. D. G. 'The Messianic Secret in Mark', *TynB* 21 (1970), 92–117.

'Prophetic "I" Sayings and the Jesus Tradition: The Importance of Testing Prophetic Utterances within Early Christianity', *NTS* 24 (1978), 175–98.

'Jesus and Ritual Purity. A Study of the Tradition History in Mark 7,15', in F. Refoulé (ed.), *A cause de l'évangile: mélanges offerts a Dom Jacques Dupont*, Saint André: Cerf, 1985, pp. 251–76.

Christology in the Making, London: SCM, [2]1989.

The Partings of the Ways, London: SCM, 1991.

'Jesus Tradition in Paul', in B. D. Chilton and C. A. Evans (eds.), *Studying the Historical Jesus: Evaluations of the State of Current Research*, Leiden: E. J. Brill, 1994, pp. 155–78.

Dupont, J. 'Le logion des douze trônes (Mt 19,28; Lc 22,28–30)', *Bib* 45 (1964), 388.

Eisler, D. L. 'The Origin and History of Zion as a Theological Symbol in Ancient Israel' (unpublished Th.D. dissertation, Princeton Theological Seminary, 1978).

Elliot, J. K. 'Jerusalem in Acts and the Gospels', *NTS* 23 (1977), 462–9.
Ellis, E. E. *The Gospel of Luke*, London: Oliphants, 1974.
    'Gospels Criticisms: A Perspective on the State of the Art', in P.
    Stuhlmacher (ed.), *Das Evangelium und das Evangelien*, Tübingen:
    Mohr & Siebeck 1983, pp. 27–54.
Emerton, J. A. 'The Aramiac Underlying τὸ αἷμά μου τῆς διαθήκης in Mk
    XIV.24', *JTS* 6 (1955), 238–40.
    'ΤΟ ΑΙΜΑ ΜΟΥ ΤΗΣ ΔΙΑΘΗΚΗΣ: The Evidence of the Syriac
    Versions', *JTS* 13 (1962), 111–17.
    'Mark XIV.24 and the Targum to the Psalter', *JTS* 15 (1964), 58–9.
Ernst, J. *Das Evangelium nach Lukas*, Regensburg: Friedrich Pustet,
    1976.
Evans, C. A. 'Jesus' Action in the Temple: Cleansing or Portent of
    Destruction', *CBQ* 51 (1989), 237–70.
    'Jesus' Action in the Temple and Evidence of Corruption in the First-
    Century Temple', in D. J. Lull (ed.), *SBL 1989 Seminar Papers*,
    Atlanta: Scholars Press, 1989, pp. 522–39.
    'Appendix: The Recently Published Dead Sea Scrolls and the Historical
    Jesus', in B. D. Chilton and C. A. Evans (eds.), *Studying the Historical
    Jesus: Evaluations of the State of Current Research*, Leiden: E. J. Brill,
    1994, pp. 547–65.
Evans, C. F. *Saint Luke*, London: SCM, 1990.
Fee, G. D. *1 Corinthians*, Grand Rapids: Eerdmans, 1987.
Feldman, L. H. *Jew and Gentile in the Ancient World: Attitudes and
    Interactions from Alexander to Justinian*, Princeton: Princeton Univer-
    sity Press, 1993.
Finegan, J. *Die Überlieferung der Leidens- und Auferstehungsgeschichte
    Jesu*, Giessen: A. Töpelmann, 1934.
    *Archaeology of the New Testament: The City of Jesus and the Beginning
    of the Early Church*, Princeton: Princeton University Press, 1969.
Fischel, H. A. 'Martyr and Prophet (A Study in Jewish Literature)', *JQR*
    37 (1946–7), 265–80; 363–86.
Fitzmyer, J. A. 'The Use of Explicit Old Testament Quotations in Qumran
    Literature and in the New Testament', *NTS* 7 (1960–1), 297–333.
    The Gospel According to Luke, 2 vols., New York: Doubleday, 1981–5.
Fohrer, G. and Lohse, E. 'Σιών', *TDNT* VII, pp. 293–319.
Ford, J. M. 'Money "bags" in the Temple (Mark 11:16)', *Bib* 57 (1975),
    249–53.
France, R. T. *Jesus and the Old Testament*, London: Tyndale Press, 1971.
    'Chronological Aspects of "Gospel Harmony"', *VE* 16 (1986), 33–59.
France, R. T. and Wenham, D. (eds.). *Gospel Perspectives III: Studies in
    Midrash and Historiography*, Sheffield: JSOT Press, 1983.
Fuller, R. H. *The Foundations of New Testament Christology*, London:
    Lutterworth Press, 1965.
    'The Criterion of Dissimilarity: The Wrong Tool?', in R. F. Berkey and
    S. A. Edwards (eds.), *Christological Perspectives*, New York: Pilgrim's
    Press, 1982, pp. 42–8.
Funk, R. W. 'A Forum for Informed Discussion', *Forum* 1 (1985), 1–2.
Garland, D. E. *The Intention of Matthew 23*, Leiden: E. J. Brill, 1979.

Gärtner, B. *The Temple and the Community in Qumran and the New Testament*, Cambridge: Cambridge University Press, 1965.

Gaston, L. *No Stone on Another*, Leiden: E. J. Brill, 1970.

Giblin, C. H. *The Destruction of Jerusalem According to Luke's Gospel: A Historical-Typological Moral*, Rome: Biblical Institute Press, 1985.

Gnilka, J. *Jesus von Nazaret*, Freiburg: Herder, 1990.

Goetz, S. C. and Blomberg, C. L. 'The Burden of Proof', *JSNT* 11 (1981), 39–63.

Goldstein, J. *1 Maccabees*, New York: Doubleday, 1976.

Goodman, M. *The Ruling Class of Judaea*, Cambridge: Cambridge University Press, 1987.

Mission and Conversion: Proselytizing in the Religious History of the Roman Empire, Oxford: Clarendon Press, 1994.

Goppelt, L. 'Zum Problem des Menschensohns: Das Verhältnis von Leidens- und Parusieankündigung', in *Christologie und Ethik*, Göttingen: Vandenhoeck & Ruprecht, 1968, pp. 66–78.

Theology of the New Testament I: The Ministry of Jesus in its Theological Significance, Grand Rapids: Eerdmans, 1981.

Goulder, M. D. *Luke, A New Paradigm*, Sheffield: JSOT Press, 1989.

Gowan, D. E. *Eschatology in the Old Testament*, Philadelphia: Fortress, 1986.

Green, H. B. *The Gospel According to Matthew*, London: Oxford University Press, 1975.

Green, J. B. *The Death of Jesus*, Tübingen: Mohr & Siebeck, 1988.

Grimm, W. 'Eschatologischer Saul wider eschatologischen David. Eine Deutung von Lc. xiii 31ff', *NovT* 15 (1973), 114–33.

Grundmann, W. *Das Evangelium nach Lukas*, Berlin: Evangelische Verlagsanstalt, ^{3}1966.

Das Evangelium nach Matthäus, Berlin: de Gruyter, 1968.

Guelich, R. A. *The Sermon on the Mount*, Waco: Word Books, 1982.

Guignebert, C. *The Jewish World in the Time of Jesus*, London: Kegan Paul, Trench, Trubner & Co., 1939.

Gundry, R. H. *The Use of the Old Testament in St. Matthew's Gospel*, Leiden: E. J. Brill, 1967.

Matthew: A Commentary on his Literary and Theological Art, Grand Rapids: Eerdmans, 1982.

Mark: A Commentary on His Apology for the Cross, Grand Rapids: Eerdmans, 1993.

Haenchen, E. 'Matthäus 23', *ZTK* 48 (1951), 38–63.

Hahn, F. *The Titles of Jesus in Christology*, London: SCM, 1969.

Hamilton, N. Q. 'Temple Cleansing and Temple Bank', *JBL* 83 (1964), 365–72.

Harnack, A. *The Mission and Expansion of Christianity* I, London: Williams & Norgate, 1908.

Harrington, D. J. 'The Jewishness of Jesus: Facing Some Problems', *CBQ* 49 (1987), 1–13.

Hartman, L. 'Ἱεροσόλυμα, Ἱερουσαλήμ', in H. Balz and G. Schneider (eds.), *Exegetical Dictionary of the New Testament* II, Grand Rapids: Eerdmans, 1991, pp. 176–9.

Harvey, A. E. *Jesus and the Constraints of History*, London: Duckworth, 1982.

Hasel, G. F. *The Remnant: The History and Theology of the Remnant Idea from Genesis to Isaiah*, Berien Springs: Andrews University Press, 1972.

Hayes, J. H. 'The Tradition of Zion's Inviolability', *JBL* 82 (1963), 419–26.

Hendin, D. *Guide to Biblical Coins*, New York: Amphora Books, 1987.

Hengel, M. *Was Jesus a Revolutionist?*, Philadelphia: Fortress, 1971.

The Atonement, London: SCM, 1981.

The Zealots, Edinburgh: T & T Clark, 1989.

Herzog III, W. R. 'Temple Cleansing', in J. B. Green, S. McKnight and I. H. Marshall (eds.), *Dictionary of Jesus and the Gospels*, Leicester: Inter-Varsity Press, 1992, pp. 817–21.

Hiers, R. H. 'Purification of the Temple: Preparation for the Kingdom of God', *JBL* 90 (1971), 82–90.

Higgins, A. J. B. *The Lord's Supper in the New Testament*, London: SCM, 1952.

Jesus and the Son of Man, London: SCM, 1964.

Hill, D. *The Gospel of Matthew*, London: Oliphants, 1975.

New Testament Prophecy, London: Marshall, Morgan & Scott, 1979.

Hoehner, H. *Herod Antipas*, Cambridge: Cambridge University Press, 1972.

Hoffmann, P. *Studien zur Theologie der Logienquelle*, Münster: Verlag Aschendorff, 1972.

Holladay, W. L. *Jeremiah 2*, Minneapolis: Fortress, 1989.

Hollenbach, P. 'The Historical Jesus Question in North America Today', *BTB* 19 (1989), 11–22.

Holm-Nielsen, S. *Hodayot: Psalms from Qumran*, Aarhus: Universitet-forlaget, 1960.

Holz, T. 'Paul and the Oral Gospel Tradition', in H. Wansbrough (ed.), *Jesus and the Oral Gospel Tradition*, Sheffield: JSOT Press, 1991, pp. 380–93.

Hooker, M. D. *The Son of Man in Mark*, London: SPCK, 1967.

'On Using the Wrong Tool', *Theology* 75 (1972), 570–81.

'Traditions About the Temple in the Sayings of Jesus', *BJRL* 71 (1988), 7–19.

Horbury, W. 'The Temple Tax', in E. Bammel and C. F. D. Moule (eds.), *Jesus and the Politics of His Day*, Cambridge: Cambridge University Press, 1984, pp. 265–86.

Horsley, R. A. 'Popular Prophetic Movements at the Time of Jesus: Their Principal Features and Social Origins', *JSNT* 26 (1986), 3–27.

Jesus and the Spiral of Violence: Popular Jewish Resistance in Roman Palestine, San Francisco: Harper & Row, 1987.

Horsley, R. A. and Hanson, J. S. *Bandits, Prophets and Messiahs: Popular Movements in the Time of Jesus*, San Francisco: Harper and Row, 1985.

Hurst, L. D. 'The Neglected Role of Semantics in the Search for the Aramaic Words of Jesus', *JSNT* 28 (1986), 63–80.

Idinopulos, T. A. 'Religious and National Factors in Israel's War With

Rome', in S. Talmon (ed.), *Jewish Civilization in the Hellenistic Roman Period*, Sheffield: JSOT Press, 1991, pp. 50–63.

Isaac, E. '1 (Ethiopic Apocalypse of) Enoch', *OTP* I, pp. 5–89.

Ito, A. 'Matthew's Understanding of the Law With Special Reference to the Fourth Antithesis' (unpublished Ph.D. dissertation, CNAA, 1989).

Jaubert, A. *La notion d'alliance dans le Judaisme aux abords de l'ène chrétienne*, Paris: Du Seuil, 1963.

Jeremias, J. 'The Last Supper', *JTS* (old series) 50 (1949), 1–10.

Jesus' Promise to the Nations, London: SCM, 1958.

The Parables of Jesus, London: SCM, 1963.

Abba. Studien zur neutestamentlichen Theologie und Zeitgeschichte, Göttingen: Vandenhoeck & Ruprecht, 1965.

The Eucharistic Words of Jesus, London: SCM, 1966.

Jerusalem in the Time of Jesus, Philadelphia: Fortress, 1969.

'Die Drei-Tage-Wörte der Evangelien', in G. Jeremias (ed.), *Tradition und Glaube*, Göttingen: Vandenhoeck & Ruprecht, 1971, pp. 221–9.

New Testament Theology I: The Proclamation of Jesus, London: SCM, 1971.

Jonge, M. de. *The Testaments of the Twelve Patriarchs: A Study of their Text, Composition and Origin*, Leiden: E. J. Brill, 1953.

'The Testaments of the Twelve Patriarchs: Christian and Jewish', *Jewish Eschatology, Early Christian Christology and the Testaments of the Twelve Patriarchs*, Leiden: E. J. Brill, 1991, pp. 233–43.

Jesus, the Servant-Messiah, New Haven and London: Yale, 1991.

Kadman, L. 'A Coin Find at Masada', *IEJ* 7 (1957), 61–5.

Käsemann, E. *Essays on New Testament Themes*, London: SCM, 1964.

Kee, H. C. 'Testaments of the Twelve Patriarchs', *OTP* I, pp. 775–828.

Kilpatrick, G. D. *The Eucharist in Bible and Liturgy*, Cambridge: Cambridge University Press, 1983.

Kim, S. *The 'Son of Man' as the Son of God*, Tübingen: Mohr & Siebeck, 1986.

Klinzig, G. *Die Umdeutung des Kultus in der Qumrangemeinde und im Neuen Testament*, Göttingen: Vandenhoeck & Ruprecht, 1971.

Kloppenborg, J. S. *The Formation of Q*, Philadelphia: Fortress, 1987.

Klostermann, E. *Das Matthäusevangelium*, Tübingen: Mohr, 1927.

Knibb, M. A. 'The Date of the Parables of Enoch: A Critical Review', *NTS* 25 (1978–9), 345–59.

The Qumran Community, Cambridge: Cambridge University Press, 1987.

Koch, K. *The Growth of the Biblical Tradition*, London: SCM, 1969.

Kraus, H. J. *Theology of the Psalms*, Minneapolis: Fortress, 1986.

Psalms 60–150. A Commentary, Minneapolis: Fortress, 1989.

Kuhn, K. G. *Konkordanz zu den Qumrantexten*, Göttingen: Vandenhoeck & Ruprecht, 1960.

Kümmel, W. G. *Promise and Fulfilment*, London: SCM, 1957.

Kwaak, H. van der. 'Die Klage über Jerusalem (Matt 23.37–39)', *NovT* 8 (1965), 156–70.

Lane, W. L. *The Gospel According to Mark*, Grand Rapids: Eerdmans, 1974.

Lehne, S. *The New Covenant in Hebrews*, Sheffield: JSOT Press, 1990.

Levenson, J. D. 'Zion Traditions', *ABD* VI, pp. 1098–102.
Sinai and Zion: An Entry into the Jewish Bible, Minneapolis: Winston Press, 1985.
L'Heureux, C. E. 'The Biblical Sources of the Apostrophe to Zion', *CBQ* 29 (1967), 60–74.
Lightfoot, J. *Horae Hebraicae et Talmudicae* II (ed. R. Gandell), Oxford: Oxford University Press, 1885.
Lindars, B. *The Gospel of John*, London: Oliphants, 1972.
Jesus Son of Man, London: SPCK, 1983.
Lohmeyer, E. *Das Evangelium nach Matthäus* (ed. W. Schmauch), Göttingen: Vandenhoeck & Ruprecht, 1956.
Lührmann, D. *Die Redaktion der Logienquelle*, Neukirchen-Vluyn: Neukirchener Verlag, 1969.
Luz, U. *Matthew 1–7*, Edinburgh: T & T Clark, 1990.
Maccoby, H. 'Paul and the Eucharist', *NTS* 37 (1991), 247–67.
MacDonald, J. I. H. 'New Quest – Dead End? So What about the Historical Jesus?', in E. A. Livingstone (ed.), *Studia Biblica 1978 II. Papers on the Gospels*, Sheffield: JSOT Press, 1980, pp. 151–70.
McEleney, N. J. 'Matthew 17:24–27 – Who Paid the Temple Tax? A Lesson in Avoidance of Scandal', *CBQ* 38 (1976), 178–92.
McKelvey, R. J. *The New Temple*, Oxford: Clarendon Press, 1969.
McKinnis, R. 'An Analysis of Mark 10.32–34', *NovT* 18 (1976), 81–100.
Mann, C. S. *Mark*, New York: Doubleday, 1986.
Manson, T. W. *The Sayings of Jesus*, London: SCM, 1949.
'The Cleansing of the Temple', *BJRL* 33 (1950–1), 272–98.
Mare, W. H. *An Archaeology of the Jerusalem Area*, Grand Rapids: Baker, 1987.
Marshall, I. H. 'The Synoptic Son of Man Sayings in Recent Discussion', *NTS* 12 (1966), 327–51.
'Slippery Words I: Eschatology', *ExpT* 89 (1977–8), 243–4.
The Gospel of Luke, Exeter: Paternoster, 1978.
Last Supper and Lord's Supper, Exeter: Paternoster, 1980.
Martinez, F. G. 'The "New Jerusalem" and the Future Temple of the Manuscripts from Qumran', in Martinez, *Qumran and Apocalyptic: Studies on the Aramaic Texts from Qumran*, Leiden: E. J. Brill, 1992, pp. 180–213.
Marxsen, W. *The Lord's Supper as a Christological Problem*, Philadelphia: Fortress, 1979.
Mealand, D. L. 'The Dissimilarity Test', *SJT* 31 (1978), 41–50.
Meier, J. P. *A Marginal Jew: Rethinking the Historical Jesus*, New York: Doubleday, 1991.
Mejia, J. 'La problématique de l'ancienne et de la nouvelle alliance dans Jeremie xxi 31–34 et quelques autres textes', in J. A. Emerton (ed.), *Congress Volume: Vienna 1980*, Leiden: E. J. Brill, 1981, pp. 263–77.
Mendels, D. *The Land of Israel as a Political Concept in Hasmonean Literature*, Tübingen: Mohr & Siebeck, 1987.
Metzger, B. M. *A Textual Commentary on the New Testament*, Stuttgart: Deutsche Bibelgesellschaft, 1975.
'The Fourth Book of Ezra', *OTP* I, pp. 517–59.

Meyer, B. F. *The Aims of Jesus*, London: SCM, 1979.

Miller, P. D. *Sin and Judgment in the Prophets*, Chicago: Scholars Press, 1982

Miller, R. J. 'The Rejection of the Prophets in Q', *JBL* 107 (1988), 225–40.

Minear, P. S. 'Yes and No: The Demand for Honesty in the Early Church', *NovT* 13 (1971), 1–13.

Moessner, D. P. *The Lord of the Banquet*, Minneapolis: Fortress, 1989.

Moo, D. J. *The Old Testament in the Gospel Passion Narratives*, Sheffield: JSOT Press, 1983.

Morris, L. L. *The Gospel According to John*, Grand Rapids: Eerdmans, 1971.

Luke, Grand Rapids: Eerdmans, 1974.

Moule, C. F. D. 'On Defining the Messianic Secret in Mark', in E. E. Ellis and E. Grässer (eds.), *Jesus und Paulus*, Göttingen: Vandenhoeck & Ruprecht, 1975, pp. 239–52.

Murphy-O'Connor, J. 'John the Baptist and Jesus: History and Hypotheses', *NTS* 36 (1990), 359–74.

Myers, J. M. *I & II Esdras*, New York: Doubleday, 1974.

Neill, S. and Wright, N. T. *The Interpretation of the New Testament 1861–1986*, Oxford: Oxford University Press, 1988.

Neirynck, F. 'Recent Developments in the Study of Q', in J. Delodel (ed.), *Logia*, Leuven: Leuven University Press, 1982, pp. 29–75.

'Paul and the Sayings of Jesus', in A. Vanhoye (ed.), *L'apôtre Paul*, Leuven: Leuven University Press, 1986, pp. 265–321.

Neusner, J. 'Money-changers in the Temple: The Mishnah's Explanation', *NTS* 35 (1989), 287–90.

Neusner, J., Green, W. S. and Frierichs, E. S. (eds.). *Judaisms and their Messiahs at the turn of the Christian Era*, Cambridge: Cambridge University Press, 1987.

Neyrey, J. 'Jesus' Address to the Women of Jerusalem (Luke 23:27–31) – A Prophetic Judgment Oracle', *NTS* 29 (1983), 74–86.

Nicholson, E. W. *God and His People: Covenant and Theology in the Old Testament*, Oxford: Clarendon Press, 1986.

Nickelsburg, G. W. E. *Jewish Literature Between the Bible and Mishnah*, London: SCM, 1981.

Nolland, J. *Luke 9:21–18:34*, Dallas: Word Books, 1993.

Luke 18:35–24:53, Dallas: Word Books, 1993.

Noth, M. 'Jerusalem and the Israelite Tradition', in Noth, *The Laws in the Pentateuch and Other Essays*, Edinburgh: Oliver & Boyd, 1966, pp. 132–44.

Oakman, D. E. *Jesus and the Economic Questions of His Day*, New York: Edwin Mellen, 1986.

Ollenburger, B. C. *Zion, the City of the Great King*, Sheffield: JSOT Press, 1987.

O'Neill, J. C. *Messiah. Six Lectures on the Ministry of Jesus*, Cambridge: Cochrane Press, 1980.

Orton, D. E. *The Understanding Scribe*, Sheffield: JSOT Press, 1989.

Otto, E. 'Silo und Jerusalem', *TZ* 32 (1967), 65–77.

Page, S. H. T. 'The Authenticity of the Ransom Logion (Mark 10:45b)', in

R. T. France and D. Wenham (eds.), *Gospel Perspectives I: Studies of History and Tradition in the Four Gospels*, Sheffield: JSOT Press, 1980, pp. 137–61.

Parrot, A. *The Temple in Jerusalem*, London: SCM, 1957.

Patai, R. *Man and Temple in Ancient Jewish Myth and Ritual*, New York: Ktav Publishing, 1947.

Patsch, H. *Abendmahl und historischer Jesu*, Stuttgart: Calwer Verlag, 1971.

'Der Einzug Jesu in Jerusalem', *ZTK* 68 (1971), 1–26.

Perkins, P. *Resurrection: New Testament Witness and Contemporary Reflection*, London: Geoffrey Chapman, 1984.

'Taxes in the New Testament', *JRelEth* 12 (1984), 182–200.

Perrin, N. *Rediscovering the Teaching of Jesus*, London: SCM, 1967.

What is Redaction Criticism?, London: SPCK, 1970.

Pesch, R. *Das Abendmahl und Jesu Todesverständnis*, Freiburg: Herder, 1978.

Das Markusevangelium II, Freiburg: Herder, ²1980.

'Das Evangelium in Jerusalem: Mark 14,12–26 als ältestes Überlieferungsgut der Urgemeinde', in P. Stuhlmacher (ed.), *Das Evangelium und die Evangelien*, Tübingen: Mohr & Siebeck, 1983, pp. 113–55.

Petersen, D. L. *The Roles of Israel's Prophets*, Sheffield: JSOT Press, 1981.

Pfeiffer, R. H. *History of the New Testament Times*, London: A & C Black, 1949.

Piper, R. A. *Wisdom in the Q Tradition*, Cambridge: Cambridge University Press, 1989.

Plummer, A. *St Luke*, Edinburgh: T & T Clark, 1922.

Polkow, D. 'Method and Criteria for Historical Jesus Research', in D. J. Lull (ed.), *SBL 1987 Seminar Papers*, Atlanta: Scholars Press, 1987, pp. 336–56.

Porteous, N. W. 'Jerusalem-Zion: The Growth of a Symbol', in Porteous, *Living the Mystery*, Oxford: Blackwell, 1967.

Rad, G. von. *Old Testament Theology* II, Edinburgh: Oliver & Boyd, 1962.

Rajak, T. *Josephus: The Historian and His Society*, London: Duckworth, 1983.

Reifenberg, A. *Ancient Jewish Coins*, Jerusalem: Rubin Mass., 1947.

Reiling, J. and Swellengrebel, J. L. *A Translator's Handbook on the Gospel of Luke*, Leiden: E. J. Brill, 1971.

Reimarus, H. *Reimarus: Fragments* (ed. C. H. Talbert), Philadelphia: Fortress, 1970.

Rese, M. 'Einige Überlegungen zu Lukas xiii.31–33', in J. Dupont (ed.), *Jésus aux origines de la christologie*, Gembloux: J. Duculot, 1975, pp. 209–12.

Riches, J. *Jesus and the Transformation of Judaism*, London: Darton, Longman & Todd, 1980.

'Works and Words of Jesus the Jew', *HeyJ* 27 (1986), 53–62.

'Apocalyptic – Strangely Relevant', in W. Horbury (ed.), *Templum Amicitiae*, Sheffield: JSOT Press, 1991, pp. 237–63.

Riesner, R. *Jesus als Lehrer*, Tübingen: Mohr & Siebeck, 1981.

Ringgren, H. *The Faith of Qumran*, Philadelphia: Fortress, 1963.

Roberts, J. J. M. 'The Davidic Origin of the Zion Traditions', *JBL* 92 (1973), 329–44.

'Zion in the Theology of the Davidic–Solomonic Empire', in T. Ishida (ed.), *Studies in the Period of David and Solomon and Other Essays*, Winona Lake: Eisenbraun, 1982, pp. 93–108.

Robinson, J. A. T. '"His Witness is True." A Test of the Johannine Claim', in E. Bammel and C. F. D. Moule (eds.), *Jesus and the Politics of His Day*, Cambridge: Cambridge University Press, 1984, pp. 453–76.

Robinson, J. M. *A New Quest of the Historical Jesus*, London: SCM, 1959.

Rohland, E. 'Die Bedeutung der Erwählungstradition Israels für die Eschatologie der alttestamentlichen Propheten' (unpublished D.Theol. dissertation, University of Heidelberg, 1956).

Roloff, J. *Das Kerygma und irdischen Jesu*, Göttingen: Vandenhoeck & Ruprecht, 1970.

Rosner, B. S. *Paul, Scripture and Ethics: A Study of 1 Corinthians 5–7*, Leiden: E. J. Brill, 1994.

Roth, C. 'The Cleansing of the Temple and Zechariah xiv.21', *NovT* 4 (1960), 174–81.

Rowland, C. C. *Christian Origins*, London: SPCK, 1985.

'The Second Temple: Focus of Ideological Struggle?', in W. Horbury (ed.), *Templum Amicitiae*, Sheffield: JSOT Press, 1991, pp. 175–98.

Sanders, E. P. *The Tendencies of the Synoptic Tradition*, Cambridge: Cambridge University Press, 1969.

Paul and Palestinian Judaism, London: SCM, 1977.

Jesus and Judaism, London: SCM, 1985.

Judaism: Practice and Belief 63 BCE – 66 CE, London: SCM, 1992.

The Historical Figure of Jesus, London: Penguin Books, 1993.

Sanders, J. A. 'A New Testament Hermeneutic Fabric: Psalm 118 in the Entrance Narrative', in C. A. Evans and W. F. Stinespring (eds.), *Early Jewish and Christian Exegesis*, Atlanta: Scholars Press, 1987, pp. 177–90.

Sanders, J. T. *The Jews in Luke–Acts*, London: SCM, 1987.

Sawyer, J. F. A. *Prophecy and the Prophets in the Old Testament*, Oxford: Oxford University Press, 1987.

Schaubert, J. 'בָּרַךְ' (*brk*), *TDOT* II, pp. 279–307.

Schiffmann, L. *The Eschatological Community of the Dead Sea Scrolls*, Atlanta: Scholars Press, 1989.

Schmidt, K. L. *Der Rahmen der Geschichte Jesu*, Berlin: Trowitzsch & Sohn, 1919.

Schnabel, E. J. 'Jesus and the Beginnings of Mission to the Gentiles', in J. B. Green and M. Turner (eds.), *Jesus of Nazareth: Lord and Christ*, Grand Rapids: Eerdmans, 1994, pp. 37–58.

Schnackenburg, R. *God's Rule and Kingdom*, Freiburg: Herder, 1963.

Schneider, G. *Evangelium nach Lukas*, Gütersloh: Mohn, 1977.

Schnider, F. *Jesus der Prophet*, Göttingen: Vandenhoeck & Ruprecht, 1973.

Schniewind, J. *Das Evangelium nach Matthäus*, Göttingen: Vandenhoeck & Ruprecht, 1968.

Schreiber, R. 'Der Neue Bund im Spätjudentum und Urchristentum' (unpublished Th.D. dissertation, Eberhard-Karls-Universität, Tübingen, 1954).

Schreiner, J. *Sion-Jerusalem: Jahwes Königssitz. Theologie der heiligen Stadt im Alten Testament*, Munich: Kösel-Verlag, 1963.

Schulz, S. *Q – Die Spruchquelle der Evangelisten*, Zürich: Theologischer Verlag, 1972.

Schürer, E. *The History of the Jewish People in the Age of Jesus Christ (175 B. C. – A. D. 135)*, 3 vols. (eds. G. Vermes, F. Miller and M. Black), Edinburgh: T & T Clark, 1973–87.

Schürmann, H. *Der Einsetzungsbericht Lk 22,19–20*, Münster: Aschendorffsche Verlagsbuchhandlung, 1953.

'Wie hat Jesus seinen Tod bestanden und verstanden? Eine methodenkritische Besinnung', in Schürmann, *Jesu ureigener Tod: Exegetische Besinnungen und Ausblick*, Freiburg: Herder, 1975, pp. 26–33.

Schwartz, D. R. 'On Sacrifices by Gentiles in the Temple', *Studies in the Jewish Background of Christianity*, Tübingen: Mohr & Siebeck, 1992, pp. 102–16.

Schweitzer, A. *The Quest of the Historical Jesus*, London: A & C Black, 1910.

Schweizer, E. *The Lord's Supper According to the New Testament*, Philadelphia: Fortress, 1967.

The Good News According to Matthew, Atlanta: John Knox, 1975.

The Good News According to Luke, Atlanta: John Knox, 1984.

Scobie, C. H. H. 'Jesus or Paul? The Origin of the Universal Mission of the Christian Church', in P. Richardson and J. C. Hurd (eds.), *From Jesus to Paul*, Waterloo, Ontario: Wilfrid Laurier University Press, 1984, pp. 47–60.

Seebass, H. 'בחר, *bachar'*, *TDOT* II, pp. 73–82.

Smallwood, E. M. *The Jews Under Roman Rule from Pompey to Diocletian*, Leiden: E. J. Brill, 1976.

Smith, D. M. *John Among the Gospels*, Minneapolis: Fortress, 1992.

'Historical Issues and the Problem of John and the Synoptics', in M. C. de Boer (ed.), *From Jesus to John: Essays on Jesus and New Testament Christology in Honour of Marinus de Jonge*, Sheffield: JSOT Press, 1993, pp. 252–67.

Smith, M. 'Zealots and Sicarii, their Origins and Relation', *HTR* 64 (1971), 1–19.

Smith, R. L. *Micah-Malachi*, Waco: Word Books, 1984.

Soggin, J. A. 'Der offiziell geförderte Synkretismus in Israel während des 10. Jahrhunderts', *ZAW* 78 (1966), 179–204.

Stanton, G. N. 'Form Criticism Revisited', in M. D. Hooker and C. J. A. Hickling (eds.), *What About the New Testament? Essays in Honour of C. F. Evans*, London: SCM, 1975, pp. 13–27.

'The Origin and Purpose of Matthew's Gospel: Matthean Scholarship from 1945 to 1980', *ANRW* 25.3, pp. 1889–951.

'Aspects of Early Christian-Jewish Polemic and Apologetic', *NTS* 31 (1985), 377–92.

'Matthew', in D. A. Carson and H. G. M. Williamson (eds.), *It is*

Written: Scripture Citing Scripture, Cambridge: Cambridge University Press, 1988, pp. 205–19.

The Gospels and Jesus, Oxford: Oxford University Press, 1989.

'Jesus of Nazareth: A Magician and a False Prophet who Deceived God's People', in J. B. Green and M. Turner (eds.), *Jesus of Nazareth: Lord and Christ*, Grand Rapids: Eerdmans, 1994, pp. 164–80.

Steck, O. H. *Israel und das gewaltsame Geschick der Propheten*, Neukirchen-Vluyn: Neukirchener Verlag, 1967.

'Theological Streams of Tradition', in D. A. Knight (ed.), *Tradition and Theology in the Old Testament*, Philadelphia: Fortress, 1977, pp. 183–214.

Stein, R. H. *The Method and Message of Jesus' Teaching*, Philadelphia: Fortress, 1978.

'The "Criteria" for Authenticity', in R. T. France and D. Wenham (eds.), *Gospel Perspectives I. Studies of History and Tradition in the Four Gospels*, Sheffield: JSOT Press, 1980, pp. 225–63.

The Synoptic Problem: An Introduction, Grand Rapids: Baker, 1987.

Strauss, D. F. *The Life of Jesus Critically Examined*, London: SCM, 1973.

Strecker, G. 'The Passion- and Resurrection Predictions in Mark's Gospel', *Int* 22 (1968), 421–42.

'Die Antithesen der Bergpredigt (Mt 5.21–48 par.)', *ZNW* 69 (1978), 36–72.

The Sermon on the Mount, Edinburgh: T & T Clark, 1988.

Strugnell, J. and Qimron, E. 'An Unpublished Halakhic Letter from Qumran', in J. Amitai (ed.), *Biblical Archaeology Today: Proceedings of the International Congress on Biblical Archaeology, Jerusalem, April 1984*, Jerusalem: Israel Exploration Society, 1985, pp. 400–7.

Stuart, D. *Hosea–Jonah*, Waco: Word Books, 1987.

Stuhlmacher, P. 'Zum Thema: Das Evangelium und die Evangelien', in P. Stuhlmacher (ed.), *Das Evangelium und die Evangelien*, Tübingen: Mohr & Siebeck, 1983, pp. 2–12.

'Die Stellung Jesu und des Paulus zu Jerusalem', *ZTK* 86 (1989), 140–56.

Styler, G. M. 'The Priority of Mark', in C. F. D. Moule, *The Birth of the New Testament*, San Francisco: Harper & Row, [3]1982, pp. 285–316.

Suggs, M. J. *Wisdom, Christology and Law in Matthew's Gospel*, Cambridge, MA: Harvard University Press, 1970.

Sweet, J. 'The Zealots and Jesus', in E. Bammel and C. F. D. Moule (eds.), *Jesus and the Politics of His Day*, Cambridge: Cambridge University Press, 1984, pp. 1–9.

Revelation, London 1990.

Sylva, D. D. 'Ierousalem and Hierosoluma in Luke–Acts', *ZNW* 74 (1983), 207–21.

Talmon, S. *Eschatology and History in Biblical Judaism*, Jerusalem: Tantur, 1986.

Tatum, W. B. *In Quest of Jesus*, Atlanta: John Knox, 1982.

Taylor, V. *The Formation of the Gospel Tradition*, London: Macmillan, 1933.

The Gospel of Mark, London: Macmillan, 1952.

Telford, W. R. *The Barren Temple and the Withered Tree*, Sheffield: JSOT Press, 1980.

Theissen, G. 'Die Tempelweissagung Jesu: Prophetie und Spannungsfeld von Stadt und Land', *TZ* 32 (1976), 144–58.

The Shadow of the Galilean, London: SCM, 1987.

Social Reality and the Early Christians: Theology, Ethics and the World of the New Testament, Edinburgh, T & T Clark, 1993.

Thrall, M. E. *Greek Particles in the Greek New Testament*, Leiden: E. J. Brill, 1962.

Tiede, D. L. *Prophecy and History in Luke–Acts*, Philadelphia: Fortress, 1980.

Tödt, H. E. *The Son of Man in the Synoptic Tradition*, London: SCM, 1965.

Tuckett, C. M. *The Revival of the Griesbach Hypothesis*, Cambridge: Cambridge University Press, 1983.

(ed.). *Synoptic Studies. The Ampleforth Conferences of 1982 and 1983*, Sheffield: JSOT Press, 1984.

Turner, M. 'Atonement and the Death of Jesus in John: Some Questions to Bultmann and Forestell', *EQ* 62 (1990), 99–122.

Tyson, J. B. 'Jesus and Herod Antipas', *JBL* 79 (1960), 239–46.

Urbach, E. E. *The Sages – Their Concepts and Beliefs*, Jerusalem: Magnes Press, 1975, 1979.

Vermes, G. *Jesus the Jew*, London: SCM, 1973.

The Dead Sea Scrolls: Qumran in Perspective, London: SCM, 1977.

The Gospel of Jesus the Jew, Newcastle upon Tyne: University of Newcastle upon Tyne, 1981.

Weinert, F. D. 'Jesus' Saying About Jerusalem's Abandoned House', *CBQ* 44 (1982), 68–76.

Wellhausen, J. *Das Evangelium Lucae*, Berlin: Georg Reimer, 1901.

Wenham, D. *The Rediscovery of Jesus' Eschatological Discourse*, Sheffield: JSOT Press, 1984.

'Paul's Use of the Jesus Tradition', in D. Wenham (ed.), *Gospel Perspectives V: The Jesus Tradition Outside the Gospels*, Sheffield: JSOT Press, 1985, pp. 7–37.

'2 Corinthians 1.17,18: Echo of a Dominical Logion', *NovT* 28 (1986), 271–9.

Wensinck, A. J. *The Ideas of the Western Semites Concerning the Navel of the Earth*, Amsterdam: Johannes Müller, 1916.

Westerholm, S. *Jesus and Scribal Authority*, Lund: Gleerup, 1978.

White, S. A. 'A Comparison of the "A" and "B" Manuscripts of the Damascus Document', *RevQum* 48 (1987), 537–53.

Wilson, S. G. *The Gentiles and the Gentile Mission in Luke–Acts*, Cambridge: Cambridge University Press, 1973.

Witherington III, B. *The Christology of Jesus*, Philadelphia: Fortress, 1990.

Wright, N. T. 'Jesus, Israel and the Cross', in K. Richards (ed.), *SBL 1985 Seminar Papers*, Atlanta: Scholars Press, 1985, pp. 75–95.

The New Testament and the People of God, London: SPCK, 1992.

Wright, R. B. 'The Psalms of Solomon', *OTP* I, pp. 639–70.

Yadin, Y. *The Temple Scroll: The Hidden Law of the Dead Sea Sect*, London: Weidenfeld & Nicholson, 1985.

Young, J. C. de. *Jerusalem in the New Testament*, Kampen: Kok, 1960.

Zeitlin, I. M. *Jesus and the Judaism of His Time*, Cambridge: Polity 1988.

Zeller, D. 'Entrückung zur Ankunft als Menschensohn (Luke 13,34f; 11,29f.)', in F. Refoulé (ed.), *A cause de l'évangile: mélanges offerts à Dom Jacques Dupont*, Saint André: Cerf, 1985, pp. 513–30.

INDEX OF PASSAGES

INDEX OF MODERN AUTHORS

INDEX OF SUBJECTS